HENRY BRA
SOCIETY

ffounded in the year of Our Lord 1890
for the editing of Rare Liturgical Texts

VOL. LXVIII.

PUBLISHED FOR THE SOCIETY

BY

THE BOYDELL PRESS

THE MARTYROLOGY OF TALLAGHT

From the Book of Leinster and Ms 5100–4

Richard Irvine Best

Hugh Jackson Lawler

LONDON

First published for the Henry Bradshaw Society 1929
Transferred to paperback and digital printing
by The Boydell Press 2010
an imprint of Boydell & Brewer Ltd
PO Box 9, Woodbridge, Suffolk IP12 3DF, UK
and of Boydell & Brewer Inc.
668 Mt Hope Avenue, Rochester, NY 14620, USA
website: www.boydellandbrewer.com

ISBN 978 1 870 252 97 3

ISSN 1352–1047

A CIP catalogue record for this book is available
from the British Library

This publication is printed on acid-free paper

CONTENTS.

PRINCIPAL AUTHORITIES.

AA.SS. The Bollandist *Acta Sanctorum.*

ANAL. BOLL. *Analecta Bollandiana.*

AU. = *Annals of Ulster*, ed. W. M. Hennessy and B. MacCarthy, 1887-1901.

COLGAN. *Acta Sanctorum veteris et majoris Scotiae seu Hiberniae.* Lovanii, 1645.

D., Donegal. *The Martyrology of Donegal* [Compiled by Michael O'Clery], ed. J. H. Todd and William Reeves, 1864.

DCA. *A Dictionary of Christian Antiquities*, ed. by William Smith and Samuel Cheetham, 1875-80.

DCB. *A Dictionary of Christian Biography*, ed. by William Smith and Henry Wace, 1877-87.

DUCHESNE. *Martyrologium Hieronymianum ad fidem codicum, adiectis prolegomenis*, ed. I. B. de Rossi et L. Duchesne, in *AA.SS.* Nov. ii.

EUS. *H.E., M.P.* = Eusebius of Caesarea, *History* and *Martyrs of Palestine.*

FM. *The Annals of the Kingdom of Ireland of the Four Masters*, ed. John O'Donovan, 1851.

GEBHARDT. O. von Gebhardt, *Acta Martyrum selecta*, 1902.

HOGAN. *Onomasticon Goedelicum locorum et tribuum Hiberniae et Scotiae*, 1910.

LAWLOR-OULTON. H. J. Lawlor and J. E. L. Oulton, *Ecclesiastical History and the Martyrs of Palestine*, 1927-28.

LIETZMANN. Die drei ältesten Martyrologien, ed. H. Lietzmann, 1911 (Kleine Texte).

O'HANLON. *Lives of the Irish Saints*, by Very Rev. John O'Hanlon, i.-ix.

P. L. Migne's *Patrologiae Cursus completus*, Series Latina.

PLUMMER. BNE = *Bethada Náem nÉrenn. Lives of the Irish Saints*, ed. Charles Plummer, 1922.

PLUMMER. MHH. = *Miscellanea Hagiographica Hibernica* . instruxit Carolus Plummer . . . Accedit Catalogus Hagiographicus Hiberniae, 1925.

PLUMMER. VSH = *Vitae Sanctorum Hiberniae partim hactenus ineditae*, ed. Charles Plummer, 1910.

PLUMMER. Lit. = *Irish Litanies*, ed. Charles Plummer, 1925 (H.B.S., vol. lxii).

RC. *Revue Celtique.*

RICEMARCH. *The Psalter and Martyrology of Ricemarch*, ed. H. J. Lawlor, 1914 (H.B.S., vol. xlvii-xlviii).

RUINART. *Acta Primorum Martyrum sincera et selecta*, ed. T. Ruinart, Amstelaedami, 1713.

MANUSCRIPTS AND TEXTS.

B. Codex Bernensis 289 : end of cent. viii. Printed in Duchesne.

Br. Brussels MS. 5100–4 (Royal Library), O'Clery's abstract of the Martyrology of Tallaght.

Carth. *Martyrology of Carthage*, in Lietzmann. Die drei ältesten Martyrologien, 1911 (Kleine Texte).

Ch. *Ch. Mart.* = *Book of Obits and Martyrology of the Cathedral of Christ Church, Dublin*, ed. J. C. Crosthwaite, 1843.

Drum. = Calendar in the *Drummond Missal*, ed. G. H. Forbes, 1881.

E. Codex Epternacensis (Paris 10837) : cent. viii. Printed in Duchesne.

G, Gorman. *Martyrology of Gorman*, ed. Whitley Stokes, 1895 (H.B.S., vol. ix).

Gelasian Sacr. Liber sacramentorum Romanae Eccl., ed. H. A. Wilson, 1894.

H. = BEW when in agreement.

L. Fragmentum Laureshamense (Vat., *Pal.* 238) : cent. viii or ix. Printed in Duchesne.

LB. Leabhar Breac, the Speckled Book. Facsimile publ. by the Royal Irish Academy, 1872–6.

LL. The Book of Leinster. MS. in Library of Trinity Coll., Dublin. Portion edited here in Library of the Franciscan Convent, Merchants' Quay, Dublin.

— *Facs.* The Facsimile by Joseph O'Longan. Publ. by the Royal Irish Academy, with introd. by Robert Atkinson, 1880.

O, Oengus. (1) *The Calendar of Óengus*, ed. Whitley Stokes. Roy. Ir. Acad. Trans. Irish MSS. Ser., vol. i, 1880 ; (2) Félire Óengusso Céli Dé. *The Martyrology of Oengus the Culdee*, ed. Whitley Stokes, 1908 (H.B.S., vol. xxix).

R. The Martyrology of Ricemarch (Trinity College, Dublin A. 4.20) ; c. 1079. Collotype facs. in *Ricemarch* ii.

Rawl. B. 502. Rawlinson B.502. A collection of pieces in prose and verse in the Irish language. Publ. in Facsimile from the original MS. in the Bodleian Library, with introd. and indices by Kuno Meyer, 1909.

S. Codex Richenouiensis (Turin, *Hist.* 28) : cent. ix. Printed in Duchesne.

Rom. Roman Martyrology of 354, in Lietzmann.

Syr. *Syrian Martyrology* of 411, ed. *ib.*

T. Martyrology of Tallaght in Book of Leinster.

T.[1 2 3] Abstracts of same in MS. 1140. Trin. Coll. Dublin.

W. *Martyrologium Wissenburgense* (Wolfenbüttel, *Wissenb.* 23) : A.D. 772. Printed in Duchesne.

INTRODUCTION.

THREE Martyrologies or Festologies have come down to us from the early Irish Church, namely, the metrical Félire, or Festology, of Óengus,[1] composed between the years 797 and 808,[2] that of Gorman, also metrical, composed between 1166 and 1174,[3] and the Martyrology of Tallaght, contemporary with Óengus. This Martyrology, which has survived in a single recension, preserved in two manuscripts, both unfortunately defective, namely, the Book of Leinster (*LL.*) belonging to the twelfth century, and Brussels 5100-4 (*Br.*), an abstract of the seventeenth century, is here fully edited for the first time. It is the oldest Irish compilation of the kind. In the metrical martyrologies only a few of the principal foreign saints are mentioned. In the Martyrology of Tallaght, however, a full list of the Roman Calendar was apparently aimed at. The earliest reference to it by name is that of Gorman in the Preface[4] to his Félire (p. 4), where he states that Óengus composed his Félire from the Martyrology of Tamlachta Mael Rúain, that is Tallaght, *see infra* p. xx. The connection of our Martyrology with Tallaght is, however, established on internal evidence by the entries under Aug. 10 : " Mael Rúain cum suis reliquiis sanctorum martirum et uirginum ad Tamlachtain uenit " ; and Sep. 6 : " Aduentus reliquiarum Scethi filiae Méchi ad Tamlachtain."

The Monastery of Tallaght was situated close to Dublin, in the present parish of that name. During the lifetime of Máel Rúain (d. 792) its founder, it attained to some eminence as an abode of piety and learning ; witness the ancient *Missal*

---

[1] Edited and translated by Whitley Stokes, (1) " On the Calendar of Óengus," *R. Ir. Acad. Trans.* 1880 ; (2) " The Martyrology of Óengus the Culdee." *H.B.S.*, vol. xxix, 1905.

[2] Thurneysen, " Die Abfassung des Félire von Óengus," *Zeitschr. f. Celt. Philol.* vi, 6–8, 1907.

[3] " The Martyrology of Gorman," ed. and transl. by Whitley Stokes, *H.B.S.*, vol. ix, 1895.

[4] O'Curry, *Lectures on the MS. Materials of Ancient Irish History*, p. 362, fell into the error of supposing this Preface to be the composition of Michael O'Clery, who was merely the scribe or editor.

(now known as the Stowe Missal[1]), and the *Rule* and *Penitential*[2] in which the austere practices of Máel Rúain are embodied. Four of its abbots are commemorated in this Martyrology in addition to Máel Rúain himself, also certain others who were members of the community. These three Festologies are among the chief sources used by John Colgan in his *Acta Sanctorum Hiberniae* (Louvain, 1645), where they are in turn described and their authority weighed. The account of our Martyrology will be found on p. 4, §25.[3] As Colgan's work is of great rarity, and not generally accessible, it will be convenient to quote the passage here :

" Martyrol. quod Tamlachtense vocamus, author, vel interpolator scripsit circa ann. 900. Meminit enim Carbraei Abb. Cluan. qui 6 Mart. an. 899 decessiit, & aliorum qui usque ad istum annum obierunt : non tamen S. Cormaci aliàs celeberrimi viri, putà Regis Arch[i]episcopi, & Martyris, qui occubuit an. 903 vel ut alii. 908. Nec alicuius qui ab an. 900. vixerit. Caeterum Martyrologium ipsum est egregium, & Martyrologio Romano, omnique alio quod viderim, longè copiosus. Post alios sanctos ad singulos dies in magno numero recensitos, subiungit semper seorsim Sanctos Hiberniae. Sed cum magna antiquitatis iactura hinc inde in exemplari peruetusto, quod paenes nos est, desunt multa, nunc plures dies, nunc integri menses, & hoc est, quod luce publica, qua alios dignissimum est, retardat aureum opus donari, donec integrum reperiatur. Operi praefigitur talis titulus : *Incipit Martyrologium Aengussii filii Hua-obhlenii, & Molruani hic.* Constat tamen totum opus non esse ab his compilatum ; cum in eo designentur natales multorum Sanctorum, qui post vtrumque floruerunt, imò & ipsius S. Aengusii natalis ad ii. Martii, & S. Molruani ad 7. Iulii in eo obseruatur. Vnde, quia ambo simul in eodem Tamlactensi monasterio floruerunt, & versimile istt opus illud esse posteà auctum ab aliquo eiusdem monasterii monacho, placuit illud Martyrologium Tamlactense nuncupare. Addo quod praefatio vetusti scholiastae ad festilogium Mariani Gormani faciat mentionem Martyrologii Tamlactensis his verbis ; *quia sic*, inquit, *reperit in Martyrologio Tamlactensi, ex quo suum festilogium desumpsit.* Vnde illud non aliud à praesenti iudicamus, quod in eodem loco compilatum esse ex dictis constat."

For convenience of reference and to avoid confusion with the Martyrology of Óengus, Colgan decided to call our Martyrology the Martyrology of Tallaght, by which name it has been known ever since.

---

[1] Ed. with Facsimile for the *H.B.S.*, vols. xxxi–xxxii, by Sir George F. Warner, 1906, 1915.

[2] Cp. "The Monastery of Tallaght," by E. J. Gwynn and W. J. Purton (*R. Ir. Acad. Proc.*, xxix, C.), 1911. "The Rule of Tallaght," ed. by E. J. Gwynn, 1917 (Suppl. to *Hermathena*, xliv). "On the Céli-dé, commonly called the Culdees," by William Reeves (*R. Ir. Acad. Trans.*, xxiv, 1864). "An Irish Penitential," ed. and transl. by E. J. Gwynn, *Ériu* vii, 121 ff.

[3] It is also described by Soller in his preface to the *Acta Sanctorum Bolland.* tom. vi, June.

Further on, in the life of Óengus, Colgan refers again (pp. 581-2), to the Martyrology of Tallaght, which he endeavours to show was a copy of an older Irish Martyrology, that associated with St. Willibrord, to which the Irish commemorations were added for each day. This is the well-known Codex Epternacensis (now Paris Bibl. Nat. MS. Lat. 10837),[1] a MS. of the early eighth century, written in Anglo-Irish minuscules. Colgan believed that St. Willibrord actually brought this MS. to Echternach out of Ireland where he had spent ten years in study. The following passage (p. 583, note 10) refers to our two MSS. :—

" Duo eius [*sc.* Codicis Epternacensis] exemplaria, licet in quibusdam diuersa, juxta dicta supra, reperta sunt diebus nostris in Hibernia, quorum unum mutilum penes nos Lovanii extat in antiquissimo codice membraneo, et alterum ex quo sanctos Hiberniae jam excerptos accepimus, in dies expectamus."

The Martyrology of Tallaght is again referred to in a document of no small interest now preserved in the Bodleian Library in a miscellaneous volume formerly belonging to Sir James Ware, now Rawl. B., 487.[2] This contains a detailed account (*Catalogus*) of the various works bearing on Irish ecclesiastical history and antiquities, then ready for press, or in course of preparation by the Irish Franciscans at Louvain, including O'Clery's Irish glossary (*Foclóir nó Sanasan Nua*), subsequently printed in 1643 ; the *Acta Sanctorum*, published in 1645, etc. The document was thus written prior to 1643. Though the handwriting is not Colgan's, but rather that of a scrivener, there can be no doubt that it was drawn up by Colgan, and in all probability addressed to Ware. Charles O'Conor, influenced evidently by Colgan's preface to the *Acta Sanctorum* (p. 6), attributed this *Catalogus* to Michael O'Clery, observing, however, that Edmund Gibson (afterwards Bishop of Lincoln) ascribed it to Thomas Ware in his *Catalogus MSS. Codicum Bibliothecae Tenisonianae*, Lond. 1692, p. 7, No. 21. But it is pretty obvious from the last sentence quoted below, which was omitted by O'Conor, that the writer was not O'Clery, but Colgan. The passage relating to the Martyrology of Tallaght is as follows :[3]

" 2ᵐ est Martyrologium Tamlachtense ab eodem S. Aengusio et S. Malruano compositum, et ab eorum discipulis postea auctum. In

---

[1] A facsimile page will be found in the New Palaeographical Society, pl. 183*a*.

[2] Cited by Charles O'Conor, *Rerum Hibernicarum Scriptores Veteres*, tom. i, Prolegomena, p. lxii, 1814 ; and printed in full in *Analecta Hibernica*, No. 1, 1930, p. 143 ff. by Charles McNeill.

[3] Here printed from a rotograph.

quo ad singulos paene mensis dies, praeter multos nostrates sanctos, ponuntur plurimi alii sancti qui nec in Romano Martyrologio nec in alio edito, quod nouerim habentur ; sed proh dolor ! hoc habemus tantum mutilum in vetustissimis pergamenis, ita quod integri aliquando desiderentur menses. Sed audio aliud extare exemplar in finibus Lageniae penes quendam Presbyterum qui si recte nomen retinuerim vocatur *Donaldus Coemhanach mac Briain Ruaidh*, quem nunc audio obiisse, et codicem illum retineri apud eius cognatos. Rem mihi longe gratum, sed et Deo eiusque sanctis gratiorem faceret, qui mihi transcriptum mitteret.''

This *exemplar* said to be in the possession of Domnall Caomhanach mac Briain Ruaidh is beyond doubt the one Colgan referred to in the *Acta Sanctorum*, and which he was awaiting from day to day (*in dies*), having received in the interval an abstract of the Irish saints. The volume itself apparently never reached him, and is now lost. Happily, however, the *codex antiquissimus membraneus* still survives, and to it we now pass.

When visiting the Irish College of St. Isidore, Rome, in the year 1862, the Rev. J. H. Todd, the well-known Irish scholar, was shown the books and manuscripts that had been transferred thither in the early part of the century from the College of St. Anthony at Louvain, among them the vellum leaves containing the Martyrology of Tallaght. Dr. Todd at once recognized them as belonging to the Book of Leinster, preserved in the Library of Trinity College, Dublin, of which he was a Senior Fellow.[1] They are now deposited in the Franciscan Convent, Merchants' Quay, Dublin, together with other MSS. and documents relating to the Order.[2]

DESCRIPTION OF THE MANUSCRIPTS.

The Book of Leinster (LL.), earlier known as the Book of Glendalough, is so well known that the briefest mention must suffice here. A lithographic Facsimile[3] of it, executed by Joseph O'Longan, was published by the Royal Irish Academy in 1880, with an Introduction and List of its contents by Professor Robert Atkinson ; and a large part of it has since been edited and translated in various places. It is one of the greater Irish codices, a compilation of the latter half of the

---

[1] See his account of the discovery in his Introduction to the *Martyrology of Donegal*, p. xiv.
[2] They were transferred to Dublin in 1872. For an account of them, by Sir John Gilbert, see *Historical MSS. Commission,* App. 4, Report, p. 599 ff.
[3] In the following pages this is referred to as *Facs.*

twelfth century. The compiler and scribe was Áed Mac Crimthainn (*Facs.*, p. 313, marg. inf., where he writes himself Aed mac meic Crimthaind). His date is inferred from three marginal entries. The first of these (*Facs.*, p. 288, marg. inf.) is a letter addressed to Áed by Find [Mac Gormáin], bishop of Kildare, who refers to him as lector of the High-King of Southern Ireland and coarb or successor of St. Colum, son of Crimthann, *i.e.* of Terryglass in Lower Ormond. Now as Áed's predecessor in office, Find grandson of Celechar, died in 1152 according to the Four Masters, and as Find the writer died in 1160, the date of this portion of the codex can be fixed to within a few years. The second entry (*Facs.*, p. 49, marg. sup.) records the death, the day before, of Domnall mac Congalaig, King of Offaly, which took place in 1161. The third entry (*Facs.*, p. 275, marg. sup.) is a scribe's lament for the banishment of Diarmait, King of Leinster, over sea, which event is recorded in the Annals under 1166.

Like the main codex, the leaves in the Franciscan Convent are unbound. They are enclosed in a vellum wrapper, rudely inscribed on the outer cover in a hand apparently of the seventeenth century : '' Martyrol. Tamlactense et opuscula S. Aengusii Keledei.''

There are two gatherings of ten leaves. The eleventh leaf which is not in the same hand, and is mutilated at one side, has no connection with the Book of Leinster ; but none the less it is included in the Facsimile, along with the others. The leaves measure 13 by 9¼ inches, and are foliated like the main codex in Old-English characters. But the foliation is obscure and in some instances illegible. The first gathering, fol. cxx–cxxix, which formed a quinio, contains the Martyrology. Folios cxxi and cxxviii formed a diploma and are missing ; they contained Jan. 30 to Mar. 11, Nov. and Dec. 1–16. Folios cxxiv and cxxv formed the middle diploma, and are also wanting ; they contained May 20 to July 31. The remaining leaves of this gathering are diplomas : cxx/cxxix : cxxii/cxxvii. The second gathering comprises four disconnected leaves, foliated cxxxvi–cxxxix, mounted on guards and stitched together. The whole has been paged 1–20. The additional leaf is unpaged. In the Facsimile they form pages 355–76, concluding the Book of Leinster proper. The Martyrology is followed by lists of Irish bishops, deacons, homonyms (Comainmnigud) of Irish saints, *etc.*, a description of which will be found in Atkinson's List of Contents prefixed to the Facsimile, p. 76 ff. As Atkinson has observed, the last two leaves, fol. cxxxviii and cxxxix, should more properly precede the Martyrology. The foliation throughout the main codex is irregular and confusing.

On the lower margins of two leaves, cxx and cxxi, is inscribed in the handwriting of Colgan, " Ex Libris Conuentus Dungallensis " (the second omitted in *Facs.*), and on a third, cxxxix (*Facs..* p. 374) " Liber Conuentus Dungallensis." O'Clery's practice, as related in his Preface to the *Genealogiae Regum et Sanctorum Hiberniae*,[1] which he completed in 1630, was to collect and assemble in one place whatever material he could find bearing on the saints of Ireland. In this way no doubt he acquired the portion of the manuscript now known as the Book of Leinster. He can hardly have obtained it direct from the codex itself, otherwise why should he have omitted to take the gathering that immediately preceded the Martyrology, no less important for his purpose, as it contains the pedigrees of the saints of Ireland, of which he had himself prepared an edition? The explanation would seem to be that the portion containing the Martyrology, etc., had already been sundered from the main codex when it came into O'Clery's hands and was brought to Donegal. This is further borne out by the state of the opening page, which is much rubbed and illegible in places, owing to its having been long without a protecting cover, as will be seen later on when the evidence of the Brussels MS. comes under review. From the Book of Leinster itself we learn (*Facs.*, p. 259, marg. inf.) that in 1583 a portion of it was loaned by its then owner, the " Calbach," to one Seán O'Cheirin, that is, as Atkinson observes (Introd., p. 8), some fifty years before Colgan obtained the fragment containing the Martyrology, the source of which was unknown to him (*cp.* Atkinson, Introd., p. 5), and also to Fr. O'Sheerin, who catalogued the contents of Colgan's cell after his decease. See *infra* p. xvi.

The writing of this portion is in the scribe's best manner, large and smaller script alternating. There is no trace of haste as is observable elsewhere in the main codex. The names are written in narrow columns, from six to eight on a page, varying in width. As a rule there are two names on a line, but frequently one only, occasionally three. There are fifty lines

---

[1] *Genealogiae Regum et Sanctorum Hiberniae*, ed. from the manuscript of Míchél O Cléirigh, with appendices and an Index by Rev. Paul Walsh, M.A., 1918.

or more to a column. Ruling with a sharp stylus has actually cut through the lower margin of fol. cxxiii (*Facs.*, pp. 359–60). The rulings and boundary lines are often ignored by the scribe. Not to disturb the linear arrangement of the names, the local designation is made to overflow into the interlinear space either above or below the line, generally the former, as circumstances permit, and is often enclosed in a border which makes it clear to which name a locality refers, and the absence of which is at times a cause of confusion. Frequently it invades the space belonging to the next column, so that a name there appears out of alignment. The initial letter of the first name is almost always a capital, and is often dabbed with colour, particularly when it begins a day or a list, Roman or Irish ; the second or third name has generally a small initial. The Irish groups are, with a few exceptions, preceded by a paragraph symbol, indicated by ¶ in this edition. The margins of some pages are filled with scholia and verse (*infra*, p. 92 ff.), to which there are " signes de renvoi " of various kinds in the text. The days of the month are rubricated, the calends being distinguished by a large ornamental K, embellished with colour.

Certain practices of the Book of Leinster scribe may be mentioned here, as they have not attracted attention hitherto. They are, the use of the paragraph symbol already referred to, in the various forms which it assumed towards the end of the eleventh century ; the frequent use of an oblique hyphen to mark a divided word at the end of a line ; the inverted semicolon (:′) at the end of the first distych of a quatrain. These signs are not met with in other secular Irish codices, such as Lebor na Huidre (*c.* 1100), Rawlinson B. 502 (*c.* 1180), or in the later Books of Lecan, Ballymote, Yellow Book of Lecan, Lebar Brecc. They point to Anglo-Norman influence. The inverted semicolon occurs as a mark of punctuation in King Diarmait's Foundation-charter of the Monastery of Duisk, *c.* 1160 (Gilbert's *Facsimiles*, Pt. II, pl. lxii), and in that of Henry II to his Bristol men in Dublin, A.D. 1171–2 (*ib.*, pl. lxiii), both of which are in the Anglo-Norman style. It is also common as such in liturgical manuscripts, *e.g.* the Gospels of Máel Brigte, A.D. 1138, in the British Museum ; the Corpus Christi Coll. Oxford Missal, *c.* 1150, and the Rosslyn Missal, late thirteenth cent. (*H.B.S.*, vol. xv).

Brussels 5100–4 (*Br.*).—This is a paper manuscript of 214 leaves in 4to, preserved in the Royal Library, Brussels. From it Whitley Stokes edited the Martyrology of Gorman (*H.B.S.*, vol. ix), in the preface to which he described the MS. and provided a full list of its contents, mainly religious. The volume is almost wholly in the handwriting of Brother Michael O'Clery, popularly known as the chief of the Four Masters. To judge by the colophons it consists of fair copies of transcripts made by O'Clery in various places, and of some made direct from manuscripts assembled in the Convent at Donegal, and dated between the years 1627 and 1636.

There are annotations in the handwriting of Colgan and his associates. The Martyrology of Tallaght occupies folios 209 to 224 (with a later separate foliation of its own). There are two columns to the page. In addition to the usual Roman notation, the day of the month is provided in Arabic numerals. It is not a complete copy of the Martyrology, but an abstract, the saints of the Roman calendar being omitted. It is altogether in the hand of Michael O'Clery down to Oct. 30, where he breaks off in the middle of a sentence, adding at the foot of the page the following note, which has been cut into by the binder, leaving only the upper portions of the letters in the lower line : " *ni fuarus an cuid ele don martarlaic san seanleabar i cCill Dara* 22 *A*(   )," " I did not find the rest of the Martyrology in the old book in Kildare 22 A(pril ?)." Another hand, seemingly that of Colgan, completes October, with the exception of two words, and adds December 17 to end, stating as his source for the added matter : " *Asan leabar mor so sios*," " From the Big Book what follows."[1] The month of November and the first sixteen days of December are wanting as in LL.

---

[1] The *Leabar Mòr* referred to here is the *Liber Magnus* or *Liber Major*, a paper manuscript found in Colgan's cell after his death. It is described in the list drawn up by Fr. O'Sheerin at the time, now preserved in the Franciscan Convent, Merchant's Quay, Dublin, and printed by Gilbert in the Appendix to the Historical MSS. Commission, 4th Report, p. 611. The entry is as follows : " Liber Magnus, in fol., continens martyrol^m. partim Hibernicè partim Latinè." It was evidently a transcript of the St. Isidore or Book of Leinster leaves, made by O'Clery before he fell in with the " Seanleabar " in Kildare ; for when transcribing from the latter the entries for April 17 and October 21, he remembered having already copied the lists there of the communities of Eig and Tech Munnu, and so did not trouble to repeat them ; see Notes, *infra* pp. 182, 190. These lists were again copied by another hand, that of Fr. Anthony O'Docharty, O.F.M., the same as that reproduced in Gilbert's *Facsimiles of the National MSS. of Ireland*, pt. iv, pl. l. Cp. p. xx. They are now preserved in the Royal Library, Brussels, MS. 5301-20, pp. 235-9. Colgan evidently found it more convenient to add the missing portions of October and December from this transcript, now lost, than from the original leaves. Among his manuscript volumes there was also a " Liber in 4° continens Martirologium Tamlactense, marginalia ejusdem et opuscula de matribus sanctorum." This also is lost.

This is the abstract referred to by Colgan in the *Acta Sanctorum* (p. 582, note 10), the original of which he was awaiting *in dies* (*supra*, p. xi). A transcript of it was made in 1850 by Eugene O'Curry, for Dr. J. H. Todd, when it was deposited in Dublin by the Belgian Government for this purpose, and with the help of it the Rev. Dr. Matthew Kelly published his edition of the Brussels abstract in 1857.[1] The unsatisfactory nature of this edition has been frequently adverted to ; but it has not been observed hitherto that the important colophon just quoted is silently omitted ; nor is there any indication that the completion of October and the month of December is by another hand and from another source. Dr. Kelly's edition in short implies a homogeneous text in which merely the month of November and the first sixteen days of December are wanting. Dr. Todd, when in Rome in 1862, made a careful collation of Dr. Kelly's printed text with the Book of Leinster leaves,[2] and was accordingly, in the absence of the colophon, misled into supposing the abstract to be a direct transcription from these leaves. Furthermore, Dr. Todd has fallen into complete confusion of the two MSS. in his account of them prefixed to the Martyrology of Donegal (p. xiv ff.). Had he used the transcript made for him by O'Curry in 1850, or better still O'Clery's original, it might have been otherwise. Professor Atkinson in his Introduction to the Facsimile of the Book of Leinster (p. 9 ff.) exposes Dr. Todd's errors, and discusses at some length the relation of the Brussels MS. to the Book of Leinster version, in which, however, he has himself been led into error.

Having compared Dr. Kelly's edition of the·Brussels MS. with the Facsimile of the Book of Leinster, Dr. Atkinson observed that the former begins with January the first, the Feast of the Circumcision, whereas the latter begins with the Nativity. He further noted certain omissions in the abstract, together with a few additional entries, not to speak of certain discrepancies in the dates, which are adscripts in the Brussels abstract, though not indicated as such in Dr. Kelly's edition. Dr. Atkinson accordingly arrived at the conclusion that the abstract could not have been copied from the Isidore leaves as

---

[1] *Calendar of Irish Saints, the Martyrology of Tallagh ; with notices of the patron saints of Ireland . . .*, Dublin, [1857].

[2] See his *Introduction* to the Martyrology of Donegal, 1864, p. xv. Todd's copy with the LL. (or St. Isidore) readings neatly written in is preserved in the National Library of Ireland.

Dr. Todd had asserted. As he was not aware of O'Clery's colophon, which was omitted from Dr. Kelly's edition, he sought for some other possible source of this abstract. He turned to the passages above quoted (p. x–xi) in Colgan's *Acta Sanctorum* and O'Conor's Prolegomena to the *Rerum Hibernicarum Scriptores* (1820), the latter of which he strangely mistook for a personal account of O'Conor's, notwithstanding that the latter expressly ascribed the document in question to O'Clery. Dr. Atkinson conjectured that the " codex alterum " which Colgan was awaiting from day to day (*in dies*) was possibly the one referred to as being in the possession of Domnall Caomhanach mac Briain. So far he was right, though he was pushing all the time at an open door, as he would have seen had he read the passage aright, and consulted the original document in the Bodleian Library.

Dr. Atkinson confined his comparison of the two documents to noting certain divergences without seeking to explain them. A comparison, however, of the Brussels abstract with the Book of Leinster leaves—the original, not the Facsimile—leads to the conclusion that although this abstract was not copied from them as Todd had supposed, its exemplar, the version in the " Seanleabar " or old book in Kildare, was a direct transcript from them, made not later than the fifteenth century, as it was presumably on vellum. This is manifest from certain blunders of the " Seanleabar " scribe, which can in many instances be traced to a misreading of LL. Particular attention is directed to the following, explained with others in the Notes (*infra*, p. 178 ff.). They furnish decisive proof that LL. was being copied:

Jan. 12. Nemainn *for* Brenaind ;
— 15. presbi *for* presb. ;
Mar. 17. Nasar *for* Nasci ;
— 22. ofeidh *for* deeid ;
Ap. 8. Suibne *for* Duibni ;
— 21. Maolrubach *for* Maele Rubi ab ;
— 28. tritu *for* Tratho ;
May 1. Gaibnidi *for* Gobnini ;
— 6. Ethin *for* Echin ;
Aug. 1. om. of ł " uel " ;
— 8. *qui* symbol ;
Sep. 17. Riacc insi *for* Muccinsi ;
Oct. 5. Olma *for* Abna.

It is not contended that all the variations of *Br.* can be explained as mistranscriptions on the part of the " Seanleabar "

CORRIGENDUM

p. xviii, l. 9, *for* " codex alterum " *read*
" exemplar alterum."

scribe. Some are mere modernizations due to the copyists, here passed over as irrelevant. Others can be laid to the charge of O'Clery, due undoubtedly to the *Br.* abstract being a fair copy of a draft made by him on the spot. This may be inferred from the form of the colophon, which does not imply that O'Clery was actually in Kildare at the time of writing. Moreover, it is evident from the displacement of certain names, to which attention is drawn in the Notes, *infra*, p. 178 ff. A similar error occurs in those entries copied from the Leabar Mór by Colgan, *e.g.* Aedani Magni cancelled under Dec. 24, where it had intruded from the following day.

As to the difference in the opening day, it may be explained thus. The Kildare scribe finding the work beginning Dec. 25 in his exemplar, with neither title nor preamble, supplied a title, and then adopted what appeared to him the more natural order, that of Óengus and Gorman, namely, to commence with the first day of January, the Feast of the Circumcision. December 25 to 31 were doubtless added by him at the end only to disappear later on with the last few leaves of his transcript.

From the above remarks it is evident that the Brussels abstract has no independent value.

Trin. Coll. MS. 1140 (*T*).—This is a small paper manuscript (7¾ by 6 inches) of 46 leaves, bound out of order, and preserved in the Library of Trinity College, Dublin. It consists of extracts, turned into Latin, from the Martyrology of Tallaght and that of Gorman made at Louvain by Colgan and his associates for the use of Joannes Bollandus, " Pro R. P. Bolando," two of the sections being inscribed " Accepi Lovanio à PP. Minor. Hibernis, 1658," presumably by Bollandus, who has added notes here and there. It includes (1) Jan. 1–28, both Roman and Irish lists, from the Book of Leinster leaves, in a flowing hand resembling that of Hugh Ward (*T*[1]) ; (2) the Irish entries of January and February, from Br., in Colgan's hand (*T*[2]) ;[1] (3) Irish entries, Jan. 1–9, also in Colgan's hand (*T*[3]) ; (4) the Irish entries for March, from *Br.* ; (5) March 11–31, Roman and Irish lists from Book of Leinster, " Ex Martyrol.

---

[1] In the Library of the Société des Bollandistes at Brussels is preserved a latinized transcript of the months of January and February, MS. 213, fol. 105r–107v, made from the above evidently by one unfamiliar with Irish names, to judge by the errors committed, *e.g.* Feb. 19, Barthinus for Baethinus, Feb. 28, Comfrirlani for cum Firlani ! For drawing our attention to this and also to the lists of the communities of Eig and Tech Munnu (*supra*, p. xvi, n.), and for most kindly sending rotographs of them, we are indebted to the Rev. Paul Grosjean, S.J.

antiquo Tamlachtensi in pergameno " ; (6) " Ex Martyrologio Mariani Gormani abb. Luthensis Martii." The last three are in the hand probably of Fr. Anthony O'Docharty. In the March extract from LL. he records the death of Colgan : Orate pro anima R.P. Joannis Colgani piae memoriae qui obiit die 15 Januarii 1658.

COMPILATION AND SOURCES.

Date of Compilation.—From the fact that only a few names subsequent to those of Máel Rúain and Óengus are found in the Martyrology—the latest according to Colgan (*supra*, p. x) being that of Coirpre of Clonmacnois, who died in 899—and further, that many of the saints occurring in the lists of homonyms, " *Comainmniugad nóeb Herenn,*"[1] preserved in the Book of Leinster and elsewhere[2] are omitted, it may reasonably be inferred that the Book of Leinster recension represents in substance the original compilation. Between the early ninth and the late twelfth century, the Irish language and Irish orthography underwent some change, scribes naturally adopting, as O'Clery and his associates at a later period, the spelling of their own day, especially in the writing of proper names. The scribe of the Book of Leinster was no exception to this rule. In a single instance, however, an obsolete Old-Irish form has survived, owing to a scribal confusion. *A uitren loco anchoritae* (June 3) for *Aui Trenloco,*[3] preserves the Old-Irish *aui*, gen. sg. of *aue* " descendant, grandson," which later developed into *húa,* gen. sg. *huí.* This is the form that occurs in the Félire of Óengus (A.D. 797–808). Here, however, owing to a faulty division of words in an early copy its signification was obscured, and so it survived like a fly in amber, after every other *aui* had in the course of successive transcription been changed to *huí* or *uí.* It thus furnishes decisive evidence of the antiquity of the Martyrology, and would appear to corroborate Gorman's statement already referred to, that it was from it Óengus derived his Félire. Gorman averred in his Preface that the reason that impelled him to compose his Félire was the paucity of the saints of Ireland that Óengus brought into his work, and the multitude of the saints of the rest of the world that he left out ; also that the days which

---

[1] Ed. by Denis T. Brosnan, in *Archivium Hibernicum,* vol. i, 314 ff.
[2] See Plummer, *Miscell. Hagiographica Hibernica,* p. 229.
[3] The solution of this cryptic entry is due to the Rev. Paul Grosjean, S.J.

Óengus assigned for the festivals of a great number were not those appointed by the Church. The reason being that Óengus, as he had ascertained, composed his Félire out of the Martyrology of Tallaght of Máel Rúain. That Óengus should have based his Festology on the Martyrology of Tallaght is after all but natural, as he was a member of that community and the pupil of Máel Rúain its founder. The Martyrology in its original form was unquestionably contemporary with the Missal, already referred to, and to which a date can be assigned hardly later than the first decade of the ninth century. This Missal, with its numerous additions and interpolations, represents, according to Sir George Warner (vol. ii, xxxvii), an attempt " to provide the monastery of Tallaght, which at the beginning of the ninth century was comparatively new and of growing importance, with an authoritative ritual."[1] The same remark may also be applied to the *Rule of Tallaght* and the *Penitential* (*supra,* p. x).

As for the paucity of names in Óengus, it is to be explained by the nature of the work. It is a metrical abridgment, in which a single quatrain (*rinnard*) is allotted to each day, whereas in Gorman the stanzas are of uneven length, four to fourteen lines (*rinnard mór*), permitting of greater fullness. His is therefore the most complete Festology we have of purely Irish commemorations, which it was its aim to be. In the ground covered by the Martyrology of Tallaght, Gorman has added upwards of one hundred names.

There is undoubtedly some variety in the days of celebration, and also some duplication, as Gorman complains, but the amount is exaggerated. The reasons given by Gorman for embarking on a new Martyrology would appear to be rhetorical rather than real, for even he has not utilized all the material which must have been at his disposal in the various lists of homonyms, etc. He names but one Irish martyrology other than Tallaght—that of Óengus, unsatisfactory not because of the alleged source from which it was drawn, but by reason of the restrictions imposed by the metre. The eleventh-century Martyrology of Cashel, described by Colgan (*Acta Sanctorum,* p. 5 ; cp. *Mart. of Donegal,* p. xvi), would seem to have been based on that of Óengus, and the Calendar of Irish saints preserved in the Drummond Missal, a MS. of the eleventh

---

[1] For another view *cp.* J. F. Kenney, *Sources for the early history of Ireland,* i, 699.

century, is taken direct from Óengus, with the addition of a few names incorporated from the Scholia. This is evident not only from the total omission of Irish names on those days on which they are wanting in Óengus, but from the inclusion on Jan. 21 of a name *Feinmi*, which is nothing more than a transformation of the substantive *feidm*, in the cheville *feidm as uaisliu* "effort that is highest." The Irish names were therefore added from Óengus to a Roman Calendar identical with the Martyrology of Christ Church.

Sources.—There is no Preface giving in the traditional Irish manner, the place, time, author, and cause of writing, such as is provided in the works of Óengus and Gorman. From the abrupt way in which the Martyrology opens, on a fresh gathering, without any title, it is not too much to assume that a single leaf containing the Preface was removed from the main codex (Book of Leinster), at the same time as the Franciscan leaves, but being unattached it got lost. At all events it was not available to the scribe of the "Seanleabar," who had to copy from a rubbed and partly illegible opening page, which he rearranged and provided with a title.

Although we are thus deprived of information as to the sources from which the Martyrologist drew, there is little reason to suppose that such would have been more precise than that given by Óengus and Gorman. The former, after enumerating in his Epilogue (137 ff.) "the vast tome of Ambrose, the Sensus of pious Hilary, the Antigraph of Jerome, and the Martyrology of Eusebius" as his foreign sources, vaguely refers to the native as "Ireland's host of books whose troop is wise, we have searched multitudes of them, the festologies (félire) of the Gaels." Gorman (Preface, pp. 4–5) also states that it was "in the ancient books of the Gaels themselves that we found the knowledge of the festivals of the Gaelic saints." No doubt most of these old sources perished in the destruction of the monasteries during the Norse invasions.[1] They would have included the diptychs or litanies of the dead contained in the various missals, such as have survived in the Stowe (or Tallaght) Missal (vol. ii, pp. xxiv, 14), and in the Antiphonary of Bangor (vol. ii, p. 33).

---

[1] In the eleventh century the Annals of Ulster record the burning of Durrow with its books in 1095, and of Monasterboice two years later.

ROMAN CALENDAR.

On a glance through the Roman lists in our Martyrology one is surprised at the number of doublets. The cause of their lavish abundance is partly explained when we place the Martyrology of Epternach beside that of Tallaght. Let us restrict our view to doublets whose members are confined to lists of single days. As a rule one member is a name borrowed from E, while another is derived from a source akin to BW. Thus the scribe of T creates some 57 doublets.[1] It must be admitted that the names in E are not always in exact agreement with their counterparts in T. But these slips are slight and not numerous.[2] Moreover we must take into account the transit from E to T in its original manuscript, and from it to LL. It was inevitable that blunders should occur. The main conclusion is that the Tallaght scribe used the Epternach manuscript, though perhaps at second hand.

We should expect that many more names would have crept from E into T than would give rise to doublets. And the expectation is sound. On the days in T from Dec. 25 to Jan. 29 we find twelve doublets. The intruders in that period, apart from the twelve mentioned, number no less than thirty-two.[3] And we must note that of these, only five differ in spelling from E.[4] If this borrowing continued at the same rate throughout the remainder of the Roman lists of the Martyrology the scribe must have introduced from E to T more than 250 names.

It is obvious that the scribe regarded E as a most valuable manuscript. But it would be wrong to suppose that he used it as the foundation of his work. It is seldom that he displaced a name in BW in favour of E. The foundation of T is BW, E is a source from which fresh names of the Martyrology are culled.

In *Ricemarch*, pp. xxv–xxxiv, there is an attempt to exhibit the relations between B, E, W, R and S.

It may be well to say a few words on the place-names in T. In every list of BEW we find cities or districts, each following the names of one or more saints commemorated on the day.

---

[1] Dec. 29, 30, 31, Jan. 2, 5 (2), 6, 7, 10, 17 (2), 27, Mar. 17, 21 (2), 22, 23, 24, 26, 27, Ap. 1, 11, 16, 18, 20, 23, 24, 27 (3), May 5, 9, 10, 19, Aug. 5, 18, 23, 24, 26, 27 (3), Sep. 7, 13, 15, 16, 17, Oct. 2, 11, 12, 13 (2), 14, 20, 22, 25, 27.

[2] Jan. 2 *esiridoni* (*is-*), 17 *mucci* (*muci*), Mar. 23 *agatani* (*-tini*), Ap. 16 *cantonis* (*-oris*), *antonii* (*-tani*), May 19 *proni* (*prenni*), Aug. 26 *coloceri* (*eleotheri*), Oct. 11 *taci* (*taraci*), 13 *martialis* (*marc-*), *andrae* (*ad-*), 25 *gauani* (*-ini*), 27 *leogi* (*ogi*) : thirteen in all.

[3] Dec. 31 (4), Jan. 8 (3), 20, 21 2), 22, 23, 24, 26 (11), 27 (5), 28 (3).

[4] Jan. 8 *euchti* (*eucti*), 26 *telliani* (*taeli-*), *taeliptae* (*tellyp-*), *uicturinae* (*-tor-*), 27 *celiani* (*cael-*).

This method is to a large extent discarded in T. It seems
obvious that the scribe desired to do away with the numerous
place-names of BEW. He wished to record the names of the
saints, but not their dwellings. Moreover, he may have felt
that his knowledge of geography was insufficient to enable him
to put down on his vellum the correct spelling of the cities of
Europe, Asia, and Africa. An instance of his carelessness, or his
ignorance, may be mentioned. In BW April 14 we have
" Rome via Appia in cimiterio Praetextati sancti Tiburtii."
T omits " in cimiterio," changes " via Appia " into " Apati,"
and gives us, in wrong order, " Tiburtii Apati . . . Romae
Pretextati." The result is that a casual reader would imagine
that Praetextatus, Apatus, and even Roma, were martyrs.
The phrase "in cimiterio" does not appear in T. Evidently
the scribe was not aware that the Roman cemeteries were
designated by the word *cimiterium*, followed by a personal name.

But if the scribe intended to get rid of the place-names
borrowed from BW, why did he preserve so many as we find in
our Index of Places ? The answer may be found in the lists
of T Dec. 25–Jan. 29. Let us note that " Eductio Christi ex
Aegypto " (W Jan. 7, T Jan. 11), " Cathedra Petri in Roma "
(Jan. 18), " Conversio Pauli in Damasco " (Jan. 25), or the
like, are not our quest. These place-names have nothing to
do with the martyrs. Setting them apart we find about 140
place-names in BW between Dec. 25 and Jan. 29, and about
twenty in T. Some of these are in tatters. The scribe cut out
the words " in cimiterio," and he left in T three or four personal
names. No doubt he supposed that they were martyrs. They
are Priscilla (Dec. 31, Jan. 16, 18), Calustus (Jan. 16, 20), and
Vetera (Jan. 23). Corruption in a document used by the
scribe made place-names into personal names : Turonus
(Dec. 30), Bononus (Dec. 31, Jan. 1), Parisilis (Jan. 3), Redon-
tius (Jan. 6), Antichinus, Clericus (Jan. 7), Agustus (Jan. 8),
Ravianus (Jan. 25) ; in all eight. Four place-names rightly
spelt, which might be supposed to be personal names, are
Retariae (Dec. 31), Galatiae (Jan. 23), Puteolis (Jan. 25), and
Treveris (Jan. 29). The only names which certainly are those
of places, are Augusti Duno (Jan. 1), Lugdonagal (Jan. 20 :
Lugdunum Galliae) and Tarracona (T Jan. 21, BW Jan. 22).

The Index of Places indicates similar facts in the latter part of
our manuscript. We find nine spurious martyrs based on the
names of the cemeteries and roads of Rome : Apatus, Balbina
(-lui-), Basilla, Calapotius (-lepod-, -lipod-), Calistus (-les-,-lius-,

Caulist-), Laurentius, Ostensus, Pretextatus (Prot-), Vetera. Moreover we discover at least twelve place-names certainly borrowed from BEW : Acaunum (Sacina), Africa, Cesseria, Effesus, Libia Superior, Macidonia, Necomedia, Parisii, Phrygia (Frig-), Puteolis, Roma, Scythia (Sceth-). Finally, there are some eighty or more names having counterparts in BEW, many of which may have been counted personal by the scribe.

THE PRESENT EDITION.

Text.—In the printed text it will be observed that the Roman and Irish lists are treated somewhat differently. In the former, abbreviations have been for the most part silently expanded, there being seldom any doubt as to the form intended : " presbi " and " mār " are throughout extended *presbiteri, martiris*. In the Irish entries, on the other hand, italics are more frequently used, as questions of orthography or grammatical form were involved. Further, the corruptions and confusion in the Roman lists being so numerous and perplexing, it was deemed more convenient to refrain from all attempt at emendation in the footnotes, reserving this for the critical notes at the end. But the Irish entries being more susceptible of direct emendation, a different practice has been adopted : occasionally a letter has been supplied between square brackets. Obscure letters are enclosed within round brackets. In addition, Irish phrases, generally the local designations, or terms of kindred, are rendered in the footnotes as they occur, the identification of the place being given, where known, in the Index.

The punctuation of the manuscript (LL.) has not been rigidly adhered to. The point, followed occasionally by a virgule at the end of a paragraph or section, is the sole punctuation used. As often as not it is omitted by the scribe at the end of a line, in which case it is here silently added. Frequently, however, it is wrongly inserted to the detriment of the sense, in which case it has been retained, as it might be held to imply a certain interpretation on the part of the scribe. The same remark applies to the use of capitals, as already observed (p. xv). Following the usual Irish practice, a full-point is placed before and after certain symbols and letters, *e.g.* .*m*. .*mc*. (mac, meic), .*h*. (hūa, huí), etc., but these are not reproduced in the edition when the abbreviated word is written out. The Roman numerals are almost invariably flanked by points, and these have been reproduced, even in the days of the

TALLAGHT

e

month, which are rubricated, and where the first point is
frequently omitted. The names of the months in the MS.
alternate between Latin and Irish.

The Latin abbreviation symbols are those usually found in
Irish manuscripts, and call for no special mention, except the
sinuous suprascript stroke, denoting syllabic *ui*, in Natiu*i*tas,
Datiu*i*, not unlike the *m*-stroke, for which the scribe of T^1 has
mistaken it ; further, the insular з and ei3 both occurring
for " eius " ; ⁊ " etiam," id̄ " idem " ; both .i. and 12, **12**
" id est " ; in̄ " inde " ; m̄ syllabic " met " in Mamm*et*is ;
p̨ " per," with p̨ᵣ as a syllabic symbol.

In the Irish lists *ab.* is printed for ab where it was not clear
as to whether the Irish gen. *abbad* or the Latin *abbatis* was
intended ; similarly *eps.* and *sac.* (Br.), which might represent
Latin *episcopus*, *sacerdos*, or Irish *epscop*, *saccart*. Further,
as the expansion of these abbreviations depends on the case
of the governing name, a difficulty frequently arose in names
formed with the diminutive suffixes *-án*, *-óc* uninflected in early
Irish, but later developing a gen. sg. *-áin, óic*, both forms
occurring in our text. In such instances the word expressing
the office or dignity is either left in its abbreviated form, or
the case of the adjoining names, frequently in the nomina-
tive, has been the determining factor. Strictly speaking all
the proper names commemorated should be in the genitive,
but the practice of the scribe varies. Again, owing to the
position of the *n*-stroke, it has not been easy at times to deter-
mine whether Lat.-*ani*, or Ir. *-ain* was intended by the scribe.
This is especially the case in Br. where the abbreviation stroke
is frequently extended over both letters, āī.

Certain interlinear glosses in LL., though undoubtedly by
the text hand, are printed between angular brackets ⟨ ⟩ where
there might be a question as to their having been added
subsequently. As a rule, however, the scholia were written
at the time of transcription (*cp. supra*, p. xv).

The aim has not been to present a diplomatic transcript
of the original, as such is already supplied by the lithographic
Facsimile of O'Longan (*Facs.*),[1] but rather to exhibit the
evidence of the manuscript in an intelligible form and, it is
hoped, with accuracy.

---

[1] The misreadings of the Facsimile are not recorded in depreciation of
O'Longan's work, but solely to indicate to those that may have recourse to it,
that the differences of reading are not accidental. On the other hand, we have
not always indicated those instances where we have succeeded in deciphering
what was obscure to the Facsimilist.

As regards the Irish commemorations, the lacunæ in LL have been supplied from Br.,[1] and these portions, though printed in the same type, will be easily distinguished by the absence of the Roman entries, also by the days of the month printed alongside in arabic numerals, which, being in the MS., are not within square brackets.

Indexes.—In the Index of Irish Places are included not only the names occurring in the printed text, but also those referred to in the footnotes and in the Index of Persons, followed by their source, *GDO*, as the case may be. As the local designations are rarely given in Gorman's text, it will be readily understood that when such are cited as *G* the reference is to the scholia, which there is no reason to doubt O'Clery found in his exemplar, now lost. They correspond closely with those in O'Clery's compilation, *Martyrology of Donegal* (*D*), which is derived to a large extent from Gorman (*Cp.* Stokes, Preface, p. 1, and Todd, *Mart. Donegal*, p. xvii), but may also have embodied scholia in the lost Martyrology of Cashel (*c.* 1030), a transcript of which Colgan had before him.[2] Many of these scholia may date from an early period.

As regards identification, Hogan's *Onomasticon Goedelicum* has been followed in the main. But in many instances no help was forthcoming from that invaluable work. These must be solved, if at all, by local investigation, where tradition may survive attached to wells and holy places, or in annual "patterns." A muster-roll of the latter is much needed.

In the Irish Index of Persons, where several of the same name occur, the arrangement is (1) parentage, (2) locality, (3) title, and (4) bare names. Also, as in the text, pet-names formed by prefixing the possessive pronouns *Mo* " my," *Do,* Teo, " thy," are printed in the combined form by which they are best known, *e.g.* Mobí (= Mo Bí), Móedoc (= Mo Áedóc). Dobí (= Do Bí), Teochonna, Tochonna (= Do Chonna), Dochumma (= Do Chumma), etc. In some cases, however, especially when there is a diminutive suffix *-án, -éne, -íne, -ín, -óc,* the name appears under various forms, *e.g.* Ernán, Erníne, Mernóc, Lugaid, Molúa, Molúóc, etc. For a classification of Irish saints' names

---

[1] They have been edited from rotographs to which we are indebted to the kindness of the Rev. Paul Grosjean, S.J. The complete text of the Brussels manuscript was transcribed by R. I. B. in 1910, when it was deposited in the Bodleian Library for the use of the late Rev. Charles Plummer. From this transcript the readings on p. 178 ff. are derived.

[2] It was among the MS. volumes found in Colgan's cell after death. See the list published by Sir John Gilbert in Appendix to Fourth Report of Hist. MSS. Commission, p. 612.

and their formation the reader is referred to Whitley Stokes's preface to the Martyrology of Gorman (pp. xxiii–iv, xlvii ff.).[1]

This Index does not purport to be more than an alphabetical list of the names occurring in the text. To have supplied dates and bibliographical references to each name, even were this possible, would have been outside its scope. For such particulars recourse must be had to the *Acta* or *Vitae* of Colgan, Plummer, etc., to O'Hanlon's *Lives*, the Annals, also to the various lists of saints, bishops, priests, deacons, etc., cited in these pages,[2] to Kenney's invaluable *Sources for the Early History of Ireland*, vol. i, Ecclesiastical, and to Dom Louis Gougaud's *Gaelic Pioneers of Christianity*, etc.

The Editors feel that an apology is due to the Members for the long delay in issuing this volume, the passage of which through the press has involved a greater expenditure of time and labour than they had foreseen when embarking on the task. In this, however, they have been greatly aided by the kindness of friends, to whom their cordial thanks are due. They are much indebted to the Rev. Paul Grosjean, S.J., of the Société des Bollandistes, who not only read through the entire proof-sheets, making many helpful suggestions, but also co-operated in the most friendly manner by gifts of rotographs from manuscripts in the Brussels Collections, as did also the Rev. P. Le Gaiffier, S.J., and the Rev. Norbert Polet, S.J.; to Professor Osborn Bergin, who most kindly read over the Marginal Notes and Poems in manuscript, solving more than one obscure passage and correcting some minor errors ; to the late Miss Mary Byrne, M.A., for help kindly given in the same portion of the work ; and to the Rev. Paul Walsh, M.A., for his identifications of several Irish place-names. They also desire to express their obligations to the learned librarian of the Franciscan Convent, Merchant's Quay, the Rev. Gregory Clery, O.S.F., for the abundant facilities he afforded them at all times in transcribing and collating the original MS. and having it photographed. Finally, special acknowledgment is due to the Royal Irish Academy for their furtherance of the work by a generous grant to the Society in aid of publication.

R. I. B.

H. J. L.

---

[1] See also Kuno Meyer, *Die Koseformen irischer Personennamen* (Zur kelt. Wortkunde II, §33, Sitzungsber. d. Kgl. Preuss. Akad., 1912).

[2] A critical edition of these is, we learn, in preparation by the Rev. Paul Grosjean, S.J.

[Dec. 25]   Uiii. kł. Ianuarii.

Natiuitas Domini nostri Iesu Christi.   Iunii.   Pastoris.
Bassilei.   Achillei.   Appromiani.   Uictorianae.   Euticitae.
Heliae.   Eufegiae.   Dorozoli.   Simfroniani.   Saturnini .bis.¹
Teuinidi.   Ignatii.   Ciriacii.   Zachii.   Ianuariae.   Datiui.
Eugeniae uirginis.   Anastasiae.   Anastasii.   Iuliani.   Marciani.
¶ Diucaill meic Nemáin.   Iarlathi eps.   Maelani episcopi.
Aedani magni.

¹ in marg.

[26]   .uii. kł. Ianuarii.

Zephani protomartiris.   Dionisii episcopi.   Nichandri
episcopi.   Iuliani.   Martini.   Dorozoli.   Eliae.

¶ Commani in Rois.¹   Molibae Enaig Elti.²   Cada Dromma
Tuircc.³   Mochommoc.⁴   Mogenoc .i. i Cill Duma Gluind.⁵
Lasriani abbatis.   Eugeni perigrini.

¹ ' of the Ros.'   ° ' of Enach Elti.'   ³ ' of Druim
Tuirc.'   ⁴ in marg. (. . .) episcopi.   ⁵ ' i.e. in Cell
Duma Gluind.'

[27]   .ui. kł. Ianuarii.

Iohannis apostoli et euangelistae assumptio et ordinatio¹
Iacobi apostoli.

¶ Colman mac Dairchill.   Tipraiti Maigi Ratha.²
Mofhiacha m.h.³ Cormaic.

¹ in marg. ó(   )s Iohannis.   ² ' of Mag Rátha.'   ³ m.h.
here and passim for ' meic huí,' g.sg., ' great-grandson,' but represents
moccu ' of the gens.'

TALLAGHT.   B

[28]   .u. kł.

Infant*um* pro Christo occisarum.[1] Castorii. Octouiani.
Uictoris.[2] Gade. Probati.[2] Rogati. Ianuarii. Saturi.
Eutitii. Eusebii.[2] Uict*u*riae. Donati.[3]

¶ Sneidairl(e)[4] m*ei*c Comrisi.[5]   Fechini m.h. Lugbe.[6]
Cilline m*ei*c Bregdae.[7] Maele Coisni.[8]

     [1] *second* c *leg., om. Facs.*   [2] *barely traceable.*   [3] Oci[   ]
Facs.   [4] rl *traceable* ; *final* e *obscure.*   [5] Comrig *Facs.*   [6] Lugbe
faint, om. Facs.   [7] Dregdae *Facs.*   [8] Mele *Facs. ; marginal
note illeg.*

[29]   .iiii. kł. Ian*uarii*.

Uictoris (   )[1] [col. *b*] Demetri. Crescentis. Primiani.
Catonis. Librosi. Uictori. Secundi. Saturnini. Honorati.
Uictoriae. Saturi. Felicis ⟨b*is*⟩.[2] Bonifatii. Domicii.

¶ Mancheni. Enani sancti .i. Glinni Faidli.[3]   Ailerain.
Moedoic .i. Liss Móir.[4] Crummini Lecne Mide.[5] Uinniauii
senis. Eulaing.

     [1] *a few letters illeg.*   [2] .b. *passim* = bis, *generally interlined,
occasionally in marg.*   [3] 'i.e. of Glenn Faidle.'   [4] 'i.e. of
Less Mór.'   [5] 'of Lecan Midi ;' *also under June* 28.

[30]   .iii. kł. Ian*uarii*.

Manseti. Seueri. Securi. Appiani. Donati. Honorati.
Policleti. Florentii. Pauli. Rerenei. Pauli. Cleti. Papiani.
Turoni. Zefani.

¶ Conlaei episcopi Aroscaig.[1] Ailbi episcopi Imlecha.[2]

     [1] *sic.* a Ruscaig *Br., etc.,* 'from Rúscach ;' *sic leg.*   [2] 'of
I*i*nlech.'

[31]   .ii. kł.

Donati.   Celestini.   Saturnini.   Siluestri pa*pae*.[1] Paulinae
Donatae.   Rusticanae.   Nominandae.   Serotinae.   Saturninae.
Hilariae.   D( )ti.[2]   P*r*iscillae.[3]   Rogatae.   Bononi
Aggagi.   Pauli.   Ermetis.   Cintiani.   Ret(i)a(ria)e.[4] [*col. c*]
Pontiani.   Attali.   Fabiani.   Cornolii.   Sixti.   Floridi.
Cintiani.   Menernini.   Simforiani.   Ammoni.   Exoperati.
Euelpisti.   Fortunati.   Seq*u*entis.   Opiones.   Kalendionis.
Saturnini.   Agnetis.   Sexti.

¶ Columbae uirginis secht n-eps*coip* impe i nDomnuch
Mor Liphi.[5] Lochani.   Endei Cilli Manach.[6] Lugnei diaconi.
Finnio Airne.[7]

---

[1] p*ū* *Facs.*   [2] *resembles* Dati ; *Facs.* T[   ].   [3] *faint,*
om. Facs.   [4] Re[   ] *Facs.*   [5] ' seven bishops around her
in Domnach Mór Liphi.'   [6] ' of Cell Manach.'   [7] ' of Arann.'

[Jan. 1]   **Kł.** Ian*uarii*.

Circumcisio Domini.   Zephani.   Effroseni episcopi.
Priminiani et aliorum .uiii.   Euantii.   Hermetis.   Uictoris.
Felicis.   Bononi.   Agaci.   Acti.   Eracli.   Narcissii.   Argiri
et aliorum .uii.   Papatis.   Primiani.   Saturnini.   Uictoris.
Honorati.   Leusii.   Hermetis.   Coronae.   Prisci et militis et
aliorum .xliii.   Seueri.   Augusti Duno c*u*m sociis suis
Agripini.   Natal*is*.

¶ Broccani m*eic* Ennae.   Fintain m*eic* Toic*h*thig.   Scethae
uirginis .i. o Fert Sceithe.[1] Aedani h*uí*[2] Fiacnae.   Euchaid.
Tobiae.   Ossine Cl*úana* Mor.[3] Comnatan u*irgo*.   Fintan *in*ac
Echdach o Belach.[4] Findchi Locha Rí.[5] Colman Muli*n*d.[6]
Crone Galma.[7] [*col. d*] Ernan m*ac* Eogain.   Aed L*o*cha
Gei*r*g.[8] Airmedach abb Craibi Lasri.[9] M*a*c Deicill hui
Echdach Usnig.   Colman m*ac* Ech*dach*.

---

[1] ' i.e. from Fert Scéithe.' Cp. Sep. 6.   [2] ' descendant of Fíachna.'
[3] *sic for* Móir, ' of Clúain Mór.'   [4] ' from Belach ;' Bealach
Facs.   [5] ' of Loch Rí.'   [6] ' Colman of Mulenn or of the Mill.'
[7] ' of Galam.'   [8] ' of Loch Geirg.'   [9] ' abbot of Cráeb Laisre.'

[2]   .iiii. Non*as.*

Esiridoni[1] episcopi.   Stratonici.   Saturi.   Sircioni.
Antecíuti.   Possessoris.   Acutionis.   Timothei.   Herisi.
Artaxis.   Uitalis.   Acutae.   Tobiae.   Eugendae.   Rutulae.
Claudiae.   Aurigae.   Zephani.   Uitalis.   Abbani.   Macari.
Marciani.   Firmi.   Maximiani.   Siritioni.   Amphitinae uirginis.

¶ Scothini.   Mancheni sapientis.   Ingena Baeth i mMaig
Liphi.[2] Lochait abb Maige Bili.[3]

[1] Ess[   ] *Facs., re-inked and obscure, as obverse shows through.*
om. T.   [2] 'The daughters of Báeth in Mag Liphi.'   [3] 'abbot
of Mag Bile.'

[3]   .iii. Non*as.*

Ciriacii.   Primi.   Caudionis.   Eugenii.   Rodii 7 trium
fratrum.   Argei.   Argenni.   Primae.   Narcisi.   Marcialis.
Marcelli.   Sca*t*uliani.   Pueri.   Constantii.   Christiani.
Possessoris.   F*i*lii episcopi.   Hilarii.   Teogenis.   Firmi.
Eugetii.   Candidi.   Rodonis.   Rogatiani.   Eugeniae.
Lucidae.[1]   [col. *e*] A(c)utae.[2]   Peoni.   Parisil*is*.   Florenti
episcopi.   Genouefae uirginis.

¶ Fintani.   Cilline m.h.Colla.   Findlugo Duin Blesci
.i. Blesc ainm muccida rig H*u*a Cuanach is é ro boi[3] isind
dunud sin ar tus unde nominatur.[4]

[1] Lucida*ę Facs.*   [2] A[   ]te *Facs.,* c *illeg.*   [3] bui *Facs.*
[4] 'Findlug of Dún Blésci, i.e., Blesc the name of the King of Uí
Cúanach's swineherd, 'tis he who was in that encampment first
of all, *unde nominatur.*'

[4]   .ii. Non*as.*

Aquilini.   Argenti.   Gemini.   Marciani.   Eugetii.
Hermetis.   Gugi.   Aggei.   Quinti.   Teothoti.   Trifinae.

¶ Aediui[1] episcopi.   Mochomma Dromma Ailche.[2]   Maelan
Enaig.[3]   Fiadnatan uirginis.

[1] Aedini *Facs.*   [2] 'of Druim Ailche.'   [3] 'of Enach.'

[5]   Non*as.*

Semionis ⟨b*is*⟩. Marci. Felicis. Sereni. Floriae.
Secundi. Honori. Luciani. Candacii. Anastasiae uirginis.
Ianuariae. Ianuarii. Acuti. Petri. Anastasii. Iocundi.
Telefini.

Ciaran m*ac* Aeda. Airendani. M*ac*c Oge m*eic* Echdach ⟨o
Loch Meilchi.[1]⟩ Ciar ingen Duib Rea.[2] Ioseph eps. Tamlachta.[3]

   [1] ' from Loch Meilge.'   [2] ' daughter of Dub Rea.'   *Also Oc'.* 16.
   [3] ' of Tamlachta.'

[6]   .uiii. Idus.

Epifania Domini. Iuliani. Antoni. Celsi et aliorum
.uiii. Telisfori. Anastasii et aliorum .x. Sinfori. Maelani
episcopi cum sociis suis. Euliae. Acuti. Petri. Iulii. Honorii.
Redontii. Antonini. Iocundi. Anastasiae. Marci.
Marcianillae. [col. *f*] Ianuariae.[1] Basillae. Sabastiani.

¶ Diarmait m*ac* Echdach o Airiud Ind(aich).[2]   Lassar
Achaid Fo(ta).[3]   Digdi c*h*erclach 7 ingen Nad Fraich i
nEnuch Aird.[4]   Tulilatha ab.   Lugidon m*ac* D(e)cla(in).[5]
Caurnan Bec.⟩[6] Dianach ep.   Dimmae Duib.[7]   .

   [1] A[   ] *Facs.*   [2] *faint,* ' from Aired Indaich.'   [3] c[   ]
Facs. ' of Achad Fota.' *Br.*   [4] ' Digde the circular and the
daughters of Nad Fráech in Enach Ard.'   [5] *sic Br.*   [6] ' the
Little.'   [7] ' the Black.'

[7]   .uii. Idus.

Luciani presbiteri. Lucei diaconi. Poliucati. Clerici.
Felicis. Ieiunarii. Deoclati. Policostini. Palladii. Corcani.
Candidae. Poliarti. Philoronis. Candidi. Sión. Euduti.
Lucei. Antichini. Spolicasti et aliorum .x.

¶ Cronani episcopi. Modici. Corcani. Donnani Inse
Aingi*n*.[1] Daloe Tige Breta*n*.[2] Ingena Fergnae.[3] Molocae
Liphechair.[4]   Ailithri ab.   Brige. Corp*re*[5] 7 Dimae (?)[6].
Emeni sancti. Cormaic ep.

   [1] aigi *Facs.* ' of Inis Aingín.'   [2] ' of Tech Bretan.'   [3] ' the
daughters of Fergna.'   [4] ' of Liphechar.'   [5] *trace of abbrev.*
stroke over p *om. Facs.* Corpre *is a place name TGD,* ' Brig of
Coirpre.'   [6] *obscured by re-inking* ; Druit *Facs.*. Dimae *Br.*,
Dimiae *Todd,* Dimaei *T²*, Dima seu Dimeus *T³,* Dinnii *T¹.*

[8]   .ui. Idus.

Euchti.   Rustici.   Phissei.   Timothei.   Iocundidi.
Ratidis.   Petri.   Luci.   Florii.   Anastaciae.   Floritidis.
Sathei.   Agusti.   Egemoni episcopi.   Uitalis.   Ieiunarii.
Felicis.   Anastasii.   Euticii.

¶ Finani episcopi.   [col. *g*] Cuaca(e) uirginis.   Cilleni
(abba*tis*) (   )at.[1]   Sara(ni) Cule (Crema).[2]   N(echt)an
ner (   ).[3] Mo(sacra) m*ac* Be*n*(nain).   Molibae (m*eic*
Colmodha fratris Dagain i nGlinn) da (L)och*a*.[4]

   [1] *read* Ercnat *OGD, om. Br.*   [2] ' of Cúil Crema.'   [3] Nechtan
an ner *Br. ;* ner de Albae *O.*   [4] *MS. very faint and obscure, portions
within round brackets supplied from Br.* ' in Glenn dá Locha.'

[9]   .u. Idus.

(.   )   (   )   (   )
Martia(lis).   Reuocati.   Possesso(ris).   Ianuarii.   Quinti.
(   ) Furtu(nati).   (   ) Saturni(ni).
Saturi.   (   ).

¶ Faelan Clúa*na* Moescna.[1]   Lomchon[2] sancti.   Finani
saxonis.   Suaibsigi[3] uirginis.   Ciaran Ruis C*u*mulca.[4]
Brendini 7 Baetini.   Guaire Bic.[5]   *in marg.* ¶ To (   )

   [1] ' of Clúain Móescna.'   [2] Lommchú *n.sg.*   [3] Súaibsech
n.sg.   [4] ' of Ros Cumulca.'   [5] ' Gúaire the Little.'

[10]   .iiii. Idus.

Firmi.   Militiadis (ep*iscopi*)[1] et confessoris.   Reuocati.
Clisti.[2] Mirti.   Possessoris 7 aliorum .u.   Saturi.   Uitaliani.
Felicitatis.   Quinti.   Melciadis.

Dermoto Insi Cloth*rann*.[3]   Dimman Insi Cain.[4]   Mosenoc.
Tommine comarb*ae* (   ).[5]   Maelodran.

   [1] *illeg., space for* epi.   [2] *sic, read* Calisti.   [3] ' Diarmait
of Inis Clothrann.'   [4] ' of Inis Caín.'   [5] *obscure ;* Tomini
Arda Macha, *Br. T* ; comarbae Patraicc. *GD.* ' successor of Patrick.'

[11]   .iii. Idus.

Educt(io)¹ Christi ex Egipto.² Petri. A(   )i.³
Philoromi.   Felicis.   Filori.   Seueri.   Lucii.   Zemin(i).⁴
Filoroni. Ingenui.⁵ Ianuarii.   Saturnini. Augenti. Donati.
Eugeni.   (   ) Quinti.   Uincentii et Felicitatis.
(   ) Pausalini.   Sefa(   )⁶ Hortensi.
Er(   ). Ciriaci. Arab(   ). Ebiciani.   (   )
Castoli. (c   ) Modesti. (   ) Castolini.
     [p. 2 a ; Facs. p. 356] ¶ Ernine Clúana Deochra.⁷ Ernine
mac Coemain. Anfudain ep. Glinne da Locha.⁸ Subni ab Iae.⁹
Ronáni. Alteni. Carthinisii episcopi. Feidelma¹⁰ uirgo.

     ¹ over Eductio,c(   ).   ² Et ceti[   ] Facs.   ³ L[   ]
Facs.   ⁴ Zei Facs.   ⁵ Ingeniǫ Facs.   ⁶ faint, sic T.
⁷ ' of Clúain Deochra.'   ⁸ ' of Glenn dá Locha.'   Marginal entry
here illegible.   ⁹ ' of I.'   ¹⁰ sic, Feidelmai Br, om. GD.

[12]   .ii. Idus.

Muscenti.   Saturi.   Zotici.   Ciriaci.   Castuli ⟨bis⟩.
(   )¹ Rogati.   Ualentianae.   Modesti.   Ebiciani.
Petri.² Corotici.   (   )ici³ et aliorum .x. 7 .uiii. Castulini.⁴
Filorini.
     Laigne mac Garbain.   Faelani sancti.   Conain Ega.⁵
Cummini meic Duib o Druim Druith.⁶   Baitheni ab. ⟨.i. mac
Brenaind⟩.⁷   Laidcend mac Báith.   Sinilli ⟨o Chill Airiss⟩⁸
7 Locheni.

     ¹ obscure, perhaps Quinti T.   ² barely traceable.   ³ [   ] bici
Facs. Arabici T.   ¹ Cassulini Facs.   ⁵ ' Conán of Eig.'   ⁶ ' from
Druim Druith.'   ⁷ See Marginal Notes.   ⁸ ' from Cell Airis.'

[13]   Idus.

Ingenui.   Satii.   Uincentii.   Saturi.   Felicitatis.
Cymmini.   Zoticii.   Ciriacii.   Erisini.   Glicerii.   Felicis.
Ianuarii.   Coronae.   Secundi et aliorum .xxu.
     ¶ Hilarii episcopi Pictauis.
     ¶ Colmain.   Manchin mac Collain.   Ronani 7 Colmain Chirr
o Dergderc.¹ Mochónae ep. Lemchailli.² Supplicii.³ Ailello
ep. Saraini episcopi. Teochonnae Cuairne⁴ 7 Deuraith.

     ¹ ' from Dergderc ' ; cp. Mar. 8.   ² ' of Lemchaill.'   ³ sic.,
out of place.   ⁴ ' of Cúairne.'

[14]   .xix. kł. Feb*ruarii*.

Gliceri discipuli et diaconi.   Felicis martiris qui fecit
librum Fel*icis*. Clerici. Diaconi. Pauli. Successi. Uictorini.
Saturi. Missoris. Gerontii. Lucreti. Ianuarii. Agapiti.
Crucessii. Eufrae. Floridae. Tueus. Casiae et aliorum
.uiii.

¶ Sancti Lugei ⟨i nInis Moir.⟩¹ 7 Baetain Me*i*c Lugei
episcopi. Diblini sancti. Fland Find i Cullind i fail² Chorcaigi.³
Latharnis 7 Itharnais i nAchud Fherta.⁴

        ¹ ' in Inis Mór.' *There is confusion here ; see Notes.*   ² fall
Facs.   ³ ' in Cullenn near Corcach.'   ⁴ ' in Achad Ferta.'

[15]   .xuiii. kł.

Supplicii episcopi et confessoris.   Crisconi.¹   Tirsi.
Menelaui.   Lauci.   Gaunitii.²   Mauricii (M)aur(i)³
(d)isci*puli* Bene*dicti* abbatis. (Ce)lesti.⁴ Lucerti. (   )mi⁵
7 aliorum .u. [col. *b*] Ambucuc et Michiae profetarum.

¶ Airechtaig 7 Robartaig i nInis Móir.⁶ *Secht* n-eps*coip*
Dromma Airbelaig.⁷   Dormitatio Itae et filiarum Cairpre.
Bricc Fheli o Bel*uch* Fheli.⁸ Diarmait presbiter. Darerca
uir*go*. Findchritan Craibige.⁹

        ¹ Prisconi *Facs.*   ⁹ G *and* u *obscure.*   ³ aur *obscure.*
⁴ Ce *illeg.*   ⁵ ? (   ) emi *or* (   ) imi ; . . emi *T.*
⁶ ' in Inis Mór.'   ⁷ ' seven bishops of Druim Airbelaig.'
⁸ ' Brcc Féle from Belach Féle.'   ⁹ ' of Craíbech.'

[16]   .xuii. kł.

Marcelli episcopi et confessoris.   Saturnini ⟨b*is*⟩ Faustini
et aliorum .uii. Calesti. Priscillae. Ememriani et aliorum
.xui. Fabiani. Honorati et aliorum martirum .xxix. Honorii
et aliorum martirum .xiiii.

¶ Sancti Faelani. Cilleni. Ninnida Laebd*e*rcc.¹ Dianach
ep. Dromma Móir.²   Iarloga ⟨Liss Moir.³⟩   Sancti Lithgein
Clúa*na* Moir i nU*i*b Falgi.⁴   Dormitatio Fursei.   Diarmait
m*a*c Mechair. Monua Maigi Niad.⁵ Me*i*c Ailella Dromma
Bairr.⁶

        ¹ ' Ninnid Squint-eyed.' *Cp. Jan.* 18.   ' ' of Druim Mór.'
³ ' of Less Mór.'   ⁴ ' Lithgen of Clúain Mór in Uí Failgi.'
⁵ ' of Mag Níad.'   ⁶ ' Ailill's sons, of Druim Bairr.'

[17]   .xui. kł.

Germanorum trium id est Speusepi. Helapi. Munici.
Uictoris. Fortunati. Mucci. Teucisii. Martini et aliorum
.xlii. Miccae. Mistriani. Marcelli. Salui. Sulpicii. Mesalani.
Teusae. Uictoricii. Ueneriae. Satae. Leonillae. Iunillae.
Ingenulae. Uictoriae. Saturnini. Albae. Hortisiani
Uincentiae. Leucii. Rubenti. Misuriani. Timosei.
¶ Ernain 7 Herni*nn* o Thig[1] Ultain m*eic* Ethechtaig i Cúil
Chorra.[2] In Clarenech Dromma Bidc.[3]
¶ Antonii monachi ap*ud* Tebaid*em* Egipti.   Molasse
Cilli Molassi[4] depo*sitio*.[5] Sanctae Micae.

  [1] Ernain o Thig Ernain, *O* (*n*) *GD.* ' Ernán from Tech Ernáin '
Herninn *is evidently a misreading of* Ernain *written above the line
in the exemplar, and here inserted out of place.*   [2] 'Ultán son of
Ethechtach in Cúil Corra.'   [3] ' the Table-faced of Druim Bidg.'
[4] ' of Cell Molassi.'   [5] depo*sitio is out of place, it goes with* Antonii
monachi.

[18]   .xu. kł.

Sanctae Mariae matris Domini.   hoc die eius dormitatio
in Roma audita est., [col. *c.*] Cathetra Petri in Roma.
Fortunati. Astéri. Priscillae. Moysei. Ammoni. Micetae.
Senonis. Zerseni. Menelampi. Dedali. Ualentis martiris.
Tyrsei cum sociis suis. Leucii. Gallinicii. Sconisii. Luricii
et aliorum .xiiii. Successi. Florinae. Ualenti. Bauli.
Telariani. Priscillae. Maluli. Luricii. Uictorini. Floridae.
Honorati. Saturnini.
¶ Nannid Insi Sam for Loch Erni.[1]   Aedammair *ingen*
Aeda. Cobba *ingen* Baetain.   Scoth 7 Femmair.   Mochua
7 Rotan. Blath 7 Ana i Clú*ain* Grenaich.[2]

  [1] ' of Inis Sam on Loch Eirne.'   [2] ' in Clúain Grenaich.'

[19]   .xiiii. kł.

Pauli. Quinti. Gerontii. Ianuarii. Saturnini ⟨b*is*⟩.
Successi. Marii et Marthae sororis Lazari. Gagiae.
Saturninae. Floridae. Calizae. Piae. Priscariae. Tertuli.
Tiberii. Tanmaioli. Uictoriani. Honorati. Fortunati.
Iulii. Lucii. ⟨Natiuitas Sancti Gemanici.⟩ Marcisii.

¶ Pauli senis heremitae.⟩ Puplii. Felicis. Uitalis.
Casiani. Secundi. Uictoris. Primi. Hispani. Luci.
Cacumari. Molendionis. Zosimi. Menelampi. Tubartini.
Furtunati. Sabastiani. Niceti et aliorum martirum .xxxuiii.
¶ Factna ep. ó Nuachongbail Réid Bairend.¹ [col. *d*]
Suibni m*eic* Eogain. Molassi m.h. Nechti.² Ochtidi sancti.

¹ 'from Núachongbail Réid Bairend.' ' = moccu Nechte.

[20] .xiii. kł.

Fabiani. Sabastiani. Uincentii. Calesti. Adaflexi.
Mariae. Marthae. Agnetis uirginis. Celidonae. Marciae.
Lugdonagal. Clementis presbiteri. Leontii. Biti. Ciriacii.
⟨b*is*⟩ Ursi. Gallinici. Marcialis item Felicis. Uiti.
Candei. Florae. Leonti. Ciriaci. Taracona.
¶ Ecca m.h. Chae i Lath Chaín.¹ Oenu m.h. Laigsi a*b*
Cl*úana*.² Fechini Fobair.³ Locheni fili Duib Dligid.⁴ Lugna
crumth*er* o Chill Tarsna.⁵ Cronani. Ferg*us*. Sara*ni*.

¹ 'Ecca moccu Cáe in Lath[rach] Caín,' *i.e. Féchín of Fobar,*
mentioned again below. ² ' Oenu moccu Laigsi abbot of
Clúain [maccu Nóis].' ³ ' Féchín of Fobar.' ⁴ *See Index.*
⁵ ' presbyter, from Cell Tarsna.'

[21] .xii. kł.

Fructuosi episcopi. Felicis. Celsionis. Ciciliani. Auguri.
Martialis. Fulogiae. Eulogiae. Uincentiae. Agnae uirginis
in Roma.¹ Repositae. Felicis. Emerentianae. Uincentii.
Cendeni. Flori. Uiti. Leontii. Puplii. Ciriacii. Uincentis.
Faustaci. Eustacii. Salutoris.² Hermetis. Fructuosii.
Augorii. Diacii. Uitalis et aliorum.u. Patroclii. Auiti
episcopi. Saturnini. Quintini. Marini. Datii. Rutiri.
Gaddani. Caeliani. Seruulii. Rogati. Uictoris. [col. *e*]
Primi. Lucii. Maiulini. Honorati. Secundi. Nasc*ussi*.
Castini. Zatii. Celestini. Hermis. Eglinnae uirginis.

¶ Segain Cilli Segain.³ Ingena Feradaig.⁴ Fainche
Cl*úana* Cae i nEoganac*ht* Casil.⁵ Flaind m*eic* Laich a*b*
Findglassi.⁶

¹ *See Marginal Notes.* ² Saluatoris *Facs.* ³ ' of Cell
Ségáin.' ⁴ 'The daughters of Feradach.' ⁵ 'Fainche of Clúain
Caí in Eoganacht Caisil.' ⁶ *Read* ' son of Cellach abb. of
Findglaiss.'

[22]   .xi. kł.

Ualerii episcopi. Ianuarii. ⟨bis⟩ Uincentii et aliorum
.xuiii. Quintiliani. Cassiani. Matutini. Paulini. Urbani.
Martialis. Fausti. Successi. Felicis. Pauli. Petri martiris.
Primitiui. Cediani. Booti. Optati. Frontonis. Iulii.
Bellici. Municipi. Tetotici. Orionis. Memonis. Hermetis
et aliorum .xix. et Felicis cum sociis suis.

¶ Mocholmoc ..i. Liss Móir⟩ m.h. Beonna.¹ Lonan Find.²
Amalgaid 7 Guaire et filiarum Comgaill id est Lasii et Columbae
et Bogae.

¹ 'i.e. of Less Mór moccu Beonna.'   ² 'Lonán the fair.'

[23]   .x. kł.

Seueriani. Cornelii. Saturni. Castuli. Belli. Minuci.
Aquiliae. Ueterae. Basillae. Eugenii. Galatiae. Macarii.
Papiae. Clemati. Exorcizae. Castuli. Florii. Secundi.
Neonis.

¶ Lucain Tamnaigi.¹ Lucas 7 Cainech. Mochelloc o
Thilaig Ualand.² Mocnopae.

¹ 'Lucán of Tamnach.'   ² 'from Telach Úalann.'

[24] [col. f]   .ix. kł.

Panes.   Babilli episcopi et trium paruulorum eius.
Mardon[i]. Eutasii. Hermetis et aliorum .xxii. Mussuri.
Eugeni. Metelli. Epictiti. Rupi. Memae. Pupliani.
Fustaci confessoris. Uincentiae. Galei. Dati. Maximi.
Saturnini. Marini. Agniti. Saturi. Gaudiani. Felicissimi.
Celiani.

¶ Baetan Methuis Truim.¹ Epscop Guasacht o Granarit.²
Manchan Leith mac Indaigae.³

¹ 'of Methus Truim.'   ² 'Bishop Gúasacht from Granard.'
³ 'Manchán of Líath son of Indach.'

[25] .uiii. kł.

Policarpi. Pauli apostoli conuersio in Damasco. Uitii.
Donati. Secundi. Sidonis. Bitii. Tirsii. Ypictiti.
Arthemini. Pupliani. Faminiani.[1] Raumani. Sadonis.
Sabiani. Puteol*is* Antimasii. Sabiani. Leodocii. Rauiani.
Teoginis.

¶ Mochonnae Ernaide[2] 7 Mochuae. Epsco*p* Guaire i
ṅGobuil.[3] Mc.h. G*r*eccae i Findchill.[4] Findche u*ir*go Slebi
Guaire.[5] Sancti Aeda episcopi.,

[1] *MS. rather* Famimani   [2] 'of Ernaide.'   [3] 'in Gobol.'
[4] 'Moccu Greccae in Findchell'; *see Notes.*   [5] 'of Slíab Gúaire.'

[26] .uii. kł.

Policarpi episcopi. Datiui. Iuliani. Paulae uirginis.
Telliani. Reot*r*i. Rodonis. Taeliptae. Uincentiae.
Uict*uri*nae.[1] Papae. Arthemati. Secundi. Emiliani.
Teoginis. [col. *g*] Sabinis et aliorum .xxxuiii.

¶ Epsco*p* Calb o Thulaig Carpait i mMenna Tiri i nU*i*b
Meith.[2] Erneni episcopi.

[1] n-*stroke faint, om. Facs.*   [2] 'Bishop Calb from Tulach
Carpait in Menna Tíre in Uí Méith.'

[27] .ui. kł.

Furtunati. Agnetis uirginis. Ueneriae. Marinae.
Fortunatae. Tecussae. Secundae. Perpetuae. Iulianae.
Uincentiae. Uict*uri*ae. Donati. Uiti. Saturnini. Messuriani.
Puplii. Festi. Uictoris. Quintilli. Rogati. Felicis.
Publicani. Bonosii. Processi. Egotis. Pictuli. Uincentii.
Primi. Aurilii. Secundi. Hilarii. Uictoris. Leoci. Dati.
Iuliani. Celiani. Saturi. Calleniti. Lucii. Honorati.
Marosi. Casti. Gaii. Gagi.

¶ Noe Findglassi.[1] Lucann sac. Findbeo Inbir Melgi.[2]
Croni Insi Locha Croni.[3] Noele Inbir.[4] Murgeni abbatis
Glinni Uisen.[5]

[1] 'of Findglaiss.'   [2] 'of Inber Melgi.'   [3] 'of Inis
Locha Cróni.'   [4] 'of Inber [Nóele].'   [5] 'abbot of Glenn
Uissen.'

[28] .u. kł.

Messoriani et aliorum .xxu. Uictoris. Festi. Perpetuae.
Marinae. Agnatae. Teliptae. Messoriani. Uincentianae.
Canti et aliorum .xxxu. Uictoriae. Papae. Genuinii.[1]
Secundi. Infirmi sacerdotis.

¶ Aedlug Aird Chassain.[2] Cainer ingen Chruthnechain
meic Laigne i fail Fhobair.[3] Eochaid epscop 7 abb Tamlachta.[4]
Melliani .i. i Cill Rois.[5] Accobrani. Commani.

[1] reading doubtful; Geniunii Facs. [2] 'of Ard Chassáin.'
[3] 'Cainer daughter of Cruthnechán s. of Laigne near Fobar ;'
see Notes. [4] 'of Tamlachta.' [5] 'i.e. in Cell Rois.'

[29] .iiii. kł.

Pauli episcopi. Ypoliti episcopi et episcoporum trium.
Constantini. Uictoris. Honorati. Constantinae uirginis.
Perosiae. Treueris.

¶ Na trí clarenig .i.[1] Baitheni 7 Segini 7 Cronani.
Mochonna. Blatha uirginis. Gildae episcopi et sapientis.
Dallan mac Forgaill ó Magin.,[2]

[1] ' The three table-faced ones, i.e.' '' from Maigen.'

* * * * * * * *

[1] [Br. 30 .iii. kł.

Cruimthir[2] Ailbhe. Huarani. Cronani sacerdotis. Ternoc.
Barinn Insi Domle.[3] Enani sancti Rois Móir.[4]

[1] Leaf lost here, LL., Brussels MS. fol. 4. [2] 'presbyter.'
[3] ' of Inis Domle.' [4] · of Ros Mór.'

31 .ii. kł.

Lug Tire da Craebh .i. mac Eachdach.[1] Cairnain et
Sillan Cilli Delga.[2] Taeda meic Colgan. Oebhnat Finn o
Ros na Seanchae.[3] Eda episcopi Ferna.[4] Maol Anfaidh
Dairinsi.[5] Cainnichi presbiteri. Docaemi episcopi.
Dochumma Noendrom[a].[6]

[1] ' Lug of Tír dá Chráeb, i.e. s. of Eochaid.' [2] 'of Cell
Delga.' [3] 'Óebnat the Fair from Ros na Seanchae ' (Ros
Enche, GD). [4] ' Áed (i.e. Máedóc) of Ferna.' [5] ' of
Darinis.' [6] ' Do Chumma (or Mo Chumma) of Nóendruim.'

[Feb.] 1   **Kł.** Feb*ruarii.*

Dormitatio sancti Brigitae lxx° anno aetatis suae.
Derlugach.   Beonni uirginis.   Cinni sac.   Airenna[n] .h.[1]
Foduibh.

    [1] · Airennán moccu (*reading* m.h. *GD*) Foduib.'

2   .iiii. N*onas.*

Mothrianoc m*a*c Aengasa.   Colmani.   Illadhon on Disert.[1]
Aithmet Clochair.[2]   Finnchi Duirn.[3]   Colma*n*i.

    [1] 'from the Dísert.'   [2] ' of Clochar.'   [3] · Finnech of
Dorn.'

3   .iii. N*onas.*

Colman m*a*c Duach.   Cuana ⟨.i. Glinni⟩[1] a*b* Maigi Bile.[2]

    [1] ' i.e. of Glenn.'   Cuanan *GD.*   [2] ' i.e. of Glenn, abbot of
Mag Bile.'

4   .ii. N*onas.*

Lomman et Colman o Tamlac[h]ta Gliadh.[1]   Cor*c* et Cóta
o Drui*n*n.[2]   Cuanna Lis Moir.[3]   Fuidbech m*a*c Illadan.

    [1] · from Tamlachta Glíadh.'   [2] *sic,* ' from Druinn.'
    [3] ' of Less Mór.'

5   Nonas.

Liadnan a*b* Fob*air*.[1]   Caerae o Rait[h] Moentich.[2]   Baetain
m*ei*c Colmain.   Fingin m*a*c Odrain Febla.[3]   Dubt[h]ach sac.
Hechtach uirgo.

    [1] · abbot of Fobar.'   [2] ' from Ráith Móentich.' .n̄. *add. in marg.*
    [3] *sic GD* ; Febla *precedes* Fingin *in Br. MS.*

6　　　　　.uiii. Idus.

Durán mac Colaim ó Druim Chrema.¹　Colman 7 Brandubh
o Loch Munremuir.²　Meli episcopi.

　　¹ ' from Druim Crema.'　　² ' from Loch Munremair.'

7　　　　　.uii. Idus.

Tri meic Daire, Lonán 7 Critan et Maolan Mona Maolain.¹
[f. 4ᵛ] Mellan Insi .i. mc. h. Cuinn.²　Fintan sac. Clúana Cain.³
Maenucan Atha Liac.⁴　Lomman Locha hUair.⁵　Colmani
episcopi. Brigit ingean Droma.⁶　Aidi episcopi Slebti.⁷
Colmani episcopi.

　　¹ ' Dáire's three sons, Lonán, Critán, and Máelán of Móin
Máeláin.'　² ' of Inis, i.e. moccu Cuin.'　³ ' of Clúain Caín.'
⁴ ' of Áth Liacc.'　⁵ ' of Loch Uair.'　⁶ sic, leg. Domma,
GD, ' daughter of Domma.'　⁷ ' of Slébte.'

8　　　　　.ui. Idus.

Colman mc. h. Thelluibh.¹　Fiachra ab Iraird.²　Mac Liac
espoc Liathdromma.³　Cére sanctae uirginis.　Hua ind
ecis⁴ qui congregauit reliquias sanctorum.　Ruidchi uirginis.
Airdoni. Falbe.⁵　Ternoc anchorita.

　　¹ ' moccu Telduib.'　　² ' abbot of Irard.'　　³ ' bishop,
of Líathdruim.'　　⁴ ' The grandson of the poet ' (i.e. Onchú
OGD).　⁵ Falbe ⟨Erdoim⟩ G, i.e. Falbe of Erdam.　Cp. Failbe
Erdaim, Ap. 8, infra.

9　　　　　.u. Idus.

Cuarani¹ sapientis qui et Cróna[n]² mac Nath Seman dicitur
uel mac Netha.　Cairech Dergain.　Sancti Ronani Lis Móir.³
Moc[h]olmoc Clúana Iraird.⁴　Crumthir Finnai Droma Licci.⁵

　　¹ corr. from Caurnani.　² Cronan OGD.　³ ' of Less Mór.
⁴ ' of Clúain Iraird.'　⁵ ' Presbyter Finne of Druim Licce.'

10   .iiii. Id*us*.

Crónani filii Mellani isna Deisibh, 7 i lLios Mór.[1] Darluga
u*irg*o o Lemmaig[2] [3].i. Modúit o Chill Moduit i níbh Maine.
Sillani episcopi Gli*nne* da Locha.[4]   Becga inghen Gabrain.[5]
Airenda*ni* ep. Tamlac[h]ta.[6]

   [1] 'in the Déssi [Muman] and in Less Mór.'   [2] 'from
Lemmag.' [3] *supply* Simplex (?) ' i.e. Modúit from Cell Modúit in
Uí Maine.' Cp. Ó (*n*) D, Feb. 12.   [4] 'of Glenn dá Locha.'
[5] 'daughter of Gabrán.'   [6] 'of Tamlachta'

11   .iii. Idus.

Mogobóc Ratha Lamraige[1] *nomen* idem et Gobán.   Lappáni
m*ei*c Ciarain.   Luchta At[h]a Ferna.[2]   Dubáni sacerdotis.
Iarlaithi.   Senachi sacerdotis.   Etchani episcopi.   Gobnat
Ernaidhe i Múscr*aigh*e Mitine.[3]   Finnani episcopi 〈Maighe
Bile〉 [4] uel Finnian Cl*úana* Iraird.[5]

   [1] 'of Ráith Lamraige.'   [2] 'of Áth Ferna.'   [3] 'Gobnat
of Ernaide in Muscraige Mitine.'   [4] 'of Mag Bile.'   [5] 'of
Clúain Iraird ' *corr. from* Maighi Bile, *expuncted*.

12   .ii. Idus.

Siatal epi.   Aedh Cael m*ac* Feradhaigh.   Cronani.   Sancti
Fethgnai.   Lugaidh Cule Ruscaigh.[1]   Cumman Glinni Mona.[2]
Coníni.   Beologa.   Fina*ni* m*ei*c Airennáin.   Aedhan Cl*úana*
Dartadha.[3]

   [1] 'of Cúil Rúscach.'   [2] 'of Glenn Móna.'   [3] 'of Clúain
Dartada.'

13   Idus.

Modimóc Tibrat Fachtna.[1] [f. 5] Domhangin.[2]   Cruachnat
oc Ros Fac[h]tna.[3]   Sancti Darii.   Sancti Finani.

   [1] 'of Tipra Fachtna.'   [2] *an alias for* Modomnóc *or* Modímmóc.
   [3] 'at Ros Fachtna '; *read* Cuachnat of Ros Raithe GD.

14   .xui. kł.

Manchani Maethla[1] cum soc[i]is suis.   Sínach Sratha
Irenn.[2] Commani.

    [1] 'of Máethail.'   [2] 'of Srath Irenn.'

15   .xu. kł.

Fergus mac Aengusa.   Berrech Cluana Cairpthi.[1] Forannan
mac Aedha.

    [1] 'of Clúain Cairpthe.'

16   .xiiii. kł.

Oengas espoc Ratha na nEspoc   Áed Glas.[2] Robni aḃ.

    [1] 'bishop, of Ráith na nEpscop.'   [2] 'Áed the Grey.' *Also*
Oct. 29

17   .xiii. kł.

Fintan Clúana Eidneach[1] aḃ.   Dac[h]onna mac Odrain.
Brelach mac Fichellaigh.   Midu mac Fac[h]tna oc Sligid.[2]
Fidchellaig.   Ossani episcopi.   Loman i nAth Truim[3] cum
sociis .i. Patricii hostiari.   Lurech mac Cuanach.   Fortchern
7 Cael Ochtra.   Aeda.   Aeda.   Aeda.   Cormacci episcopi.
Conani.   Cumeane episcopi et Lacteani sacerdotis.   Ossani
et Sarani.   Conaill.   Colmani et Lactani episcopi.   Finnsigi
uirginis.   Hi omnes in Áth Truim requiescunt.

    [1] 'of Clúain Eidnech.'   [2] 'at Slige.'   [3] 'in Áth Truim.'
Also Oct. 11.

18   .xii. kł.

Colman i mMuríab fri Móna ituaidh ata Colman.[1] Molibba
i nUíb Eachach Ulad no i nUíb Garrchon.[2] Oengus. Danielis
episcopi.   Nem espoc Droma Bertach quinta feria semper
ante quadragesimum.[3] Huidhrín o Dhruim Dresna.[4] Sanctae
Lasre uirginis i nGlinn Medhoin.[5]

    [1] 'in Muriab to the north of Mona is Colmán.'   [2] 'in Ui
Echach of Ulster or in Uí Garrchon.'   [3] *sic.*   [4] 'from Druim
Dresna'; Dresa GD.   [5] 'in Glenn Medóin.'

19   .xi. kł.

Baeithin meic Cuanach episcopi.   Maol Dobarchon.
Nodtat episcopi.   Dego meic Nemuaill.   Fechine mc. h.
Cainchi o Leammaigh.¹ Odrán Tíre Óenaigh.²

  ¹ 'Féchín moccu Cainchi from Lemmag.'   ² 'of Tír
Óenaig.'

20   .x. kł.

Cronani. Colgu mc. h. Dunechda.¹ Espoc Olcán.²

  ¹ 'Colgu moccu Dunechda.'   ² 'Bp. Olcán'; Bolcán GD.

[f. 5ᵛ] 21   .ix. kł.

Fintain Coraigh .i. i lLemhc[h]aill nó i Clúain Eidhnech.¹
Colman Airdi Bó for brú Locha Eachach.²   Cronan Cilli
Bicci.³

  ¹ 'i.e. in Lemchaill or in Clúain Eidnech.'   ⁿ 'of Ard Bó
on the brink of Loch nEchach.'   ³ 'of Cell Becc.'

22   .uiii. kł.

Caemhan Maighi Mennota.¹ Guirminni inghen Conghaili.
Míadhnat Airid Droc[h]ait.² Maelan Achaid.³ Feicin sac.

  ¹ 'of Mag Mennota'; Mag Maic Dodon GD.   ² Midabair
Rind Droichit GD; 'of Aired Drochait.'   ³ 'of Achad';
Achaid Gobra GD.

23   .uii. kł.

Cass Lethglinne.¹ Mannán 7 Tiaman Airid Suird.² Ingena
Oengassa.³ Cruimther Connrach.⁴ Findchadan na hArda.⁵
Colmain. Ernine Lethglinni.⁶

  ¹ 'of Lethglenn.'   ² Tian GD; 'of Aired Suird'; Airid
hUird GD.   ³ 'the daughters of Óengus.'   ⁴ 'Presbyter
Connrach.'   ⁵ 'of the Árd.'   ⁶ 'of Lethglenn.'

24   .ui. kł.

Cuimine Find mac Fiachna meic Feradhaigh[1] ab Iae.
Ciaran hua Mesa .i. Aird Fhota.[2]

[1] 'Cummine Find s. of Fíachna s. of Feradach, abbot of Í.'
[2] 'descendant of Mesa (?) i.e. of Ard Fota.'   Heise⟨Airidh
Fota⟩D. . . Ciaran⟨Uamha⟩G : *a corruption of Ua Mesa.*

25   .u. kł.

Cianani abbatis.   Caimsae uirginis.   Croni Tamhlachta.[1]
Ciarani sancti.

[1] ' of Tamlachta.'

26   .iiii. kł.

Cornani[1] sancti Glinni Esa.[2]   Beccani Chind Ṡali.[3]
Moennae. Ethni. Sancti Aedlugha.

[1] *sic, for* Cronani.   [2] ' of Glenn Esa ' ; Aesa *GD.*   [3] ' of
Cenn Sáile.'

27   .iii. kł.

Comgain Glinni Usin.[1]   Comman mc. h. Themhni.[2]

[1] ' of Glenn Uissen.'   [2] Commán moccu Temne.

28   .ii. kł.

Cruimt[h]ir Domhnaigh[1] cum Firlain h. Faelain.[2]   Ternoc
et Diuchaill meic Maelduibh i nAiriudh Muilt oc Lochaibh
Eirne.[3] Aedo meic Bricc.[4] Mosinu mc. h. Mind .i. Sillan ab.
Bennchair.[5] Ernini ingen Airchinnig eadem et Febair.

[1] ' of Domnach.'   [2] ' descendant of Fáelán ' ; *om. GD.*
[3] ' in Aired Muilt at Loch Erne.'   [4] *Also May* 4, *July* 30, *where
om. GD. His day is Nov.* 10, *OG.*   [5] ' Mosinu moccu Mind, i.e.
Sillán abbot of Bennchor.'

[March] 1   **Kł.** Marta.

Sarain episcopi. Dauid Cille Mune.[1] Moinend episcopi.
Senani episcopi. Me*i*c Nisi episcopi. Banfota. Enani.[2]
Cassan m*a*c Nemain. Baítani episcopi Cl*ú*ana.[3] Columbae
Cinn Garadh.[4]

[1] 'of Cell Mune.'   [2] Enan gl. mac Nissi *GD*.   [3] 'of
Clúain.'   [4] 'of Cenn Garad.'

2   .ui. N*onas*.

Fergna aƀ Iae.[1] Finniaui. Lughaidh sac. Mantan.
Conuill. Cuain Chain.[2]

[1] 'Abbot of Í.'   [2] 'Cúan the Fair.'

[f. 6] 3   .u. N*onas*.

Moṡacru m*a*c Senain i Tigh Thacru.[1] Connae uirginis.
Ereclach. Foilend. Fachtna ó Chraebaig.[2] Cilline Inse
Domle.[3] Mochua Cl*ú*ana Dobtha.[4] Conaill sancti. Deochain
Reat.[5] Modímoc episcopi. Concrada. Celi Cri*st*.

[1] 'in Tech Tacru ; ' Sacru *GD*.   [2] 'from Cráebach ; ' ó
Crebhicc *GD*.   [3] 'of Inis Domle.'   [4] 'of Clúain Dobtha.'
[5] 'deacon Reat.'

4   .iiii. N*onas*.

Mucini Maighni.[1] Noebepscop o Clochar Bainni.[2]

[1] 'of Maigen.'   [2] 'a holy bishop from Clochar Bainne.
Pilip eps. Cluana Bainb *GD*.

5   .iii. N*onas*.

Ciaran Saighre et Carthach i Saighir[1] in uno die 7 Cárthach
m*a*c Oengusa Droma Ferdaim.[2] Colma*n*i. ifīr.[3]

[1] 'Cíarán of Saigir and Carthach in Saigir.'   [2] 'of Druim
Ferdaim,' Fertáin *GDO*(*n*).   [3] *sic*, Isirni *Kelly* ; *om. TGD ; perhaps
for* infirmi.

6   .ii. Nonas.

Odrani sancti.   Furb*aide*.¹   Maol Ruain Droma Ratha.²
Inghena Lenini.³   Carp*re* Crui*nn*.⁴   Múadain Cairn ⟨Fur-
b*aide*⟩.⁵ Maeldub mac B*er*rain.

¹ *om. TGD, here evidently inserted in error from Muadán entry
below.*   ² 'of Druim Ráithe.'   ³ 'the daughters of Leníne.'
⁴ *sic, read* Cruimm ; Coirpre Crom ' the Bent,' *O* (*n*) *GD.*   ⁵ 'of
Carn Furbaide.' Furb*aide* add. *Colgan.*

Nonas.

7   .uiii. Idus [*recte* Nonas.]

¹ Senani Insi Cathaigh.² Beoaedo Aird Carna.³ Mocellócc.
Metan o Thuaim Athi.⁴ Caritan Droma Lara.⁵

¹ *Both Senan and Beóáed are out of place here, their day being
.uiii. idus. See Notes.   Under* Nonas *a blank space.*   ² 'of Inis
Cathaig.'   ³ 'of Ard Carna.'   ⁴ 'from Túaim Átha.'   ⁵ 'of
Druim Lara.'

8   [.uiii. Idus.]

Moconna Essa mac nEirc.¹   Cronani Airdni.²   Colmani
Chirr.³   Libra*nn*i sancti.   Molaisi mac Aeda.   Ailgniad.
Curchach Cl*úana* Lothor.⁴   Ciaran.   Conanla Eassa Ruaidh.⁵
Liberi sancti.   Siadail Chinn Locha.⁶   Mochua mac Nemain.
Moconna Daire.⁷   Neman ⟨.i. Dairinse⟩.⁸ ⁹Mac Colaim Chirr.⁹

¹ 'of Ess mac nEirc.'   ² 'of Airdne.'   ³ 'Colmán
Cerr ; ' *om. GD., cp. Jan.* 13.   ⁴ 'Curcach of Clúain Lothair ; '
cp. Aug. 8.   ⁵ 'of Ess Rúaid ; ' *nom.* Conandil *OG,* Conan *D.*'
⁶ 'of Cenn Locha.'   ⁷ 'of Daire ;' *also May* 3.   ⁸ 'of Dairinis.'
⁹⁻⁹ *om. GD.*

9   .uii. Idus.

Brigit inghen Doma i Maigh Liphi.¹   Setna Droma m*ei*c
Blae.²   Brigit Mona Milain.³   Lugida Cille Cule.⁴   Setna Chilli
Ané i Sleibh Bregh.⁵   Sillain.   Colmain Cl*úana* Tibrinni.⁶
Dimmae.   Mellae.   Tosai Droma Laidcinn.⁷

¹ 'd. of Doma in Mag Liphi ; ' *cp. Feb.* 7.   ² 'of Druim
maccu Blai ; ' mc Ublai *TGD.*   ³ 'of Móin Miláin.'   ⁴ 'Lugaid
of Cell Cúle.'   ⁵ 'of Cell Aine in Sliab Breg.'   ⁶ 'of
Clúain Tibrinne ; ' *also Mar.* 13 ; *under* 10 *March GD.*   ⁷ 'of
Druim Laidcinn.'

10   .ui. Idus.

Silu*ester* ep.   Torman et Mac Crúadeni.¹   Sancti Setnae.
Failbe Bec ab Iae.²   Fir Fuighill ep.

    ¹ Meic Thormain me*ic* Cruaidhen *D and gl. G* ; Torman *om. T.*
    ² ' Failbe the Little, abbot of Í.'

[f. 6ᵛ] 11   .u. Idus.

Constantini Briton † me*ic* Fergusa do Cruth*nechaib*.¹
Librani.   Libren Cl*úana* Fota.²   Cuannae ceci.³   Findcain
aircisiremh.⁴   Mosenoc † Sena*n*i Bethrech.⁵   ]
⁶[p. 3*a*. ; *Facs.* p. 357]   Oengusa episcopi hu*i* Oibleain.⁷

    ᴸ ' or son of Fergus of the Picts.'   ² ' of Clúain Fota.'
    ³ ' Cúanna the Blind.'   ⁴ ' Findchán the much
    tortured ' (?) ; *in marg. man. al.* .i. Finchani qui fuit in
    cruciatibus diuturnis.   ⁵ ' or Senán Bethech ' (*sic leg.*
    GDT).   ⁶ *Here LL resumes.*   ⁷ ' grandson of Oibleán.'

[12]   .iiii. Idus.

Grigo*rii* papae Romae.   Ost*e*nsio Petri Grigorio recusanti
principatum.   Muridani episcopi et aliorum .lx.   Egoni et
aliorum .ui. Donatae.   Basilissae filiae Cionis.   Zoni.   Duni.
Alaxandri.   Iohannis et aliorum .xliiii.   Siluani.   Innocentii.
Rasii.   Migdoni.   Maci.   Dorothi.   Gorgoni.   Macedoni.
Eunci.   Maximi.   Rugini.   Petri et aliorum .x.   Iouiani.
Ilarii.   Concessi.   Spirnae.   Pioni.   Smragdi.⁴   Eradi.   Eracli.
Marias.   Nestorii.   Eugenii.   Quirini.   Zefani.   Felicis.
Pilippi   Antonii.

    ¶ Garalt Maigi Eó¹ cum suis.   Mochua Ailiuin.²   Dagani
episcopi.   Cilleni Lilchaig.³   Sancti Maele Corgais.

    ¹ ' of Mag Eó.' *Mar.* 13, *GD.*   ² Dochualen *G*, Dachuailen
    mac Guaire *D. read* (?) Mochuailén.   ³ ' of Lilchach.'   ⁴ Sinragdi
    Facs.

[13] .iii. Idus.

Macedoni et uxoris eius. Patriciae et filiae. Modestae.
Chioni. Saturnini. Silui. Ianuarii. Petroni. Zosimi.
Modestini. Saliui. Cioni. Castacii.

¶ Mochaemoc Leith Móir.[1] Conchend m*eic* Lucennain.
Cuangusa m*eic* Aile*l*la. Colman ⟨bdíc⟩[2] Cl*úana* Tibrinne.[3]

[1] 'of Líath Mór.' *See Marginal Notes.*   [2] Beithech *T.*
Mar. 10, *GD.*   [3] ' of Clúain Tibrinne.'

[14] .ii. Idus.

Dionisii episcopi. Eufrosii. Felicissimi. Dati*ui*. Alax-
andri. Pionis. Furmini. Dionisii. Alaxandri. Saluatoris.
Frontinae. Hursiniae. Dionae. Pelliotae. Rabae. Dionae.
Faustae. Saluae. Ingenuae. Palidi. Pallitani. Innocentii
episcopi. Eufrasiae. Petri. Mammerii. Naborii. Lucae.
Iacobi. Frontoni. Fi*r*mini. Lucii. Uincentii. Marci.
Pauli. Teophili. Petroni.

¶ Sancti Talmachi. Flannan Cilli Aird.[1] Cu*m*nig.
Coímani. Ultani.[2] h. Aignig.

[1] ' of Cell Aird.'   [2] *supply* .m. = moccu ' Ultán moccu
Aignich (*or* Eignich)' ; Maighnidhe *GD.*

[15] Idus.

Iacobi apostoli fratris Domini. Ordinatio Lucae euan-
gelistae. Longini. Lucii martiris. Salui. Pauli. Silui.
Saturnini. Ingenuae. Spinosi. [col. *b*] Innocentii. Efiro.
Reguli et aliorum .iiii.

¶ Et filiorum iii. Nesani id est Monissu ⁊ Sessloga[1] ⁊
Diucaill. Trenech.[2] ⟨deirg.⟩[3] Tiu[4] ingen Eltine. Sancti
Eugenii.

[1] Nesslug *GD, gen. sg.* Neslogha *O* (*n*) ; *read* Nessloga.   [2] *om.*
TGD.   [3] deirg *over* Trenech *MS., but is the epithet of* Diucaill
GDO(*n*), *read* Diucaill deirg ' the Red.'   [4] 'd. of Eltíne.'
Tui *Br.* Trí hinghena Eltín ' three daughters of Eltín ' *G gl. & D.*
Trium filiarum Eltini *T.*

[16]   .xuii. kł.

Hilarii. Titiani. Tasiani ⟨bis⟩. Castoris. Dionisii ⟨bis⟩.
Noni. Sireni. Eugenii. Iuliani. Iouani. Amphi. Curiacae.
Mariae. Milisae. Ascliophidoti. Sampiliani. Sereni ⟨bis⟩.
Grignei. Eugeniae et aliorum .x.¹

¶ Denach Insi Détna.² Abbani m.h.³ Chor*maic.* Finani
loboir Suird *no* Clúana Mó[i]r.⁴ Curitani sancti episcopi et
ab*batis* Ruis Mind Bairend.⁵ Episcopi Feithmeic o Chill
Tuama.⁶ ⟨Laudani.⟩⁷

¹ *See Marginal Notes.* ² ' of Inis Détna ' ; Setna *GD.*
³ = moccu ; *also Oct.* 27. ⁴ ' Fínán the Leper of Sord or of Clúain
Mór.' ⁵ ' of Ros Mind Bairend.' *G has* Barrfind, *a separate com-*
memoration ; so also D. ⁶ ' from Cell Túama ' ; Tua*mma Facs.*
⁷ *om. GD.*

[17]   .xui. kł. Ap*rilis.*

Patricii episcopi. Mariae. Uictorinae. Ciriacae. Nó*nn*ae.
Dionisii. Ianari. Uictorini. Largii. Largi. Ilarii. Titiani.
Alaxandri. ⟨Zefani.⟩ Teodoli. Petri.

¶ Nessain Corcaige.¹ Failtige*rn* uir*go.* Tige*rn*ach eps.
Beccan Ruimni.² Gobbain m*eic* Nasci.

¹ ' of Corcach.'   ² ' of Ruimen.'

[18]   .xu. kł.

Collegi. Pamporii. Ninepti. Rogati. Mariae. Rogatae.
Aureliae. Saldae. Quartildae. Coloti. Capilidae. Coloti.
Quartini. Saturi. Marini. Ingenui. Aurelii. Capilledi.
Dionisii et aliorum .uii. Ap*rilis.* Seruuli et xx. milites.¹
Honorii. Ierolii. Tithei. Martii et aliorum .xliii.

¶ Conaill episcopi. [col. *c*] Ericbirt sax*onis.* Moedóc Clú*ana*
Escrach.² Tommain ep. Coemain sancti.

¹ *sic.* ² ' of Clúain Escrach.'

[19]   .xiiii. kł.

Ioseph sponsi Ma*riae*. Grigorii ordinatio. Teodori. Basi.
Bucelli. Fisciani. Auxilii. Poemi. Iosepi. Britoniae.
Basillae et aliorum .uii. Uonechtae. Rogatae. Quartillae.
Auxulae. Apollonii. Ammoni. Saturnini. Marci et aliorum
.ix. Florentii. Collectici. Aprilis. Seruuli. Quinti.
Ingenui. Dionisii. Ianuarii. Uago. Uictorii. Nuncti.
Samfo*ri*. Rogati et aliorum .xxui. Bassilii.

¶ Auxilinus.[1] ¶ Lachtain Achaid Úir.[2] Mella Cl*úana*
Hí.[3] Mochua Árasnai.[4]

¹ *See Marginal Notes.*   ² ' of Achad Úr.'   ³ ' of Clúain Hí.'
⁴ ' of Arasnae.'

[20]   .xiii. kł.

Iosephi. Pauli. Quirilli. Eugenii. Ioseph. Serapionis.
Tygini. Claudii. Exs*upe*ri. Uictorini. Ualentini. Domini.
Teodori. Bassii et aliorum .xx. Grigorii. Commodi. Fisciani.
Pomeri. Tillae. Basillae. Quartillae. Unoetae. Catulini.
Leotini. Sorentii et aliorum .uii. Quinti. Marci. Quintilli.
Florentii et aliorum .ix. Policroni. Parmeni. Helii. Criso-
theli. Lucae.

¶ Mucci*n*. Cutbricti sax*onis* .i. Insi Menóc.[1] Aedan
Cl*úana* Maelain.[2] Canan m*ac* Corae. Cathchan Ratha
Dirthaigi.[3]

¹ ' i.e. of Inis Menóc.'   ² ' of Clúain Máeláin.'   ³ ' of Ráith
Derthaige.'

[21]   .xii. kł. Ap*rilis*.

Serapionis ⟨bis⟩. Iosephi. Uoluntiani. Ammoni. Poli-
carpi. Amatoris. Pauli. [col. *d*] ¹Amatoris. Pauli.¹ Quirilli.
Grigorii. Eugenii. Tigrini. Claudii. Exs*upe*ri. Uict*ur*icii.
Ualentini. Do*m*ini. Olimpiacis. Maximi. Iosephi. Uolusii.
Filocali. Filocarpi. ⟨Momatiae uirginis.⟩ Monachi et aliorum
.u. Be*ne*dicti abbatis.

¶ Lucill m.h. Chiara.[2] Ennae Áirni[3] m*eic* Ainmire m*eic*
Ronain de Cremthannaib.[4]

¹⁻¹ *dittography*.   ² = moccu Cíara.   ³ ' of Árann.'
⁴ ' of the Cremthanna.'

[22]   .xi. kł.

Secundi. Paulini. Aronis. Pauli. Saturnini et aliorum
uiii. Drecóni. Orionis. Serapionis. Iosippi. Iacobi.
Acclusi. Uolusi. Philocali. Contii. Filocarpi. ⟨Honis.⟩
Uolutiani. Nomini. Luci. Ammonis. Ammoni. Amatoris.
Felicis et aliorum .xiiii.
    ¶ Failbe ab Iae.¹ Dimmae. Treno meic Deeid.
Molocae meic Colmain Find Lilchaig.² Derercae. Ilinni
7 Degitge. Egressio familiae Brendini.

    ¹ · of Í.'   ² ' of Lilchach.'

[23]   .x. kł.

Felicis. Secundi. Paulini. Arionis et aliorum .xix.
Cessariae. Saturnini. Pauli. Iuliani. Agatani. Alaxandri.
Augustini. Tinomi. Dionisii et aliorum .ix. Felicis. Agatii.
Dreconii. Orionis. Felicis. Zefani. Albini. Laurentii.
Teodoriae.

    ¶ Sancti Treno Cilli Daelen.¹ Lassar ingen Fintain.²
Baetain Monan.³ Trian. Cairlain. Fergusa. Failbi. Darerca
uirgo. Ingen Feradaig.⁴ Momedoc Feda Duin⁵ .i. Midúi
meic Midgna.

    ¹ ' of Cell Dáelen.'   ² ' daughter of Fintan.'   ³ ' of
Monu.'   ⁴ ' the daughter of Feradach.'   ⁵ ' of Fid Dúin.'
Also May 18, Aug. 13.

[24] [col. e]   .ix. kł.

Cena Domini. Seleuci. Agapiti. Albini. Timolaii.
Romuli. Diopi. Catulae ⟨bis⟩. Aprilis. Aliundo. Saturnini.
Sali et aliorum .xui. Molei. Romuli. Pisoni. Alaxandri.
Diopi. Rogati. Uictorini. Uiti. Ioseph. Sancdioli.
Secunduli. Ueroli. Salitoris. Felicis episcopi. Ambrosii.

    ¶ Mochta Lugmaid¹ Cumman nomen matris eius. Scire
uirgo. Epscop² Cairlán. Fergusa. Domongart mac Echdach.
Epscop² Mac Carthind. Lugaid · mac Echach o Chlúain Laeg.³

    ¹ ' of Lugmad ' ; see Marginal Notes, also Aug. 19.   ² bishop.
³ ' from Clúain Laíg.'

[25]   .uiii. kł.

Dominus noster Iesus Christus crucifixus est. et conceptus. et mundus factus est.   Passio Iacobi fratris Domini.   Et conceptio Mariae.   Et immolatio Isaac a patre suo Abraam in Monte Morae.   Pasio Dulae uirginis.   Ancillae militis. ⟨Cartulae.⟩ Eufatae.   Caustratae et aliorum .cccc.   Teodolae. Nicustratae.   Eufratae.   Lucellae.   Uictorini.   Alaxandri. Castoli et aliorum .x.   Iunii et aliorum .ccc. martirum.

¶ Cammini sancti Cumman nomen matris eius.   Enan mac Muadan.   Columb ingen Buti.

[26]   .uii. kł.

Castoli.   Montani et Maximae uxoris eius.   Petri episcopi. Mariae.   Marci.   Cassiani.   Saturnini.   Saluatoris., [col. f] Timothei et aliorum .xii.   Diogenis.   Teodori.   Iereni diaconi. Serapionis.   Ammonii.   Uictorini.   Uictoris.   Saluatoris ⟨bis⟩ et aliorum .xiiii.   Madiariae.   Maximae et aliorum .xl.   Hermes.
    Sinchelli abbatis Cilli Achid.[1]   Cilliani meic Tulodrain ⟨no Mochelloc⟩ .i. o Chathir Meic Conaich.[2]   Carthac meic Airbertaig.   Molocga ⟨.i. Lilchaig.[3]   Garban Achid[4].⟩   Fintain Achid.[4]   Gobban ab Airdni Dairind[si].[5]   Lappani.   ⟨Cilleni. Cenannain.⟩

    [1] 'of Cell Achaid.' See Marginal Notes.   [2] 'or Mochellóc, i.e. from Cathair Meic Conaich.'   [3] 'i.e. of Lilchach.' [4] 'of Achad.'   [5] 'of Airdne Dairinse.' Also May 30.

[27]   .ui. kł.

Resurrectio Domini.   Acuti.   Pinnarii.   Successi.   Romuli. Miriae.   Misiae.   Successae.   Marioli.   Matutinae.   Doti. Alexandri.   Saturnini.   Donati et aliorum .xii.
    Mochonne Maige Eo.[1]   Suairlech episcopi.   Fintan os psalmorum.   Aduentus reliquiarum Sillani.

    [1] 'of Mag Eó.'

[28]   .u. kł.

Mariae Magdalenae.   Rogati.   Successi.   Dorothei. Alexandri.   Castori.   Mariae.   Audachtae.   Guntari.   Miniregis.   Grigorii.   Pronati et aliorum .xu.
    Sillain.   Conaill episcopi.   Carnig episcopi.   Cassan Imduail.[1]

    [1] 'of Imdúal.'

[29]   .iiii. kł.

Pastoris. Liberii. Uictorini. Saturnini. Teucri. Medicii.
Dolae. Iuliae. [p. 4*a*; *Facs*. p. 358] Iulianae et aliorum .iiii.
Iuliani et aliorum .ccxliii.   Achatiae.   Ordinatio *Grigorii*.
*Gri*gorii Nazareni in Armenia.

¶ M*ei*c Lumnain łiaich.[1]   Ingena Baiti[2] quae nutriebant
Christum Ethni et Sodelb nomina earum.   Aedan Daire
Bruchais.[3] Lassar. Algasach.   Fulartach m*ac* Bric.   Lesra[4]
uir*ginis*.

    [1] ' Mac Lumnáin, physician.'   [2] ' the daughters of Baíte.'
[3] ' of Daire Bruchaisi.'   [4] = Lasre *g.sg.* of Lassar, *already
mentioned.*

[30]   .iii. kł.

[1]Dom*ni*ni. Dom*ni*ni. Pillo. Poli.[1] Achaici. Tacaici. Liberi.
Pallatini. Uictoris. Marcellini. L*in*i. Satuli. Crusis.
Agathoniae. Eulaliae. Eufeniae. Aquilinae. Saturnini.
Auriliani. Pastoris et aliorum .ii. B*e*n*e*dicti.

¶ Cronan Ballni .i. i Cera i Connactaib.[2] Colmain Linni
Duachail ⟨.i. nomen demonis .i. Cassan Linni.⟩[3]   Tolai ep.
craibdig.[4] Gobbain 7 Ferg*ui*s episcopi. Cronai*n* 7 Fiachnai.
Sancti Colmani. Fer da Chrich. Liber Lethdummi.[5]

    [1-1] *sic*, forte Philopoli *T*; for Domnini Philippoli, *see Notes.*
[2] Balli *Facs.* ' of Ballna, i.e. in Cera in Connacht.'   [3] ' of Linn
Dúachail, i.e. Cassán Linne.'   [4] ' Tóla, a pious bishop.'   [5] ' of
Lethduma.'

[31]   .ii. kł.

Annisii. Felicis. Teodoli. Pauli. Uictoris. P*r*otidae.
Corneliae. Ualeriae. Mariae. Eufemiae. Abdae et aliorum
.u. Iohannis.

¶ Faelani filii Aeda.[1]   Féthaido.[2]   Senioris M*ur*maige.[3]
Colman Camachaid.[4] Mella Daire Melli.[5]

    [1] ' Fáelán, Aed's son.'   [2] Féthaed *n.sg.*   [3] ' Senóir of
Múrmag ; ' na sin maithe a Murmaig *G* ' the good seniors from
Múrmag.'   [4] ' of Cammachad.'   [5] ' of Daire Melle.'

[April 1]   Kł. Ap*rilis*.

Sanctae Mariae natiuitas. Agapae. Chionae. Erennae.
Maii. Ingenianae. Brigitae. Partini. Pantenei. Uictoris.
Quintiani. Herenei. Ingeniani. Saturnini. Alaxandri.
Secundi ⟨b*is*⟩. Zefani. Dionisi Pantini. Pa*t*erni et aliorum . x.
Sancti Ambrosii episcopi. *in marg.* ¶ Erectio tabernaculi.
¶ Gobbani sancti. Aedan laech.¹ Tuan m*a*c Cairill
⟨o Thamlactain Bairchi.⟩² M*ei*c Geráin.³

   ¹ 'laicus.'   ² 'from Tamlachta [*in*] Bairche.'   ³ 'Gerán's sons.'

[2] [col. *b*]   .iiii. N*onas*.

Amphiani. Proculi. Uictoris. Satuli et aliorum .x.
Marcellini. Saturnini. Teodoli. Ciriacii et aliorum .uiii.
Reginae. Agathopi. Proculae. Ciricae. Macidoniae.
Procliuiae. Marcisii. Mastisii.¹ Puplii. Ualerii. Orbani.
Iuliani. Proculi. Gagi. Agapitis ⟨b*is*⟩ et aliorum .xxx.
Dionisii. Amisiani. Dioscori. Gomisii. Nicae episcopi.
Austasii. Dionisii. Gordiani et aliorum .xiii.
¶ Conall m*a*c Aeda. Brónchi u*irginis*.

   ¹ Mastasii, a *expuncted, with* i *over it.*

[3]   .iii. N*onas*.

Euagri. Benigni ⟨b*is*⟩. Agathae uirginis. Sinnidiae.
Tomae. Teosiae. Meri. Cresti. Euagristi. Meriti et aliorum
.ccxl. Amphiani. Pauli. Urbani. Saturnini. Puplii.
Quintiliani. Uictoris. Successi. Iuliani. Palatini et aliorum .ii.
¶ Comman m*a*c Domongin.

[4] [col. *c*]   .ii. N*onas*.

Teodoli. Agathopi. Pauli. Matutini. Urbani. Satur-
nini. Successiae. Iulianae. Quintiliani. Uictoris et aliorum
.xii.
¶ Tigernach¹ epi*scopus* Cl*úa*na Eois.² Gall Locha Teiget.³
Coíne Cille Coíne.⁴ Colmain Find.⁵ Ultan m*a*c Caitte.
Cronsichi. Cru*m*thir Corc Cilli Móre.⁵

   ¹ *See Marginal Notes.*   ² 'of Clúain Eois.'   ³ 'of Loch
Teiget.'   ⁴ 'of Cell Coíne.'   ⁵ 'the Fair.'   ⁵ 'Presbyter
Corc of Cell Mór.'

[5]   Non*as.*

Claudiani. Marciani. Nicanoris. Apollonii. Didimi
presbiteri. Quinti. Chioniae. Herennae. Pancrati. Agape.
Successii. Pauli. Honorii. Hireni. Traci. Probi. Anfiani.
Andronici. Probi. Karuli. Marciani. Nicandri. Apollonii.
Babilli episcopi cum suis. Nicanoris. Fatuelis saxonis cuius
caput decollatum locutum est in Scetha et dixit Libera nos a
malo.

Baptisma Patricii uen*ientis* ad Hiberniam. Becgain m*e*ic
Culae nomen matris eius.[1] Antiosi[2] episcopi.

> [1] *See Marginal Notes.*   ' *sic, om. rell.*

[6]   .uiii. Idus.

Herensi. Berenei. Firmi.[1] Solutoris. Quartilae. Ciriacii.
Moysi. Moderatae. Rufinae. Successiae et aliorum .uii.
Florentii. Geminiani. Epifani. Rufini. Modesti. Serapionis.
Teodori et aliorum .xuii. Romani ⟨b*is*⟩. Gaii. Donati.
Uictoris. Xixti. Secundi et aliorum .uii. Timothei. Ciri
et aliorum .xii. Zefani. Florentini. Ambrosii et aliorum
.xxxu. Germaniani.

¶ Sancti Aedeai ⟨† Aidech⟩.   Cronbice ab Cl*úana*.[2]
Cathubi episcopi. Ordinatio P*a*tricii.

> [1] f *with suprascr.* i.   [2] ' Crónbec, abbot of Clúain.'

[7] [col. *d*]   .uii. Idus.

Timothei. Eleusii. Pel*u*ssi. Philosii. Ciriacis. Dioginis.
Siriae. Macariae. Maximae. Libiae. Eleusii. Capricae.
Firmani.[1] S*u*p*e*rioris. Uictoris.

¶ Senani abbatis.   Ruissine Insi Pích.[2] M*e*ic Liac o
Daire.[3]   Finani Caimm.[4] in oculis eius fuit ista obliquitas.
Senani episcopi.

> [1] f *with suprascr.* i.   [2] ' of Inis Pich.'   [3] ' Mac Liac
> from Daire.'   [4] ' the squinting.'

[8]   .ui. Idus.

*Co*nnexi. Ianuarii. Macarii. Micarii. Maiori. Concesii.
Successii. Saluatoris. Maximae ⟨*bis*⟩. Concessae. Pinnari.
Ammoni. Regani. Timothei.

¶ Aedani m.h. Duibni.[1]   Cathubi episcopi.   Failbe
Erdaim.[2] Tigernach Airid.[3] Ronani m*eic* Fe*r*gusa.   Cind
Ḟaelad ab Ben*n*chai*r*.[4]

   [1] 'Áedán moccu Duibni.'   [2] 'of Erdam.' Cp. Feb. 8.
   [3] 'of Aired.'   [4] 'Cenn Fáelad abbot of Bennchor.'

[9]   .u. Idus.

.Uii. uirgines quae in unum merueru[n]t coronari. Dimetri.
Hilarii. Concessi. Macharii. Dedici. Si*m*mi*m*onis. Fortu-
nati et aliorum .uii. Donati. Saturi. Piloti et uirginum .u.
Quadrati cuius sang*u*is adhuc remanet. Hilarii.

¶ Broccani.   Aedach m.h. Echdach Elich.[1]   Senani.
Colma*n*i.

   [1] echdach *is cancelled, perhaps* = moccu Féchach Éle.

[10]   .iiii. Idus.

Apollonii. Repensi. Diaconi. Ilarii. Saturnini. Pin-
nadi. Teodori. Donatae. Concessae. Successae. Mariae.
Pinnadii. [col. *e*] Marcelne et aliorum .xuii. Gagiani. Teodori.

¶ Erednaton uir*ginis* et Sancti Midgussa. Berchani Aego.[1]
Cuannae uirginis i mMaig Locha i mBregaib .i. i rR*us* Eo.[2]

   [1] 'of Eig.'   [2] 'in Mag Locha in Brega i.e. in Ros Éo.'

[11]   .iii. Idus.

Hilarii. Saloniae. Maximi. Concessi. Domi*n*ni. Petri.
Iohannis. Mariae. Dalmat*h*ae. Teclae. Fortu*n*atae.
Domitionis et multa milia cum eo. Fortunati. Eustorgii.
Nestoris. Filonis et aliorum .ccxluii. Ruphi martiris.

Concessi cum ceteris sociis. Dalmat*h*i. Patricii cum sociis
eorum. Aduentus reliquiarum apostolorum et sanctorum.

¶ Moedoc h*ua* Dunl*aing* i Cl*úain* Mór.¹ Aida*n*i Echdromma
7 Echf*o*raid.² Scellain. Salemonis. Senani. Broccani.
Frossaig anchoritae. Dadnan ep. Cilli Cunga.³ Senior m*ac*
Mael Da Lua.

¹ 'descendant of Dunlang in Clúain Mór.'   ² 'Áedán of
Echdruim and of Echforad.'   ³ 'of Cell Cunga.'

[12]   .ii. Idus.

Iulii episcopi Ro*m*ae. Carpi. Pauli. Isaac. Agothonis.
Musculae. Donatae. Noueliae. Proclinae. Calepodi.
Agapi. Ualeri. Bassi. Puplii. Iuliani. Felicis. Pauli.
Mauri. Celsi. Cipriani et aliorum .xluiii. Quarti confessoris.
Annodi. Zefani.

¶ Erneni episcopi. Co*n*nathi ab Dairi la Ultu.,¹

¹ ' abbot of Daire in Ulster.'

[13] [col. *f*]   Idus.

Eufemiae uirginis. Eucarpiae. Bassae. Caritae. Parurae.
Calipodi. Castonicae. Secutoris. Agathonicae. Leonitidis.
Pauli diaconi. Karuli. Ianuariae. ⟨Policarpi.⟩ Accoli.
Arobi.

¶ Riaguil m*eic* Buachalla. Mochammóc Insi Caín.¹ Me*ic*
Tairchair Locha m*ac* Ni*n*a.²

¹ 'of Inis Caín.'   ² 'the sons of Tairchar of Loch mac
Nen.'

[14]   .xuiii. k⫟. Maii.

Tiburtii. Apati. Ualeriani. Ro*m*ae. Pretextati. Marciae.
Corneliae. Fortunatae. Dom*n*ae cum suis uirginibus simul
coro*n*atae. Maximi ⟨bis⟩. Ciriaci. Donati. Patii. Saturnini.
Prontii ⟨b*is*⟩. Canditoris. Tituli. Tiburtii. Ualeriani.
Ualenti. Pr*o*duci. Liurni. Archilai. Dioclitiani. Foebi.
Simfronii. Proculi. Ualenti. Optati. Saturnini.

¶ Sancti Tassagi. Colma*n*i. Cilline m*eic* Lubnain.

[15]   .xuii. kł.

Maronis.   Messoris.   Mossitis.   Archilaii.   Cipriani.
Proclinae.   Lotae.   Tertiae.   Acutae.   Dionicae.   Potamicae.
Predentii.   Dioginis.   Diaconi.   Felicis.   Marciani ⟨bis.⟩
Fausti.   Marcial*is*.   Siluani.   Fortunati.   Luciani.   Leonidis.
¶ M*eic* Draigin o Chill Roa.¹   Ruadani Lothra.²   G*re*llan
m*ac* Rotain.   ⟨Dubta.⟩   Sarnat Darinsi Cétnae.³

¹ ' Draigen's sons from Cell Róa.'   ² ' of Lothra.'   ³ ' of
Dairinis Cétnae.'

[16]   .xui. kł.

Carisae.   Lectoris.   Christianae.   Calistae.   Teodorae.
Gallidae.   Niciae.   Call*m*iae.   Monicae.   Nigiae.   Basiliae.
Leonidis.   Uincentii.   Caritonis cum aliis .u.   Uincentii.
Marciani ⟨b*is*⟩.   [p. 5*a* ; *Facs.* p. 359]   Martirialis cenobieris.
Antonii.   Felicis.   [*in marg.*]   Tertii.   Eniani.   Martialis.
Siluani.   Lucani.   Canto*n*is.   Calisti et aliorum .xu.
¶ Felicis diaconi .i. i nU*í*b Diarmata i Connact*aib*.¹
Hermogenis.²   Tetgall m*ac* Colbraind.   Falbi.,

¹ ' in U*í* Díarmata in Connacht.'   ² *out of place.*

[17]   .xu. kł.

Petri diaconi.   Furtunati.   Quinti.   Marciani.   Baruci.
Mapolicii.   Galli.   Uictoricii.   Donati.   Ianuarii.   Maconi.
Hermoginis.   Ministri.   Marciani.   Iacobi.
¶ Locheni Cu*n*gi.¹   Donnani Ega²   ⟨nomen fontis⟩ cum
suis id est lii.   Hi sunt Aedani.   Iarloga ⟨b*is*⟩.   Mairic.
Congaile.   Lonain.   M*eic* Lasre.   Iohain ⟨b*is*⟩.   Ernain.   Ernini.
Baethini.   Rotain.   Andrel*is*.   Caril*is*.   Rotai*n*.   Fergusai*n*.
Rectaire.   C*on*nidi.   Éndae.   M*eic* Loga.   Gure*n*tii.   Iuneti.
Corani.   Baetani.   Colmai*n*.   Iernlugi.   Lugaedo.   Luctai.
Grúcind.   Cucalini.   Cobrai*n*.   C*on*mind.   Cummini.   Baltiani.
Senaig.   Demmain.   Cummeni.   Iarnlugi.   Finai*n*.   Find-
chai*n*.   Findchon.   Cronani.   Modomma.   Crónain.   Ciaráin.
Colmain.   Nau*er*mi.   Demmani.   Ernini.   Ailchon.   Donnani.
¶ Eochaid Liss Móir.³   Aedan m*ac* Garbain.   Lugaid m*ac*
Garbain.   Lugaid m*ac* Dructa.

¹ ' of Cunga.'   ² ' of Eig ' ; lii *repeated in marg.* ; liv. O. *See
also Marginal Notes.*   ³ ' of Less Mór.'

[18]   .xiiii. kł.

Septimi. Diaconi. Ianuarii. Uictoris. Pa*ter*ni. Uictoricii.
Calocerii. Pampi. Lycii. Donati. Iuliani. Micionis.
Do*m*ni. Hermoginis. Pamphil*i*. Turini. Mumi. Siri*c*i.
Prisciani et aliorum .xu.
¶ Moninnsen o Manist*ir*.[1] Molassi Lethglinni.[2] Cogitosi
sapientis. Lassar i*ngen* Eccain ó Magin.[3] [*in marg.*] ¶ Eugeni
episcopi.

  [1] 'from Mainistir.'   [2] 'of Lethglenn.'   [3] 'd. of Eccán from
Maigen.'

[19] [col. *b*]   .xiii. kł.

Hermoginis.[1] Expediti. Aristonici. Zefani. Gagi.
Mariae. Galatae. Militinae. Arminiae. Rufi. Donati.
Elladii. Ilarii. Uincentii. Allicionis. Exsuperi. Liberi et
aliorum .x.
¶ Lasse uir*go* Clú*ana* Mind.[2] Me*i*cc Erca ó Dermaig.[3]
Sancti Cilleni.

  [1] *See Marginal Notes.*   ^ 'of Clúain Mind.'   [3] 'the sons
of Erc from Dermag '; M͞c cerca *MS.*

[20]   .xii. kł.

Passio Heradii. Acceti. Siluani. Fortunati. Iohannis
⟨b*is*⟩. Marciae. Gemnae ⟨b*is*⟩. Comiliae. Corniliae.
Donate. Fortunatae. Papiae. Romae. Mariae. Orati.
Donati. Accessi. Uictoris. Felicis. Alaxandri. Ciriacii.
Aradi. Acciei. Meriani. Maximi et aliorum .uiii.

[1]Communis sollemnitas omnium sanctorum et uirginum
Hiberniae et Brita*nn*iae et totius Europae et specialiter in
honorem Sancti Martini episcopi. et familiae Ego eliuatio.
Et Sancti Sobarthei*n* et Sancti Sedrac ep. Sínaig 7 Flaind et
Maeli Ochtraig.,[2]

  [1] *See Marginal Notes.*   [2] 'Sínach and Flann and Máel
Ochtraig.'

[21] .xi. kł.

Cessari. Aratoris. Felicis. Silui. Uitalis. Ualeriani. Maximi. Mariae. Fortunatae. Papiae. Tiburtii. Cesari. Eugenii. Uictoris. Petri et Pauli cum suis omnibus. Aprunculi.

Maele Rubi ab Bennchair.[1] Edilaldi saxonis. Ninnid. Búgno i tír Bretan.[2] Beraich ab Bennchair.,[3]

[1] 'Máel Rubi abbot of Bennchor.'   [2] 'in the land of Britons.'
[3] 'Berach abbot of Bennchor.'

[22] [col. c] .x. kł.

Pilippi apostoli natiuitas. Gaii. Leonis. Tubiani. Papiae. Basillae. Felicis. Gerapuli. Leonidis. Epipodi. Aratoris. Ciriaci. Rogati. Primoli. Mucae. Parmeni. Lucae. Elimae. Caulisti.

¶ Rufin Glinni da Locha.[1] Tommae Bennchair.[2] Abel mac Aeda. Nechtan m.h. in Baird.[3] Saignen 7 Lachain Armaige.[4] Epscop Cuilen i lLemchaill.[5]

[1] 'of Glenn dá Locha.'   [2] 'of Bennchor.'   [3] = moccu in Baird.   [4] 'of Armag ;' án maige G, anmhaighe D.   [5] 'in Lemchaill.'

[23] .ix. kł.

Catuli. Saturnini. Felicis. Theoni. Chori. Teodori. Uictori. Theonae. Mariae. Uenusti. Uictori. Soluti. Pleni. Silui. Nabori. Cori. Iuberii. Catulini. Felicis. Saturnini. Saluni. Faustini. Uictori. Uitalis. Ranastini. Agripini. Iohannis. Zefani.

¶ Sancti Ibari episcopi. Macc Oge 7 Soairlech isind Ednean.[1] Miannach 7 Deitche 7 Rian i Fothirbe Liathain.[2]

[1] 'in the Eidnén.'   [2] 'in Fothirbe Líatháin.'

[24] .uiii. kł.

Passio Georgii cum .xxx m ddcclxxix. Fortunati. Donati. Felicis. Secundi. Coronae. Uictoris. Rofinae. Naboriae. Carionae. Mariae. et trium puerorum de camino ignis Sedrac.

Misac. Abdinago. Militi ⟨bis⟩. Saturnini. Siluani. Liberalis.
Meturi. Tomini. Baradii. Donati. Floriani. Fortuni.
Fusci. Germani. Donati. Florii. Ualerii. Felicis. Ursi.
Clioni. Silui. Uitalis et aliorum .xxuiii. Zotici. Secundi.
Saturnini. Lauri. [col. d] Barachi. Silutani. Liberalis.
Meturii. Tommodi. Firmani. Zefani. Iohannis. Mam-
metis. Tonicisi. Barthoci et aliorum .xxii.

¶ Ecbrichti saxonis. Uldbrithi.

¶ Coemnat Cula Cichmaig[e].¹   Coip ingen Charnain² et
Sectan 7 Sechtmisid.   Fuilen Drommfota.³   Meic Coelbad.⁴
Diarmait ep.   Lugaid presbiter.   Meicc Baetain.⁵   Finceille
uirginis.   Eicnech mac Con Catrach.

¹ ' of Cúl Cíchmaige.'   ² ' d. of Cáernán.'   ³ ' of Druim
Fota.'   ⁴ ' Cóelbad's sons.'   ⁵ ' Báetán's sons.'

[25]   .uii. kł.

Marci euangelistae. Hermoginis. Euodi. Memfi. Geurgii.
Nobilis. Calistae. Marciae. Fortunati. Rustici et aliorum
.ii.

¶ Mac Caille ep. Digde uirgo. Dechonen Clúana Arathair.¹
Lugna Lettrach.² Ingena Cuanain.³ Matoc ailithir.⁴ Ailither
Clúana Gési.⁵

¹ ' of Clúain Arathair.'   ² ' of Lettir.'   ³ 'Cúanán's
daughters.' Ap. 26, GD.   ⁴ ' pilgrim.'   ⁵ ' of Clúain Géise.'

[26]   .ui. kł.

Cirilli. Etuniae. Leonidis. Uindei. Iulii. Uictoricii.
Siricii. Honorati. Felicis. Maximi. Pauli. Uitii. Uictoris.
Simplicis. Pollionis. Kalendini. Apollionis. Marciani.
Laetissimi. Ructi. Leonis. Apollonii.

¶ Caiss Bennchair.¹ Isaac. Conain. Beccain Clúana.²
Modimmóc Clúana Cáin.³ Cronain. Senain.

¹ ' Cass of Bennchor.'   ² ' of Clúain.'   ³ ' of Clúain
Cáin.'

[27]   .u. kł.

Alaxandri. [col. *e*] Euentii presbiteri. Teodoli presbiteri
et aliorum .iiii. Castori. Anchimi. Zenoni. Generi. Zefani.
Sodalis. Antonii heremitae. Antonini. Maurimi. Cutici.
Zotici. Elipidii. Antimi. Epei. Senoni. Genesi. Euticii.
Capti. Maurii. Hirudini. Priami. Uictoris. Maximi.
Hermetis. Pauli. Hermogini. Mariae. Germanae. Liph-
andiae. Militanae. Brigitoniae.¹ Laetissimae. Feliciae.
Mediae. Gemellinae cum aliis .u. Germani. Felicis. Achimi.
Senori. Assani. Anathasii.

¶ Baain. Ultain. Fergusa. Furudrain.

¹ Brigtomae *Facs.*; *second* i *subscr.*

[28]   .iiii. kł.

Egressio Noe de arca. Cristifori cum suis .xmcccciiii.
Omnis qui ieiunat in feria eius requiem inueniet apud Deum.
Uictorini. Eufrodisii. Eusebii. Tabilli. Uictoris. Pilippi.
Cari ⟨bis⟩. Pollionis et aliorum clxxxii. Agapi. Malinae.
Niciae. Uictorinae et aliorum .lxx. Lictoris et aliorum .lxx.
Luciani et aliorum .lxxx. Eunuchii. Augustini sacerdotis.
Donati. Tomae. Erasmi. Mauilii. Iuliani. Celsii. Eueni.

Cronain Ruis Cré.¹ qui prius Mochua dictus est. Suibni
in Scelic.² Conchind Cilli Achid.³ Luchthigern maccu Tratho.
Caurnan Clúana Ech.,⁴

¹ 'of Ros Cré.'   ' 'of the Scelec.'   ³ 'of Cell Achid.'
⁴ 'of Clúain Ech.'

[29] [col. *f*]   .iii. kł.

Germani diaconi. Prosodoci. Uictorini. Marciasii.
Sabbati. Códñi. Nonnae. Matrinae. Basilii. Theusii.
Ualentini. Tigusti. Marciani. Uictorini. Maulini. Augusti.
Uitalis. Bononiae et aliorum lxxxiii.

¶ Fiachnae. Coningen .i. Cuach .i. Cilli Findmaige.¹
Breccani abbatis Maigi Bili.² Domungin o Thuaim Muscraige.³
Luccraid Cilli Luccraide.⁴ Donnani sacerdotis. Fálbi i nInis.⁵
Enani. Ega.⁶

¹ 'i.e. of Cell Findmaige.'   ² 'of Mag Bile.'   ³ 'from
Túaim Muscraige.'   ⁴ 'of Cell Luccraid.'   ⁵ 'in Inis.'
⁶ Enan Insi Áego *GD*, ' of Inis Eig.'

[30]   .ii. kł.

Affrodisii. Quirini. Pap*ae* et aliorum .xxx. Dorothae.
Uiatoris. Terentii. Martini ⟨ter⟩. Uictorii. Claudii.
Maioricae. Claudii. Siluani. Orim*enti*. Onoragi. Dagarii.
et aliorum .xluii. [*in marg.*] ¶ Lucini. Saturnini. Clementis.
Meturi.
    ¶ Ciaran Clúana Sasta.¹ Failchon episcopi. Luta² uirginis
Dromma Dairbrech.³ Rónái*n* Liathrois.⁴ Familia Ega ut
alii dicunt.

    ¹ ' of Clúain Sasta.'   ² Luit *n.sg.*   ³ ' of Druim Dair-
brech.'   ⁴ ' of Líathros.'

[May 1]   **Kł. Maii.**

Initium predicationis Iesu Christi. Natiuitas Pilipi
apostoli. Iacobi apostoli fratris Domini. Nicodimi. Proculi.
Quintiani. Eleutherii. Alaxandri. Saturnini. et milites¹
.xxui. Felest*ini*. Agapiti. Quintiniani. et xxiii. *m* Gaii.
Germani. Apollonii. Petri. Renouati. Iohannis. Frigiae.
Zefani.
    ¶ Mochoemi Tíri da Gl*as*.² Colmani ⟨.i. Gobnini.⟩ Oseni.
Ultain m*eic* Mael Snechtai. Mancheni. Braccani episcopi.
Ronani. Dicollo Clúa*na* Brain.³ Cellain h*uí* Fiachrac*h*.⁴
[*in marg.*]   ¶ Banbai*n* eps. Aedgein Fobair.⁵

    ¹ *sic.*   ² ' of Tír dá Glas.'   ³ ' of Clúain Brain.'
⁴ ' descendant of Fiachra.'   ⁵ ' of Fobar.'

[2]   .ui. N*onas*.¹

Saturnini. Hippoliti. [p. 6*a* ; *Facs.* p. 360] Eupolitis.
Elpidii. Hermoginis. Zefani. Celestini. Germani. Quintini.
Urbani. Belleci. Alaxandri. Mariae. Priuatae. Transillae.
Saturnini et aliorum .ui.
    ¶ Nechtain o Chill Unci i Conaillib.¹ Aedain m*eic* Cuansae.
Enain. Colmain.

    ¹ *obscure* ; K† *Facs.*   ² ' from Cell Uinche in Conailli.'

[3]   .u. Nonas.

Crucis Christi inuentio. Mariae uirginis conceptio. Euentii.
Teodoli. Ambrosii. Rufinae. Musae. Saturnini. Mariani.
Fortunati.

ᶠ Condlaed ⟍Roncend prius⟩ Cilli Dara.¹   Scandal Cilli
Conbraind.² Barrfind Dromma Culinn.³   Clothaig sancti.
Carpre episcopus Maige Bile.⁴   Aithgin Bothi.⁵   Aedani.
Neccain. Mochonnae Daire.⁶   Ingena Ossine.⁷   Dairchella
Glinni da Locha.⁸

    ¹ 'of Cell Dara.'   ² 'of Cell Conbraind.'   ³ ˙of Druim
Culinn'; *also May* 21.   ⁴ 'of Mag Bile.'   ⁵ 'of Both
[Domnaig].'   ⁶ 'of Daire.'   ⁷ 'Osséne's daughters.'   ⁸ 'of
Glenn dá Locha.'

[4]   .iiii. Nonas.

Antherii papae et aliorum .xt.   Siluani.   Urbani ⟍bis⟩.
Antoninae.   Celestinae.   Mariae.   Romulae.   Romani.
Floriani.   Emetuni.

    ¶ Mochua mac Cummine .i. i Sleib Ebline.¹   Aedo meic
Bricc.²

    ¹ ˙i.e. in Slíab Eblinne.'   ² *See also Feb.* 28, *July* 30, *where*
om. GD.

[5]   .iii. Nonas.

Ascensio prima Domini nostri Iesu Christi.   Herennae.
Gallae. Felicissi. Eutini et non Iustini. Grigorii. Hilarii.
Petiui. Belli. Petri. Marciasi. Erennei. Archilai. Necturi.
Niceti. Eutemi. Iohannis. Petri. Zefani et aliorum .ui.

    Euchbrit saxonis.   Faelan Find Cilli Colmai.¹   Senani.

    ¹ 'Fáelán the Fair of Cell Colmai.'

[6]   .ii. Nonas.

Mattei. Secundiani. Iacobi et translatio Iohannis filii
Zachariae. Gerontii. Iacobi. Saturnini. Mauriani et aliorum
.lxxx. Heliodori. Concordii. Marinae. Mariae. Curice.
Brigitonae. Ausidiae. Iudith. [col. *b*] Emeriae. Acacae.
Faustinae. Uictoris. Felicis. Marcelli. Maximi. Augustini.
Ualeriani. Gaiani et aliorum .lxxii.

¶ Colmain Locha Echin.[1]

[1] 'of Loch Echin.'

[7]   Nonas.

Agnitio sanctae crucis. Conceptio Mariae .i. ut*ero*. Flaui.
Afrodisti. Macrobii. Augustini. Marcellini. Pudentellae.
Postellae. Allae. Flauiae. Septi*m*nae. Dextrae. Quintae.
Scolasticae. Rogatae. Celerini ⟨bis⟩. Maximi. Uict*u*ri
⟨bis⟩. Marcialis. Augustini et trium fratrum. Gaginati.
Frontoni. Quinti. Priuatiani. Arnesii. Donati ⟨bis⟩.
Nauigii. Puluini. Octouiani. Marini. Zefani. Felicitatis.

¶ Breccan .i. Echdromma[1] et Quiarani ⟨idem et
Mochuaróc⟩. Lasrae uirginis.

[1] 'i.e. of Echdruim.'

[8]   .uiii. Idus.

Uictoris ⟨bis⟩. Maximi. Cessi. Donati. Lucii. Iohannis.
Saliuae. Secundilae. Marciae. Daticae. Uictoriae. Ster-
titiae. Rogatae. Floridae. Ninae. Flauiae. Iuliae. Famosae.
Mariae. Processae. Secundae. Feliciae. Eupiae. Maximae.
Cutidi. Sincliticae. Fortunati. Saturnini. Tertuli. Arestini.
Tamphi. Marini. Luci. Donati. Rustici. Marciani. Dati.
Batizi. Militi. Uictoriani. Ianuarii. Odróni. Cap*it*is.
Cessi et aliorum .x. Lurentii.[1]

¶ Odrani episcopi. Commani oc Tig M*ei*c Findchon.[2]

[1] *See Marginal Notes.*   [2] 'at Tech Meic Findchon.'

[9]   .uii. Idus.

Reuelatio Míchaelis archangeli.   Festiuitas apostolorum.
id est reliquiarum Tomae et Iohannis et Andreae.   [col. *c*]
Quirilli passio.   Gindei.   Zenonis.   Affrodisii.   Cendei.   Effenici.
Timothei.   Gordiani.   Beati et aliorum .ccxiiii. et aliorum
martirum .xxui.

¶ Lamruaid.   ¶ Brenaind Biror.[1]   Dabreccoc Tuamma
Dracon.[2]   Banban sap*iens*.   Santan ⟨Cendmar⟩ i Cill da
Les.[3]

Memmertius episcopus et confessor qui ob imminentem
cladem sollennes an*te* ascensionem Domini letanias instituit
cantari.

¹ ' of Biror.'   ² ' of Túaim Dracon.'   ³ ' Sanctan
Big-head, in Cell dá Les ; ' *before* da Les *Facs. has* .i.

[10]   .ui. Idus.

Gordiani.   Epimacis.   Midoris confessoris.   Protextati.
Quarti.   Quinti.   Maioris.   Petri.   Diutii.   Teclae.   Furionis.
Mariae.   Lucellae.   Probatae.   Mocae.   Maximae.   Iusti.
Matronae.   Iacobi.   Ianuarii.   Quirilli.   Gindei.   Dioni*n*i.
Ac*h*aci.[4]   Crispionis.   Zenonis.   Affrondisii.   Primitii.

¶ Comgaill B*e*nnchair¹ .xči. anno aetatis¦ eius principatús
au*tem* .l. anno et mense iii° et decimo die.   Aedo.   Corma*i*c.
Fintain.   Condlai episcopi.   Mc Lemnae.²   Mosínóc .i.
Cl*úana* Caichni.³

¹ ' of Bennchor.'   ² ' Son or sons of Lemain ; '   *see Index*
of Names.   ³ ' i.e. of Clúain Caichni.'   ⁴ i *subscr. om. Facs.*

[11]   .u. Idus.

Iob profetae.   Antimi.   Dimetri.   Attici.   Maii.   Monta-
niani.   Iulii ⟨*bis*⟩.   Uicturini.   Fortunati.   Comini.   Septimi.
Primuli.   Montani.   [col. *d*] Nerei.   Attici.   Inerti.   Marnili.
Martini martiris.   Uicturinis et ceterorum fratrum translatio.

℣ Coemgini abbatis. Findlogo. Critan mac Illadon. Cormac i nAchud Findnaige.¹ Lugair infirmus. Loegaire lobor.² Colum cáin.³ Lasrae uirginis. Fintain Clúana Cain.⁴ Mael Doid. Aeilgnei. Mochritoc .i. Critán mac Illadon 7 Crummthir Cormaic⁵ 7 i nÁraind atá.⁶ Is é ro chomarc de Diabol cinnas rasossed nem.⁷ ad quem Diabolus dixit [*marg. inf.*] Dia mba cleirech etc.⁸

¹ 'in Achad Findnaige ;' Findnaigi *Facs.*   ² ' the leper' ; *om. GD.*   ³ ' the fair.'   ⁴ ' of Clúain Caín.'   ⁵ ' presbyter Cormac.'   ⁶ ' and in Árann he is.'   ⁷ ' It is he who asked the Devil how he might attain Heaven.'   ⁸ *See Marginal Notes.*

[12]   .iiii. Idus.

Pancrati. Nerei. Aquilei fratrum. Ciriaci qui crucem Domini inuenit et .cccui. cum eo passi sunt. Maximi. Ciriaci.¹ Gratii. Pancratii. Rotheris. Moisitis. Iohannis. Affroditi. Achilis. Zefani. Alaxandri.

¶ Dimmae meic Caiss. Ailithir Muccinsi.² Herc Nasci ⟨.i. i Tilaig Léis.⟩³ Lugaeth mac Oengusa. Hernéni.

¹ Ciriacii. *Facs.*   ² ' of Muccinis.'   *See Marginal Notes.*
³ ' Erc of the tie, i.e. in Telach Léis ;' *there is a stop after* Herc *in MS.*

[13]   .iii. Idus.

Taraci. Probi. Andronici. Affrodissii. Sabini. Agripae. Mariae. Lucii. Credulae. Quirillae. Perpetuae. Grissi. Lucii. Gerbassi. Saturnini. Alaxandri. Sabini et aliorum .dui. Maximi.

¶ Sancti Mochonnae 7 Maeli Doid.   Dublittrech Find.¹

¹ ' Dublittir the Fair.'

[14]   .ii. Idus.

Coronae. Uictoris. Secundini. Quarti. Uictorini. Taraci. Militis. Ianuarii. Madiani. Alaxandri. Affronnidis. [col. *e*] Maximini. Pali. Adacti. Eutherii.

Carthagi .i. Mochutu Lis Móir.¹ Garbani 7 Lasre. Mael Chethair meic Ronain.

¹ ' Carthach, i.e. Mochutu of Less Mór.'

[15] Idus.

Primus Penticosti. Timothei. Alexandri. Rosulae. Populae. Andrae. Bamororae. Cotiae et uii. uirginum. Digni. Simplicii. Felicis. Uictoris. Cirici. Ianuarii. Pauli. Aquilini. Petri. Andreae. Dionisii. Heroli. Minerui. Eradii.

¶ Saráin meic Airechair .i. ó Inis Moir i nUíb Maic Caille la Híiu Liathán.¹ Tochonne ep. Dublitri ab Findglasi.² Colum mac Failgusa. Colman m.h. Laigsi.³ Cainnech Airecuil.⁴ Comman mac Dimmae. Columb Insi Locha Cré.⁵

¹ ' i.e. from Inis Mór in Uí Maic Caille in Uí Líatháin.'
² ' abbot of Findglais.'   ³ = moccu Laigsi.   ⁴ ' of Airecul.'
⁵ ' of Inis Locha Cré.'

[16] .xuii. kł. Iunii.

Dioclitiani. Florentii. Aquilini ⟨bis⟩. Uictorini. Heradi. Paulini ⟨bis⟩.¹ Menserini.² Florentii. Gaiani ⟨bis⟩. Uincentii. Minerii. Pauli. Minorgi. Auriani. Uicturiae. Ioueni. Herilii. Niderni. Basillae et aliorum .xii.

¶ Brendini Clúana Ferta.³   Boetii .i. cuius nomen erat Bregbesach filii Bronaig. Fidmuni .i. huí Suanaig.⁴ Meic Lasre ab Bennchair.⁵ Cairnig o Thuilén.⁶ Ernán mac Aeda. Odrán sac. Mochamail.⁷ Duthracht Liathdromma.⁸ Findchad episcopus. Fintan Clúana Cruich.⁹

¹ om. Facs.   ² m̄, resembling ir̄.   ³ ' of Clúain Ferta.'
⁴ ' i.e. úa Súanaig, descendant of Súanach.'   ⁵ 'abbot of Bennchor.'   ⁶ Chuilén Facs. ' Cairnech from Tuilén.'
⁷ Mochamil Facs.   ⁸ ' of Liathdruim.'   ⁹ ' of Clúain Cruich.'

[17] .xui. kł.

Andrionis. Uictoris. Basillae. Basiae. Caloceri. Gallicorii. Liberii. Adomnini. Pauli ⟨bis⟩. Aquilini. Uictoris. [col. f] Arthemi. Primi. Eponi. Heracli. Potomonis. Minerii. Hiemi et aliorum .uii. ⟨Calori.⟩

¶ Sillani episcopi. Finnén. Critan. Epscoip Findchain Dromma Enaig 7 Dromma Feise.¹ Ingena Garbain.² Mc̄ Guaslaingi o Chluanaib.³

¹ ' bishop Findchán of Druim Enaig and Druim Feise.'
² ' Garbán's daughters.'   ³ ' from Clúana '; meic ua Slainge ó Chlúain Aírbh G, mec ua Slaincce D.

[18]   .xu. kł.

Marci euang*elistae*.   Potomonis.   Bostasii.   Hortasii.
Serapionis presbiteri.   Pantini.   Dicorii.   Palmi.   Datiui.
Mariae.   Maximae.   Lucianae.   Agnae.   Urbanae.   Luci.
Hermoni.   Zefani cum aliis quattuor.   Discori.   Pantomoni.
Pedecladi.   Marciani.   Luciosi.   Casii.   Uictoris.   Michaelis.
¶ Fir da Chrich.   Momedóc Feda Dúin.[1]   Modomnóc
Tiprat Fa*chtna*.[2] Eps*coip* Colmain.   Brain Bic o Chloenad.[3]
Midgus m*ac* Eirc Cilli Talten.[4]   Bresal o Durthach.[5]

[1] 'of Fid Dúin'; *also Mar. 23, Aug. 13.*   [2] 'of Tipra
Fachtna'; *also under Feb.* 13.   [3] 'Bran the Little from Cloenad.'
[4] 'of Cell Talten.'   [5] 'from Durthach.'   *See also Sept.* 30.

[19]   .xiiii. kł.

Urbani confessoris.   Decii regis.   Eunucorum martirum.
Calocerii.   Pa*terni*.   Proni.   Galli.   Curii.   Iudicii.   Urbanae
‿bis⟩.   Coloniae.   Iuliae.   Sarrae.   Selincii.   Seleucii.   Felicis.
Dominici.   Crescenti.   Alaxandri.   Areni ‿bis⟩.   Quinti.
Fortunati.   Emelii.   Basilii.   Decii.   Clorini.   Florini.   Pullioli.
Fausti episcopi.   Pudentianae.
¶ Diuir Enaig.[1]   Ceir.   Ciaran m*ac* Colgan.   Ricille
uirginis.   Caradíc.   Brittán Ratha.[2] T*ri* m*eic* Eogain.[3] Cum-
mine m*eic* Baetain.   Mochonna Cilli Comarthai.[4]

[1] 'of Enach.'   [*] 'of Ráith.'   [3] 'Eogan's three sons.'
[4] 'of Cell Comarthae.'

[20]   .xiii. kł.

Marcellosae.   Uictoriae.   Salsae.   Basillae.[1]

*   *   *   *   *   *

(*Br.* fol. 9 v) [Laidcind.[2] Cruimm Dit[h]ruib o Inis Croind.[3]
Colman Daire Móir.[4] Dainel Tulcha.[5] M*ac* Laithbe Dom*naig*
Moir.[6]

[1] *Two leaves lost here, supplied from Brussels MS.*   [*] *above*
line.   [3] 'from Inis Crainn.'   [4] 'of Daire Mór.'   [5] 'of
Tulach.'   [6] 'of Domnach Mór.'

21 .xii. kł.

Colman Crón. Cummine mac Luigdeach. Colman lobor
i mMaigh Eó.[1] Moenind 7 Polan. Maeli Doid o Lis Mor.[2]
Barrfinn Droma Cul*inn*.[3] Brigit ingen Dimmain.[4] Finnbarri
Corcaigi.[5]

   [1] 'the leper, in Mag Éo.'   [2] 'from Less Mór.'   [3] 'of
Druim Culinn.'   [1] 'daughter of Dímmán.'   [5] 'of
Corcach.'

22 .xi. kł.

Baithini m*eic* Finnach. Ronani Find o Lainn Ruadain.[1]
Luigsech uir*go*. Eodusa o Maigin.[2] Na teora cailleacha Droma
da Dart.[3] Conaill Insi Cáil.[4] Caisin Sendumae.[5]

   [1] 'from Lann Rúadán ; ' *alongside* Ruadain *another hand has
written* Ronain, *which read, with* OGD.   [2] *over* Eodusa, UII,
with date 23 *alongside, has been cancelled.* Read Secht meic Eodusa
' the seven sons of Éodus from Maigin.'   [3] ' the three nuns
of Druim dá Dart.'   [4] ' of Inis Cáel.'   [5] ' of Senduma.'

[f. 10] 23 .x. kł.

Gobani Mairgi o Tig Scuithin.[1] Cremt[h]and Maighi Duma.[2]
Faol*chon*. Comman. Strofan Cl*úana* Móir.[3] Nechtlaicc eps.

   [1] 'Gobbán of Mairge from Tech Scuithín.'   [2] 'of Mag
Duma.'   [3] ' of Clúain Mór.'

24 .ix. kł.

Colman. Sillani. Aedbi aḃ Tire da Ghlas.[1] Stellain i
nInis Celtra.[2] Berchain Cl*úana* Caí.[3] Segin Aird Macha.[4]
Secht n-ingena Fergasa i nInis Cealtra.[5]

   [1] ' of Tír dá Glas.'   [2] ' in Inis Celtra.'   [3] ' of Clúain
Caí.'   [4] ' of Ard Macha.'   [5] ' the seven daughters of
Fergus in Inis Celtra.'

25   .uiii. kł.

Duncad ab Iae[1] .i. mac Cinn Faela*dh*. Mocholla *ingen*
Doma.[2] Modomnoc. ūc.[3] Cruimt[h]ir Cáel Cilli Móiri.[4]

　　[1] 'abbot of Í.'　　[2] *sic, read (G)* 'daughter of Dímma.'　　[3] *sic,*
om. Kelly ; *entry om. GD.*　　[4] 'Presbyter Cáel of Cell Mór.'

26   .uii. kł.

Colman Stellain Tíri da Ghlas.[1]   Becain Clú*ana* Aird.[2]

　　[1] 'of Tír dá Glas.'　　[2] 'of Clúain Aird.'

27   .ui. kł.

Esp*oc* Cillin o Tigh Tálain.[1]   Commaigh inghen Eachdach[2]
7 Maelan 7 Cuint oc Snamh Luthair.[3]   Echbritan m*a*c Óssu.
Esp*oic* Ethirn o Dhomhnach Mor.[4]

　　[1] 'from Tech Táláin.'　　[2] 'daughter of Eochaid.'　　[3] 'at
Snám Luthair.'　　[4] 'from Domnach Mór.'

28   .u. kł.

Maelod*r*an. Sillan. Eog*an* sap*iens*. Furudrain hi lLai*n*n
Tuirriu.[1]   Secht n-esp*oic* o Tigh na Comairce.[2]

　　[1] 'in Lann Tuirriu.'　　[2] 'Seven bishops from Tech na
Comairce.'

29   .iiii. kł.

Cumne uirginis .i. ingen Ailleain i nAird Ula*dh*[1] Darii.[2]
Maele Tuile 7 Mobeccu. Brun*n*seci[3] uirginis.

　　[1] 'Cumman uirgo, i.e. daughter of Aillén (from Daire Ingine
Aillén) in Ard Ulad.'　　[2] Darii, *here taken as a n. pr., is part of the*
place-name: ó Dhoire i. Aillen i nAird Uladh *GD* ; ic Daire in.
Aillein ic Ard Ulad ata *O* (*n*).　　[3] Briuinsech cael 'the
slender,' *GD.*

30 .iii. [kł.]

Goban Airdni .i. Dairinsi.[1] Saergusa.[2] Bile. Érnine.

[1] 'of Airdne i.e. of Darinis.' Also Mar. 26. [2] Saerghos Droma
GDOn, Saergussius de Druim-bile T. Bile is part of the place-name
Mag Bile, properly belonging to the following day, and here treated
as a saint's name.

31 .ii. [kł.]

Fir da Crich. Eogan episcopus et sapiens Maigi Cremc[h]aill.[1]
Maelodrain Slaani.[2]

[1] Maighe Bile GD ; Cremchaill goes with Ernín in GD : Ernin
Cremhcaille G, Cremchoille D. But T has Eugenius episcopus et
sapiens de Magh Creamh-chaill. The interlineation in the lost original
occasioned the confusion; read with GD. [2] added here by later
hand and cancelled at beginning of the entry ; 'of Sláne.'

[June] 1 **Kł.** Iunii.

Cronani Lis Moir.[1] Egol Disirt Fegoilsi.[2] Leban Atha
Egais.[3] Cummini.

[1] 'of Less Mór.' [2] 'of Dísert Fegoilse.' [3] 'of
Áth Egais.'

2 .iiii. Nonas.

Senani. Nainnid o Clúain Usend.[1] Foim.[2]

[1] 'from Clúain Usend ;' read Uinsenn O(n)GD. [2] sic, (?)
scribal error for Forondán Luac 'of Lúa,' O(n)GD.

3 .iii. Nonas.

Etchii. Zefani. Caemgin ab Glinne da Locha.[1] Didae
uirginis. Aui Trenloco anchoritae.[2] Affine 7 Glunsalaich.
Espoc Sillen. Espoic Branduibh.[3]

[1] 'abbot of Glenn dá Locha.' [2] Auitren loco MS.
'The descendant of Trénlug.' [3] Also under June 13.

4   .ii. *Nonas.*

Finncháin. Molua Etardroma.[1] [f. 10ᵛ] Colmain cru*im*thir.[2]
Colum sac. Cl*úana* Emain.[3] Cassain Domn*aigh* Moir.[4] Petair.
Mochuae Cichech.[5] Faithlenn m*ac* Aoda Damhain.

¹ 'of Etardruim.'   ² 'presbyter.'   ³ 'of Clúain Emain.'
⁴ 'of Domnach Mór.'   ⁵ 'of the paps.'

5   *Nonas.*

Finnloga 7 Leain i Cill Gobuil.[1]   Brocan Cl*úana* me*i*c
[Feicc].[2] Niad. Berchaini.[3]

¹ 'in Cell Gobuil.'   ² '*supply* Féicc *GD*, 'of Clúain meic
Féicc.'   ³ Niad 7 Berchan ó Chlúain Aedha Aithmet i
Luighne *GD.*

6   .uiii. Idus.

Coccae. Clarainech Cl*úana* Cain.[1]   Lonain.   Mael Aith-
geain. Faelain. Medrain episcopi. Esp*oic* Colmain.

¹ 'The Table-faced one of Clúain Caín.'

7   .uii. Id*us.*

Columbae mon*achi.* Mochonne. Caemhán Airdni Caemain.[1]
Colum Gobbae.[2] Moc[h]olmóc Dromma Moir.[3]

¹ 'of Airdne Cáemáin.'   Cp. *June* 12.   ² 'Colum the smith.'
³ 'of Druim Mór.'

8   .ui. Id*us.*

Murchon mc. h. Machteni.[1]   Corm*ac* h*úa* Liat[h]ain.[2]
Medran. Broen esp*oc* Caisil.[3] Luait[h]rind Achaid Coraind.[4]
Airmidach a Cunga.[5]

¹ = Murchú moccu Machthéni.   ² *also under June* 21,
more correctly.   ³ 'bishop of Caisel.'   ⁴ 'of Achad Coraind.'
⁵ 'from Cunga ;' abb Cunga 'abbot of Cunga,' *GD.*

9   .u. Idus.

Columbae Cille et Baithini.   Umalgaid mac Eac[h]dach.
Dafinna mac Declain.   Mothorae Domnaig Cliabra.¹   Cruimther
mc. h. Nessi.²

   ¹ ' of Domnach Clíabra.'   ² = Cruimther (presbyter) moccu
Nessi.

10   .iiii. Idus.

Ainmerech Ailich.¹   Santan espoc.   Illadan mac Eac[h]dach
o Raith Liphiten.²   Forcellach Fobair.³   Senbeirech Chuile
Dremni.⁴   Maeli Dúin sancti.   Rétach mac Caemain.   Sancti
Ferdomnuigh.

   ¹ ' Ainmere of Ailech.'   ² ' from Ráith Liphthen.'   ³ ' of
Fobar.'   ⁴ ' of Cúil Dremni.'

11   .iii. Idus.

Mac Táil Cille Culinn¹ qui et Eogan prius dictus est.
Riagail Bennchair.²   Inghena Laisren i cCill Cule.³   Tochum-
racht uirgo.

   ¹ ' of Cell Culinn.'   ² ' of Bennchor.'   ³ ' Laisrén's
daughters in Cell Cúle.'

12   .ii. Idus.

Cóemani Airdni .i. Santlet[h]an.¹   Tommeni mc. h. Birn
.i. ailithir Locha Uane.²   Diucaill Achaid na Cró.³   Locheni.
Cronani.   Murchon.   Tarannan ab Bendchair.⁴

   ¹ ' of Airdne i.e. Santlethan.'   " ' Tomméne moccu Birn
i.e. a pilgrim, of Loch Uane.'   ³ ' of Achad na Cró.'   ⁴ ' abbot
of Bennchor.'

   TALLAGHT.   E

13   Idus.

Meic Nisi ab Clúana meic Nois.¹ Carilla i Tir Ross.² Damnat
Sleibhe Betha.³   Espoic Branduibh.⁴   Mocumae cruimthir
Clúana Tiprat.⁵

¹ ' abbot of Clúain meic Nóis.'   ² sic, ' Cairell in Tír Rois.'
³ ' of Sliab Betha.'   ⁴ ' bishop Brandub ; ' om. GD ; also under
June 3, more correctly.   ⁵ ' Mochumma, presbyter, of Clúain
Tiprat.'

[f. 11] 14   .xuiii. kł. Iulii.

Ném mc. h. Birn.¹   Colmán mac Luacháin.²   Ciaran
Belaigh Duin.³   Cuman Becc o Tamnaigh.⁴

¹ = moccu Birn.   ² also under June 17, more correctly.
³ ' of Belach Dúin.'   ⁴ ' Cummán the Little, from Tamnach.'

15   .xuii. kł.

Sinell húa Liathain.¹   Colman mac Corardain o Imleach
Brēn.²

¹ ' descendant of Líathán.'   ² sic, ' from Imleach Brēn ; '
ó Miliuc i nDartraige Coininnsi O(n)DG ' from Míliuc in Dartraige
Coininnsi.'

16   .xui. kł.

Cethig episcopi Sancti Patricii. Sétna ep. mac Treno.
Aitheachain Colptho.¹   Colman mac Roe o Rechraind.²   Lugo
sac.

¹ ' Aithcáin of [Inber GD] Colptha.'   ² MS. has Roe
brechraid, with e corr. to a by another hand, and n added above
line, evidently a mistranscription of o Rechraind, ' from Rechru,'
so GD.

17   .xu. kł.

Edani nigri.¹   Cellain meic Finain.   Totholain.   Colmain
meic Luac[h]ain.   Meic Nechtain Droma Bricci.²   Moling
Luaim.³   Mochommóc mac Doborchon.

¹ ' Áedán the Black.'   ² ' Nechtan's sons, of Druim
Bricci.'   ³ sic MS., read Luachair.

18   .xiiii. kł.

Furodrain 7 Báithin dá m*a*c Mainain.¹   Colman m*a*c
Micii.

    ˡ ' two sons of Máenán.'

19   .xiii. kł.

Cassani Cl*úana* Raitte.¹   Failbe o Thaliucht.²   Caelai*n*n
Daire Chailai*n*ne.³   Molommae Domnaig Imlech.⁴

    ¹ ' of Clúain Ráithe ; ' *under June* 20 *in GD, probably the true
day, as also that of* Molomma.   ² Thobucht *GD* ' from Tobacht.'
³ ' of Daire Cáelainne.'   ⁴ ' of Domnach Imlech ; ' *under June* 20
in GD.

20   .xii. kł.

Faelain amlabair i Sraith Eret i nAlb*ain*.¹

    ¹ ' Faelán the Dumb, in Srath Eret in Alba ; ' i rRáith Erenn.
G, Erann *D,* o S*h*rath Herenn *O(Rn*¹*).*

21   xi. kł.

Corm*a*c h*úa* Liat[h]ain i nDermaigh.¹   Diarm*a*it on Disiurt.²
Suibne eps. o Chobran.³

    ¹ ' descendant of Líathán, in Dermag.'   ² ' from the
Dísert.'   ³ ' from Cobran.'

22   x. kł.

Mochuae Luachra,¹ idem et Cronan ó Ḟerna.²   Suibne ab.
Guaire Bic.³   Crunnmaeil m*ei*c Ronain.

    ¹ ' of Lúachair.'   ² ' from Ferna.'   ³ ' Gúaire the
Little.'

23   ix. kł.

Mocoe sac. ab Noendroma.¹   Faelani sancti et filiarum
Moinani.

    ¹ ' abbot of Nóendruim.'

                                                        E 2

24 .uiii. kł.

Cormac Sencometa.[1] Lon Cilli Gabra.[2] Gabrini.

¹ ' of Senchoimét.'   ² ' of Cell Gabra.'

25 .uii. kł.

Sinc[h]ill Cilli Achid.[1] Moluoc Lis Moir.[2] Ingena Minguir.[3] Ailill mac Segini.

¹ ' of Cell Achid.'   ² ' of Less Mór.'   ³ ' Mingor's daughters.'

26 .ui. kł.

Soadbair episcopi. Colman Partraighi.[1] Lac[h]tain.

¹ ' of Partraige ; ' proinntighe, *GD* ' of the refectory.'

27 .u. kł.

Aeda. Scandail .i. Clúana.[1] Dimmain. Brocain

¹ ' i.e. of Clúain.'

[f. 11ᵛ] 28 .iiii. kł.

Cruimmine i lLecain Midi.[1] Ernine Clúana Find.[2] Bigsigi uirginis.

¹ ' in Lecan Midi.'   ² ' of Clúain Find.'

29 .iii. kł.

Maele Doid .i. Falbhe meic Dara et Faeldobor et Cochae Ruis Bendchair.[1] Caincomrac Chinn Clair.[2] Connain eps. o Tigh Collain.[3]

¹ ' of Ros Bennchair.'   ² ' of Cenn Cláir ; ' ó dísert Cinn Cláir *GD* ' from Dísert Cinn Cláir.'   ³ Connáin *GD*, ' from Tech Colláin.'

30   .ii. kł.

Coelan Dachoe.[1]   Falbe o Chill Eó.[2]   Sporoc ingen Choluim.[3]

   [1] *sic, om. GD.*   [2] ' from Cell Éo.'   [3] Sproc *GD,*
' daughter of Colum.'

[July] 1   **Kł.** Iulii.

Commai eps.   Lugidii me*i*c Lugei.   Ultani.   Aile*ll*a esp*uic*
Cl*úana* Emai*n.*[1]   Bairinn.   Sillini.   Cathbadh.   Ultain.

   [1] ' of Clúain Emdin ' ; Arda Macha *GD.*

2   .ui. N*onas.*

Ternoc Cl*úana* Mór.[1]   Ingena Cat[h]badh i nAiriud.[2]

   [1] *sic,* ' of Clúain Mór.'   [2] ' Cathbad's daughters in Aired.'

3   .u. N*onas.*

Dartinni [1]uirginis 7 Colmani .i. Guaire[1] i cCill Aird i n*Uíb*
Ercain.[2]   Cilline ab Iae.[3]   Ultan.

   [1-1] *om. GD.*   [2] ' in Cell Aird in Uí Ercain ;   ' Garrchon
GDO (*n*).   [3] ' abbot of Í.'

4   .iiii. N*onas.*

Finnbairr ab Insi Domle.[1]   Bolcan[2] i cCill Chúle.[3]

   [1] ' of Inis Domle.'   [2] Boloan *MS.*   [3] ' in Cell Chúle.'

5   .iii. N*onas.*

Fergusa o hUamaigh.[1]   Etain uirginis Tuama Noadh.[2]

   [1] ' from Uamag.'   hó Hummigh *G.*   [2] ' of Túaim Nóa.'

6 .ii. N*onas*.

Moninni Sleibi Cul*inn*[1] quae et Darerca prius dicta est.
Tri ingena Ernin oc Enuch Dirmaighi.[2]   Fedchonn niadh.[3]
Fuidbec.[4]   Tri hingena Maine i nAiriud Boinne[5] .i. Dermór
7 Et[h]ne 7 Cumman.

¹ ' of Slíab Culinn.'   ² ' Ernín's three daughters at
Enach Dirmaige.' *om. GD.*   ³ ' Fedchú the champion.'   ⁴ *om.*
GD.   ⁵ ' Maine's three daughters in Aired Bóinne.'

7   N*onas*.

Sancti Tiugmaich[1] episcopi. Maol Ruain eps. Tamlac[h]ta.[2]
Cronae Bicce.[3]   Fiadabuir Uachtair Achaid.[4]   Comgell inghen
Diarmata.[5]

¹ Trigmech *GD.*   ² ' of Tamlachta.'   ³ ' Cróne the
Little.'   ⁴ ' of Uachtar Achaid.'   ⁵ ' daughter of
Díarmait.'

8   .uiii. Id*us*.

Broccán scribnidh.[1]   Diarm*a*it Glinne hUisen.[2]   Colman
imramha.[3]   Trea Aird Trea.[4]   Sancti Celiani Scotti martiris
cum suis fratribus Aed 7 Tadg et Amarma coniuge regis
Gothorum truncati a *p*reposito do*m*mus regiae in ippodoronia[5]
palatii regii.

¹ ' a scribe.'   ⁴ ' of Glenn Uissen.'   ³ ' of the Voyage.'
⁴ ' of Ard Trea.'   ⁵ *sic, read* hippodromo.

9 [f. 12]   .uii. Id*us*.

Garban sac. Cinn tSaile.[1]   On*ch*on.   Condmach Atha
Silain.[2]   Broccaid.

¹ ' of Cenn Sáile.'   ² ' of Áth Siláin ' (?) ; Átha Blair *GD*,
of Áth Blair.'

10 .ui. Id*us*.

Cuain h. Airbir i n*Uib* Cendsel*aigh*.[1] Aodh deochain i cCrich Mane.[2] Ultain. Senain.

Read i nAirbir 'in Airbre (?) in Úí Cennselaig'; Cúán Airbhri *G*, Airbre *D*. [2] 'Áed deacon in Crích Maine.'

11 .u. Idus.

Mac Con Lóc[h]ae, Falbi nomen eius i nDis*iurt* me*i*c Con Lochae i Curchibh.[1] Colman m*a*c Cronain. Sanctae Gabtinae uirginis. Lonan Arda Cruinn.[2] Berran.

[1] 'Cú Lóchae's son, Failbe his name, in Dísert meic Con Lóchae in Cuircne;' Curcne *O* (*n*), Cuircne *GD*. [2] 'of Ard Cruinn.'

12 .iiii. Id*us*.

Nazair o Liath.[1] Colman Bruicisi.[2]

[1] 'from Líath [Mór].' [2] Cluana Bruchas *G*, Cluana Bruchais *D*, Cluana Bruch*us* *O* (*n*); 'of Clúain Bruchais.'

13 .iii. Id*us*.

Mosiloc Cluana Daetcain.[1]

[1] 'of Clúain Dáetcain (?); ' o Cluain da aithgeid *O* (*Fn*), Cluana daithgen *D*, Chluana deochra *O* (*Ln*).

14 .ii. Idus.

Onc[h]on me*i*c Blait[h]mic. Colman m*a*c Andgein.

15 Id*us*.

Rónain me*i*c Mági. Comman m*a*c Dimmai. Me*i*c Ercain o Bruigh Long.[1]

[1] *sic*, Lóeg *G*, Laog *D*; 'Ercan's sons from Brug Lóeg.'

16   .xuiii. [*recte* xuii] kł. Aug*u*ist.

Gobbain. Torptha. Maolodhar o Brí Molt.[1]   Hilarmi.[2]
Breccan Cathe.[3] Scoth Cl*úana* Moescna.[4]

    [1] ' from Brí Molt.'   [2] *read* Hilarini ; Hilarianus G.   [3] Cluana
Catha GD, ' of Clúain Catha.'   [4] ' of Clúain Móescna.'

17   .xui. kł.

Flainni Inber Becce.[1] Corpnatae.[2] Sistan sac. for Loch
Melge.[3]

    [1] *sic*, ' Flann of Inber Becce.' Flann Becc GD.   [2] Craebnat GD.
[3] ' on Loch Melge.'

18   .xu. kł.

Failbe m*a*c Cruaich dibich.[1]   Dubh[2] m*a*c Comardae.
Cellach m*a*c Dunc[h]ada regis.   Cronan mc. h. Lugada.[3]
Miannach m*a*c Failbe.

    [1] Craicdibhigh GD.   [2] Dubogan G, Dobogan D.
[3] Laigde G = moccu Laigde.

19   .xiiii. kł.

Fergusa sancti. Coibran Cl*úana*.[1]   Ciaran o Tigh h*ua*
nGortigh.[2] Ossino[3] Thergaidh 7 cáeca man*ach* imbi. Moc[h]-
olmóc mc. h. Amla.[4]   Aedan ab Lis Moir.[5]

    [1] ' of Clúain.'   [2] ' from Tech Úa nGortig.'   [3] *sic* ; ' Ossíne
of Tergad (Tengaidh GD ' of Tenga ') and fifty monks around
him.'   [4] = moccu Amla.   [5] ' of Less Mór.'

20   .xiii. kł.

Faelchon. Curifini. Molocae Sleibhe Bladma.[1] Caramnani.
Failbe.

    [1] ' of Slíab Bladma.'

21   .xii. kł.

Secht n-eps*coip* Tamhnaighe.¹   Lugan Sax*o*.²   Buadge.³
[f. 12ᵛ] Sillan Gl*inne* Munire.⁴   Curcaine Cille Curcaine.⁵

¹ ' Seven bishops of Tamnach.'   ² ' a Saxon ; ' sacc*art GD*.
³ *om GD, probably* = Buada, *belonging to* Tamnach Buada, *sic GD*.
⁴ ' of Glenn Munire.'   ⁵ ' of Cell Curcaine.'

22   .xi. kł.

Dobi Insi Causcraidh.¹   Dabeoodóc.   Colum.   Oiseni ep.
Moronóc Droma Samr*aidh*.²   Moroecha macnaeb.³   Colmani.
Lugidii.

¹ ' Dobí (or Mobí) of Inis Causcraid.'   ' ' of Druim Samraid.'
³ ' a boy-saint.'

23   .x. kł.

Lasre.   Cronsigi.   Banbnatan.   Runach Insi Moire ¹
Fullenn Atha Innich.²   Caincomrac Insi Oendaimh.³   Esp*oic*
Fethc[h]on.⁴

¹ ' of Inis Mór.'   ² ' of Áth Innich ; ' Atha ind eich *G*,
an eich *D*, i.e. Ford of the Horse.   ³ ' of Inis Éndaim.'
⁴ ' bishop Fethchú.'

24   .ix. kł.

Declan Airde Móir.¹   Lugbei Droma Bó.²   Corodni.
Crónain. Blait[h]m*ec* m*ac* Flainn.   Comgall m*ac* Táde³
ó Cl*úain* Diamhair.⁴   Satanal martir.   Oilleóc Cl*úana* Etch*éin*.⁵
Fergusa.

¹ ' of Ard Mór.'   ² ' of Druim Bó.'   ³ mac Tadéin *G*.
⁴ ' from Clúain Díamhair.'   ⁵ ' of Clúain Etchéin (?).'

25   .uiii. kł.

Colman idem et Mocholmoc hua Fiachrach.[1] Fiachrach.
Colain.[2] Deocain Nesain.[3] Finnbairr sac. Fiachra Cael
Clúana Cain.[4] Mosilóc .i. dalta Moling.[5] Ninnio senoir.[6]
Cristain. o Teni.[7]

[1] sic, read húa Liatháin O(n)D ; úa Litáin G ' descendant of
Liathán.' [2] = Coelán G. [3] ' deacon Nessán.' [4] ' Fiachra
the Slender of Clúain Cain ; ' Clúana Cactni G, Caichtne D.
[5] ' i.e. fosterling of Moling.' [6] ' the aged.' [7] oteni MS.; ' from
Teni (?).'

26   .uii. kł.

Tommain.[1] Nessain Mungarit.[2] Furudrain ep.

[1] Tomman Mungairti GO(n) ' of Mungarit.' [2] ' of Mungarit ; '
i.e. deacon Nessán, entered here again in error.

27   .ui. kł.

Beogain ab Maigi Bile.[1] Lasrain Tiprat Oss.[2]

[1] ' of Mag Bile.' [2] ' of Tipra Oss ; ' Thiprat Rois rain
GD.

28   .u. kł.

Furudrani sancti.   Colman[1] Gabla Liuin.[2] Liuican.
Uisseoit.

[1] Comgall GD. [2] ' of Gabal Liúin.'

29   .iiii. kł.

Biti Insi Caumscraidh.[1] Coelain Insi Celtra.[2] Cummine
mac Araide. Coman mac Finnba[i]rr. Iustan Lene manach.[3]

[1] ' of Inis Caumscraid.' [2] ' of Inis Celtra.' [3] ' of
Lene, monk.'

30   .iii. kł.

Colmain eps*coip*.   Maol Tuile m*a*c Mochuire.[1]   Sarani.
Febrithea.   Cobarchar Gulbain Guirt m.h. Gairb[2]   Aodh
m*a*c Bricc i Sleibh Liacc.[3]   German m*a*c Guill.

[1] mac Nochaire *GD.*   [2] ' of Gulban Guirt moccu Gairb ;' *see
Notes.*   [3] ' in Slíab Liacc.'   *See also Feb.* 28, *May* 4, *om. GD.*

31   .ii. kł.

Colman ,m*a*c Darane o Daire Mór.[1]   Sancti Natali i Cill
Manach.[2]   Íarnoc ailithir uagh ina curp.[3]   Papan i Sentreibh.[4]
7 Follamon mac Nath Fraich.[5]

[1] ' from Daire Mór.'   [2] ' in Cell Manach.'   [3] Iarnóc
a pilgrim, chaste in his body ; uithir ' sickly ' *OGD.*   [4] ' in
Sentreib.'   [5] mac *corr.* mic *man. rec.*

[Aug. 1]   **Kł.** Aug*uist.*]

[*p. 7a* ; *Facs.* p. 361] ¶ Columbae episcopi m*ei*c Riaguil.
Morioc Insi m*ei*c Lugein.[1]   Arun ep. Cl*úa*na Cain.[2]   Micae
Airdni ‹ł Ernaide.›[3]   Sarain B*e*nnch*air*.[4]   Trí m*ei*c L*u*ssen
Insi Móri .i.[5] Lib*er* 7 Falbe 7 Olbe.   Nath Í Cule
Sachaille.[6]   Lacteni Fothirbi.[7]

[1] ' of Inis meic Lugein ; ' mc. Ualaing *GD.*   [2] ' of Clúain Caín.'
[3] ernaid *Facs.* ' of Airdne or Ernaide.'   [4] ' of Bennchor.'   [5] ' the
three sons of Lussén of Inis Mór, i.e.,' *etc.*   [6] ' of Cúil
Sachaille.'   [7] ' of Fothairbe.'

[2]   .iiii. No*n*as.

Teothotae cum tribus filiis.[1]   Zefani episcopi.   Zefani
diaconi.   Felicis.   Luciani.   Musitaniae.   Nicetae.   Pauli.

¶ Comgan celi Dé.   Cobran Cl*úa*na Cuallacta.[2]   Lonan
m*a*c Lasre.   Fechine sac.

[1] fúís *Facs.*   [2] ' of Clúain Cúallachta.'

[3]   .iii. Non*a*s.

Inuentio corporis Zefani.   Hermelii.   Efronii episcopi.
Acellae.   Drogenis.   Zefani.   Nicodemii.   Samuelis.   Ermilii.
Effronii.   Iohannis met*r*apol*i*s.

¶ Trea i*n*gen Chairthind.   Mochua Crochain.[1]   Aedan
Cl*úana* Tarbfethi[2] Limmid Cilli Mair.[3]

  [1] ' of Crochán ; ' i.e. Crocán ' pitcher ' *GD*.   [2] *sic, read* ' of
Cl*ú*ain Tarb ; ' Cl. Cairbre *GD*.   [3] *sic, read* Fethlimmid ' of Cell Már.'

[4]   .ii. Non*a*s.

Iusti.   Crescentionis.   Sacinthi.   Iustini   Heremeti.
Floriani.   Eracli.   Isei.   Philistinae.   Mimi episcopi.   Zefani.
[*in marg.*] Laurenti.

¶ Moluae me*i*c Ochae Cl*úana* Ferta.[1]   Berchan Cl*úana*
Sasta.[2] Midnat Cilli Luci*n*ni.[3]

  [1] ' of Cl*ú*ain Ferta.'   *See Marginal Notes*.   [2] ' of Cl*ú*ain
Sasta.'   [3] ' of Cell Lucinni.'

[5]   Non*a*s.

Herentii.   Dassii   Heraclii ⟨b*is*[1]⟩.   Bassi.   Affri.   Augusti.
Leonis.   Irinei.   Floriani.   Filistini.   Tethasii.   Cassiani
episcopi.

¶ Osuualdi regis et aliorum .ii.   Ni*m*ni episcopi.   Donati.
Irennei.   Aradi.   Dasi.[2]

  [1] *in marg*.   [2] *There is confusion here.   See Aug.* 6, 9.

[6]   .uiii. Idus.

Sixti episcopi in Ro*m*a ⟨.i. in Roma⟩.   Felicis.   Agapiti.
Donatiani.   Laurentii.   Ypoliti.   Sanctae Affrae et milites[1]
.clxx. [col. *b*] Sanctae Affrae.   Mariae.   Cirillae.   Ueneriae.
Faustini.   Marci.   Caliusti.   Pretextati.   Cronani[1] et aliorum
.cxl.

¶ Cronani f*i*lii Lugada*ch*. idem et Mochua Cl*úana* Dolc*ain*.[3]
Lugaid Cl*úana* Fobuir.[4]   [2]Duissech for Loch Cúan.[5]   [2]Erne
Cl*úana* Railgech.[6]   [2]Molibba Guirt Chirb.[7]   [2]Echi i Cill Glassi.[8]

  [1] *sic*.   [2] *Under Aug* 5, *GD*.   [3] ' of Cl*ú*ain Dolcáin.'   [4] ' of
Cl*ú*ain Fobair.'   [5] ' on Loch Cúan.'   [6] ' of Cl*ú*ain Rail-
gech.'   [7] ' of Gort Cirb.'   [8] ' in Cell Glassi.'

[7] .uiii. Idus.

[1]Septem fratrum dormientium in Effeso. id est : Maximianus. Malchus. Dionisius. Ianuarius. Iohannes. Serapion. Constantinus . qui in tempore Decii morientes post .clii. annos resurrexerunt predicare mundo . regnante Teothosio filio Arcadii. Sopronii. Donati episcopi. Uastini. Ausenti. Affrae. Ueneriae et aliorum .l. martirum.

¶ Molóce ⟨.i. o Tilaig Ólaind⟩.[2] Senain. Temnani Linni Duachail.[3] Darii dōr.[4] Cronain Maige Bile.[5]

[1] *See Marginal Notes.*   [2] 'i.e. from Telach Olaind.'
[3] 'of Linn Dúachail.'   [4] *sic, om GD. cp. Aug.* 8.   [5] 'of Mag Bile.'

[8] .ui. Idus.

Secundi. Seriani.[1] Uictoriani. Ostensi. Albani ⟨bis⟩. Ciriaci. Largi. Crescentiani. Smragdi. Secundi. Faustini. Felicis. Nazari. Eutiani. Iulianae. Trifoniae. Mariae. Donatae. Mecronae. Agapae uirginis et aliorum .xuii. Choruntonis. Diomedis. Secundini. Corpofori.

¶ Colmani episcopi Insi Bó Finni.[2] .lxxx. anno etatis eius quieuit. Darii uirginis. Curchach Clúana Lothur.[3] Beoani filii Nessani i Fid Chuilend.[4]

[1] *sic.*   [2] 'of Inis Bó Finne.'   [3] 'of Clúain Lothur ; '
Lothair *GD.*   [4] 'in Fid Chuilenn.'

[9] .u. Idus.

Passio Antonii. Firmi. Rustici. Permonii. Crescentiani. Largi. Tiburti. Tiberiani. Teodori. Iuliani. Laudaici. Primi. Policarpi. Sixti. Nemiodani. Indaci. Fintinni et aliorum .xi.

¶ Nath Í presbiteri i nAchud Chonaire.[1] Tri ingena Ailella.[2] Barran uirgo. [col. c] Crumthir Riagáin.[3] Feidlimthe. Ultain. Laeban. Moloce. Mac Liac. Cethri meic Ercain.[4] Cethri meic Dimmain.[5] Breccain. Ciarain. Udnochtain. Coritain . hi omnes i Cill Móir Dithruib[6] quiescunt. [9]Rathnat Cilli Rathnaite.[7] [9]Colman mac Baeith i nDruim Rathe.[8]

[1] 'in Achad Conaire.'   [2] 'Ailill's three daughters.'
[3] 'presbyter Riagán.'   [4] 'Ercán's four sons.'   [5] 'Dimmán's four sons.'   [6] 'in Cell Mór Díthruib.'   [7] 'of Cell Rathnaite.'
[8] 'in Druim Ráithe.'   [9] Rathnat *and* Colman *under* Aug. 5. *GD.*

[10]   .iiii. Idus.

Laurentii archidiaconi et martiris in Ro*ma* et uirorum
.xi. et uirginum .xiii. Felicissimi. Zefani. Crescentionis.
Arcarei. Quirilli. Quinti. Gemini. Agapae. Perpetuae.
Petronillae. Crispinae. Menellae. Mariae. Iulianae. Inno-
centiae. Terentiae. Isiodorae. Ostensae. Affrae. Cres-
centiae. Perpetuae. Felicitatis. Portiani. Cresti et aliorum
.xxuiii. Ciriaci. Cirici. Exsuperati. Eugenii. Pastoris.
Pontiani. Largi. Leocis. Leocipi. Seui. Cassiani et
aliorum .xxx. Annae matris Samuel*is.*

¶ Blaan*i* episcopi Cind Garad i ṅGallgaedel*aib*.[1]   Mael
Ruain cum suis reliquiis sanctorum martirum et uirginum ad
Tamlachtain uenit. Cummine aƀ Dromma Bó.[2]

[1] ‘ of Cenn Garad in Gallgóedil.’   [2] ‘ of Druim Bó.’

[11]   .iii. Idus.

Tiburti et Ualeriani. Ciciliae. Susannae. Mariae.
Munisanae. Teclae. Cassiani. Zefani. Cornilii. Gauricii
episcopi. Gairi et aliorum multorum.

¶ Airerain sapientis et abbatis Tamla*chta* post Mael Ruain.
Etractae uirginis. Indectae uirginis. Banbnatan. Toidiliae.
Ingena Dútu.[1] Ingena Senaich.[2] Ingena Donnain.[3]

[1] ‘ Dútu's daughters.’   [2] ‘ Senach's daughters.’   [3] ‘ Donnán's
daughters.’

[12] [col. *d*]   .ii. Idus.

Macarii. Iuliani. Crisanti. Ui*n*ciae. Agnae. Ueneriae.
Clariani et milites[1] .lxx. Ciciliae. Dariae. Agathae. Iuliani.
Eupuli. Marci. Macarii. Columbae. Clarinae. Radic*un*dis et
aliorum .lxxii.

¶ Molassi m*eic* Declain Insi Muridaig.[2]   Segeni aƀ Iae.[3]
Murchad o Chill Alaid.[4]

[1] *sic.*   [2] ‘ of Inis Muredaig.’   [3] ‘ of Í.’   [4] ‘ from
Cell Alaid.’

[13]   Idus.

Hipoliti.   Pontiani episcopi.   Luciani.   Antici.   **Cornilii.**
Calisti.   Ipolissi et aliorum .ii.

¶ Momedoc Feda Duin.[1]   Brigitae Cl*úana* Dianlama.[2]
Moloca m*a*c Caetren ⟨ᵗ Carthind.⟩

    [1] ' of Fid Dúin.'   *Also Mar.* 23, *May* 18.   [2] ' of Clúain
Dianlama.'   *See Notes.*

[14]   .xix. kł. Septim*bir*.

Assumptio Mariae uirginis.   Fortunati.   Dimetri.   Felicis.
Euticii.   Fortunae.   Iulianae.   B*e*rmiae.   Pauli.   Eracli.
Dissi.   Pari*n*i.   Possessoris.   Pr*o*salm ⟨b*is*⟩.   Si*n*laiae.
Uincentiae et aliorum .iii.[1]

¶ Fachtna m*a*c Mongaig o R*u*s Ailithir.[2]   Dinil m*a*c in
tŝáir.[3]   [4]Mac in tsáeir eps. 7 aƀ Darinsi Maeli Anfaid.[4]   Broc-
cain m*ei*c Lugda*ch.*   Cummini.   Coemain.   Aicclig.

    [1] ui. *Facs.*   [2] ' from Ros Ailithir.'   [3] ' son of the
wright,' *sic, dittography.*   [4—4] Mac in tsáeir = Fachtna mac
Mongaig *OG,* ' bp. and abbot of Darinis Máeli Anfaid.'

[15]   .xuiii. kł. Sep*timbir*.

Stratonis.   Ignati.   Pilippi.   T*u*rsi.   Iohannis.   Aciani.
Ciricii.   Laurentii.   Zefani.   Quintini.   Cornilii.   Celsi.
Georgii.

¶ Fir da Chrich.   Colmai*n* o Achud[1] et Sancti Sara*n*i et
filiarum Cairp*r*i.

    [1] ' from Achad.'

[16]   .xuii. kł.

Natiuitas sanctae Mariae.   Arionis.   Ignatii.   **Agniti**
cum suis.   Ossi.   Ignatii.   Tirsi.   Zefani.   Ciciliae.   Iuliae.
Iulitae.   Eulali.   Anastasii.   Hirundinis.   Musae.

¶ Lugani et sancti Cona*n*i.

[17] .xui. kł.

Eufemiae uirginis. [col. *e*] Dissiae. Romulae. Mammetae. Eli. Emilianae. Gallae. Iohani. Transillae. Orionis. Mammetis mon*achi*. Desei. Zefa*n*i.

¶ Beccain. Sancti Eoani me*i*c Cairlaind. Foirthetho. Ernáin. Tuchai. Beccáin. Te*m*miani monachi.

[18] .xu. kł.

Agapiti. Panteni. Pontimi. Martini. Marcianae. Palanciae. Scolasticae. Marciae. Mosae. Maciae. Candidae. Cristinae. Luciae. Helianae. Amantiae. Talamae. Taianae. Sincliticae. Candidi. Erennae. Potomi. Dasci ⟨b*is*⟩. Romani.

¶ Daig m*a*c Cairill Insi Cáin.[1] Martan. Ernine m*a*c Cresine o Raith Nui i n*U*í*b* Garrchon.[2] Colman Cúle.[3]

[1] 'of Inis Caín.' *See Marginal Notes.* [2] ' from Ráith Noí in Uí Garrchon.' [3] 'of Cúil.'

[19] .xiiii. kł.

Magni martiris. Silonis. Quirilli. Gelasii. Timothei. Pontoni. Filionis. Rosini. Leontii. Orionis. Eogeniae. Marcioani. Teodotae. Gaddae. Magni. Philonis. Laurentii. Sancti Crucis. Zefani. Quintini. Iuliani. Antonii. Passio Osuuini regis. Pauli.

¶ Mocta Lugmaid.[1] Enani Dromm*a* Rathi.[2]

[1] 'of Lugmad.' *Also Mar. 24.* [2] 'of Druim Ráithe.' *Also Sep.* 18.

[20] [col. *f*] .xiii. kł.

Dioscori ⟨b*is*⟩. Iulii. Uincentii. Augurii. Iuliani. Ipoliti. Tragani. Quadrati. Zetici. Angeli. Ualentini. Leontii. Mamm*é*tis. Pampilii episcopi cum clero suo. Quintini. Zeli. Coloni. Maximi. Ualentionis. Alexandri. Pistriardi. Mathei. Diomidis. Luxorii et aliorum .u.

¶ Mothrianoc Ruscaig.[1] Lassar o Chill Archalgach.[2] Conchand o Chaelchad.[3]

[1] 'of Rúscach.' [2] 'from Cell Archalgach.' [3] 'from Cáelchad ; ' ó Chaolachadh *GD.*

[21]   .xii. kł.

Uincentii.   Iuliani.   Ualentiani.   Seui.   Quadrati.
Timothei. Leontiani. Luxori. Leontii. Artosii. Diomedis.
Sotici. Ualentini.

¶ Sinachi episcopi Clúana Iraird.¹   Mogin Mór.   Celbae²
7 Masse.   Uncan Tugneda.³

¹ ' of Clúain Iraird ; ' *see Index.*   ² Coelba *G.*   ³ ' of Tugnid.'

[22]   .xi. kł.

Timothei discipuli Pauli ⟨*in* uia Ostensi⟩.   Expectiti.
Saturnini. Aprilis. Felicis. Tasseusi. Meneruii. Emiliani
cum suis. Simfroniani. Pigrini. Martialis. Nectiui. Mar-
celli. Aurelii. Felicis. Ipoliti. Nect*uri*. Medardi. Marini.
Sedrac episcopi. Natani. Emiliani cum uii.¹ filiis.

¶ Cummeni et Sanctae Sinchi. Sedrach epi. Beogaes m*eic*
Daigre ab Benn*chair.*²

¹ luii. *Facs.*   ² ' of Bennchor.'

[23]   .x. kł.

Fortunati et aliorum .u. Hermoginis. Sirti. Martialis.
Zefani. Hermog*er*atis. Laurentii. Abundi. Inocentii.
[col. *g*] Mirendini. Ipoliti. Ciriaci ⟨*bis*⟩. Archilaii. Laudi.
Timothei. Apollinaris. Augusti. Flauiani. Sidonii. Ermo-
deri. Munni. Neonis. Archei. Ypoli cum suis. Ciciliae.
Mariae. Basillae. Dom*n*inae et aliorum .xiii. Laurenti.
Claudii. Asteri. Dm̄o.¹ Arafranis. Sidoni episcopi.

¶ Eogain ep. Aird Sratha.²   Secht n-eps*coip* Domnaig
Móir Aelmaige.³

¹ *or* Dnio (?).   ² ' of Ard Sratha.'   ³ ' Seven bishops
of Domnach Mór Áelmaige.'

[24]   .ix. kł.

Zenoni.   ¹¶ Iulii.   Italicae.¹   Capitolini.   Genobii.
Emeritae. Iunillae. Genesi. Partholomei.² Zenoui. Mage-
noli.

¶ Patricii abbatis et episcopi Ruis Dela.³ Patricii hostiarii
et abbatis Aird Ma*cha.*⁴ Gelldarii. Faelani. Segini. Abbai*n*.

¹⁻¹ *in marg.*   ² *sic.*   ³ ' of Ros Dela.'   ⁴ ' of Ard Macha.'
TALLAGHT.   F

[25] .uiii. kł.

Passio Bartholomei apostoli. Iuliani. Eptati. Genesi. Iulii. Patricii. Euticitis. Reuersinae. Eoticae. Mariae. Italicae. Rufine. Iunillae. Zefani. Timothei. Iohannis. Ioseph et aliorum .u.

¶ Sillain me*ic* Findchain episcopi et abbatis Maig[e] Bile.[1] Broccain I*m*gain.[2]

[1] ' of Mag Bile.' [2] ' of Imgan ; ' i Maigin *Br.*

[26] .uii. kł.

Quinti. Zefani. Quarti. Maximiani. Anastasii. Seueri. Cinti. Mercurii. Uictoris. Coloceri ⟨b*is*⟩. Bassi. Meroni. Primi. Celsi. Eleutheri episcopi cum s*uis* ( )[1]. Rufini. Basillae.

[p. 8*a* ; *Facs.* p. 362] ¶ Faelan Cl*úana* Moescna.[2] Comgall h*úa* Sarain.[3]

[1] *a few letters illegible, resembling* ret. (?) *reliquiis.* [2] ' of Clúain Móescna.' *Also Jan.* 9. *See Marginal Notes.* [3] ' descendant of Sarán.'

[27] .ui. kł.

Rufi. Sabbati. Alexandri. Sabasti. Felicis. Potenti. Zefani ⟨b*is*⟩. Laurenti. Sabiani. Honorati. Rufini. Hermetis Tribuni. Clerici. Petri et aliorum .x. Dionisii. Cesarii episcopi. D*o*mini. Gauiniani. Castori. Mariae. Teodoriae. Iohannae . militis. Cesarii. Sauiani martiris et aliorum .xxu. [*in marg.*] Marcellini. Basillae. Baluinae.

¶ Usailli m.h. in Baird.[1] Adain.[2]

[1] = moccu in Baird. [2] *sic , leg.* Aida*ni Br.*

[28] .u. kł.

Hermis in Affrica. Hermetis. Heliae. Basilei. Zefani ⟨b*is*⟩. Serapionis. Constantii. Alexandri. Augustini.[1] episcopi. Fausti episcopi. Excellentissimi episcopi. Laurenti martiris. Ciriaci martiris et aliorum .dcccciiii. Scribae. Basillae uirginis.

¶ Feidlimid m*ac* Crimtha*inn.*

[1] *in marg.* magni.

[29]   .iiii. kł.

Passio Iohannis Baptistae in Emisma ciuitate Feniciae.
Dormitatio Helesei profetae.   Receptio Heli.   Pauli ⟨bis⟩.[1]
Felicis.   Zefani.   Nat*alis* et aliorum .dcccc.   Gemillinae.
Concordiae.   Mariae.   Elizabeth.   Coronae.   Basillae.

¹ *in marg.*

[30]   .iii. kł.

Passio Agapae et Chionae et Herennae et Gaudentiae.
Eufemiae.   Mariae.   Cirillae.   .uii. sorores Agapae.   Felicis.
Geurgii.   Adauti.   Paulini.   Zefani.   Quintini.   Cirici.
Ioseph ⟨bis⟩.   Iohannis et aliorum .iii *m* ccc.

¶ Fir da Chrich.   Cronan Cl*úana* Andobor.[1]   Muadan
Aricail Muadán.[2]   Loarn sac. Achaid Móir.[3]

¹ ' of Clúain Andobor ; ' Andobair *GD*.   ² ' of Airecul
Múadáin.'   ³ ' of Achad Mór.'

[31] [col. *b*]   .ii. kł.

Paulini episcopi Nolanae urbis qui se tradidit in seruitutem
pro filio uiduae.   Lini episcopi.   Gaiani.   Triu*eris*.   Zefani.
Iuliani.   Rufini.   Collociae.   Mariae.   Iustae.   Marialitae.
Fithioniae.   Humilianae.   Iulianae.   Iohannis.   Brigitoniae.
Italicae.   Uincentii.   Siluani.   Uitalici.   Emiliani.   Florentii.
Antin*chi*.   Antiochi cum suis o[*mn*]ibus.

¶ Aedani episcopi Insi Medcóit.[1] et Sancti Cronani diaconi
Senan Atha Omna.[2]   Aed mar*tir*.   Aed m*a*c Maine.

¹ ' of Inis Medcóit.'   ² ' of Áth Omna.'   Seiséin *G*, Sessén *D*.

[Sept. 1]   **Kł.** Sep*timbir*.

Ciciliae uirginis.   Calistae.   Tonsae.   Musae.   Mariae.
Agnae.   Donatae.   Teclae.   Fortunatae.   Prisci martiris et
aliorum martirum iii *m* cccc.x.   Marci.   Felicis.   Torentiani.

F 2

Donati. Zefani. Euodii. Egidii abbatis. Laurentii. Her-
moginis. Dubitati. Ualenti. Nausi. Iesu Naue. Fortunati.
Donati. Felicis. Gedeon profetae. Cleomannis. Constantini.
Feliciani. Sisinni. Amansi. Uictorii. Uincentii. Donati
subdiaconi.¹

*   *   *   *   *   *

¹ *Remainder of this day, also* 2, 3, *and portion of* 4 *wanting ;*
but there is no break in the MS.

[4]   [.ii. Nonas.]¹

¶ Ultan m.h. Conchobair i nArd Brecain.² Comgelli .i.
Bothi Conais.³ [col. c] Senain. Fiachrach. Commein ab
Dromma Snec[h]ta.⁴ Sairbile uirgo Fochairde Murthemni.⁵
Falbe mac Ronain i Clúain Airbelaig.⁶

¹ *See Notes.* ² 7 soror eius Cron i ñGalaum Lagen *add. in marg.*
' Ultan moccu Conchobair in Ard Breccáin.'   ³ ' i.e. of Both
Conais.'   ⁴ ' of Druim Snechta.'   ⁵ ' of Fochard Murthemni.'
⁶ ' in Clúain Airbelaig.'

[5]   .iiii. Nonas [*recte* Nonas].

Taurini. Herculini. Zefani. Quinti. Donati. Arcontii.
Saturnini ⟨bis⟩. Mariae. Iuliae. Iulitae. Tauri. Ingenui
episcopi cum suis. Saturnini. Memorati. Arapolini episcopi.
Ferrucionis. Nimpi. Quintiani. Torsi et aliorum .iiii.

¶ Elacho¹ ⟨ł Eolang⟩ Achaid Bó² Eolog³ anchorita et Duib
Scuili. Faithlenn dechoin.⁴

¹ Deocain Indecht Eolach G.   ² ' of Achad Bó.'   ³ *Under*
Elacho *and* Eolog *are two points. See Notes.*   ⁴ ' deacon.'

[6]   .iii. Nonas [*recte* .uiii. Idus].

Eleutherii episcopi. Cotidi cum sociis suis. Zefani cum
suis.

¶ Meic Culind ep. Lusca.¹ Coluim ⟨.i. Crossaire⟩ ó Russ.²
idem et Colman Midísil.³ Giallain. Tochunni. Scíath o
Firt Sceithi i mMúscraige tri Maigi.⁴

Aduentus reliquiarum Scethi filiae Méchi ad Tamlachtain.

¹ , of Lusca.'   ² ' from Ros.'   ³ ' of Midísel.'   ⁴ ' from
Fert Scéithe in Muscraige trí Maige.'

[7]   .ii. Non*as* [*recte* .uiii. Idus].

Senoti.   Festi.   Ianuarii.   Acuti.   Desiderii.   Lauani.
Sinoti.   Capudaci.   Laurenti.   Anathasii cum suis.
¶ Ultain.   Sillain episcopi.   .i.¹   Toitae for Loch Ech*ach*.
Elair Locha Cré.²   Molassi sancti.   uel híc M*a*c Culind.

¹ *supply* Toite Inse ' i.e. Toite of Inis Toite on Loch Echach.'
² ' of Loch Cré.'

[8]   Nonas [*recte* .ui. Idus].

Natiuitas Mariae matris Iesu.   Eulaliae.   Anastasiae.
Britoniae.   Hirundinis.   Fausti.   Serapionis.   Pii ⟨*bis*⟩.
Teophili. [col. *d*] Piotheri et aliorum .xii.   Nemesis.   Arioni.
Ammoni.   Iohannis.   Petri.   Seuerini.   Dimetri et aliorum
.xᵗ.   Dedimi.   Nistori.   Mistori.   Orosei.   Isiodori.   Sera-
pionis.   Siluini.   Metri.   Orobionis et aliorum .cxxii.   Seueri
et aliorum .xi.   Ammonis.   Zefani.   Pampili.   Neotini.

¶ Fintan Airde Cain.¹ et m*eic* Talaraig.² et Maeli Caisni.
Fergus cruthnech.³   Crumthir Catha⁴ m*eic* Oengusa i Cl*úain*
Eorainne.⁵

¹ ' of Ard Caín.'   ² ' and the sons of Talarag ' ; meic
Thalairc *GD*.   ³ the Pict.   ⁴ ' presbyter Catha.'   ⁵ ' in Clúain
Eorainne ' ; Eossain *GD*.

[9]   .uiii. [*recte* .u.] Idus.

Gorgoni martiris.   Hacunti.   Alexandri.   Tiburti.   Donati.
Eleasi.   Iacinti.   Fortunati.   Liberati.   Deusii.   Geurgii.
Damiani martiris et aliorum .dccc.   Eugulfi.   Cirici.
Iohannis.

¶ Ciaran m*a*c in tś*á*er.¹   Findbarr ⟨.i. Broednea⟩ Cilli
Cuńge² et Fer da Chrích et Sanctae Cerae.   Mochotae
⟨.i. m*a*c Dergain⟩ Dromma.³   Sanctae Darercae.   Conall
m*a*c Oengussa ⟨.i. in t-eices⟩.⁴   Aithgen ep. Maige Bile.⁵
Noebingena Enaig Lóeg.⁶

¹ ' son of the wright.'   ² ' of Cell Cunga.'   ³ ' of
Druim.'   ⁴ ' i.e. the poet.'   ⁵ ' of Mag Bile.'   ⁶ ' the
saintly maidens of Enach Lóeg ' ; noémhinghen og Enaig *G*,
inghen Enaigh *D*.

[10]   .uii. [*recte* .iiii.] Id*us*.

Euepiae et aliorum .dccc.   Cursici.   Hisici.   Siluasii.
Hielini.   Dedi*m*i.   Meref*o*ri.   Augusti.   Nectari episcopi.
Depletori.   Mauriolioris.   Zarii.   Salui.   T*u*rsi.   Zefani.
Merosori.   Hilarii papae.   Iohannis et Pauli.

¶ Finnio m.h. Fiatach.¹   Senaig Gairb ⟨† me*i*c Buidi⟩.²
Findbair Maigi³ et Sancti Segeni abbatis Benn*ch*ai*r*.   Ailbi
Imlig.⁴   Lucill et Odran.   Fergus m*a*c Guaire.

¹ = moccu Fíatach.   ² 'Senach the Rough, or Buide's son.'
³ 'of Mag [Bile].'   ⁴ 'of Imlech ;' *cp. Sep.* 12.

[11] [col. *e*]   .ui. [*recte* .iii.] Idus.

Prothi.   Iacinthi.   Eugeniae.   Siri.   Euleliae.   Mariae.
Musae.   Basillae.   Ypoliti.   Serapionis.   Felicis.   Militiadis.
Patientis.   Donati et aliorum .xxx.   Petri.   Iohannis.   Tomae.

¶ Sillain i nImlich Cassain i Cualṅgi.¹   Colmain ep. Ailbi.²
Conamail.   Daniel ep. Benn*ch*ai*r*.³   Mośinu.

¹ 'in Imlech Cassáin in Cúalnge.'   ² 'of Ailbe.'   ³ 'of
Bennchor.'

[12]   .u. [*recte* .ii.] Idus.

Timothei.   Siri.   Epuli.   Serapionis.   Petri.   Ipoliti.
Sanetinae.   Mariae.   Teclae.   Herclii.   Transili.   Teophili.
Eusebii episcopi.   Zefani.   Iuliani.   Laurentii.   Celsi.

¶ Molassi ⟨m. Nad Fraich⟩ Daminsi.¹   Ailbei eps.
Imlecha.²   Colma*n*i episcopi ⟨Ablae.⟩³   Me*i*c Lasre.

¹ 'of Daminis.'   ² 'of Imlech [Ibair].'   ³ 'of Abla ' (?)

[13]   .iiii. Idus [*recte* Idus].

Felicissimi.   Secundini.   Teodoli.   Timothei.   Litori.
Agusti.   Nectari.   Marulionis.   Sec*u*ndi.   Depletori.   Pectori
episcopi.   Beati.   Parmenii.   ⟨Quinti⟩.   Lodori.   Geurgi.

¶ Dagan presbiteri me*i*c Colmada Inbir Dóile.¹   Neman m.h
Duib.²

¹ 'of Inber Doíle.'   ² = moccu Duib.

[14]   .iii. Idus [*recte* .xuiii. kł. Octimb*ir*].

Cornelii ⟨papae in Ro*ma*⟩ et Cipriani episcopi ⟨in Cartagine⟩. Dionisii ⟨b*is*⟩ episcopi et aliorum .iii. Saturi. Felicis. Honori. Dimetri. Zetae. Mariae. Romulae. Epartii et aliorum .xuiii. Iohannis. Petri. Zefani. Mathei.

¶ Coeman Brecc ic Ross Ech i Cailli Follomuin.[1] Ingena Coluim i Cremthannaib.[2] Mael Tolaig o[3] Dromma Faindle.[4]

¹ ' at Ros Ech in Caille Follamain.'   ² ' Colum's daughters, in the Cremthanna.'   ³ o *sic, omitt.* ; ' of Druim Faindle ; ' ó Druim Níad *GD*, ' from Druim Níad ; ' *om. Br., the last two entries are under Sep. 13 in GD.*   ⁴ *Two lines erased here.*

[15] [col. *f*]   .ii. Idus [*recte* .xuii. kł.].

Dedicatio basilicae Mariae.   Cirini episcopi.   Serapionis. Leonti. Epacti episcopi. Zefani. Croci. Seleuci. Arthei. Ualerii.   Cirionis.   Merobi.   Stratoris.   Pauli episcopi. Gordiani episcopi. Arcioni. Paulini episcopi. Constantii. Ioseph. Maglaconi. Galitiae. Mariae. Sincliticae. Nicodimi. Serapionis. Leonti et aliorum .ix.

¶ Lassar Cl*úana* Mór.[1]   Ainmere Cl*úana* Fata.[2]   M*eic* Taidc.[3]

¹ *sic* ' of Clúain Mór.'   ² ' of Clúain Fota.'   ³ ' Tadg's sons.'

[16]   Idus [*recte* .xui. kł.].

Felicis ⟨b*is*⟩. Alexandri. Zefani. Uiatoris.   Spepati. Lolati.   Prisciani.   Tussi.   Iohannis.   Salui.   Iohannis. Prisizati. Papiae. Sec*un*dae. Mariae. Donatae. Bessiae. Generosae.   Ciciliae.   Romulae.   Gallae.   Emerentianae. Merentianae. Eufemiae.

¶ Monenn Cl*úana* Conaire.[1]   Lasrian*i* abbatis in Hí Col*uim* Ch*ille*.[2] Molasse m*ac* Lugair.[3]   Critain Aireni.[4] Senain. Sarain. Cathboth. Colma*n*. Coeman. Anfodan. Auxilii.

¹ ' of Clúain Conaire.'   ² ' in Í Coluim Chille.'   ³ = Molasse moccu Lugair.   ⁴ ' of Airene ' ; Critain *om. Br.*

[17]   .xuiii. [*recte* .xu.] kł. Octimbir.

Ualeriani. Gordiani. Magrini. Constantii. Sancтini.
Paulini. Maronii. Gaudiani. Dordiani. Laurentii. Isici
episcopi. Calcidoni. Socratis. Zefani. Paliosi. Petri.
Mauricii. Eufemiae uirginis pass*io*. Constantiae. Mariae.
Trinsille.

¶ Broccain .i. Rois Toirc.[1] Grellain episcopi .i. o Laind.[2]
Herci episcopi o Domnuch Mór Maigi Coba.[3] [col. *g*] Cummine
aƀ .i. Damoirne.[4] Riaguil Muccinsi.[5]

[1] ' i.e. of Ros Tuirc.'   [2] ' i.e. from Lann.' *Also Sep.* 18.
[3] ' from Domnach Mór Maige Coba ; ' Maige Damhairne *GD*.
[4] ' of Damoirne ; ' Bennchair *GD* ' of Bennchor.'   [5] ' of Muccinis.'

[18]   .xuii. [*recte* .xiiii.] kł.

Trofimi. Ociani. Sisti. Eustorgi episcopi. Saturi ⟨*bis*⟩.
Dimetri. Pallei. Nibi. Heli. Primadi. Pauli. Castoris.
Niceti. Ianuarii. Angi. Iuliani. Paterni et aliorum .cl.
Felicis. Eutropii. Medeti et aliorum .dxiii.[1]

¶ Enain Dromma Rathe.[2] [3]Gemmae uirginis. Dedicatio
basilicae Martini.[3] Mael Canaig. Fergnai presbiteri. Grel-
lain Lainni.[4] Foindelaig.,

[1] .dxui. *Facs.*   [2] ' of Druim Ráithe.'   [3]-[3]*Out of place.*
[4] ' of Lann.'

[19]   .xui. [*recte* .xiii.] kł.

Ianuarii martiris. Dimetri. Castoris. Aniceti. Diapoli.
Palei. Nilii. Pari. Madieli. Saturi. Trofi. Ferili. Militi.
Iorgii episcopi.

¶ Meic Cúigi presbiteri. [1]Zefani. Anci.[1] Fintani
abbatis. Comgell uir*go*.

[1]-[1] *Out of place.*

[20]   .xu. [*recte* .xii.] kł.

Daromae. Constantiae. Priuatae. Priuati. Felicis.
Dionisii. Iohannis. Celsi.

Aedain. .

[21]   .xiiii. [*recte* .xi.] kł.

Mattei apostoli et euangelistae et Lucae euangelistae.
Edoni. Uictoris. Sedrac episcopi.   Eufemiae et aliorum
xxui. martirum. Iohannis. Iuliani. Zefani. Petri. Cirici.
Mammetis. Clementis.

[*in marg.*] ¶ Saran m*ac* Tigernain m*eic* Móinaig.[1]

    [1] ' Sarán son of Tigernán [Tigernach *GD*] son of Móenach.'

[22]   .xiii. [*recte* .x.] kł.

Mauricii martiris. Expueri. Candidi. Uictoris.   Inno-
centii. Uitalis cum omnibus sociis eorum id est ui. *m* dclxui.
in Sacina ciuitate super fluuium Rodanum.   Pantaleonis
martiris et Hermologi presbiteri.   Herinipi .i. in Necomedia.
Ipoc*r*ati cum suis. Basillae. Mariae. Transillae. Sidonis.
Zefani. Uelensi. Pauli. Geurgii. [p. 9*a* ; *Facs.* p. 363]
Martini. Erasmi et aliorum martirum u. *m* dcccclxxxi.

Barrind.   Aed m*ac* Senaig m*eic* Ernini.[1]   Colman m*ac*
Cath*bad* i mMidisiul.[2]

    [1] *sic, but GD have* Meic Ernín *a separate commemoration ; om.*
Br.   [2] ' in Midísel.'

[23]   .ix. kł.

Marci euangelistae.   Liberi episcopi.   Sosii.   Teclae
uirginis Euasnit.

¶ Adomnani abbatis Iae et Sancti Sarani et Cóimnatan.
Conich[1] m*eic* Luachanain.[2]

    [1] *gen. sg.* ; Conaing *GD*.   [2] *second* a *subscr.* ; Lucunáin *GD*.

[24]   .uiii. kł.

Conceptio Iohannis Baptistae.   Siri.   Andoci.   Martialis.
Tuitsi. Felicis. Lupi episcopi.   Uictoriae.   Secundolae.
Mariae.   Faustinae.   Elizabeth.   Secundae.   Uictoriae.

Rustici episcopi. Siluani. Zefani. Silurini. Iuliani. Iohannis.
Crizofori. Marci. Stragili. Liberi episcopi. Nobilis. Petri.
Lini. Cornilii. Priscillae et xxii.
¶ Cailchon Clúana Airthir.¹   Cellachan Clúana Tiprat.²
Failchon Findglasi³ et filiarum Cainig o Maig Locha.⁴

¹ ' Cailchú of Clúain Airthir ; ' ó Lúi Airthir GD, o Lui
Erthir O(n).   ² ' of Clúain Tiprat.'   ³ ' Failchú of
Findglaiss.'   ⁴ ' and Cainnech's daughters from Mag Locha.'

[25]   .uii. kł.

Bardoniani. Carpi. Eucarpi et aliorum .xxui. Eusebii
episcopi. Senatoris. Zefani. Pauli. Timothei. Titi.
¶ Modai ⟨.i. i nAilbe¹⟩. Ruine. Colmani sancti. Barrind
Corcaige.² Senan ep. Corcaige.² Imchad. Caelan. Sinell
Dromma Broon.³ Colman Comraire.⁴

¹ ' i.e. in Ailbe.'   ² ' of Corcach.'   ³ ' of Druim Broon.'
⁴ ' of Comrar.'

[26]   .ui. kł.

Eusebii episcopi et confessoris. Senatoris. Faustini.
Luxurii. Migni. Zefani. Nabartii. Cirici. [in marg.]
Iohannis.
¶ Colmani Lainni Elo¹ ⟨lu° anno aetatis.⟩ Colmani Ruis
Branduib² uel hic Barrind Corcaige.³

¹ ' of Lann Elo ; ' also under Oct. 3.   ² ' of Ros Branduib.'
³ ' of Corcach.'

[27]   .u. kł.

Timothei discipuli Pauli. Cosmae et Damiani pasio.
Eleuterii. Taraci. Probi. Andronici. [col. b] Florentiani
et aliorum .xx. martirum. Iohannis. Celsii. Laurentii.
¶ Suibni sancti. Columbani eliuatio. Finniaui. Erneni
hui Briuin.¹ Fintanne meic Copain.

¹ ' descendant of Brion.'

[28]   .iiii. kł.

Marcialis.   Laurentiae.   Uictoriae.   Donatae.   Leae.
Luciosae.   Mariae.   Longiosae.   Scolasticae.   Teothosae.
Candidae.   Cristinae.   Ualeriae.   Sincliticae.   Longae.
Uictoriae.   Gurgelli.   Marii.   Zefani.   Fausti.   Prisci.   Placidi
et aliorum .xx.

¶ Finnio.   Diarmait mac Lucraid o Clúain Fidnaige.[1]
Gildae.   Iunilli ⟨.i. infirmi⟩.   Fiachraich episcopi.

    [1] 'from Clúain Fidnaige.'

[29]   .iii. kł.

Dedicatio basilicae Michaelis archangeli in Monte Gargano.
Euticii.   Sosii.   Placidi.   Ianuarii.   Ampuli.   Heracliae.
Eugeniae.   Mariae.   Traciae.   Humilianae.   Teothotae.
Traciae.   Celidoni.   Zefani.   Fraterni.   Iohannis.   Iamputiani.
Ambodi.   Geurgii.   Euteci.   Martini.   Paluti.   Patricii.   Ciricii.

¶ Columbae sancti.   Murgaile.   Comgilli militis Christi.
[col. c] Sedrac cum suis reliquiis.   Meic Ieir episcopi.   Nessan
Ulad.[1]

    [1] 'of the Ulaid.'

[30]   .ii. kł.

Ieronimi presbiteri in Bethleem.   Antonini translatio.
Licasti.   Celsii.   Fictoris.   Zefani.   Desidei.   Iohannis.
Desiderii.   Honorii episcopi.   Noe.   Mariae.

¶ Failani.   Connae sanctae.   Creber.   Brigitae.   Senan.
Mochonna Chuairne.[1]   Lassar ingen Lochain.   Bronchein
Lethet Corcaige.[2]   Ailither ep.[3]   Lugaid Airthir Achaid.[4]
Mobí Clairenech[5] Domnaig Broic.[6]   Comsid sac. Domnaig
Aires.[7]   Rothan 7 Daigri o Clúain Acuir.[8]   Bresal o Derthaig.[9]
Faelan Ratha Aidme.[10]   Airmer Craibdech o Bréchmaig.[11]
Loegaire ep. o Loch Con.[12]

    [1] 'of Cúairne ; '   Clúana Airdne 'of Clúain Airdne ' GD.
[2] 'of Lethet Corcaige.'   GD have Corcan n. pr.   [3] 'pilgrim,'
a gl. on Corcan. GD.   Achaid is written under ep. and immediately
over Airthir, and goes with the latter in GD.   [4] 'of Airther
Achaid.'   [5] Mobí cailleach ' nun ' GD.   [6] 'of Domnach
Brocc.' Mobí Clairenech, ' table-faced,' is also under Oct. 12.
[7] 'of Domnach Aires.'   [8] 'from Clúain Acuir.'   [9] 'from
Derthach.' Also May 18.   [10] 'of Ráith Aidme ; ' Aidne GD.
[11] 'the pious from Bréchmag.'   [12] 'from Loch Con.'

[Oct. 1]   **Kł.** Oct*imbir.*

Lucae euangelistae.   Aduentus reliquiarum Iesu Christi et Mariae et apostolorum et martirum et profetarum et uirginum.   Prisci martiris.   Crescentii.   Petri.   Euagri. Faustini. Iohannis. Marcialis. Ianuarii. Pauli. Alexandri. Eupropii. Zefani. Remedii. Pignae. Catiae.   Basillae. Basilissae. Crescentiae. Gotiae.   Transillae. Denegotiae. Musae. Eugeniae. Brigitoniae. Baluinae. Geurgii. Saturnini.   Spei. Casti. Primi. Ciricii. Donati.   Christi et aliorum .xuiii. Autisii. Laurentii. [col. *d*]   Faustini cum suis. Germani episcopi. Doctoris episcopi.

¶ Doithnennaig Feda Duin.[1]   Clothrainne .i. Insi Duine.[2] Sinell sac. Maigi Bile.[3]   Colman.   Fintan.   Columbae abbatis Benn*chair*[4] [5]*fratris* Glassain.[5]   Fidairle h*úa* Suanaig.[6]

[1] 'Doíthnennach of Fid Dúin.'   [2] ˙ Clothrann i.e. of Inis Dúine.'   [3] 'of Mag Bile.'   [4] ' of Bennchor.' [5]–[5] *om. G*, Glassan *D*, Colmán m*ac* Duach *frater* Cassain *Br*. [6] ' descendant of Súanach.'

[2]   .ui. N*onas.*

Euliter. Primici. Aurilli. Epetini. Eusebii. Gaiani. Secundiani. Pitini. Primi. Cirilli. Martini. Pantaleonis. Eusebii episcopi.

¶ Herci episcopi.   Onme ⟨.i. simul⟩ ł Omne ⟨.i. Giallan.⟩[1] Odran Lettracha.[2]   Maelduib Bic[3] et Liadnain abbatum.

[1] *See Marginal Notes.*   [2] ' of Lettracha.'   [3] ' Máeldub the Little.'

[3]   .u. N*onas.*

Candidae. Teuthotae. Marcianillae. Felicis. Teodosti. Marciani. Amboni. Casti. Geni. Leodargi.   Urbani. Celsii. Spargi. Felicis. Marcelliani.   Natale Marci euangelistae.

¶ Colma*ni* Elo[1] nat*iuitas.* ⟨Mac Rethi.⟩[2] Nuadu anch*orita.* Secht n-eps*coip* Cl*úana* Caa.[3]

[1] ' of Elo,' *also under Sep.* 26.   [2] *interlined*, Ternoc *gl*. mac Raite *G*, Raithe *D*.   [3] ' Seven bishops of Clúain Caa.'

[4]   .iiii. N*onas.*

Marcelli episcopi. Marci. Marsini. Marciani. Dassi
Audacti. Baluinae. Iunillae. Leonillae. Heuualach ⟨b*is.*⟩
¶ Colmai*n* ep. Finani. Senai*n*. M*eic* Caille.¹ Modgrinn.
Mofinoc m*ac* Cuacha.

¹ Senán mac Caille *GD.*

[5]   .iii. N*onas.*

Placidi. [col. *e*] Euticii et aliorum .xxx. Baraci. Fi*r*mati.¹
Uictorini. Quintini Pelagii. Ualenaci. Apollinaris. Zefani.
¶ Aduentus reliquiarum Sanctorum Hibernensium quas
Mac ind éicis² congregauit. Colmani episcopi. Forirthich.³
Sinche uir*go* ingen Fergnai o Chruachan Maige Abna.⁴ Da
Lócha. Duib.⁵ Baethellaig.

¹ F *with supras cr.* i *MS.*   ² 'Son of the poet.'   ³ Fortech *G,*
Fortach *D.*   ⁴ ' d. of Fergna from Crúachu Maige Abna ; '
Alna *Facs.*   ⁵ *sic, read* Duib dá Locha.

[6]   .ii. N*onas.*

Casti. Emelii. Saturnini. Zefani. Marci. Rogati.
Ianuarii. Saturnini. Ammoni. Romani. Felicis. Fausti.
Marcialis. Baluinae. Teodorae. Mariae. Concordiae.
¶ Aedo. Baithine. Colmani. Diureni. Lugech sancti.
Fir da Chrich Dairi Eidnig.,¹

¹ ' of Daire Eidnech.'

[7]   N*onas.*

Mattei euangelistae. Marci episcopi. Marcelli. ⟨Carti⟩.
Marcellini. Figii. Baricii. Augusti. Dionisii. Ianuarii.
Zefani. Iohannis. Marcialis. Priuati. Tutillae. Mariae.
Pelagiae. Coronae. Iuliae. Rusticae. Eracli. Iuliani.
Martini. Laurentii ⟨b*is*⟩. Martini. Apulei. Iosippi
diaconi. Rustici. Celsii et aliorum .uiii. Muricii sancti.
¶ Colmani sancti. Cellaigi diaconi ⟨.i. saxonis⟩ i nGlind
da Locha.¹ Comgilli abbatis.

¹ ' in Glenn dá Locha.'

[8] .uiii. Idus.

Fausti. Eusebii Iuliani. Eracli. Diodari. Pilagiae.
[col. *f*] Chionae. Agapae. Herennae. Romae. Frigiae.
Attici. Luduli . Iulii. Septimi. Agripi. Dionisii. Eliut*eri*.
Rustici. Marcillieni. Genuini. Nubii. Probii. Iohannis.
Tracii. Eusebii. Martialis. Priuatis et aliorum martirum.

¶ Cellai*n* presbiteri. Mochritoc. Ciarain. Conamlo.¹

¹ *n. sg.* Conamail.

[9] .uiii. Idus.

Eusebii. Eraclii. Dionisii. Diodori. Attici. Secundae.
Frigiae. Mariae. Laudae. Lucidae. Eufemiae. Cirillae.
Petri. Buti. Duoli. Septimi. Iulii. Acripini et aliorum
.cccxuii. Eleutri. Parisii. Pauli. Parisaci. Quintini.
⟨Antonici.⟩ Iuliani. Antonii.

¶ Fintani abbatis. Aedani m.h. Chuind.¹ Dinertaig
Cl*úana* Mór.² Me*ic* Tail.³

¹ = moccu Cuind. ² *sic,* 'of Clúain Mór.' ³ 'Mac
Táil,' i.e. Fintan *GD*.

[10] .ui. Idus.

Eusebii. Eracli. Dionisii. Zefani. Fústi. Diodoris.
Secundae. Salsae. Marthae. Trifoniae. Perpetuae. Pauli.
Ianuarii et aliorum martirum .cccxxxiii.

¶ Fintani Dromma Iṅg.¹ Sillani abbatis. Sennan ep.

¹ 'of Druim Ing.'

[11] .u. Idus.

Taci martiris. Probi. Andrioni. Ampodi. Placidi.
Fausti. Iohannis. [col. *g*] Celsii. Ianuarii. Marcialis. Mar-
celli. Eracli. Andoci. Antoni. Uenusti. Petri. Faustini.
Uincentii. Danais et aliorum .iii. Uenantii. Quintini.
Quinti.

¶ Cru*m*thir .i. Fergnae. Lomman i nAth Truim¹
cum suis omnibus et Fortchern. ¶ Abel m*ac* Adae.
¶ Cainnig .m̄² Daland lxxx° iiii° anno etatis suae.

¹ 'in Áth Truim.' *Also Feb.* 17. ² *sic, supply* ua
(= moccu Dalann) *O*, mc.h. *Br*.

[12]   .iiii. Idus.

Hedisti monachi. Heustasii. Euasii. Zefani. Euagri.
Siriae.   Prosiriae.   Mariae.   Petronillae.   Fortunatae.
Eucharisti. Fortunati. Prisciani. Pauli. Celesti. Laurentii.
Mamedisti. Saturi. Bet*u*ricae. Pilionis. ⟨Donati.⟩ Burri.
Secundi.

¶ Mobí Clar*enech* mac Beoaid de Chorco Thrí de Lugnib
Connac*ht* Uan Find *ingen* Barrfind a mát*hai*r.[1]   Berchan
ab Glassi Noeden.[2]   Fiac et Fiachra eius filius cum eo i
Sleibti.[3]   Sillnatain. ⟨Bécc.⟩ Aedáin. Diarmait. Baitheni.
Failain. Breccain.

[1] ' Mobí Clarenech (table-faced) s. of Beóaid of Corco Trí of the
Lugni of Connacht. Uan Find d. of Barrfind was his mother.'
[2] ' Berchán, abbot of Glass Noíden;' this was Mobí's real
name, O(n)G.   [3] ' in Slébte.'

[13]   .iii. Idus.

Marcelli episcopi. Martialis.[1] Fausti. Andrae. Musae.
Proseriae. Perpetuae. Felicitatis. [col. *h*] Mariae. Marciae.
Munesanae. Marci episcopi. Agripiani. Ianuarii. Simplicii.
Probi.[2] Aciriani. Rústi. Andriani. Achanusti episcopi
et aliorum .u.

¶ Finnsige uir*ginis* .i. inna Hírnaide.[3] Comgani cele Dé.[4]

[1] *over* ti *an* n-*stroke MS.*   [2] P*r*obci *MS. with* c *expuncted.*
[3] ' i.e. of the Irnaide.'   [4] ' the culdee.'

[14]   .ii. Idus.

Calisti episcopi. Celesti episcopi. Calapotii. Saturi.
Lupili. Ampodi. Mogemoci*n*eicaill.[1] Luciani. Saturnini.
Prociui. Iusti. Paulini episcopi. Luppi.

[*in marg.*]   ¶ Colum sac. Insi Cáin.[2]

[1] *sic, Facs ; obscure, partly in ras. and retraced. Read* Mocholmóc
[i.e. Colum] Insi Caín.   [2] ' of Inis Caín.'

[15]   Idus.

Maurorum. Cecae cum aliis .x. Sussi et aliorum .lxx.
Lupi. Mirei. Aufichi. Saturnini. Nerei. Zefani. Agripini.
Patricii. Donaetae. Fortunatae. Mariae. Brigitoniae.
Saetaminae uirginis.

¶ Sancti Tommeni. Cuani. Maele Coisni. Coronae
uirginis. Fintianae ⟨sanctae⟩ uirginis. Natiuitas Colmain
meic Lenin. Bóithine. Cormani Galmae¹ et soror Ultain.

¹ ' of Galam,' *cp. Sep.* 4.

[16]   .xuiii. [*recte* .xuii.] kł. *Nouimbir*.

Caere in Africa et aliorum martirum .ccclxxx. Leudgari.
Martini et multorum militum in Roma. Siasii. Iohannis.
Zefani. Mariae. Heraclae. Meri. Transillae. Saturni.
[*in marg.*] ¶ In Ticina urbe honorati Michaelis archangeli.

¶ Lucinnani abbatis. Riaguil Muccinsi.¹ Colmain Cilli
Ruaid.² Coemgeni. Critani sancti. Ceire filiae Duib Reae.
Bricc.³ Taicthig. Cóimani sancti. Columbae sancti. Coib-
senaig ep. Eogan Lis Móir.⁴

¹ ' of Muccinis.'   ² ' of Cell Rúad.'   ³ ' the speckled,'
epithet of Cóemgen *GD.*   ⁴ ' of Less Mór.'

17   .xuii. [*recte* .xui.] kł.

[p. 10a ; *Facs.* p. 364]

Nicodimi martiris. Alexandrini. Nobilitani. Zefani.
Ueneriae. Agnae. Uictoriae. Mariae. Mammae. Donatae.
Marialitae. Defensoris. Lucitini. Rusticiani. Socrati.
Uenerei. Petrassii. Ianuarii. Laurentii. Quintasii. [*in
marg.*] Crescentii. Accintini. Rufiani.¹ *also in marg.* uel híc
honor Michaelis.

¶ Colmani abbatis. Con Britt² anchoritae. Nóinachi³
abbatis.

¹ *cp.* Oct. 16 *above, and Sept.* 29.   ² *gen. sg.* ; Cú Bretan *GD.*
³ Nomachi *Facs.*, *read* Móinachi ; Moenach *G* ; *om. Br.*

[18]   .xui. [*recte* .xu.] kł.

Lucae euangelistae translatio.   Pilippi martiris.   Luci.
Uictorini.   Hermetis.   Taxi.   Petri.   Ianuarii.   Bressei.
Uictricis.   Leucii.   Agnae.   Uictorici.   Teclae.   Mariae.
Fithioniae.   Uictoriae.   Ciciliae et aliorum martirum.
Eunuchei. Uictoris. Faustini. Martialis. Potioli. Ianuarii.
Euticis.   Pauli.   Simfroniani.   Beresepiae.   ✠ ¶ Trifoniae
uxoris Decii.

¶ Mothecca Rúscaigi.[1]   Moluanen Tamlac*hta*.[2]   Colmani
abbatis [*in marg.*] meic Coirtgid.

¹ ' of Rúscach.'   ² ' of Tamlachta.'

[19]   .xu. [*recte* .xiiii.] kł.

Austini. Susii. Festi. Ianuarii. Desiderii. Proculi.
Prosodociae.   Nicae.   Mariae.   Humilianae.   Do*m*nae.
Agathae.   Ozi.   Nectasiae.   Pelagii.   Pelagiae et aliorum
.xliiii. Beronici. Iohannis. Auste*r*i. Tomae. Euthicitis.
Celsii.   Neapuli.   Asperi.   Puteolis.   Eustasiae uirginis et
aliorum martirum .ui.

¶ Failani sancti.   Colmani Báin.[1]   Magniu ab. Cilli Mag-
nenn.[2] Cronan Tomma Gr*é*ni.[3] Crínan Cule Lagin.[4]

¹ Colman the White.   ² ' of Cell Maignenn.'   *Also Dec.* 18.
³ ' of Túaim Gréne.'   ⁴ ' of Cúil Lagin ; ' Chule Conlaing *GD*,
Cule Connlaigh *O(n)* ; Cule Lugdidh *Br.*

[20]   .xiiii. [*recte* .xiii.] kł.

Eutici martiris.   Promicei.   Dassi.   [col. *b*] Ianuarii.
Suscemi.   Suscimi.   Luci.   Sisinni.   Marcelli.   Be*r*miaci.
Ianuarii.   Iohannis.   Caprassii.   Muriae.   Zefani et aliorum
.ui. Dorothae. Iulianae. Muriae. Dariae. Marialitae.

¶ Colmani sancti.   Colman Tomma Gr*é*ni.[1]   ¶ Fintain
Maelduib.   Aidani sancti.   Ingell Maigi Eo.[2]

¹ ' of Túaim Gréne.'   ² ' of Mag Eó.'

[21]   .xiii. [*recte* .xii.] kł.

Dasciometis cum .xii *m*. Dasi. Euteci. Zomei. Gagi.
Modesti. Desei. Maceri. Macarii. Diciei. Iusti. Iohannis.
Beati. Zefani. Pueri. Geurgii.

¶ Mc. h. Gairb ab Maigi Bili.[1] Sillan magist*er*.

¶ Fintan ⟨.i. mac Tulchain⟩[2] cum suis mo*nachis* qui sub
iugo eius fuerunt .ccxxxiii. quos non uret ignis iudicii quorum
ista sunt nomina : Lasrani. Commani. Domdachain. Com-
gain. Adomnain. Discreti. Cilleni. Broceni. Critani.
Osseni ⟨*bis*⟩. Cairilli. Sarain. Dairchelli. Cronani. Suig-
nain. Critain. Deoni. Rioli. Brandubi. Uiblani. Ailteni.
Fingailli. Segini ⟨*bis*⟩. Conmaili. Cummini. Orcani.
Oengusa. Ultain. Anfudain. Cilchini. Locheni. Emini.
Zrafain ⟨*bis*⟩. Oebleain. Conchille. Cellaig. Ernini.
Sognathi. Mailani.[3] Maeli Cosni. Nemani. Corain. Lonain.
Lonain.[4]   Colmain. Uindici. Blaithm*eic*. [col. *c*] Maani.
Sarani. Beoni. Conani. Aedgni. Alteni. Cummini.
Daborchon. Cronani. Cummeni. Murbeu. Segini. Dirathi.
Cillini. Ociani. Mael Bresail. Furudrani. Iarnbuidi.
Colmain. Goreni. Cronani. Aedain. Commain. Uilnani.
Cronani. Ailitherii. Colmain ⟨*bis*⟩. Findbairr. Noeri.
Dermata. Lannani. Maili Gaimrid. Cobrain. Commain.
Cronain. Erconi. Critani. Liburti. Cobrani. Colmani.
Hilgeni. Findichii. Berchani. Airetain. Colmain. Bricceni.
Gormurni. Colmani. Marcani. Cronani. Laesirbi. Brocani.
Co*n*bráin. Lasrain. Findchain. Mochollae. Colmain ⟨*bis*⟩.
Ménni Maelduib. Co*n*briti. Co*n*besaig. Dicullo. Co*n*amlo.
Mael Corgis. Ninmon. Co*n*ocain. Cuoc. Failani. Cilleni.
Erneni. Librani. Gobbani. Scellain. [col. *d*] Conáni. Gur-
burti. Donnani. Co*n*bruit. Colmani. Breccani. Failani
⟨*bis*⟩. Anfudain. Locheni. Beca*n*i. Saeran. Finani.
M*ei*c Lasre. Ultani. Sarani. Gu*r*chon. Columbae. Ultain.
Colmani. Huilnani. Silain. Rioci. Locheni. Maelodrain.
Morani. Octani. Echtbrain. Notani. Blaitm*eic*. Diogeni.
Gurdoci. Cumma. Uuali. Anfudain. Dicollo. Uillani.
Fiachnae. Condorchon. Setani. Samueli. Eboci. Nemani.
Mael Dogair. Airgenain. Arconi. Nói. Trianani. Commae.
Caeteni. Iucarii. Gu*r*gaile. Fergil. Condoci. Cantani.

---

[1] = moccu Gairb, ' abbot of Mag Bile.'   [2] *See Marginal*
Notes.   [3] † f *add. over* M. (*i.e.* Failani).   [4] *bis.*

Ailbicti. Murdani. Rioci. Eloci. Budgoctheni. Gaim-
dogari. Bicduelo. Artgeni. Conalto. Coilmani. Liadnachi.
Dulmeni. Iunerti. Dicollo. Failchon. Mael Rubai. Fid-
bothaig. Conbesaig. Congnathi. Duathlo. Mancheni.
Eochthech. Miuchbriti. Eugeni ⟨bis⟩. Ferdomnaig.
Finnain. Bluttini. Beoain. Toichthech. Dicollo ⟨bis⟩.
Tulchani. Coemain. Uindini. [col. e] Dermaitai. Dimmai.
Cronain. Dotain. Haec est familia Mundu.

¶ Mochuoc húa Liathain.[5]   Mancheni lobor.[6]   Mael
Aithgeain.

[5] 'descendant of Líathán.'   [6] 'a leper.'

[22]   .xii. [*recte* .xi.] kł.

Mattei apostoli. Pilippi episcopi. Eusebii. Hermetis.
Seueri. Leugadi episcopi. Hermae. Bermae et aliorum .u.
Eugathi. Tomae.

¶ Cilleni sancti. Sarani.

[23]   .xi. [*recte* .x.] kł.

Passio Longini martiris qui Christum pupugit in latus
suum. qui etiam predicauit post precisam lingam suam.
Ciciliae uirginis. Seueri. Seusepi. Dorothei. Seuersi.

¶ Dalbach Cule Collainge.[1] Cilliani meic Doidnain Colmani
sancti. Mael Tuile mac Tiain. Laidcinn.

[1] ' of Cúil Collainge.'

[24]   .x. [*recte* .ix.] kł.

Seueri et aliorum .xii. Uitalis. Iohannis. Felicis. Rogati.
Paperi. Securi. Flauiani. Zefani. Uictoris. Securi. Kari.
Epolei. Flauianae. Iuliae. Mariae. Frigiae. Iulitae.
Ciciliae. Euagri. Herapoli. Iusti. Claudiani. Uictoris.

¶ Lonain Clúana Tibrinni.[1]   Colmani meic Fuidicain.
Coeti. Findgain meic Airchinnig o Damair.[2] Epscoip Eoain
o Chill Airthir.[3]

[1] ' of Clúain Tibrinne.'   [2] *sic.* ' from Diamair ; ' ó Diamair
O(n)D, ó Dhiammair G.   [3] ' from Cell Airthir.'

[25]   .ix. [*recte* .uiii.] kł.

Maximi et aliorum.   Saturnini   Claudiani.   Primi.
Flauani. Gauani. Sauini.   Saturi. Uitalis. Felicis. Paperi.
Rogati. [col. *f*] Claudiani.   Asteri.   Neonis.   Eucharisti.
Sapiri. Crispiani.   Quinti.   Bonifati.
¶ Lasriani filii Nasci. et Maeluidir.   Conac.   Beoc.
Lasriu mac Coluim.   Duthracht Lemchaille.[1]

1 ' of Lemchaill.'

[26]   .uiii. [*recte* .uii.] kł.

Luciani.   Marciani.   Cedi episcopi Romae et aliorum
.ui. Titi. Eraclidae. Martini. Zefani. Danielis cum suis
omnibus.

¶ Nasad   Beoain .   Mellain tres sancti de Britonia
et in una ecclesia sunt i n*Uib* Ech*ach* Ulad i Tamlachtain
U*m*ail ic Loch B[r]icrenn.[1]

Filiarum Me*i*c Ieir .i. .uii.[2] Darinill et Darbelli*n*n et
Comgell i Cill Maignend.[3]

1 ' in Uí Echach Ulad in Tamlachta Humail (?) at Loch
Bricrenn ; ' Bicrenn *MS.*, Bricrenn O(*n*)GD   2 *read* iiii OGD,
and supply Cóel, O(*n*)GD.   LL. 353 *b*.   3 ' in Cell Maignenn ; '
for Maignend OGD have na n-ingen, ' of the daughters.'

[27]   .uii. [*recte* .ui.] kł.

Tarsi.   Policarpi.   Gaii.   Eumini.   Noconi.   Leogi.
Met*r*obi. Diodori. Marciani. Lucii. Euminiae. Eulaliae.
Insolae. Anastasiae. Uicti. Proti. Gaii. Silini. Ianurii
Cerionis. Longi. Medroti. Petri. Tarrei. Comini. Florentii.
Celsii.

¶ Abbain m.h.[1] Chormaic. Augusti*n* Bennch*air*.[2] Colman
h*ua* Fiach*rach* i Senbotha Fola.[3] Uii. me*i*c Stiallain o Raith.,[4]

1 = moccu.   2 ' of Bennchor.'   3 ' Colmán descendant of
Fiachra in Senbotha Fola.'   4 ' Stíallán's seven sons, from Ráith.'

[col. *g*] ¶ Epsc*op* Erc Dom*naig* Móir Maigi Luadat.[5] Odrani presbiteri i lLetracha ⟨† o Hí.⟩[6] Rectini craibdech.[7] Colmain. Airennain o Thig Airennain i mMidi.[8]

[5] ' Bishop Erc of Domnach Mór Maige Lúadat.' *See Marginal Notes.* [6] ' in Letracha or from Í.' *See Marginal Notes.* [7] ' the devout.' [8] ' from Tech Airennáin in Mide.'

[28] .ui. [*recte* .u.] k̄l.

Simonis Cannanei et Tathei apostolorum. Samaridi. Sufroni. Cinti. Amantii. Suffroniani. Marandi. Archilai.[1] Infiani. Ammaranti. Cinti. Iohannis. Pauli. Zefani. Luci. Cirillae. Hirundinis. Marinae. Bonifatii. Cartatae et aliorum martirum.

¶ Mobeóc. Conan et Nath Í. Beoan 7 Mellan. Suibni. Dorbeni aƀ Iae.[2]

[1] Archillai F*acs*. [2] ' of Í.'

[29] .u. [*recte* .iiii.] k̄l.

Quinti martiris. Sacincti. Uictoris. Lucii. Uitalis. Feliciani et aliorum. Taimthinae uirginis. Luciani.

Cuani sancti. Findchain. Aed Glass.[1] Fonere Domnaig.[2] Luaran ó Daire Lurain.[3] Caelani o Thig na Manach.[4]

[1] ' Aed the grey.' *Also under Feb. 16.* [2] ' of Domnach.' [3] ' from Daire Lúráin.' [4] ' from Tech na Manach.'

[30] .iiii. [*recte* iii.] k̄l.

Ianuarii. [col. *h*] Calendionis. Marcialis. Germani. Marciali. Teophili. Eusebii et aliorum .ccxx. Felicis. Quinti. Luciani. Uitalis. Donati. Petri. Marii. Lucae. Ianuarii. Orbani. Atici. Lucae. Romulae. Mariae. Emilianae. Firmae. Feliciani cum suis. Ianuarii. Marci. Gerbassi. Protassi. Celsii. Pu*er*i. Marcelli. Eusebii. Mundani. Butini. Saturnini episcopi.

¶ Mocholmoc ⟨aƀ Camsa⟩ m.h. Gualae. † .h. Gáili di Gáilinni di Ultaib dó 7 i lLaind Mocholmóc ata.[1] Airnich[2] m*eic* Echin.

[1] ' Mocholmóc (abbot of Cammas) moccu Gúalae, or moccu Gaile; of the Gailinne of Ulaid, and in Lann Mocholmóc is he.' *Br. has* mc.h. Gaille. [2] Ernach *OGD.*

[31]   iii. [*recte* .ii.] kł.

Quintini. Rogati presbiteri. Uincentii diaconi. Dagoni.
Iuliani. Siluani ⟨*bis*⟩. Calendionis. Felicissimi. Donati.
Rusticiani. Fortunati. Mammi. Angelari. Nundini ⟨*bis*⟩.
Zefani. Felicis. Donati. Ualerii. Castae. Secundae.
Mariae. Gallae. Celsi. Agapi.

¶ Failani martiris fratris Fursu.

Uitalis. Petri. Crescentis. Saturnini. Uigilanti. Pilippi.
Germani. Teophili. Marci. Felicis. Cirilli. Quinti.

◄ Commiani abbatis et aliorum .lxuiii. Gallicae.¹

¹ *a leaf lost here.*

*   *   *   *   *   *

[Dec. 17]   [.xui. kł. Ianuarii.]

[p. 11*a* ; *Facs.* p. 365]

Uictoriae et aliorum .xxxiii. Uictoriani. Adiutoris.
Carti. Honorati. Simplicis. Amponii. Felicis. Uincentii.
Octori. Quinti. Donati. Diosocri.

¶ Toliaci sancti. Senchaid ó Dubad¹ idem et Cail⟩.
Moedoc m*ac* Mursin. Moliac.

¹ 'from Dubad.'

[18]   .xu. kł.

Basiliani. Tarsi. Teotecti. Saluatoris martiris. Iuliani.
Teodini. Cinti. Celsii. Simplicii. Pompini. Pauli. Cresti.
Dactili. Feliciani. Nicositis. Rogatiani. Martii. Euasi.
Priuati. Digni. Tinni. Sati. Teucri. Uictoris. Martini
et aliorum .xxxiii.

◄ Maigniu o Cill Mag*nenn*.¹ Modicu. Emeni. Mael-
duib Cl*úana* Conaire.² Colmain. Cummíni Cl*úana* Már.⟩³
Libani. Senain. Rignaige i*ngine* Feradaig.⁴

¶ Flannain m*eic* Tairdel*baig*. Muniss ep. i Fergnaidi.⁵
M*eic* Cathbath ó Míliuc.⁶ Aedgein Ardda Lonain.⁷ Coeman
Ruis Chruthnechain.⁸

◄ Salutatio Mariae ab Elizab*eth* matre Iohannis.

¹ 'from Cell Maignenn.'   ² 'of Clúain Conairi.'   ³ *sic*, 'of
Clúain Már.'   *Cp.* Dec. 24.   ⁴ 'daughter of Feradach.'
⁵ 'in Fergnaide.'   ⁶ 'Cathbad's sons from Míliuc ;' ó Im-
leach *GD* 'from Imblech.'   ⁷ 'of Ard Lonáin.'   ⁸ 'of
Ros Cruthnecháin.'

[19]   .xiiii. kł.

Secundini martiris. Zosimi. Ciriaci. Uictoriae ⟨bis⟩.
Iulianae. ⟨Mariae.⟩ Brigitoniae. Marialitae. Spinae.
Anathasii. Secundini. Grigorii episcopi. Crisanti. Zefani.
Celsii. Teotini. Cinti. Simplici. Pomponi. Pauli. Cresci.
Digni. Datuli. Feliciani. Rogatiani. Martirii. Honorati.
Priuati. Tintii. Petri. Siti. Uict*u*ri. Ciciliani. Pauli.
Saturnini. Famonis. Felicis. Uincentii. Aresci. Musci.
Saturi. Uictoris. Uictorini et aliorum .lxii. Basiliani.
Honorati et aliorum .xxx. martirum. ¶ Mariae Magdal*enae*
et Elizabeth.

¶ [1]Crumthir Fraech o *Clúain* Cullaig.[2] Samthand Cl*úana*
Bron*aig*.[3] Anfudain Ruis Chré[4] et Fuinechtae. [1]Fethlug.
[col. b] [1]Eoganan m*ac* Oengusa i nArd Leccaig i mMaig Ene.[5]
[1].Uii. me*ic* Aeda Echdromma.[6]

[1] *under Dec. 20 GD.*   [2] 'presbyter Fráech from Clúain
Cullaig.'   [3] 'of Clúain Brónaig.' *See Marginal Notes.*
[4] 'of Ros Cré.'   [5] 'in Ard Leccaig in Mag Ene.'   [6] 'Áed's
seven sons from Echdruim.'

[20]   .xiii. kł.

Ignatii martiris. Iulii episcopi Antiochiae. Teclae uirg*in*is.
Uictoriae. Agathae. Bithaniae. Ciciliae. Refrini episcopi.
Anastasiae. Anastasii episcopi. Liberi episcopi. Bontiani.
Basii. Innocentii. Zosimi. Pauli. Secundi. Beati. Grigorii.
¶ Cinti.⟩ Crisantii. Darii.

¶ Feidelmtho.[1] Dáire. Diarmato.[2]

[1] Feidlimid *n.sg.*   [2] Díarmait *n. sg.*

[21]   .xii. kł.

Tomae apostoli in India. Iohannis. Sereni episcopi.
Zefani. Celsi. Teclae. Focci. Flori. Honorati. Dimetri
⟨bis⟩. Iononati. Iohannis. Mathei et aliorum .xxx.

¶ Silani episcopi Lis M*óir*.[1] Fulartaich me*ic* Bri*cc* me*ic*
Scandail.[7] ¶ Flaind me*ic* Fairchell*aig*. Molua ó Mungarit.[2]
[3]Berr 7 Churennan i rRos.[4] [3].Uii. me*ic* Dretill Insi Uachtair.[5]
[3]Mochua o Chaill Inse Ailche.[6]

[1] 'of Less Mór.'   [2] 'from Mungarit.'   [3] *under Dec. 22*
GD.   [4] 'in Ros ;' o Ros Aiss i nInis *GD* ' from Ros Aiss in
Inis.'   [5] 'The seven sons of Dretell of Inis Úachtar.'   [6] 'from
Caill Insi Ailche.'   [7] *Also Mar. 29.*

[22]   .xi. kł.

Felicis episcopi.   Fistis.   Apolloni.   Eugeni.   Flori.
Arizo et aliorum .xxxu.   Teodosiae.   Eugeniae.   Eulaliae.
Decimi.   Honori.   Dimetri.

¶ Emini Rois Glasi.[1]   Itharnaisc Cloen*ad*.[2]   Tua m.h.[3]
Roida idem et Ultan Tigi Tua.[1]   Id*eo* Tua dicitur quia lapis
in labiis eius per omne tempus *quadragesi*mae habebat ut
non posset loqui et inde Tua[5] dictus est.   Forunnan Cilli
Eae.[6]

[1] 'of Ros Glass.'   *See Marginal Notes.*   [2] 'of Clóenad.'
[3] = moccu.   [4] 'of Tech Túa.'   [5] 'the Silent.'   [6] 'of Cell Eae.'

[23]   .x. kł.

Felicis Rom*ae* episcopi.   Eurasti et aliorum .xxxu.   Uic-
torini.   Pass*io* Celsi.   Uictoris ⟨b*is*⟩ et aliorum dccxxxu.
Dimetri.   Honori.   Iohannis.   Florii.   Arizoni.   Felicis.
Zefani.   Eleutherii.   Urbani.   Cornelii.   Euaristi.   Colnilii.
Triani.   Siriani.   Flauiani.   Felicis.   Paulini.   Saturnini.
Transillae. [col. *c*] Cartulae.   Musae.   Romulae.   Mariae.
Abrahae.   Celesti.   Euticiani.   Petri.   Loni.   Teli.   Sicti.
Solani.   Zefe*r*ini.   Gallini.   Pauii.   Abilionis et aliorum
martirum.   Et magna sollemnitas omnium sanctorum totius
Africae.

¶ Mochua m*ac* Oengusa.   Mothemnioc coic Cl*úana* Ferta
Molua.[1]   Colman Cl*úana* da Fiach.[2]   Lugnath ⟨presbiter.⟩
Mernóc.   Mochellóc.   Herneni o Ros Ingite[3] 7 Anfudan.
Corconutan eliuatio eius ad coelos.   ¶ Mogoroc De*r*gne.[4]
Mosenoc.   Luchair Cilli Delg*r*aigi.[5]   Da ailithir [déc] Insi
Uachtair.[6]   Feidlimid Achaid Lurchair.[7]   Ronain Find m*eic*
Aeda.

[1] 'cook of Clúain Ferta Molúa ; ' *under Dec.* 24 G.   [2] 'of
Clúain dá Fhíach.'   [3] 'from Ros Ingite.'   [4] 'of Dergne.'
[5] 'of Cell Delgraigi ; ' Chille Elgraighe *GD.*   [6] *supply* déc O(*n*)GD
and Br., 'twelve pilgrims of Inis Úachtair.'   [7] 'of Achad
Lurchair.'

[24]   .ix. kł.

Luciani martiris. Zefani. Geurgii. Metrobii. Pauli.
Petri. Laurentii. Genoti. Ciricii. Celsii. Teothini. Timisti.
et aliorum .xliiii. et sanctarum uirginum simul numero .xlii.
et aliorum multorum martirum Christi.

¶ Mochua ‹.i. Cronan› m*a*c Lonain. ‹Fiadaili ab Cilli
Achid.›[1]   uel hic Mothemnioc.[2]   ‹Senan epi*scopus*.›

¶ Cumméni sancti ‹Cl*úana* Mair›[3] et sanctorum ceterorum
quorum Deus nomina nominauit et quos p*r*esciuit et p*r*e-
distinauit conformes fieri imaginis Filii sui in uitam eternam
in Christo Iesu. Amen.

  [1] 'of Cell Achid.'   [2] *Also under Dec.* 23.   [3] 'of
Clúain Már.'   *cp. Dec.* 18.

MARTYROLOGY OF TALLAGHT

MARGINAL NOTES AND POEMS

p. 1 ; Facs. p. 355, *marg. sup.*[1]

  l. 3 .   Be*r*tatar di*d*u amais i*n*d rig . . . .

  l. 5   Lochan m. Lugair .   .

[1] Along the upper margin are five lines so illegible that only odd words can with any certainty be deciphered. It has been possible to add here and there isolated letters and syllables to the readings of the Facsimilist, but they are quite insufficient to give a notion of the contents. It has seemed preferable therefore to refer to the Facsimile, rather than attempt a reproduction, which would serve no purpose. The few connected words given above may help towards identification, if another copy exists.

ibid. marg. inf.

        I[1] Re Chesair Aug*u*ist (   )[2]

        ( )erair[3] ce( ) tar[4] trian domain

        ocus Conchobo*r* cen fell

        i commus coicid Here*nn*

        I sechtmad[5] bli*a*dain dec

        flatha Conch*obuir* na cét[6]

        ac*h*os( )et be (   )[7]

        [   ][8]

        Da bl*iadain* dec isi*n*d (   )[9]

        do Chesair is do*n*[10] Co*m*did[11]

        (   )ré[12] fo*r* in bith buan

        do reir eolais ra imluad

        Tibir Cesair cruaid a gal

        ro gab dar es(i) (   )[13]

        ( )ob (do)[14] is Crist cen cess

        comre ropo cho( )es[15]

[1] *For* I *the Facs. has the paragraph symbol* ¶.

[2] grig *Facs.*   [3] *obscure,* [ ]er[ ] *Facs.*   [4] cintar *Facs.*

[5] *asp. mark added over* d *by retracer.*   [6] ced *Facs.*

[7] *reading doubtful ; the second letter resembles* d, *but* ch *seems more likely ; Facs. has a* doxt [ ].

[8] *verse omitted.*   [9] *illeg.*

[10] dan *MS. and Facs.* o *converted into a by retracer.*

[11] cid *Facs.*   [12] *read perhaps* i comré.

[13] *om. Facs., illeg., read doubtless* a athar, *which is translated.*

[14] *read perhaps* curob, do *following is faintly traceable.*

[15] chomæs *Facs.*

In the time[1] of Caesar Augustus .
. . .[2] over a third of the world,
and Conchobor, without treachery,
ruling over a province of Ireland.

In the seventeenth year
of the reign of Conchobor of the blows

.   .   .   .   .   .[3]
[   ]

Twelve years in (sovranty ?)[4]
were Caesar and the Lord,
(at the same time) over the lasting world,
according to knowledge, to be told.

Tiberius Caesar, hard his valour,
reigned after his father,[5]
(so that) to him and Christ, without sorrow,
          contemporary, it was

---

[1] One would expect *I rré* or *fri ré*.   [2] The reading here is very doubtful.
The idea is apparently that the Roman rule extended over a third part of
the world.   [3] As Conchobor began to reign in 30 B.C., the allusion is
presumably to the birth of the Virgin Mary.   [4] Caesar Augustus died
A.D. 14.   [5] *i.e.*, his stepfather.

p. 1 ; Facs. p. 355, *marg. inf.*—cont.

Da bliadain Tibir na tor
i comḟlaith fri Conchobor
dar esi Crist narbo holc[1]
i n-oen feil (   )[2]

[1] narbinbalc *Facs.*
[2] *In marg.* and at the commencement of the following line are several
words now undecipherable. *Facs.* has c̄c̄, but (?) com (   )ser (   )e(   ).

p. 2 ; Facs. p. 356, *marg. sup.*

E(nlaith[1]) betha[2] brig cen tair
is ar fálti[3] frisin gréin.[4]
Hi noin[5] enair cipsi uair.[6]
congair a sluaig[7] din chaill chéir.

I n-*ocht calaind* apreil áin
tecait fainnli fria nglan dail[8]
traig ardd (i   ) (c)id (n)osceil[9]
i n-*ocht*[10] *calaind* octimbir.

I feil Ruadain rád cen dis[11]
[is][12] and oslaicther[13] a nglais
hi *sechtmad déc*[14] *calaind* mái
dogair[15] in chúi din chaill chaiss.

Hi[16] noin iúil anait eoin
(do chantain) ch(iui)l lith lathi[17]
conait chet bí[18]
do[19] Mail Ruain o Thamlacti.

[1] E[   ] *Facs.*, *illeg.*, Enlaith *B.*   [2] *very faint.*   [3] fáilti *B.*
[4] ngrein *B.*   [5] *in* noin *B.*   [6] gersa fuar *B.*   [7] an sluag *B.*·
[8] na firdail *B.*   [9] *partly illeg.* ; sluag aird ibig cid nosceil *B.*, *resembles*
(d)osceil *MS.*   [10] o ocht *B.*   [11] *gan* geis *B.*   [12] is *add. B.*
[13] oslaicthir *B.*   [14] Septimb *B.*   [15] congair *B.*   [16] IN *B.*
[17] *partly illeg.* ; da chantain ciuil lith laithi *B.*   [18] *sic* ; nar rug bad bi *B.*
[19] o *B.*

Two years was Tiberius of the princes
in co-sovranty with Conchobor.
after Christ, 'twas no ill,
in one festival .

¹The birds² of the world, power without ill,
'tis to welcome the sun.
On January's nones, whatever hour it be,
the cry of the host from the dark wood.

On the eighth of the calends of noble April
the swallows come on their pure tryst
. . . . . , what hides them?³
on the eighth of the calends of October.

On the festival of Rúadán, no petty saying,
their fetters are then unloosed.
On the seventeenth of the calends of May
the cuckoo calls from the pleasant wood.

On the nones of July the birds cease
to sing the music of holydays
.   .   .   .   .   .   .ᐟ
for Máel Rúain from Tamlachta.

---

¹ Another copy in Brussels 5057–59, p. 49 (*B*).   ² *Enlaith betha* =
W. *adar byd*, Meyer, Contribb. 220.   ³ Meaning doubtless that the
swallows depart; but the passage is obscure in both MSS.; for *airdibig* cp.
adér-sa tria airdebech, H.3.18, 40b = *bid úasal, gid airdeibech*, Hib. Min. 83,
8, Meyer, Contribb.   ⁴ Verse defective, and meaning obscure.

p. 2 ; Facs. p. 356, *marg. sup.*—cont.

Hi[1] feil Ciarain mei̇c in tṡaer
    tecait giugraind dar fairge uair[2]
I feil Ciprian condelgg[3] n-oll
    (geis)id da(m) (do)nd din rái réid.[4]

Tri fichit cet mbl*iadna* ṁbán[5]
    amser[6] in domuin cen len.
memais[7] trethan dar ca*ch* n-airm[8]
    i ndeud aidchi im[9] gairm na n-én.   E.

(At)nagat[10] coṁbin̄ni cheóil
    ind eoin fri rig[11] nime nél
ic admolad ind rig reil
    coistid cleir na n-én do chéin.[12]   E.

---

¹ A *B*.   ² tic gigrainn don fairgi fuair *B*.   ³ latar *B*.   ⁴ *partly illeg.*; geisid dam don*n* do rae ruaid *B*.   ⁵ bliad*na* buan *B*.   ⁶ saegu*l̄ B*.   ⁷ muidfid *B*.   ⁸ da cech airm *B*.   ⁹ ic *B*.   ¹⁰ *partly illeg.*; At nagar *B*.   ¹¹ nem *B*.   ¹² caistid cein re cleir na n-en *B*. *The last two stanzas are reversed in B.*

ibid., marg. sin.

A(gna u)irgo (in Roma, et adoptiua filia Iesu fuit, et .xiii. annorum erat quando pasa fuit) sub (Simpronio prefec)to ur(bis Romae et ui)cario eius As(pasiaro n)om*ine* . et post[2] (mult)a tormenta[3] igne(is) arden(*tibus*)[3] missa est et de his uiua et sana rediuit, et postea commixtus[4] (gladi)us nudus in (ore eius) et usque (ad inter)io(ra eius per)uenit, (et sic) uitam suam corona (   ) (fi)niuit.[5]

---

¹ The portions within brackets are illegible, and are here supplied from the corresponding note in Fél. Óengusso (*R*) ed. Stokes, p. 50 ; *cp. ed.*¹ p. xxxix, which, however, differs slightly.
    ² per *O*.   ³⁻³ *om. O*.   ⁴ conflixus *O*(*F*), conflictus *O*(*L*).
    ⁵ *obscure* ; uitam suam finiuit *O*(*R*) ; *there is space for* sempiterna *in our MS*.

On the festival of Cíarán, son of the wright,
wild geese come over the cold sea.
On the festival of Cyprian, a great counsel,[1]
the brown stag bells from the ruddy[2] field.

.

Three score hundred fair years,
the world's age, without sorrow,
the ocean will burst over every place
at the end of the night, at the call of the birds.

Melodious music the birds perform
to the king of the heaven of clouds,
praising the radiant king.
Hark from afar to the choir of the birds.

---

[1] Strength *B.*   [2] so *B, rúaid* being required by the rhyme, and is also more appropriate here than ' level, smooth ' (*réid*).

[JAN. 21]

Agna uirgo in Roma, etc.

TALLAGHT   H

p. 2 ; Facs. p. 356, *marg. inf.*

> (Cethri) com(anm)and ro scribad.[1]
> Baithini balc buadach
> mac Finnach mac Brenaind [brígach][2]
> mac Alla mac Cuanach.

> [3]B(aethin) mac Brenaind dis*cipulus*[4] et *frater* Columbae.[5]
> Baethin mac Finnach i nInis Baithin. Baethin mac Alla i Cl*úain*
> da An(dobair). B(aethin mac) Cuanach i Tig Baithin i n-iarthur
> Mide.,

---

[1] ro rimed *LB. F.*   [2] mac Finnaig, mac Brenainn brigach *F* ; mac
Brenaind, mac Findaig *LB.*   [3] *Cp. the note in Fél. Oeng.[2] (R[2]). The
letters within brackets are illegible.*   [4] ɔis *Facs.*   [5] Colambae *Facs.*

---

ibid.

> Athair Póil dithrebaig déin.
> Iocaz cosin cheill chain
> Tabida a siur flatha fail.
> Mathatha a m*áthair* main.
> Euzar a chliamain cruaid
> dochuaid *for* seilb diabuil daeir.

---

p. 3 ; Facs. p. 357, *marg. sin.*

> Sáegul Mochaemoc Leith
> ni[1] chelat tuir na tréith
> da secht mbliadan cethri cét[2]
> ní baegul[3] ní himmarbréc.

---

[1] nocha *D.*   [2] *sic LL.* .xiiii. cccc. *MS.* ; tri bliadna decc ar ceithre
céd *D.*   [3] iarmar *LL*[1].

---

ibid. marg. inf.

> Commodus ainm ind ríg thall
> ro fáid Pilip i ferand.
> is n-airm ro lessaig Dia
> dianid ainm Mesopotamia.

[FEBRUARY 19]

> [1]Four namesakes that have been written,[2]
> Baéthíne, strong, victorious :
> the son of Finnach ; the [vigorous] son of Brénaind ;
> the son of Alla ; the son of Cúana.

(Báethín son of) Brénaind, discipulus et frater Columbae. Báethín son of Finnach in Inis Báethín. Báethín son of Alla in Clúain dá Andobair. Báethin son of Cúanu in Tech Báethín in the west of Meath.

[1] This quatrain, which is partly illegible, also occurs in the notes to Fél. Óengusso (*LB, F*) under Feb. 19.
[2] ' counted,' *LB, F.*

> The father of Paul, the austere hermit,
> Iocaz with the clear intellect.
> Tabida his sister, of the .   . kingdom.
> Mathatha his . . . mother.
> Euzar his hard relation
> went over to the ignoble Devil.

[MARCH 13]

> [1]The life-time of Mochóemóc of Líath,
> nor lords nor princes hide it :
> four hundred and fourteen years,
> 'tis no mistake, 'tis no lie.

[1] Another version, Book of Leinster *Facs.*, p. 353, *marg. inf.* (*LL*[1]), also in Mart. of Donegal (*D*), p. 74.

[MARCH 16]

> [1]Commodus the name of the king of yore,
> who sent Philip into the land,
> into the place God appointed,
> whose name is Mesopotamia.

[1] *See* the prose narrative in notes to Fél. Óengusso, under Mar. 16.

p. 3 ; Facs. p. 357, *marg. inf.*—cont.

Eugenia ingen glicc
do Chludia is do Philipp.
Prothius Iacinthus 'moalle
a da dalta derbdilse.

Seuerus Habitus cen raind
a da brathair iar colaind.
Elenus coa ro lég lind.
abb Elopol*is* primgrind.

Eugenia ba gein co ṅglóir
ro chés ar cretim ṅdermóir
fuair a garbad[1] assa lus
ros mar*bad* la Commodus.   C.

ibid. marg. sup.
Xiiii. Kł. ap*rilis.*   Auxili*n*us episcopus et coepiscopus et frater
Sancti Patricii episcopi. uel Auxili*n*us nomen eius.   Patricius
dixit.

Auxilinus t'ainm ifus
rotrigus im chomarbus ⸴̇
at m*a*c sethar a chara
at eps*cop* at anchara

Uii. filii Restiti[2] de Longbardis[3] .i. Sechnall   Nec[h]tain
Dabonna   Mogornan   Daríoc   Auxilinus . Lugnath.,

Fiacail Mochta ní blad fas[4]
trí chét bl*iadna* buan a chis
cen guth n-imruill taris súas
cen cu(it[5]) n-inmair[6] taris sis.

---

[1] ṅgarbad *MS.*, n *expuncted.*   [2] *sic, read* Restituti.
[3] *sic, read* Longobardis.   [4] *s* legible, *om.Facs.*
[5] *faintly traceable, om.* Facs.; mir *O(n)FM, supplied by Stokes.*
[6] nmmair *Facs.*

Eugenia, the discreet daughter
to Claudia and to Philip.
Protus, Hyacinthus, together,
her two rightful fosterlings.[1]

Seuerus, Auitus, inseparable,
her two brothers after the flesh.
Helenus, with whom she studied,
the abbot of Heliopolis, most fair.

Eugenia, 'twas a glorious birth,
suffered for the mighty faith,
she endured hardship on account of it,
she was put to death by Commodus.

[MARCH 19]

Xiiii. Kt. aprilis. Auxilius episcopus, etc.

Auxilius thy name here below,
I have ordained thee my successor.
Thou art a sister's son,[2] O friend,
thou art a bishop, thou art an anchorite.

[MARCH 24]

Uii. filii Restituti, etc.

Mochta's tooth, 'tis no empty fame,
three hundred years, lasting its tribute,
without a word of error over it upwards,
without a morsel of relish over it downwards.[3]

---

[1] a d[i] iunaich, ' her two eunuchs' Fél.O. (R²), p. 98.   [2] He was said
to be the son of Patrick's sister. Cp. the note on Sechnall in Fél. Óeng.,
Nov. 27.   [3] Ed. and transl. O'Donovan, FM. 534, vol. I. p. 176, also by
Stokes, Fél. Óengusso,² p. 188-9.

p. 3 ; Facs. p. 357, *marg. dex.*

Fir nimi fir thal*man*   sl*u*ag timchill
dar leo ba lá brátha   bás Sinchill.

Ni thanic ni thicfa   o Adam
bad duriu bad gúriu   i crabud.

Ni t[h]anic ni thicfa   rád n-ile[1]
sanct aile rismad failti   fir nime.,

[1] nisle *MS.* s *expuncted* ; rádh nile *D.*

p. 4 ; Facs. p. 358, *marg. dex.*

Tigernach Cl*u*ana Eouis. † Oois .i. o Oois ainm muccida ríg
Airgiall bae sin baile ria Tigernach. iss *ed* ro chunnig ar in cler*ech*
la toaeb Foch*ar*ta a ainm do bith ar in baile. † crand mor ro bói
and prius .i. Eo aisse .i. ibar. ut dicitur Eo Ross .i. eo roása. †
eó aisse .i. crand messa .i. dair. ut dicitur aiss mes forsmbít mucca
amne.,

ibid. marg. sup.

Fecht doringni Bresal m*ac* Diarm*a*ta m*ei*c Cerb*aill* fleid móir
dia athair 7 ní thestá ní aire acht bó co n-oeib ítha.   Co cuala
Bresal a bith a[c] callich Cilli Elgr*a*ig*e* i Termo*n* Cena*n*sa.   Luchair
a ainm *side*.   Co ndechaid Bresal dia cennach 7 tarcid *sec*h*t* mbú
7 tarb din chall*ich* dia cind 7 nis tarat dó.   Co tuc Bresal ar écin
in mboin.   Co tard Bresal in mboin la fleid da athair i Cenannas
ar ba rigdún tunc.   Doriacht in chaill*ech* i ndiaid a saraigthi co
Diarmait. 7 iachtais co ach*er* ara sargud do Bresal.   Unde poeta
cecinit.

Tan bo[1] áne doib 'con chomool
co cuala in nguth immuig.
doroich cuccu in chaill*ech* [cnesgel][2]
ro saraig Bresal 'moa boin.

[1] ba *Facs.*   [2] cnesgel *add B.*

[MARCH 26]

The men of Heaven, the men of earth, a surrounding host,
it seemed to them, 'twas the day of doom, the death of Sinchell.

There has not come, there will not come, from Adam,
one more austere, more strict, in piety.

There has not come, there will not come, a saying of many,
another saint more welcome to the men of Heaven.[1]

[1] Cp. the similar lines on Molúa,' Aug. 4, infra p. 113. The above have
been ed. and transl. in Mart. of Donegal, pp. 86-7.

[APRIL 4]

Tigernach of Clúain Eóis, or Oois, i.e. from Oois, the name of
the king of Oriel's swineherd, who was in that place before Tiger-
nach. What he asked of the cleric alongside Fochart was that
his name should be given to the place. Or, it was a great tree that
was there formerly, i.e. *eó aisse*, i.e. a yew, *ut dicitur* Eó Rosa,
i.e. *eo rodsa*. Or eó aisse, i.e. tree of acorns, i.e. oak, *ut dicitur*
thus, *aiss* mast on which swine are fed.

[APRIL 5]

[1]Bresal son of Díarmait son of Cerball once made a great feast
for his father, and there was naught lacking to it save a cow with
livers of tallow.[2] Bresal heard of such being with the nun of Cell
Elgraige in the sanctuary of Cenannus, Lúachair her name. So
Bresal went to buy it, and he offered seven cows and a bull to the
nun for it, and she did not give it to him. And Bresal took the
cow by force, and gave the cow with the feast to his father in
Cenannus, for it was then a royal fortress. The nun after being
outraged came to Díarmait and complained bitterly of the outrage
done to her by Bresal. *Unde poeta cecinit :*

> When they were most merry at the carousal
> he heard a voice without,
> the [white-skinned] nun comes to them
> whom Bresal had outraged over her cow.

[1] Another version in *B*. IV. 2 (R.I.A.) fol. 144a (*B*), ed. K. Meyer., ZCP.
VII 305 ff. A shorter version, omitting the verse, in Book of Lismore, fol.
94b (ed. and transl. W. Stokes, "Lives of the Saints from the Book of
Lismore," p. xxvii f.), Liber Flavus Fergussiorum (R.I.A.), fol. 20 [72] *v*, and
23P3 (R.I.A.), 11b. The story is re-told by Keating, Hist., I.T.S., vol.
iii. 67 ff., and in Mart. of Donegal (*D*), p. 94 ff.

[2] For the meaning, see Stokes, ZCP. III, 572-3.

p. 4 ; Facs. p. 358, *marg. sup.*—cont.

Ecóir 'na ndernais ar Diarmait
   a Bresail na mbriathar mbind.
tarrastar in[1] dochond detla[2]
   racha dochom éca[3] ind.

Indeo a Becain cosna buadaib
   ar *Colum Cille* cen choll.
is meisi in chommairge chenand :'
   tuc leis ar th' ferand ar th' fond.[4]

[1] ind *B*.   [2] ceilli *B*.   [3] n-écca *B*.   [4] fand *Facs.*

7 atbert Diarmait fodema do bás ara ndernais .i. sárgud na
call*ige*. Berair iar tain Bresal la Diarmait co Linn mBr*esail* for
Abaind Lorgaid coro báded and.

Ba aithrech po*st* la Diarmait bádud a m*ei*c conid and sin atbert
fri Colum Cille ac cur a chomairle chuce. In fil mo chobairse et*ir*
ar se don gním doringnius. Atá ar Colum Cille .i. eirg cossin
n-athlaech fil issind insi .i. Becan. Ni lamaim ar se techta chuce.
Ragatsa lat ar Colum Cille. O ráncatar a ndis is amne fuaratar
Becan ic figi[1] chasil 7 cuilchi fliuch imbe 7 ic irnaigthi simul. Ut
dicitur.

Sním[2] casil[3] crossigell
   slechtain irnaigthi idan.
a dera úad cen édáil
   buaid Becgain cen (cu)it (c)inad.[4]

Lám i cloich lam i n-airdde.
glún filti fri[5] cair(r)gge.
súil ic siliud[6] dér chaid(ch)e[7]
*oc*us bel ic aurnaigthe

[1] denum *B*, tógbháil *D*.   [9] Gnim *BD*.   [3] *supply* is *metr. gr.*
[4] criad *B*.   [5] coir *add D*.   [6] silled *Facs.*   [7] dér chaid de *Facs.*,
der caid ale *BD* ; *read* chaidche (*Bergin*).

'Unjust is what thou hast done,' said Díarmait,
'O Bresal of the smooth words.
There has been wanton folly,
thou shalt go to death for it.'

¹' Well, O Bécán of the virtues,'
said Colum Cille without hurt.
'I am the . . .² safeguard
that he has brought on to thy land, on to thy foundation.'

¹ This stanza out of place here ; it occurs further on in *B*, at the place where it is cited below.
² Meaning of *cenand* obscure ; ' white-faced,' in other contexts, Meyer, Contribb.

And Díarmait said, ' Thou shalt suffer death for what thou hast done, that is, for outraging the nun.' Thereupon Bresal is taken by Díarmait to Linn Bresail (Bresal's Pool) on Abaind Lorgaid, and there drowned.

Díarmait afterwards repented of the drowning of his son, and 'tis then he said to Colum Cille, taking counsel of him, ' Is there any help for me at all for the deed that I have done ? ' quoth he. ' There is,' said Colum Cille, ' that is, go to the ex-layman who is in the island, namely Bécán.' ' I dare not go to him,' said he. ' I will go with thee,' said Colum Cille.

When the two arrived they found Bécán building¹ a wall, with a wet quilt about him, and praying at the same time, *ut dicitur :*

Building² a wall, [and] cross-vigil,
prostration, pure prayer,
tears from him without avail,
the virtue of Bécán, without aught of sin.

Hand on a stone, hand upraised,
knee bent against a rock,
eye ever shedding tears,
and lips praying.

¹ Literally ' weaving.'   ² Literally ' spinning.'

p. 4 ; Facs. p. 358, *marg. sup.*—cont.

Unde dicitur Becan cosna[1] buad*aib*.

O ro dercaid Becan for Diarmait iss *ed* atbert   fon[2] tal*main*
a fingal*aig* ar se.   Dothaet Diarmait coa glune 'sin tal*main* lasin
ṁbrethir sin.   Fil Diarmait for mo faesamsa a Becain ar Colum
Cille.   Unde Colum Cille Indeo a Becain ut diximus.   Et atbert
Becan fri Colum Cille is cenand in cho*mm*airge.   Mathim n-anacuil
do Diarmait ar Colum Cille do chind mo imdergthasa.   Regaid
cid lesc ar Becan.   Tanic Diarmait chucutsu dia chomdidnad[3] .i.
do thodiuscud a me*i*c.   Tocbaid Becan a oenlaim suas 7 dogní
ern*aigthi* fo th*rí* 7 dob*er*t[4] .l.[5] Bresal a iffurn la ca*ch* n-irnaigthi
Becain.   7 aiscis a m*a*c do Diarmait.

---

¹ casna *Facs.*   ' fan *Facs.*   ³ chomditnad *Facs.*   ⁴ *sic for*
dobreth.   ⁵ .i. *Facs.*

---

p. 5 ; Facs. p. 359, *marg. sin.*

Zephán 7 Lurint 7 Geurgii 7 na naidi*n*[1] i mBethil 7 Petar decoin
7 Donnan Ego co n-ulib martirib in domuin hoc die commemorantur.,

ibid. marg. sup.

Hermogi*nis*[1] magus prius et per Iacobum Ze(b)edi filium Deo
credidit.   Et iste Fletum suum discipulum misit ad Iacobum. et
ipse credidit Deo.   Et Hermog(ines misit)[2] demones ad Iacobum
ut alligarent eum.   Sed angelus alligauit eos ignitis funibus.   Et
Iacobus misit demones ad Hermogi*n*(em) (.   g . .)[3] manibus
post tergum emexis,[4] et sic post multa tormenta *credidit* Deo[5]
et Iacob.,[6]

ibid. marg. sin.

.i.   Crand mór ro bái issin Róim 7 no adraitis in gentlidi é
coro throscsetar Cristaide na Róma fri ulib naemaib Eurpae immó
trascrad 7 fri Martan co senrudach[7]   et statim cecidit.,

---

¹ n-*stroke om. Facs.*   ² *illeg.*   ³ *end of line, partly illeg. and partly*
broken off.   ³ *illeg.*   ' connexis *Stokes.*   ⁵ do *Facs., abbrev.*
stroke faint in MS.   ⁶ *sic.*   ⁷ semnidach *Facs.*

Unde dicitur Bécán of the virtues.

When Bécán looked on Díarmait, this is what he said, ' Under the earth, thou parricide ! ' At the word Díarmait sinks to his knees in the earth. ' Díarmait is under my protection, O Bécán,' said Colum Cille. *Unde Colum Cille:* ' Indeo a Bécáin,' *ut diximus.*

And Bécán said to Colum Cille, '. is the protection.' ' Quarter to Díarmait,' said Colum Cille, ' because of my humiliation.' ' It shall be given[1] though reluctantly,' said Bécán. ' Díarmait has come to thee for solace, that is, for the raising of his son.' Bécán lifts his free hand up, and prays thrice, and fifty Bresals were brought out of Hell at every prayer of Bécán's, and he restored his son to Díarmait.

[1] Literally ' shall go.'

[APRIL 17]

Stephen and Laurence and George, and the babes in Bethlehem, and Peter the deacon, and Donnán of Eig, with all the martyrs of the world, *hoc die commemorantur.*[1]

[APRIL 19]

Hermogenes, etc.[2]

[APRIL 20]

i.e., a huge tree that was in Rome, and the heathen used to worship it. And the Christians in Rome fasted on all the saints of Europe, and on Martin in particular, for it to fall, *et statim cecidit.*[3]

[1] Ed. and transl. Stokes, Fél. Óeng.[2] pp. 114–15.
[2] Printed by Stokes, *ibid.*, p. 117 note.
[3] Printed by Stokes, *ibid*, p. 119 note. Cp. Fél. Öeng.[1] p. lxxv.

p. 5 ; Facs. p. 359, *marg. inf.*

Cia beit[1] na n-a*n*fis[2]
na nIacob n-amra n-án
nos relub dúib cen nach ńdúthi
ro legus la súdi[3] slán

Iacob m*a*c Cleopais is Maire.
cend na n-apstal n-uasal n-ard.
luid martra i n-*òcht calaind* Ap*r*eil
sech ba hacbeil ba gním garg.

Dech *calaind* Iuil la m*a*c Alphei
la Iacob caem cosin rath
iar p*r*ecept dó acon tŚiria
tuaid in Parsidia atbath.

Iacob aurdairc m*a*c Zebedei
ardaps*t*al de munt*ir* Dé.
luid martra i n-*ocht calaind* Aug*u*ist
ba cend n-áruisc for bith ché.　　C.

---

[1] *sic, for* beithe ; *verse defective*　　[2] *n*-stroke *om. Facs.*　　[3] suidi *Facs.*

p. 6 ; Facs. p. 360, *marg. sup.*

(N)am churim[1] ar co*m*mairge
Maire ogi ingini.
Brigti báne bruthmaire.
Cuangusa[2] morglaine
Moninni 7 Midnatan.
Scire . Sinchi　Samthainne.[3]
Caite . Cuacae　Coemilli.[4]
(　)nne[5]　Coppe　Cocnatan.
Nessi　Ane　Ernaigthi.
De*r*bŕiled[6] is Becnatan.
Céire is Chrone is Chailainne.
Lasrae . Locae[7] is Luathrinni.
Ruind . Ronnait . (R)ig(n)aige.
Sarnat . Segnat　Sodeilbe.

---

[1] **N** *lost in fracture.*　　[2] *obscure* ; Cua[che] *Plummer.*　　[3] Samchainne *Facs.*　　[4] Coemill *Facs.*　　[5] ｨC]raine *Plummer* ; C *faintly traceable* ; *but reading doubtful, might be* Coíne (?)　　[6] Derbŕilen *Facs.*　　[7] Lochae *Facs.*

[MAY 1]

Though you be in ignorance
of the wondrous renowned Jameses,
I will reveal them to you, without baseness.
I have studied them with full science.

James son of Cleophas and Mary
chief of the noble high apostles,
suffered martyrdom on the eighth of the calends of April,
'twas not only terrible, it was a fierce deed.

On the tenth of the calends of July, Alpheus' son,
fair James, with grace,
after he had preached in Syria
north in Persia he died.

James the distinguished son of Zebedee
a chief apostle of God's people,
suffered martyrdom on the eighth of the calends of August.
He was a head of counsel of this world.

[1]I put myself under the protection
of Mary virgin maiden,
of Brigit fair and fervent,
of Cuangus of great purity,
of Moninne and Midnat,
of Scíre, Sínech, Samthann,
of Caite, Cúaca, Cóemell,
of Craine(?), Coip, Cocnat,
of Ness the glorious of Ernaide,
of Derbfiled and Becnat,
of Cíar and Cróne and Caílann,
of Lassar, Locha, and Lúaithrenn,
of Ruinne (?), Ronnat, Rignach,
of Sarnat, Segnat, Sodelb,

---

[1] Ed. and transl. by Charles Plummer, Irish Litanies, p. 92 ff. (Henry Bradshaw Soc., vol. lxii.)

p. 6 ; Facs. p. 360, *marg. sup.*—cont.

> Is na n-óg i n-oenbailc.
> Tuaid tess tair tiar
> na*m* churim[1] ar commairgi
> na Trinóite togaide.
> na fádi . na firapstal.
> na mmanach . na mmartirech.
> na fedb is na foismidech.
> na n-og is na n-irisech.
> na nóem is na noemaiṅgel
> ar cach n-olc dom anacul
> ar demnaib ar drochdoenib.
> ar dornom ar drochamsir.
> ar galar ar gubelaib.
> ar uacht　is ar accorus
> ar anaeb . ar escuni[2]
> ar dígail　ar dairmitin.
> ar dinsem ar dercháine.
> ar mirath ar merugud
> ar theidm bratha . borrfadaig.
> ar olc iff*ir*n . ilphiastaig.
> 　co n-ilur a phian.,

---

[1] na*n*churim *Facs.*　　[2] *sic Facs.* ; *reading obscure, the letter after* u *is smudged ; final* i *subscript.*

ibid. marg. sin.

Uiii. idus maii i nGlestonia .i. i nGlestiṅṅgberg sancti Indrathi mar*tiris* .i. Indrechtaig iresaig .i. ar iriss damair martra.

ibid. marg. inf.[1]

> Diamba cleirech níba írach
> nib ard a[2] guth.　[3]Ni thoe eithech.[3]
> níba[4] santach . níba setach.[5]
> níb neóit brécach[6]
> Nib airbirech[7] fri séire.
> [3]ní ecnaige do cheile.[3]

---

[1] *LB* = Lebar Breac, Facs. p. 101, *marg.*, ed. and tr. Stokes, Félire Oeng.[1], p. clxxxiv.　　[2] nirba roard do *LB*.　　[3-3] *om. LB.*　　[4] nirba *LB*.
[5] nirba satach *LB*.　　[6] nirba neoit . nirbat breccach *LB*.　　[7] nirbat aererach *LB*.

and of the virgins everywhere,
north, south, east, west.
I put myself under the protection
of the chosen Trinity,
of the prophets, of the true apostles,
of the monks, of the martyrs,
of the widows and the confessors,
of the virgins and the faithful,
of the saints and the holy angels,
against every ill to safeguard me
against demons and evil men,
against   and foul weather,
against sickness and straits,
against cold and hunger,
against distress and .   . ,
against vengeance and dishonour,
against contempt and despair,
against misfortune and straying,
against the plague of wrathful doom,
against the evil of hell full of monsters,
with its abundance of torments.

[MAY 8]

Uiii. idus maii in Glastonia, i.e. in Glastonbury, Saint Indrath martyr, i.e., Indrechtach the faithful, i.e. for the faith he suffered martyrdom.

[MAY 11]

If he be a cleric, let him not be wrathful.
Let not his voice be raised.   Let him not swear falsely.
Let him not be greedy.   Let him not be treasure loving.
Let him not be niggardly, lying.
Let him not be fault-finding at meals.
Do not slander thy fellow.

p. 6 ; Facs. p. 360, *marg. inf.*—cont.

Do thaeb lethfas   do lige lethfuar
o¹ Crist mac Dé   rotbé² a luag.³
⁴Ingnais do *cheneoil*⁴ coll*aide*⁵
co llaithe th' éca⁶
Uir anfeóir⁷ thorut
i forciund⁸ do seta
fis . fos . feidle
toa⁹ ¹⁰cen amble¹⁰
umla¹¹   idna ainmne.¹²
⁴Nir gaba doman⁴ a bachlaig.,

¹ la *LB*.	² rotbia *LB*.	³ abb anfinc fort *add. LB*.	⁴⁻⁴ *obscure,*
membrane greasy.	⁵ duit *LB*.	⁶ co ¹laa hecca *LB*.	⁷ aniuil *LB*.
⁸ forcend *LB*.	⁹ tói *LB*.	¹⁰⁻¹⁰ *om. LB*.	¹¹ uimle *LB*.
¹² linmire *Facs*.			

ibid. marg. sin.

.iiii. idus maii.   Ailithir o Chill ind Ailithir i nGarmna i
n-iarthur Chonnacht 7 o Chluain Gési i mMaig Gési . i mMaig
Threga. 7 brathair do Muadan ailith*er* é o Chill Muadain i Sleib
Choirp*re* . 7 fert*ur* germanos fuisse. t combad di Chorco Moga
dó . 7 Lugaid a ainm.,

p. 7 ; Facs. p. 361, *marg. inf.*

Molua ba anmchara do D*au*id
dar muir modmall
is do Maedóc is dom Chaemóc
is do Chomgall.

Angelus cec*init*¹
Fir nime fir thal*man*   trén rudrach
andar leo ba lá bratha   bás Lugdach.

Ni ranic ni ricfa   réim ngaile²
sanct aile rissba mo failte   fer nime.

Nóe cét Bennchuir³
Sé chét Oentruib
cóic cét Condere na comland
Mac Carthaig cóir
ba anmchara dóib iar Comgall.,

¹ *in marg*.   ² *sic, read* ngile (*Bergin*), *which is translated.*

Thy side half-bare, thy bed half-cold
From Christ, God's Son, mayest thou have thy reward.
Absence from thy bodily family
until the day of thy death.
Grassless earth over thee
at the end of thy journeying.
Knowledge, steadfastness, patience,
Silence without muteness.
Humility, purity, patience.
Take not the world, O cleric.

[MAY 12]

[1].*iiii. idus maii.* Ailither[2] from Cell ind Ailithir in Garmna in western Connacht, and from Clúain Géise in Mag Géise in Mag Trega ; and he was a kinsman of Múadán the pilgrim from Cell Múadáin in Slíab Choirpre, *et fertur germanos fuisse.* Or, he may have been from Corco Moga, and his name Lugaid.

[1] There is a Latin rendering of this entry in the abstract preserved in the Library of Trinity College, Dublin (*T*).
[2] Alitherius seu Peregrinus de Cella duorum Peregrinorum *T*.

[AUGUST 4]

[1]Molua was soul-friend to David[2]
across the tranquil sea
and to Máedóc and to Mochóemóc
and to Comgall.

Angelus cecinit :

The men of Heaven, the men of earth, a mighty inheritance,
they thought it was Doomsday, Lugaid's death.

There has not come, there will not come, a bright course,
another saint more welcome to the men of Heaven.[1]

Nine hundred of Bennchor, six hundred of Óentreb,
five hundred of Condere of the combats,
the son of Carthach the just, was soul-friend to them after
    Comgall.

[1] These quatrains on Molúa have been edited and transl. from *F* by Stokes, Fél. Oengusso,[2] pp. 182-3.
[2] *i.e.*, of Menevia, or St. David's, in Wales.

TALLAGHT.   I

p. 7 ; Facs. p. 361, *marg. sup.*

Morfessiur de *christ*ianis dochuatar i n-uaim ar imgabail a
n-imgrema [1]fo Deic 7 Ualir.[1] ro iadad ind uaim forru . ar nocon
fes a ndola inti. Ro batar an(d)[2] 'na cotlud co cend cóic *i*nbl*iadna*
ar *coícait* ar *cet* co rragbatar[3] ríg cristaide forsin domun 7 co ragbad[4]
*for cum*tach ciuitat*um*. co ndechas cosin n-uaim i mbatar *som*
co tucait a clocha do denam cumtaig díb. Co ndechaid fer dibseom
do chennuch bíd dóib iar n-eirge assa cotlud andar leo. Co
tuargaib a argat isin chathraig. Ass a duine ar lucht na cathrach
senargat fil acut ni gebthar uait é i n-amsir Deic dorigned ar
iat. 7 atat clu. bliad*an* and o ro fogain in t-argat sain . 7 rí cristaide
fil and indiu .i. Constantin m*ac* Elenae. Conid and sin rofit*ir* a
imthus 7 ro attlaig buide do Dia 7 ro innis a scéla fira uile . 7
tucad[5] a aes cumtha assind úaim . 7 tucad post in rí dia n-acal*laim*
coro innisetar a scéla fíra dó . 7 ra[6] mórait na cristaide 7 ainm Dé
ar in mírbail sin.

[1-1] *Faintly traceable with the help of LB.*   [2] *end of line* ; isan uaim
Facs. ; *but both is and* uaim *illeg., and doubtful* ; *read* and.   [3] corrag-
natar *Facs.*   [4] coragnad *Facs.*   [5] tucai *Facs.*   [6] ro *Facs.*

ibid. marg. inf.

Nirbo doc[h]ta[1] do[2] Mochta   Lugmaid (Li)s.[3]
( ) cet[4] sacc*art* ( )cet[5] n-epsco*p*   maroen[6] fris.

Ochtmoga[7] saerchland salmach
   a theglach aidble[8] remend.
[cen ar][9] cen buain cen tirad
   cen gnimrad *acht* [mad][10] leigend.,

p. 8 ; Facs. p. 362, *marg. sup.*

Faelan Cl*úana* Moescna .i. i Feraib Mide .i. i Feraib Tulach.
Idem et Crundmael m*ac* Ronain i mBerriuch i Foth*artaib* ut alii
dicunt.

---

[1] bochtai *LB.*   [2] muinnter *C.*   [3] *illeg.*, Lis *LB.*, etc.   [4] *illeg.*,
trí chét *rell.*   [5] da cét *esp. F*, ar cet escop *LB*, um ched nespoc *C.*
[6] *obscure,* araen *LB*, maille *F.*   [7] tri fichit *D, FM.*   [8] ríoghdha *D, FM.*
[9] *om.*   [10] *om.* ; *supplied from LB*, etc.

[AUGUST 7]

[1]Seven Christians[2] went into a cave to avoid persecution under Decius and Valerianus. And the cave was closed on them, for it was not known that they had entered it. They were asleep in it[3] for a hundred and fifty-five years, until Christian kings came into power in the world and men began to build cities. And people went to the cave where they were, and took away its stones for building. And after rising from sleep, as they thought, one of them went to buy food. And he proffered his money in the city. 'Hence, O man,' said the people of the city, 'ancient coin is what thou hast ; it will not be accepted from thee ; in the time of Decius it was made,' they said, 'and one hundred and fifty-five years have gone since that money circulated, and a Christian king is here now, namely, Constantine, son of Helena.' So then he knew his situation, and he gave thanks to God. And he told his true tale in full. And his companions were brought out of the cave, and the king was afterwards brought to hold speech with them. And they told their true story to him. And the Christians and God's name were magnified because of that miracle.

[1] Ed. and transl. from the Facsimile of *LL* by Stokes, Fél. Óeng.[2] pp. 467–8; also another version, half Latin, from *F. ibid.* pp. 182–5, and a Latin version from *LB*, Fél. Óeng.[1] p. cxxix f.
[2] In *F* and *LB* their names are given.   [3] et dormierunt in ea. *LB*.

[AUGUST 19]

[1]There was no niggardliness for Mochta, of the court of Lugmad, three hundred priests, a hundred bishops were along with him.

[2]Eighty psalm-singing noble youths
his household, vastness of courses.
Without tilling, without reaping, without drying,
without toil save only study.

[AUGUST 26]

Fáelán of Clúain Móescna, i.e., in Fir Mide, i.e., in Fir Tulach. *Idem et* Crundmáel son of Rónán in Berrech in Fotharta, *ut alii dicunt.*

[1] Ed. and transl. Stokes, Fél. Óeng.[1] p. cxxxii (*LB*) ; *ibid.*[2] p. 188 (*F*) ; by Colgan, Acta Sanctt., p. 734 (*C*), cited in *D*, p. 224.
[2] Ed. and transl. Stokes *l.c.*; *D*, p. 224, Colgan *l.c.*, and O'Donovan, *FM*, I, pp. 178–9.

p. 8 ; Facs. p. 362, *marg. inf.*

Uii. id. sep. Quies Colmain cum omnibus fratribus qui fecit uinum t*er* de aq*u*a fontis .i. in cétna fecht do Cholum C*hille* in fecht aile do Fechini Fo*bair* in tan dorat a śúle dó . in tres fecht do Ruadan Lothra . 7 atá in topur sin fo themiul ar cúl licci Ruadáin anair ina relic . 7 cachoen fo tic us*ce* isind relic sin ni piantar a anim.

Colman m*ac* Echda*ch*. Macc Óige m*ac* Echda*ch*. Diarmait m*ac* Echd*ach*. Fintan m*ac* Echdach. Diucaill 7 Ternóc 7 in Clarenech .i. Fergus m*ac* Nad Slúaid. Eps*cop* G*r*ellain. 7 Eps*cop* Findchain. 7 Eps*cop* Meláin. Et Fintan os psalmorum . 7 Fechine m.h.[1] Chuinge. Odran presb*iter*. Coitchend 7 Critan Cind Locha Silend. Segan 7 Brandub. Colum 7 Ernain m*eic* Aeda. na tri ailithrig Eirne. na tri ailithrig Locha Úane. Tri m*eic* Dáre. .uii. m*eic* Niad. .uii. m*eic* Eodusa. De uirginibus au*tem* Darbile ingen M*ur*idaig Aeda*m*mair [2]( )la. Ainpthini ingen Mael Duin. Midabair Cuppa Cind Locha. Comaig *ingen* ( )[3] Sp*er*óc ingen Coluim. Cuachnat . Scoth . Femoir . Blathnat . Ana. Rígnach ingen Colchain ( ) dar ( )[4] Beoain[5] m*áthair* Cholmain. .uii. [n-]ingena Fergusa. .uii. .uii. [n-]ingena m*eic* Inguir. .uii. [n-]ingena Garbain. .uii. n-ingena Lasrén. .uii. caillecha Dromma da Dartraith Locha ⟨ꝉ hola⟩[6] 7 coica ( )[7] (Co)lman m*ac* nAeda i rRus m*ac* nAeda .i. ic Snám Luthair ic Loch Eirne requiescunt.,

---

[1] = moccu.   [2] *a few letters lost.*   [3] *space for a couple of letters left (or erasure).*   [4] *several letters lost ;* dar *sic Facs.*   [5] *or perhaps* Beoaid.   [6] *add. below line.*   [7] *several words lost*

p. 9 ; Facs. p. 363, *marg. sup.*

Onme ⟨.i. simul⟩ ꝉ Omne m*ac* ríg Lage*n* 7 doratad é i ṅgiallaigecht do ríg Lethi Cuind 7 dorat s*ide* é i llaim ṁBrigti fria réir dara chend a patre suo et aliquo die dixerunt discipulae Brigitae ei. Is álaind ar siat in giallan bec indiu. Bid é a ainm co bráth ar Brigit Giallan . 7 iss e sin fil i Cill Giallain i nU*íb* Muridaig.,

[SEPTEMBER 3]

.uii. id. sep.—Quies Colmáin cum omnibus fratribus qui fecit uinum ter de aqua fontis, i.e., the first time for Colum Cille, the second time for Féchíne of Fobar, when he gave his eyes to him, the third time for Rúadán of Lothra. And that well is in darkness behind Rúadán's flagstone on the east side in his graveyard. And every one about whom water comes in that graveyard his soul is not tormented.[1]

Colmán son of Eochaid. Macc Óige s. of Eochaid. Díarmait s. of Eochaid. Fintan s. of Eochaid. Diucaill and Ternóc and the Table-faced, i.e. Fergus s. of Nad Slúaid. Bishop Grellán, and Bishop Findchán, and Bishop Mellán, and Fintan *os psalmorum,* and Féchíne moccu Cuinge. Odrán presbyter. Coitchenn and Critán of Cenn Locha Sílenn. Segán and Brandub. Colum and Ernáin sons of Áed. The three pilgrims of Éirne. The three pilgrims of Loch Uane. The three sons of Dáre. The seven sons of Nía. The seven sons of Eodus. De uirginibus autem. Darbile daughter of Muiredach. Áedammair ( )la. Ainbthíne d. of Máel Dúin. Midabair. Cuppa of Cenn Locha. Comaig d. of (Eochaid). Speróc d. of Colum. Cúachnat. Scoth. Femoir. Blathnat. Ana. Rígnach d. of Colchán (. . . .). Beóain mother of Colmán. The seven daughters of Fergus. The seven daughters of Ingor's son. The seven daughters of Garbán. The seven daughters of Lasren. The seven[2] nuns of Druim dá Dartraith Locha (or Hola) and the Fifty . . (at) Colmán mac nÁeda in Ros mac nÁeda, i.e., at Snám Luthair at Loch Éirne *requiescunt.,*

---

[1] The above passage has been ed. and transl. by Stokes, Fél. Óeng.[2], pp. 198–9, where it is an additional note on Colmán of Druim Ferta, Sept. 3.
[2] Cp. May 22, Three nuns of Druim dá Dart.

[OCTOBER 2]

Onme (i.e. *simul*) or Omne son of the king of Leinster. And he was given as a hostage to the king of Leth Cuind, and he gave him into Brigit's hand that she might on his account obtain submission *a patre suo, et aliquo die dixerunt discipulae Brigitae ei :* ' 'tis lovely the little hostage (gíallán) is to-day,' said they. 'Gíallán will be his name for ever,' said Brigit. And that is the one who is in Cell Gíalláin in Uí Muiridaig.

---

[1] Cp. the versions ed. and transl. Stokes in Fél. Óengusso[1] (*LB*), p. cliv ; *ib.*[2] (*R*[1]), pp. 220–1.

p. 9 ; Facs. p. 363, *marg. sup.*—cont.

Brendin*us*[1] p*rofet*auit.

A Odrain bat[2] magister[3]
rimsa na fer do saebe :'[4]
Bat[5] oen ac immorchor[6] Choluim'[7]
i cind feind lam Chaeme.[8]

Dar ú Neill dar Connachta
siar[9] is tar airer na hEchtge.[10]
tassi Coluim h*ui* Chremthaind[11]
bertair[12] co hInis Celtrae.,[13]

[1] Bremuni *Facs.* ; Mocaemoc dixit fri hOdran quando fleuit ica baisted *F.*
[2] bad *F.*   [3] maigistir *F.*   [4] dogra frim na dena *F.*   [5] bad *Facs.*
[6] *asp. mark om. Facs.*   [7] bad aen oc imch*ur* Colum (*sic*) *F.*   [8] la
Mocoeme ic in*n* fena *F.*   [9] Tar uib Neill i Connachta *F.*   [10] budes
la taeb na hEchta *F.*   [11] reilgi m*ei*c h*ui* Crimtannain *F.*   [12] be*r*thai*r* *F.*
[13] Celtra *F.*

ibid. marg. inf.

Corgus aps*tal* da la déc
recair a les a c[h]omét.
.iii. láe cech rathe réim ngle
foclait faithi firinne.

Cetchetain oen diden dil.
cetna satharn in missin
acht as ó marta maith mod
a thossach a thinscetol.

[OCTOBER 27]

Brendin*us* pro*fe*tauit.

O Odrán, thou shalt be a master,
ply not thy perversities on me.
Thou shalt be one bearing Colum
.[2] with Mocháeme.

Over Uí Néill, over Connacht westwards,
and over the region of Echtge,
the relics of Colum grandson of Crimthann
shall be borne to Inis Celtra.

---

[1] This poem also occurs in the notes to the Franciscan copy of Fél. Óengusso (*F*) under Dec. 13, where, however, it is put into the mouth of Mocháemóc, when Odrán wept as he was being baptised. Stokes, Fél. Óeng,[1] p. clxxxii only refers to it, but prints the gloss on *reilgi :* .i. reliquie .i. taise Col*uim* m*eic* Crimtha*inn* r*u*ctha la Mochoemh*e* Tire da Ghlas ⁊ la hOdran maigister *for* fen tar E*ch*tge fodhes co hInis Celtra co Camini Innsi Celtra. ' The relics of Colum son (*recte* great-grandson) of Crimthann were taken by Mochóeme of Tír dá Glas and by Odrán the Master on a wain over Echtge, southwards to Inis Celtra, to Caimíne of Inis Celtra.' The pedigree of Colum of Tír dá Glas is given both here and in *LL* 351*d*, etc.

[2] The meaning is not clear. For *fén* ' waggon, wain,' see Stokes, Irish Metrical Glossaries, Phil. Soc. Trans., 1891, p. 58. The form *feind* of the text is unusual.

[1]Lent of the apostles, twelve days,
it must needs be kept
three days every quarter, a clear course
the prophets of righteousness proclaim.

The first Wednesday, Friday dear,
the first Saturday of that month,
provided it is from March, a good work,
its beginning, its commencement.

---

[1] Another copy of this poem occurs in the Book of Hui Maine (*H*) 53 *b* 2 (old fol. 109), in which the spelling is modernized.

p. 9; Facs. p. 363, *marg. inf.*—cont.

Cetain aine sathar*n* siuil
i sechtmain tan*ai*se iúil.
cetain áine sathar*n* sin.
in tres sechtmain septimbi*r*.

Ocus in tres sec*h*tmain slán
do decimbe*r*[1] digrais dál
na tri lathi cetna co[2] cóir.
aint*er* ar Mac nDé ndegmóir[3]

Iss *é* seo cóir na háine
forstabair commaine
is do deoin mo rig co rath
cen feóil cen fín cen banach.

Is noeme do neoch[4] namma
áine in quatuor *tempo*ra.
cena fochneit[5] fath cen chol
mor a fochraic fiad apstol.

Itge na dá dagfer[6] déc
co ríg nime nert nad bréc
co rius Pardus buan a blad[7]
iar n-oene corg*uis* apstal.   C.

[1] deitsimp*er* H.   [2] *om.* H.   [3] an decimpir dé degmoir H.   [4] is
naemadh o nech H.   [5] fosaic neich H.   [6] deigfer H.   [7] mblad H.

p. 10 ; Facs. p. 364, *marg. sup.*

Triur ar trichait ar díb cétaib
di munt*ir* masclaig[1] muaid.
la munt*ir* me*i*c Tulchain treoraig
ciaptar ceolaig cantais uail.[2]

Ros coimet h*ui*a Tuath*ai*l Tec[h]tmair
m*ac* Fiachr*ach* Fechtnaig co n-uaill.
Ro bruiset baig *ocus* brethir
i cend demuin teithmir thruaig.

[1] *gl.* .i. messoclaig (?) ; mescoclaig *Facs.*   [2] *gl.* .i. iar ceolaib uird 7
offrind cantais úala di gul 7 deraib ar seirc Dé.

Wednesday, Friday, Saturday of the course,
in the second week of July.
Wednesday, Friday, Saturday,
the third week of September.

And in the third full week
of December, excellent the meeting,
the three same days fittingly
are kept fasting for the Son of the good and great God.

This is the order of the fasting
upon which He puts obligation,
with the good-will of my bountiful King :
no meat, no wine, no female.

It is sanctification for one merely
to fast on the Ember days,
without murmuring, a sinless cause,
great the reward of it before the apostle.

The prayer of the twelve good men
to the King of Heaven, a strength that is not false,
May I attain to Paradise, lasting its fame,
After the fast of Lent of the Apostles.

[OCTOBER 21]

Two hundred, three and thirty
of the community of noble . . ¹
with the community of Tulchán's vigorous son,
though they were tuneful they used to sing lamentations.²

The descendant of Túathal Techtmar protected them,
Fíachra Fechtnach's son, the proud.
They broke bond and word
against the wanton³ wretched Devil.

---

¹ *masclach* or *messoclach* (gl.) obscure.   ² gl., i.e. after the music
of the Ordo and Mass they used to sing lamentations of wailing and tears
for the love of God.
    ³ For meaning of *teithmir* see Gwynn, Metr. Dinds. IV. p. 408.

p. 10 ; Facs. p. 364, *marg. sup.*—cont.

Ni agat[1] monud no mithis[2]
   no gorud fri richis[3] ruaid.
*Co*nsuidet suidi fiad a*n*glib
   iar clod chatha chai*n*gnig crúaid.

Bithbennacht Cr*ist* dona nemdai*b*
   arin scoil cáem credlaig crúaid.
Fora fóisam dún ar talmain.
   la nem thall diar n-anmain truaig.   T.

Munnu mór mac Tulchain trein
   m*eic* Trena m*eic* Dega m*eic* Déin.
m*eic* Dubthaig Duinn robo ri
   m*eic* Maain is m*eic* Roedi.

Roedi is Cond Crínna 'moalle
   dá m*ac* finna Feidilmthe.
Feidl*imid* Rech*taid* don Maig
   m*ac* Tuath*ail* m*eic* Feradaig.

Feradach Find Fec[h]t*nach* Fáil
   m*ac* s*id*e Crimth*ainn* Niad Náir.
[   ][4] os cach dind
m*ac* Lugdech m*ac* na tri Find.

Na tri Find Emna cen ail
   m*ai*cne án Ech*ach* Feidlig.
don rigraid sin is caín clú
   cen*el* mi*n*gla*n* Munnu.   M.

---

[1] *MS. has* íagat, *with* f *expuncted, and gl.* .i. ni agatar.   ° *gl.* .i. míathis.
[3] *gl.* .i. i llo bratha.   [4] something omitted ; four syllables wanting.

They fear neither wealth nor ill-fortune,
nor burning exposed to the red fire.[1]
They sit upon seats in the presence of angels,
after the victory of hard vexatious battle.

The everlasting blessing of Christ from Heaven
on the dear pious austere school.
May we be under His safeguard on earth,
with Heaven beyond for our wretched souls !

[OCTOBER 21]
Great Munnu[2] son of mighty Tulchán,
son of Trían, son of Daig, son of Dían,
son of Dubthach Donn, who was a king ,
son of Maan and son of Róede.

Róede and Conn Crínna together,
two fair sons of Feidlimid.
Feidlimid Rechtaid of the Maig,
son of Túathal, son of Feradach.

Feradach Find Fechtnach of Fál,
the son of Crimthann Nia Náir.
.   . over every height,
the son of Lugaid son of the Three Finds.

The Three Finds of Emain, without reproach,
glorious sons of Eochu Feidlech,
of that kingly host whose fame is fair,
is the noble bright race of Munnu.

---

[1] gl. i.e., on the Day of Judgement.
[2] Cp. the pedigree of Munnu in *LL* 349 f., Rawl. B. 502, 90c, and Lebaı
Brecc, 15 *e*.

p. 10 ; Facs. p. 364, *marg. inf.*

Patricius cecin*it.*

Epsco*p* hErc[1]
cach ní concertad[2] ba cert
cach óen be*r*es [co]cert[3] cert[4]
fortraib[5] bennacht Epsco*ip* hErc.[6]

---

[1] .i. br*eth*em Pat*r*a*ic LB.* [2] co ndernadh *Tig.* [3] *om. LB.* cocair
Tig. co *om. haplogr. MS.*, coicheart *FM.* [4] *what appears to be* i *is added
under* e *by a later hand ; and so Facs. ; read* coceirt ceirt ; cocert cáir *Lc.*
[5] fo*r*tbeir *Tig.*, fodreith *LB.*, fortbaid *Lc.* [6] easpuic Erc *FM.*

p. 11 ; Facs. p. 365, *marg. sup.*

Aed Alla*n* cecin*it.*

Samthand fri soillsi sainmand.
 mad ragab gensa glanbarr.
Tuaithmaig [1]Midi miad[1] n-imglan
 mór saeth f*r*i sini[2] Samthand.

Ro gab inní nad assa
 áine fri rig[e][3] slessa.
Damair fri terca tuarai :'
 roptar[4] cruadai a cressa.

Arad fri nimib[5] níthu
 glan a cridi fri baithu.
i n-ucht Fiadat fo glanbarr
 asrola Samthand saethu. S.

---

[1]–[1] imorlonad, *with* inmorlonad *added above line, Facs.* [2] fo sine *FM.*
[3] rig *MS.*, righe *FM, sic leg.* [4] batar *FM.* [5] nimhe *F.M, sic leg.*

[NOVEMBER 2]

Patricius cecinit.[1]

Bishop Erc,[2]
everything he adjudged was just.
Everyone that passes a just judgement
may the blessing of Bishop Erc be upon him !

[1] Other copies in Lebar Brecc (*LB*), Facs. p. 23, marg. inf., 220 *b*. Book of Lecan (*Lc*), 306 *b* 37 ; Annals of Tigernach (*Tig*.), RC. xvii, 126 : Annals of Four Masters (*FM*), i, 168.
[2] *gl*. Patrick's brehon, *LB* ; cp. Trip. Life, p. 264, 20, FM. i. p. 136. He is Erc of Sláne, and his day is Nov. 2 ; see Fél. Óeng. and Mart. of Donegal. His pedigree is in *LL* 349 *b*. His death is recorded in the annals under A.D. 512.

[DECEMBER 19]

Áed Allán cecinit[1] :

Samthann with noble radiance,
well has she attained the bright crown of chastity.
In the northern plain of Meath, a shining honour,
great was the suffering . . . of Samthann.[2]

She undertook, what is not easy,
fasting . .[3]
She endured against scant nourishment,
hard were her girdles.

A ladder for the assaults of Heaven,
pure was her heart against fools.
In the bosom of the Lord, under a radiant crown,
Samthann cast away tribulations.

[1] Edited with transl. by Kuno Meyer : Konig Aed Allán als Dichter, ZCP. XIII, 143 f., and by Ó'Donovan, Annals of the Four Masters, A.D. 734 (*FM*).
[2] ' War viel Mühseligkeit unter Samthanns Brüsten,' Meyer ; ' great suffering did S. endure,' O'Donovan.
[3] ' Fasten mit gestreckten Seiten,' Meyer, taking *rige* as noun to *rigim* ' strecke,' as in *hi rigi*, Ml. 99 *d* 1 ; ' fasting for the Kingdom above,' O'Donovan.

p. 11 ; Facs. p. 365, *marg. inf.*

Fingein ce*c*i*nit.*

A chlerig coisc in figill
iṅge foa thrí notairind :'
is lór celebrad chena
i feil Dega m*ei*c Cairill.

Tri coicait cloc buadach band
la cét ṁbalcbuidnech ṁbachall
la *sescait* soscela slán
do laim Dega a oenurán.

ibid. col. c.

Emianus ⟨.i. Emin án⟩ natus est de patre Hiaman. Hiaman
nomen patris Iamnat uero nomen matris eius de Chorco Solgoi*n*n
Cruaich a chen*e*l de h*uí*b Senaig in tṡainruth. Is é luid dar éis
Brain m*ei*c Conaill martra a choicait náeb dar eis ṁBrain rig Lag*en*
a choicait ríg ar in ṁbudechair.

Fingein cecinit.[1]

O cleric, end the vigil,
thrice only bow thyself down ;
enough already of celebration
on the festival of Daig son of Cairell.

One hundred and fifty bells, a triumphant achievement,
with a stout hostful hundred of croziers,
with sixty whole gospels
from the hand of Daig alone.

[1] These verses belong more properly to Aug. 18, which is Daig's day
See the notes to Fél. Óengusso, where his pedigree is given. He was the
chief artificer of Cíarán of Saiger. The second quatrain is cited in Mart. of
Donegal, p. 222.

[DECEMBER 22]

Emianus, i.e. Emín án (noble Emín), *natus est de patre Hiaman*,
etc. Of Corco Solgoinn Crúaich his kindred. Of the Uí Senaig in
particular. It is he that underwent martyrdom from the yellow
plague, on behalf of Bran son of Conall, fifty saints of them, on
behalf of Bran king of Leinster, fifty kings of them.[1]

[1] Edited and transl. by Stokes, Fél. Óengusso,[2] p. 260 f.. The story of
Emíne Bán and his forty-nine monks has been edited by J. G. O'Keeffe,
Anecd. from Irish MSS. i, 40 ff, and transl. by Charles Plummer, Ériu iv,
41 ff. Bran son of Conall died A.D. 695, AU.

NOTES AND INDICES

1. NOTES ON THE ROMAN CALENDAR.
2. NOTES ON THE BRUSSELS ABSTRACT.
3. INDEX OF PLACES (ROMAN CALENDAR).
4. INDEX OF PERSONS (ROMAN CALENDAR).
5. INDEX OF PLACES (IRISH CALENDAR).
6. INDEX OF PERSONS (IRISH CALENDAR).

NOTES ON THE ROMAN CALENDAR

Dec. 25.

iunii . iouini HLS, iuuini R. **bassilei** : basilei EWR, *om.* BLS.
achillei . agellei BL, accilae E, acellei W. **uictorianae** : uictorine L.
euticitae : euticeti BLW, eutici E. **heliae eufegiae dorozoli, iuliani
marciani** : *om.* HL. **simfroniani** : simfroniane BW, simproniane L,
simforiani E. **teuinidi** . timedi (tem- E) HL. **ignatii** : agnati W. **ciriacii** :
syriacii BLE. **zachii** : gagi BLW, zagii E. **anastasiae** : + felicitatis HLS.
Appromiani is the name of a cemetery.
For *heliae dorozoli iuliani marciani* see Dec. 26.

Dec. 26.

zephani : stephani BLW, stefani E. **dionisii** : dyonisii L. **nichandri** :
neandri (menan- E) HL. **martini** : marini martiani B, marciani, marini E,
martiniani L, martiani W, marini mār R. **dorozoli** : dorostoli HL.
eliae : heliae HL.

Dec. 28.

castorii : castoris S. **octouiani** : octaui HL. **gade** : gattae (za- E)
HL. **probati** : propati E. **rogati** : rogatae E. **saturi** : + catonis
restitutae (-uti E, *om.* L) saturninae gaiani domiciae thomae (to -E) HL.
eutitii : eutici BLW, + domitiani (-ciani H) HL. **uicturiae donati** : *om.*
HL.
Eutitii is out of place among the African martyrs.
For *uicturiae* see Dec. 29.

Dec. 29.

uictoris, uictori : uictori B, uicturini L, uictoris ES, uicturi WR.
demetri, catonis : *om.* HL. **crescentis** : criscenti BWL. **librosi** :
S, librosi HLR. **uictoriae** : uicturinae E. **saturi** : *om.* L. **felicis
bis** : felicis W, + primiani (*sec.*) BL. **bonifatii** : bonifatii (bone- B -faci
W) HL. **domicii**: domiti E.
For *catonis* see Dec. 28.
Domicii is misplaced after the Roman *felicis bonifacii*.

Dec. 30.

manseti : mansueti HLRS. **seueri securi** : seueri ER, securi BWL,
donati : + felicis BLRS. **honorati** : honori HL. **policleti** : pole ... cliti B,
polecliti LWS, policliti E, + perpetuę BS, perpetui LWS. **florentii** : *om.* E.
rerenei : sereni HL. **pauli** (*bis*) : pauli HL. **papiani** : papia api B,
pampiani W. **zefani** : stephani BWL, *om.* E.
B has *perpetuę* in the middle of *polecliti*.
Pauli cleti seems to be a duplicate of *policleti*.
T has the place-name *turoni* (Tours) : see W.

Dec. 31.

celestini : caelestini HL. **paulinae** : paulini R, pauliniae S.
rusticanae : R, *om.* BLW. **nominandae** : dominandae, nominandae BLE,
nominandae (*bis*) W, + donatae BLW. **serotinae saturninae** : R, *om.*
BLW. **hilariae** : R, hilarinae BLW, hilariae, hilarinae E. **rogatae** :
rogatae (*bis*) BW, rogatiae, rogatae L. **aggagi**: + donatae (-ti W) HL. **pauli**:

om. E. **ermetis**: hermetis HL, + stephani (stef- E) HL. **cintiani** (*bis*) :
quintiani HL. **cornolii**: cornili BW, corneli LE. **sixti, sexti** : sixti BW,
syxti L, sext: E. **floridi** : floredi W, + quottae B, gothe L, cottae EW.
menernini : meneruini BLW, minerviani E. **simforiani**: simphoriani LE,
sinfuriani W. **exoperati** : exsuperanti BL, exuperati E, exuperanti W.
euelpisti: cuelpisti B. **fortunati**: furtunati H. **sequentis**: equentis B.
opiones : apionis (app- BL) HL. **kalendionis** : calendionis BLW, kalen-
dini E. **agnetis** : agneti B. *fin.*, + columbae HLRS.

D ( )*ti* is a corruption of *depos* (H). The misplaced *siluestri papae*
should have followed it. T here has *priscillae* as a saint. It is the cemetery
in which Pope Silvester was buried (E *Rom.*). *Bononi* and *retiariae* are
place-names : Bononia (Widdon, Bulgaria), and Ratiaria in Dacia.

Jan. 1.

zephani :   stephani   BL,   stefani   EW. **effroseni** :   eufrosini   HL.
priminiani : primani B, primiani LWS, priani E. **euantii** ; euenti L.
hermetis: ermetis W. **agaci** : gagi BLW, gai E. **acti** : iacti E, appi
W. **eracli** : heracli E. **narcissii** : narcisci W. **argiri** : arciri B. **papatis** :
papa E. **saturnini** : saturnini (*bis*) HL. **hermetis** : ermetis W. **coronae
prisci et militis et aliorum xliii, natalis** : coronae et milites triginta
et martini martyris B, coronae xxx nat alamachi . . L, nt coronae
. . . , et milit xxx E, coronae milites xxx W, nat almachi . . . R, martinae
martyris S. **agripini** : agrippini BEL.

T has two place-names : *bononi* for Bononia (Widdon) and *augusti duno*
(Autun). *Bononi agaci* is also in Dec. 31.

Natalis in T is misplaced, and is an error for *natale*. *Coronae* (THL) is
probably not a personal name, but the crown of martyrdom. In this part of
the article the principal person is Priscus in T, Martinus (Martina) in BS, and
Alamachius (Almachius) in LR. It is conceivable that the latter two names
belong to a single person : *natal martini = nat almarchi*. See *D.C.A.* i. 58,
and for the group *Ricemarch* p. xxix.

Jan. 2.

esiridoni, sircioni, siritioni : siridoni BLW, isiridoni E, isiodori R,
isidori S. **stratonici** : stratoni L. **antecluti, amphitinae** : *om.* HL.
acutionis timothei : acucionis thimothei W. **herisi** : herissi LE. **artaxis** :
artaxi (arth- W) HL. **acutae** : acuti E. **tobiae** : tubiae (*bis*) BL, tubiae
W. **rutulae** : rutilae E. **zephani**: stephani BL, stefani EW. **macari** :
machari BLW, maccari E. **marciani** : R, *om.* HL. *fin.* + mancheani R.

Abbani (TE) is an error for *abbatis*. It is misplaced, before than after
macari.

Mancheanus is an Irish saint. See below.

Jan. 3.

ciriacii : cirici (cy- B) HL. **caudionis** : claudionis (-donis E) HL.
eugenii : eugenis E. **argei** : R, arget B. **argenni** : R, *om.* HL. **narcisi** :
narcissi HL. **marcelli** : marcellini HL, + cigni R. **scatuliani** : statuliani
HL. **pueri, christiani** : pueri christiani (iani *om.* B cr- W) HL. **pos-
sessoris** : possessores W. **filii**: anifili B, feli W, *om.* E, + digo iuni BW, vico
juvini L, diogini E, theogeris R, + amanti L. **hilarii** ; hilarini HL. **firmi** :
om. L. **eugetii** : eugenti BLE. **candidi** : candedi BW, *om.* L. **rodonis** :
codonis B, sodonis L. **rogatiani eugeniae** . *om.* L. **lucidae** : lucidei
BW. **acutae** : agute W, *om.* L, + antheri B, anteri R. **peoni** : pennicei
BL, paenicae E, pennici W. **florenti** : *om.* L. **genouefae** : S, genoueue,
BW, genefevae E, genufeţe R, *om.* L.

On this day the scribe of T used two lists. One of them (*a*) recorded a
group of twelve African saints, the names being in the same order as in E
but without title. The other (*b*) gave the saints in the present T, but without

the Africans. The scribe amalgamated the lists. His method was this: starting from *narcisi* (*b*) he inserted a name from *a* after each name in *b* up to *rogatiani*, when he placed the three remaining names without interruption. But he supposed that *marcelli, pueri* and *christiani* were the names of three persons, and in consequence he made confusion in T.

For this day see *Ricemarch* i. 55.

B has *x̄p̄i anifili*. The correct reading is *christiani fili*. *Parisilis* is a corruption of *parisius* (Paris).

Jan. 4.

argenti, eugetii : augenti R, eugenti HS. **hermetis** : ermetis W. **gugi** : gagi BW, gai E. **aggei** : argei W. **teothoti** : theodoti (-ci W) H. **trifinae** : S, trifonis H, arifinę, triponis R. **aediui** : aedui E, *om.* BW, *fin.* + pauli R.

aediui is in the Irish group.

The saints of Bologna (*hermetis* . . . *aggei*) are misplaced here among those of Africa.

Jan. 5.

semionis bis : symeonis (*bis*) B, simonis simionis W, simeonis (*bis*) S, simeonis ER. **sereni** : severi E, serini W, + senni BW. **floriae** : caelisfori (-floriae E) H. **candacii** : candedi (-idi E) H. **anastasiae, anastasii** : anastasiae (-si E) H. **ianuariae ianuarii** : ianuarii (-riae E) H. **acuti** : caitq W. **telefini** : *om.* H.

The two Simeons mentioned here are the prophet (Luke ii. 25) and the stylite (*D.C.B.* iv. 679). BWS have both ; E has the stylite and R the prophet.

Jan. 6.

iuliani : iuliani (*bis*) HR. **antoni, antonini** : antonini BW, antotini E. **telisfori, sinfori** : fori BW, talesfori flori E, telisfori R, telesfori S. **anastasii, anastasiae** : anastasiae BWS, anastasi E. **maelani** : meliani BR, melani ES, miliani W. **euliae, marcianillae, sabastiani** . *om.* H. **basillae** : balissę B, basilissae EWRS.

Redontii is a place-name, Redones (Rennes). For *Melanius*, bishop of Rennes, see *A A.SS.* Jan. i. 357 and *Anal. Bolland.*, ix. 437 ff.

HR have two persons named Julianus, one at Antioch and another in India. S mentions the former. Which of the two is recorded in T is uncertain.

Seven names are repeated here from the list of African martyrs in Jan. 7 (TH).

Jan. 7.

lucei (*bis*) : luceri E, liceri RS, *om.* BW. **poliucati** : poliotti B, poliucti E, piliocti W, poleucti R. **felicis** : + esidori B, ysidori R. **ieiunarii** : ianuarii EWRS, *om.* B. **deoclati, corcani, sion** : *om.* H. **policostini** : costini B, spolicosti E, polecostin W. **palladii** : palladae E, palati W. **poliarti, spolicasti** : poliasti BW, poliarti E, poliarchi S. **philoronis** : filoronis BS, filonis E. **candidi** : candediani BW, candidae E. **euduti** : eucti BW, *om.* E.

Lucianus, a presbyter of Antioch, suffered martyrdom at Nicomedia, 7 Jan. 313. Lawlor-Oulton, *Eusebius*, ii. 295 f.

Clerici is a title or, perhaps, a corruption of *in eraclea*. *Antichini* is a corruption of Antiochia.

Syr. Jan. 7 has Polyeuctus (*poliucati*) and Lucianus. *Syr.* Jan. 8 has Philoromus (*philoronis* ?)

Jan. 8.

euchti, euticii : eucti E, *om.* BW. **rustici** : rusitici W. **phissei** : phisei B, pissei E, physei W, cipisei RS. **timothei** : thimothei W. **iocundidi** : iocundi BW, secundi, iocundi E, secundi RS. **ratidis** : ratitis (rad- W) H. **florii, floritidis** : flori tilis fori BW, flori tilis floriani E, flori S. **anastaciae, anastasii** : anastasi, taciae E, anastasiẹ BW, anastasi R. **sathei** : pathei E, satthei W. **uitalis** : *om.* H. **ieiunarii** : ianuarii E, ianuarii (*bis*) R, *om.* BW, + leuci ER. **felicis** : R, *om.* BW.

Agusti is a mangled place-name. Augustiduno (Autun).
Euchti is misplaced. See Jan. 7.
Taciae (E) may have been originally a marginal correction on *anastasi*.

Jan. 9.

martialis : marcialis H. **quinti** : quinti (*ter*) E. **saturnini** : saturnini (*bis*) H. **saturi** : *om.* EW.

Jan. 10.

militiadis, melciadis : miltiadis E, melchiadis B, melciadis W. **mirti** : mirthae B, in irta E, nirthi W, nirtae S. *fin.* + artatis H, + pauli primi R, + termitii S.

Of the nine personal names recorded in T and H here six are repeated from Jan. 9 H and probably T.

Rom. has, under Jan. 10, "Miltiadis in Callisti," Thus it appears that *Clisti* (Callisti) is the name of a cemetery and is misplaced. This Pope died on 10 or 11 Jan. 314.

Jan. 11.

a(pselam)i · alsolami BW, alo lami E, absalini R, absalmii S. **philoromi, filoroni** : filoromi BERS, piloromi W. **filori** : flori H. **seueri** : *om.* E. **lucii** : leuci H. **ingenui** : *om.* H. **augenti** : agenti EW, **donati** : donati (*bis*) H, + agustini H, + gregorii nazari (-zeni S) BS, + saluii H. **felicis**: felicis (*bis*) W. **eugeni** : + uictoris BW. **felicitatis** : R, *om.* H. **pausalini** : pausami B, pati pausalini E, pausalmi W. **sefa** (   ) : stephanẹ BW, stefani E. **hortensi** : hortinsi (or- W) H. **er** (   ) **ciriaci arab** (   ) **ebiciani** (   ) **castoli** (   ) **modesti** (**castolini** : *om.* H.

Peter Apselamus suffered at Caesarea on 11 or 10 Jan. 310 (see Lawlor-Oulton, *Eus.* i. 377, ii. 331). HRS wrongly state that the martyrdom took place at Alexandria. TR alone indicate that Peter and Apselamus are names of a single person.

Carth. has Saluius on this day.
Of the last ten names of T, at least five are borrowed from Jan. 12.

Jan. 12.

muscenti: moscenti BW, + bonittẹ B. **ciriaci**: cyriaci H. **castuli bis** : castuli, castoli B, castoli (*bis*) E. **quinti** (?) : quinti HS. **ualentianae, (arab)ici** (?) : *om.* H. **ebiciani**: ubiciani B, bicciani E. **petri**: + aventinae (-ini W) H. **corotici**: carotici (gar- B) H. **castulini** : castolini EW. **filorini** : philoromi (phiromi W) H, + zotici (-iui B) H.

Apparently TH have Quintus and Petrus here, which are duplicates of the Quintus and Petrus in TH Jan. 11.

Jan. 13.

satii : satti H. **saturi** : *om.* H. **cymmini** : cymini B, cimini E, *om.* W. **zoticii** : *om.* W. **ciriacii** : cyriaci H. **erisini** : crisi B, herisi E, erisi S, *om.* W. **glicerii** : cliceri BW. **felicis** . *om.* W. **secundi** : secunde

B, + quosquoni enonis B, quosquonio enonis E, quoquomo eo nonis W. **hilarii** : helari B, elari W.
Pictaui is here one of the few place-names given as such in T.

Jan. 14.

gliceri . . . **diaconi, clerici diaconi** : cleri diaconi B, luceri diaconi E, cleridiae W, cliceri diaconi (*bis*) R, glicerii diaconi S. **uictorini** : uicturini BW. **saturi** : saturnini W. **missoris**: misoris E. **lucreti** ; lucriti BW, luctiri E. **agapiti** : S, *om.* H. **crucessii** : *om.* H. **eufrae** : eufrasi BRS, eufraxi W, euphrasi E. **tueus casiae** : theucosiae (theo- E) H.
Syr. has on this day Glycerius the deacon at Nicomedia (not Antioch, as HRS).
Carth. Jan. 14 has Felix of Nola. For Satyrus see *AA.SS.* Jan. 1. 724.

Jan. 15.

supplicii, mauricii (m)aur(i) (   )mi, michiae : *om.* H. **cris-coni** : grisogoni B, crisogoni R. **tirsi** : cyrsi B, tyrsi EW. **mene-laui** : minelampi BW, menelai ER, + cornili BW, corneli ES. **lauci** : leuci BW. **gaunitii** : gainici B, gaginici W, + genonis BWS, zenonis ER. **(ce)lesti** : caelesti (cal- W) H. **lucerti** : liceri (luc- E) diaconi H. **ambucuc** : S, abbacuc BR, ambacu E, abacus W. *fin.* + remedii H, + amanti BW.
Ch. Ch. Mart. and *Drum.* have Abucuc, Supplicius, Maurus and Machias. Mauricius and Maurus are probably a doublet. It is curious that *Syr.* has on Jan. 19 Cosconius, Zenon and Melanippus at Nicaea.
Remedius, Archbishop of Rheims, died about 530.

Jan. 16.

marcelli : + marthe audeini BW, + landoni W. **saturnini bis** : saturnini H. **faustini** : fursei R, fausti S. **ememrriani** : anani mari E. **fabiani** ; frauiani BW, naffaviani E. **honorati honorii** : honorati H.
Calesti and *priscillae* are names of cemeteries. In the latter Pope Mar-cellus was buried, who heads the list. See *Gelasian Sacr.* 162. Marcellus died in 309.
Honoratus, bishop of Arles, died on 14 or 15 Jan. 429 (*D.C.B.* iii. 138).

Jan. 17.

speusepi : speusippi H. **helapi** : helasippi (el- E) H, + melasippi H. **munici, mucci, miccae, micae** : micae B, muci E, nice W, musi R, mutii S. **fortunati** : furtunatae (for- E) H. **teucisii, teusae** : thecuse BW, teussae E. **martini** ; *om.* H. **mistriani** : mistiani B. **sulpicii** : *om.* E. **mesalani** : miseliani H. **uictorici** : uicturici BW. **satae** : sartae E. **iunillae** : S, iunellae BW, innillae E, + neonis BWS, nenonis E, neoris R. **uictoriae** : uicturiae BW. **saturnini** : saturninae B. **hortisiani** : hortisiane B, ortisiani W. **uincentiae** : uincenti BW. **misuriani** : mis-suriani BW. **timosei** : mosei BW, timothei E.
The order of the names in T differs from that of H. H brings together the members of a group of martyrs in Langres (*AA.SS.* Jan. ii. 73) : the *tergemini* (Speusippus, Elasippus and Melasippus), their grandmother Leonilla, a woman named Iunilla and Neon. T gives the names of the first two of the group, omits Melasippus and Neon, and misplaces Leonilla and Iunilla. *Ger-manorum* is an error for *geminorum*.
Micae appears also in the Irish group.

Jan. 18.

mariae : *hiat.* B. **cath. petri** : RS, *hiat.* B. **fortunati** : furtunati BW. **asteri** : + leupardi B. **moysei** : mosei HS, rusei R. **micete** : miceae B, in micea E, micęę W. **senonis** : zenonis H. **zerseni** : zesimi BW, zosomi E. **menelampi** : menelapi E. **dedali** : didali H. **tyrsei** : tyrsi (tir- W)

H. sconisii : sconis E. **luricii** (*bis*) : luci, lurici H. **florinae, floridae** : floride (-ed- W) H. **ualenti** : ualentis H. **bauli** : pauli H. **telariani:** theleriani B, teleriani E, feleriani W. **maluli** : maiuli B, iuli E, marculi W. **uictorini** : uicturini BW. **saturnini** : saturninae H. *fin.* + priscae RS. The first *priscillae* is the name of a cemetery ; the second is that of a martyr.

Jan. 19.

pauli (*bis*) : pauli H. **saturnini bis** : saturnini H. **marii** : mariae H. **gagiae** : gagi BW, gaiae E. **calizae** : calistae H. **priscariae** : picariae H. **tertuli** : zertuli E. **tiberii** : tyberitani B, tiberitani E, tiberiani W. **tanmaioli** : maioli H. **uictoriani** : uicturiani BW. **fortunati** : furtunati BW. **gemanici** : germane (-ani W) H. **marcisii** : marcusii (mor- W) H. **puplii** : publi BW. **casiani** : cassiani H. **uictoris** : uicturis BW. **hispani** : spani E. **cacumari** : ecamari B, cacinari E, cacmari W. **molendionis:** melondionis E. **menelampi** : minelampi BW, menilapi E. **tubartini** : tibariani (tub- E) H. **furtunati** : tortunati E. **sabastiani** : sebastiani BS, *om.* E.
The sequence of the names on this day in T for the most part follows that of H ; but T misplaces eight names between *successi* and *tertuli*. It has all the names in H, and has only one not in H—*pauli senis heremitae*, which is probably a doublet with the *pauli* who is the first in the list. *Tiberii tanmaioli* is a corruption of *tiberitani maioli*.
For *menelampus* see *Syr.* Jan. 19 and note on Jan. 15.
Sebastianus is also found on Jan. 20.
There are eleven names common to TH Jan. 18 and 19.

Jan. 20.

sabastiani : sebastiani BE. **uincentii** : R, *om.* BW. **adaflexi** : audifax B, audefax W, *om.* E, + abacuc B, ambacu E. **mariae** : mari ER. **marthae** : *om.* E. **agnetis** : *om.* EW. **celidonae** : caeledoniae B, celedoniae E, caeledome W, celendonii S. **marciae, marcialis** : marciae H, + tyrsi BS, tarsi E, tursi W. **leonti** (*bis*) : leonti H. **biti, uiti** : biti H. **ciriacii bis, ciriaci** : ciriaci, quiriaci B, ciriaci, kiriaci E, cyriaci, quiriaci W. **gallinici:** galinici H. **candei** : cendei (-di E) HS, + leuci (lu- W) H. **florae:** flori H.
Rom. has " Fabiani in Callisti et Sebastiani in Catacumbas," and *Carth.* has " Sancti martyris Sivastiani." *Calesti* (T) is misplaced ; it is the name of the cemetery in which Fabian was buried. For Fabian and Sebastian see *D.C.B* ii. 440, iv. 593.
The Passion of Marius (*AA.SS.* Jan. ii. 216) places the martyrdom on Jan. 19, and states that the martyrs were Marius and Martha and their sons Audifax and Abbacuc. TBW have Maria for Marius.
Syr. has on this day, at Nicomedia, Leontius, Cyriacus, Cindus, Bitius, Florus and Felix. TH has this group, with some other names, both here and on Jan. 21.
Lugdonagal (Lugduno Gall.), and probably *celidonae* are place names. Tarracona, in Spain, is misplaced ; it belongs to Jan. 21.

Jan. 21.

celsionis : celsiani E. **ciciliani** : caeciliane B, ciciliane W, celiani E. **auguri** : augori E, augerię W. **martialis** : marcialis H. **fulogiae** : fulogi B, fulogicę W, *om.* E. **eulogiae** : elogii B, eologii W, et logii S. **uincentiae** : *om.* BW. **emerentianae, eglinnae** : *om.* H. **agnae** : RS, agnetis BW. **cendeni** : candei (cen- E) H. **flori** : flore B. **puplii** : publi BW. **ciriacii** : cyriaci EW. **uincentis** : *om.* H. **faustaci** : fustaci E. **eustacii** : eostasi BW. **salutoris:** solutoris B, solutaris E. **hermetis** :

et metis W. **augorii** : auguri BW. **uitalis** : RS, *om.* BW. **quintini** : quinti BW. **datii** : dacii W. **rutiri** : saturi (-iri W) H. **gaddani** : gaddiani H. **caeliani** : celiani EW. **seruulii** : zabullii (-uli E) H, + mamas B, mammar E, mammas W. **rogati** : arogati BW. **uictoris** : uicturis B. **maiulini** : maulini E. **nascussi** : marcusi (mae- E) H. **zatii** : gagi BW, gai E. **celestini** : caelestini BE. **hermis** : ermis H.

This day is the day of the Passion of St. Agnes according to the *Gelasian Sacr.*, p. 164. For her second commemoration, see Jan. 27.

Emerantiana was a foster sister of Agnes. She is commemorated on Jan. 23, BS. See *D.C.B.* i. 62, ii. 106, *Drum., Ch. Ch. Mart.*

Diacii is an error for *diaconorum.* The deacons are Augorius and Eulogius (T *eulogiae*). They are after Fructuosus in H. We note that *uincenti arogati* (BW) and *uincentiae rogati* (E) indicate the same persons. Probably BW gives us the true names.

There is reason to believe that TH are seriously corrupt. All of them have borrowed a group of Nicomedian martyrs from Jan. 20 (*q.v.*). Again, among the first few names we find Fructuosus the bishop, and Fulogius (= Eulogius) and Augorius, with support from R and S. Further on are Fructuosus, Eulogius and Augorius. It seems that a person named Vincentius was in each group (see T : *uincentiae, uincentii, uincentis*). This is a doublet. Moreover EW place the first group at Rome and the second at Tarracona, while T (Jan. 20) connects Tarracona with the first group. RS and the *Ch. Ch. Mart.* put it in Spain. The Acts (Ruinart 219) know nothing of any martyrs save the three named above, and they imply that the three did not suffer at Rome, since the magistrate was a praeses.

Jan. 22.

ianuarii bis : ianuari, genuari B, + luberci apodimi BW. **paulini** : puluii (pal- W) H. **martialis** : marcialis EW. **cediani** : caeciliani BW. **booti** : eboti B, eopoti W. **optati** : obtati B. **bellici** : bellici (*bis*) E, *om.* BW. **municipi** : municipio BW, muci E, munici R, minucii S, + quiri gemelli saturi genuari (ian- W) H. **tetotici** : tyci B, techi E, tyrsi W, + flori (*om.* E) orionis (*om.* E, *bis* W) clementis (*om.* E) anastasi (*om.* W) H, + saturnini BWR. **memonis** : memnonis (menn- W) H. **hermetis** : ermetis E, + ianuariae H.

On this day *Carth.* has Vincentius and *Syr.* Clemens.

Jan. 23.

cornelii : cornili BW, + emerentiani (-de S) BS, + donati H. **saturni** : saturnini H. **castuli** : castoli H. **belli minuci** : bellimi nici B, belli munici W, minucii R, belli S. **aquiliae** : aquilae H. **ueterae, secundi** : *om.* H. **basillae** : basilae E. **macarii** : machari H. **papiae** : popiae B, popice W. **clemati** : climati E. **castuli** : castoli E. **neonis** : *om.* BW.

Aquila, the wife of Seuerianus (H), should have been beside him.

Exorcizae is not a martyr but the title of Cornelius the exorcist.

Veterae has its origin in *via salaria veteri* (E).

Galatiae is a place-name (B).

Jan. 24.

babilli : babili B, babilae ER. **mardoni** : marduni H. **eutasii, fustaci** : eustasi BW, eustaci E. **hermetis** : ermitis E. **mussuri** : musuni H. **rupi** : ruppi H. **memae** : mimme B, memmae E, minime W. **pupliani** : publiani B, puplicani E, publicani W. **galei** : + emetri E. **maximi** : *om.* BW. **agniti** : *om.* H. **saturi** : + iabelli H. **gaudiani** : gudodiani BW, sududiani E. **felicissimi** : S, *om.* E. **celiani** : geliani B.

For the confusion between Babylas (T *babilli*) of Antioch (HRS, Oengus, *Drum., Ch. Ch. Mart.*), and Babylas of Nicomedia (*Syr.*), see *Ricemarch*, p. 60. The confusion becomes greater by the fact that T has the place-name *Panes* before *babilli*. Possibly Panes is a corruption of Paneas (Caesarea Philippi) which was wrongly placed before *babilli* instead of *Marini*. See Eus. *H.E.*, vii. 15.

Agniti may be a couplet with *dati*.   In T *agniti* is in the same position as *dati* in H, between *marini* and *saturi*.

Jan. 25.

policarpi, arthemini : *om.* H. uitii, bitii : biti BES, uiti WR, + praeiecti B. secundi : + papiae castulae (ka- E) H. tirsii : tyrsi BW, *om.* E. ypictiti : epictiti B, epitici W, *om.* E. pupliani : publiani BW, *om.* E, + pappiae (papi- W) catine agape BW. faminiani : fauiani (fab- E) H. raumani, rauiani : sauiniani (sab- E) H. sidonis, sadonis : sodonis H. antimasii : antymasius B. sabiani (*bis*) : sabinus (sav- W) H. leodocii : leodotius B, leodocius E, leudocius W. teoginis : theugenis (te- E) H, + agilei ER.

Polycarp appears in *Syr.* Jan. 27, and in THRS, Oengus, Gorman, *Drum.*, *Ch. Ch. Mart.*, Jan. 26. BW seem to regard this Polycarp as the friend of St. Ignatius. But he suffered on Feb. 22 or Feb. 23. See note on Jan. 26.

Artheminus is no doubt the Arthematus of Jan. 26.

Carth. Jan. 25 has Ageleus.

T gives a place-name : Puteoli. Possibly *rauiani* is a corruption of Ravenna. Cp. B : *ravennae poteolis.*

Jan. 26.

policarpi : pilicarpi W. datiui iuliani : *om.* BW. paulae : *om.* EW, + anthemiasius (arth- W) sauinus (-nius W) leudocius (-tius W) BW. telliani : taeliani E, *om.* BW. reotri : E, *om.* BW. rodonis taeliptae (telly- E) uincentiae : *om.* BW, + saturi E. uicturinae (-torinae E). papae : *om.* BW, + canti victoris E. arthemati : arthematis BW, artematis ERS, + armate arthemi fabiani BW. secundi emiliani : *om.* BW. teoginis: theugenis BW, theogenis S, *om.* E. sabinis: sabiani BW, *om.* E, + sidonis BW, sindonis S.

For this day we have two overlapping lists : TE and BWRS. Of the sixteen names in T no more than six have support from BW or RS, and three of these have support from E. Moreover the last seven names in BW appear in the same order in Jan. 25; a fact which suggests corruption in our authorities. The lists of BLW on Jan. 28 are alike with E Jan. 26. See also note on Jan. 27.

Polycarp is called bishop by TBS, and W places his martyrdom at Smyrna, no doubt supposing that he was the famous martyr of the second century. B is more cautious : " *in nicea smirne* " (*sic*). But the date of the Smyrnaean martyr in *Syr.* is February 23, and there is reason to believe that it is approximately correct. See Lawlor-Oulton, *Eus.*, ii. 131 ff. The Polycarp mentioned here and in Jan. 25 is commemorated in *Syr.* Jan. 27.

Jan. 27.

furtunati, fortunatae : fortunati BLW, fortunatae E. agnetis : agnitis E, *om.* LW. tecussae : theucusae BL, theoctise, W. uincentiae : RS, *om.* BWL. uicturiae : uicotriae E, *om.* BLW, + teliptae reotri, papae emeliani S. donati : *om.* BL. uiti : *om.* L. saturnini : *om.* HL. messuriani : missuriani (misu- W) H, *om.* L. puplii : publi BW, pupliae E, *om.* L. uictoris : uictoris (*bis*) BW, *om.* L. quintilli : *om.* L. felicis : felici B. publicani : publiani (pup- E) HL. bonosii : bosoni BLW. egotis : egodditis (god- E) HL. pictuli : epictili (-uli E) HL. hilarii : helari BWL. uictoris : *om.* EL. leoci : leaci (lae- E) HL. dati : R, dauae S, *om.* BWL. iuliani, saturi : RS, *om.* BWL. celiani : R, caeliani E, ciliani S, *om.* BWL. calleniti : calenici BL, calentini E, callenici W.

marosi : matrosi E. **gaii, gagi** : gagi BL, gaii EW, + caelestini BW, caelesti E, celestini L, + sulpici BWL.
The following names in this list appear also in Jan. 26 : *uincentiae, uicturiae (uicturinae), secundi, dati (datiui), iuliani, celiani (telliani), teliptae (tealiptae), reotri, papae, emiliani.*

Jan. 28.
messoriani (*bis*) : messoriani S, censoriani R, *om.* HL. **uictoris** : + emiliani BWL. **festi**: R, festae S, *om.* BWL. **perpetuae** : R, *om.* BWLS. **marinae** : RS, *om.* BWL, + leaci callenidi lucii S. **agnatae** : agnetis BS, agnitis W, agorae ER, *om.* L, + datiui iuliani telliani seotri (sect- L reot-W) BWL. **teliptae** : *om.* ERS. **uincentianae** : uincentiae BWL, *om.* ERS. **canti** : *om.* ERS. **uictoriae** : uicturini BWL, *om.* ERS. **papae** : papiae L, *om.* ERS. **secundi** : *om.* ERS. **infirmi** : *om.* HLRS.
Here, as at Jan. 26, we have overlapping lists ; one represented by BWL, the other by ERS. They agree only on Victor and Agnes. Every name, with the exception of *infirmi* (T only), appears also on Jan. 26 or 27.
Gelasian Sacr. (p. 165) has the second commemoration of St. Agnes on this day. Thus it is misplaced in TR Jan. 27. The title of the Mass is " Item in natali eiusdem de natiuitate." Cp. BE. R has " Natale Agnę de nat(iuitate) genuinum," and E " Agnę ingenuinum." This suggests that *genuinii* (T) is corrupt and misplaced. It is not a personal name.

Jan. 29.
pauli : + papiae L. **ypoliti** : epoliti BWLR, ippolyti E, eppoliti S. **constantini, constantinae** : constanti BRS, constantini EWL.
Constantini and *constantinae* are probably a doublet ; and it is certain that both names are incorrect. The Acts of Constantius (*A A.SS.* Jan. ii. 925 ff.) agree with BRS.
Papias appears in L, Gorman, *Ch. Ch. Mart.*, Jan. 29.
Pevosiae and *treveris* are place-names : Perugia and Trèves.

March 12.
grigorii : gregorii H (gri- E). **muridani epi.** . mirdani prb. E, *om.* BW. **egoni**: egdoni B eggedoni W. **donatae**: domne BW. **basilissae filiae cionis** : baselisse (-ll- W) uxoris felicionis BW. **alaxandri** : alexandri BW. **iohannis** : neonis BS, neonas, iohannis W, + andi (-dini E) HS. **siluani** : saluiani W. **maci** : marii H. **migdoni** : migdoni (*bis*) H. **dorothi** : dorothei H. **gorgoni** : + orion (arionis E) petuni firmi (confirmi E) pauli carpi agatoni (-atho-E) H. **macedoni** : + patricie (-ci E) modesti domiciani (-tiani E) zosimi (*om.* E) eustasi H + basi E. **eunci** : eutici BW, euneni E. **maximi** . maximę W. **iouiani** : iuuiniani W. **ilarii** : hilarii (hil-, hel-) (*bis*) H. **marias** : mareas (-si E) H. **pioni** : pionis W, + metrodi B, petrodi E. **smragdi** : zmargdi E, + uingelusi B, evenguli E, uingelosin W. **eradi eracli, zefani felicis pilippi antonii** : *om.* H.
Pope Gregory I died on 12 March 604, and Pope Innocent I on 12 March 417.
Syr. Mar. 12 has nine martyrs. Eight of them appear in T : Mardonius presbyter (T *muridani epi.*, E *mirdani prbi.*), Migdonius, Dorotheus, Maximus Petrus, Hilarius, Smaragdus and Eugenius. The ninth, Domna, is found in BW.
For *basilissae filiae cionis*, see March 13.
Gorgonius appears in HS March 11, and in TH March 12. *Syr.* gives the correct day : March 11. For Gorgonius, Dorotheus and Petrus see *Eus. H.E.* viii. 6.
Spirnae is not a person, but the city of Smyrna, where Pionius suffered during the Decian persecution. See Gebhardt, p. 96, Lawlor-Oulton, *Eus.* ii. 136.

March 13.

macedoni : machedonii (-cadonis E) H. **patriciae** : matriciae W, patricii S. **modestae** : modestae, modesti H, modesti S. **chioni, cioni** : cioni BE, cyrion W. **silui, saliui** : salui H. **petroni** : petruni H. **castacii** : eustasi (ci- E) H. *fin.* + basillisse *etc.* H.

This list is parallel with the beginning of a list of Nicomedian martyrs in H. H has a long list of martyrs of Nicaea, Thessalonica and Nicomedia. R has no mention of our list, but gives a few names of the Nicaeans. S has six of our list and two of the Nicaeans.

Syr. Mar. 13 has a martyr named Modestus in agreement with S ; while TH has *filiae modestae*. This suggests that the text is corrupt. Moreover in March 12 we find *in asia. .. macedoni patricie (-ci E) modesti prbi*. H. This is obviously the same group of martyrs, on a wrong day and in a wrong place, yet (with *Syr.* S) having *modesti* instead of *filiae modestae*. Other indications might be mentioned in proof of the unsoundness of March 12, 13 ; but two are sufficient. In both we have the sequence, *zosimi eustasi basilissae* (H). Again in March 12 we find *modesti prbi. . . . basilisse uxor. felcionis (filiae cionis* E) H ; and in March 13, *modeste filiae eius cioni (cyrion* W) *prbi. . . . patrie uxor. eius claonii (om.* W) *patifrigie (party fr.* W) *it. basselisse claonii (om.* B) BW and *modestini . . . patrae claoni patyrrigiae it. basilissae* E. It is clear that in March 13 there are several duplications, and that one of the two lists has invaded its neighbour. The ease with which names take their forms is shown in *felcionis, filiae cionis, cioni, chioni, cyrion, claonii.*

March 14.

dionisii *(bis)* : dionisii BE, *om.* W. **alaxandri** : alexandri BW, alaxandri E. **pionis** : epionis B. **furmini** : frunimi E. **alaxandri** *(sec.)*: alexandri BW, alaxandri *(bis)* E. **eufrosii felicissimi datiui, saluatoris, hursiniae, rabae, faustae** saluae ingenuae, lucae iacobi, lucii *etc.* : *om.* H. **frontinae** : florentini S. **dionae** *(bis)* : dione H. **pelliotae, palidi pallitani** : palatini BES, *om.* W. **innocentii** : *om.* W. **eufrasiae** : efrasi B, eufrasi EW. **naborii** : naboris H, + comes B, comis E. **frontoni** : frontonis H. **firmini** : fronimi B, frunini E, frunimi W, + leonis B, + nicomedi (-ꭇ E -die W) H.

Faustae, etc., noted here as omitted by H, belong to March 15, and six of the names are repeated there in T.

Syr. has Fronton, a martyr at Thessalonica, on this day. B places him at Nicomedia, and EW in Africa.

March 15.

iacobi ap. : *om.* W. **lucii** : lucini W, + fauste BW, ficustae R. **salui, silui** : siluii H. **pauli** : pauli *(bis)* E, + solutoris (sal- E), alexandri (alax- E) theofili (-phili B teo -E) octaui theodoli petruni *(bis* E) H. **saturnini, spinosi innocentii** efiro : *om.* H. **ingenuae** : ingenui E. **reguli** : riguli E, *om.* BW.

T describes Jacobus as apostle and brother of the Lord. Cp. Gal. i. 19. But he was not one of the Twelve. See Acts xii. 1, 2, and Eus., *H.E.* ii. 23.

Longinus is said to have been the soldier who pierced the Lord's side (John xix. 34). See *AA.SS.* Mar. ii. 381 ff. See Oct. 23.

March 16.

hilarii : helari BW. **titiani tasiani bis** : tatiani B, tasiani datiani EW. **castoris** : castori H. **dionisii bis** : dionisi H, dionis S. **noni** : nonni H. **sireni, sereni bis** : sereni HS, sereni *(bis)* R. **eugenii, eugeniae** : eugeniae H, eugenii RS. **iouani** : iuueni E, iouuiani R. *om.* BW. **amphi, sampiliani** : pampini BW, pampiliani E, pamphiliani RS, + cassionis (casso- E) H. **curiacae** : quiriace, cyriace BW, ciriacae,

ciriaci E, quiriaci S. **ascliophidoti** : ascipiodoti BW, asclepiodoti E.
mariae, grignei : *om.* H.
  Hilarius was bishop of Aquileia, and his archdeacon was Tatianus.
Their companion martyrs were Felix, Largus and Dionysius (*AA.SS.* Mar.
ii. 418). One of the two named *dionisii* in T may be the last of the three.
  Eugeniae et aliorum x indicates a group of martyrs. They are probably
the ten given in TH : *castoris dionisii noni sireni eugenii iuliani iouani* (*om.* BW)
curiacae milisae ascliophidoti. They are a group in H under Nicomedia. But
be it noted that *Syr.* has no commemorations on this day, and that RS
divides our ten into two groups.

March 17.

  patricii : RS, *om.* EW. **mariae** : + quiriaci B. **uictorinae, uictorini**:
uicturine (-orini E) H, uicturini S. **ciriacae** : cyriacae H. **ianari** :
ianuarii H, ianuariae R. **largii largi** : largi H. **ilarii** : hilari (he- W) H.
titiani: ticiani W, + catoni B, caton W, datiani B, datiui W. **alaxandri**:
alexandri BW, *om.* E. **zefani, petri** : *om.* H. **teodoli** : theodoli BW, theo-
dori S, *om.* E.
  Seven names are misplaced here. Six are duplicates of March 16 :
Maria, Cyriaca, Nonna, Hilarius, Tatianus and Dionysius. Largus, a com-
panion of Hilarius, should have been recorded on March 16.

March 18.

  collegi : collectici ES, colestici R. **pamporii** : pamponi E, + parilis
E. **ninepti** : minepti H. **rogati** : rogati (*bis*) H, + samphorini B,
samproni W. **mariae** : + pymeni B. **rogatae** : rogati, rogate H. **aure-
liae** : aurili E. **saldae** : saldię E. **quartildae** : quartille H, + luciani
(-asi E) H. **coloti** (*bis*) : coloti H. **capilidae, capilledi** : cappelledi B,
capillidi E, capelledi W. **quartini** : quarti WS. **saturi** : + quintasi H.
marini : maniri B. **ingenui** : RS, ingenuae EW. **aurelii** : aurili H, +
saturnini uictoris mauri currenti (*om.* E) H. **dionisii** : + ianuarii uictoris
uogonocti (convoti E vogonucti W) samfori (simp- E, samph- W) H. **seruuli** :
seluoli BW, servili, servoli E, + quinti H. **honorii** : *om.* H. **ierolii** :
iemsoli BW, *om.* E. **tithei** : timothei (thi- W) H. **martii** : manti E.
  Of the fourteen names in H, and omitted here, six appear in T March 19.

March 19.

  ioseph : S, *om.* H. **grigorii** : *om.* BW. **teodori** : theodori prb.
BWRS, theodori epi. E. **basi** : bassi H. **bucelli** : lucelli H, lucillae S.
fisciani : visciani E, fissiani S. **auxilii, britoniae, rogatae, auxulae,
collectici aprilis seruuli, ingenui dionisii ianuarii uago uictorii nuncti
samfori rogati** : *om.* H. **poemi** : pomeni (-ri B) HS. **iosepi** : ioseri BW,
iosippi E. **basillae, bassilii** : basiliae (bass- B) H, + theodori epi. (prb. E)
catulini (ga- W) leonti H. **uonechtae** : uonoetę B, vonectae E, bonoetae W.
apollonii . appolloni E. **quinti** : quinti quintili B, quinti quintilli E,
quinti W. **quartillae** : quartilli E.
  Syr. has here Bassus.
  Twelve names appear here which are also found on March 18. *Uago
uictorii nuncti* is a curious doublet with *uonechtae.*
  Auxilii is no doubt Auxilius, a disciple of St. Patrick. See *Drum.*
March 19. The name is repeated as Auxilinus in the Irish group.
  Gorman has here Quintus, Quintilla, Quartilli, Auxaile, Marcus and
Joseph.

March 20.

  iosephi (*bis*) : ioseph H. **quirilli** : cyrille B, cirilli E, cyrilli WS,
aquerilli R. **tygini** : tigrini H. **exsuperi** : exuperi EW. **uictorini**: uictorici

(-tur- W) H. **ualentini**: ualenti W. **domini**: domni BE, *om.* W. **teodori** . . **¡**
commodi . . **tillae** . . . **florentii policroni parmeni helii crisotheli
lucae** : *om.* H. *fin.* + uulframni BW, + benigno W, + cuthberti E.
  The names *teodori* . . . *florentii* appear in TH March 19, with the excep-
tion of *commodi, tillae, leotini* and *sorentii.* Leotini is probably a corruption
of Leontius (Aug. 19, 20).
  Polychronius, bishop of Babylon, appears here in Oengus. He is
commemorated in E and *Ch. Ch. Mart.* Feb. 17.

March 21.

  serapionis bis : serapionis. **iosephi** (*bis*) : ioseppi (-ippi E) H.
uoluntiani, uolusii : uolusiani B, uolutiani W, uolusi ERS. **policarpi,
filocarpi** : policarpi S, philocarpi B, filocarpi E, phylocarpi W, filocarphi R.
pauli quirilli grigorii . . **domini olimpiacis maximi, momatiae
monachi** : *om.* H. **filocali** : R, philocali B, filicali E, phylocali W, + cotini
B, gothini E, chotini W, + honis (bio- E) nomini luci (lo- E) H.
  The second Serapion may be the bishop of Thmuis. See *AA.SS.* Mar. iii.
260. *Syr.* has Serapion on March 19.
  T repeats *pauli* . *domini* from March 20. Gregory I (among the rest)
is mentioned here because he wrote the life of St. Benedict in his *Dialogues.*
See *Drum.* Mar. 21.

March 22.

  secundi : RS, *om.* BW. **paulini, pauli** : paulini ER, pauli BW.
dreconi : decroni H. **aronis, orionis** : arionis BE, arionis (*bis*) S, orionis
W, aroris R. **serapionis** . **felicis** : *om.* H.
  Oengus has Secundus.
  *Serapionis iosippi, uolusi philocati filocarpi, uolutiani, ammonis ammoni,
amatoris* are repeated from T, March 21 ; and from H March 21, *contii* (*cotini*),
honis, nomini luci. There seems to be no support for *iacobi acclusi, felicis.*

March 23.

  init. + fidelis theodori (-oli B) H. **felicis secundi paulini arionis,
saturnini** : *om.* H. **agatani, agatii** : agacius B, agatini E, agatius W.
alaxandri : alexandri E. **augustini** : *om.* H. **tinomi** : phiomoli B,
thimodoli E, thyomoli W, thimioli S. **dionisii** : dionisii (*bis*) H. **felicis** :
fidelis EW. **dreconii orionis felicis zefani albini laurentii teodoriae** :
om. H.
  T borrows *felicis secundi paulini aronis, saturnini, dreconii orionis* from
March 22. *Zefani albini laurentii teodoriae* have no support.
  Cessariae is apparently a place-name. See note on March 24.

March 24.

  agapiti : agapi E, agabi R. **albini, ambrosii** : *om.* H. **timolaii,
molei** : timolai E, molai BW. **romuli** (*bis*) : romuli E, romoli BW. **diopi**
(*bis*) : diophi (-pi E, -phy W) H, + cyri B, cyrini S. **catulae bis** : catulae
H. **aprilis** : aprelis E. **saturnini** : saturnini (*bis*) H. **sali, salitoris** :
salitoris H. **pisoni** : phison B, physon W. **alaxandri** : alexandri BW.
uictorini : uicturini H. **uiti** : uti BW, auti E. **sancdioli** : coliondole
(-nidolae E) H. **secunduli** : secundole B, secundoli W. **ueroli** : ueruli H.
felicis : + saturnini soreces (socrecis E) H, + abatae E.
  Albini may be a repetition from March 23. *Aliundo* is a corruption of
Aliunde.
  Eusebius (*M.P.* 3. 3, 4) tells us of a group of martyrs who were beheaded
at Caesarea on 24 March 305. They were Timolaus, Dionysius (2), Romulus,
Paësis, Alexander (2) and Agapius. Here TH has Timolaus, Romulus and
Alexander ; and *Pisoni, Diopi* and *Agapiti* may be corruptions of Paësis,
Dionysius and Agapius. The two groups appear to be identical. But H has

Africa as the place of the martyrdom. However we find a similar group in H March 23: " In civitate Caesareae Agatius Alexandri Fidelis Thyomoli Dionisi it. Dionisi." Here we have six of the names (*fidelis* = Paësis), Caesarea instead of Africa, and a wrong date. Apparently T March 23 has wrongly appropriated *cessariae, agatani, agatii, alaxandri, tinomi, dionisii felicis.*

March 25.

iacobi : *om.* W. **immolatio isaac** : *om.* EW. **cartulae, castoli** : castulae (-li E) H. **eufatae, eufratae** : eufratae (euph- E, -thę W) H. **caustratae, nicustratae** : nicostrati H. **teodolae** : theodolae EW, *om.* B. **lucellae** : + teclę B. **uictorini** : uicturini H. **alaxandri** : alexandri BW. **iunii** : iuuini BW, *om.* E.

Neither *Ancilla* nor *Dule* (*Syr.*) is a personal name. Both mean "slave."

March 26.

castoli : castuli H. **montani** : munati BW. **patri** : + sarmate (sarmataeme W) H. **mariae, hermes** : *om.* H. **marci** : marciani BE, martiniani W. **saluatoris, saluatoris bis** : solutoris (-uris E) H. **timothei** : thimothei W. **teodori** : theodori (theu- W). **iereni** : hirini BW, hereni E. **serapionis** : sirapionis W. **ammonii** : ammomi E, amon W. **uictorini uictoris**: uictor̄ B, uictoris E, uictoriis W. **madiariae**: machariae BE. **maximae** : maximi W.

Syr. has here Marcianus.

March 27

acuti : aguti B. **successi** : *om.* W. **romuli** : romoli BW. **miriae misiae** : missę B, misiae E, missiae WS. **successae** : successi W. **marioli** : mauroli BES, maroli W, maurili R. **doti, donati** : donate B, doti E, donati WS. **alexandri** : alaxandri E, *om.* W, + solutoris BE. *Solutoris* is borrowed from March 26 (T *saluatoris*).

March 28.

mariae magdalenae : *om.* H. **successi** : RS, *om.* H. **alexandri** : alaxandri E. **mariae** : RS, *om.* BW. **audachtae** : audacte BW, audate E, audacti S. **guntari miniregis** : guntramni regis B, guntherampni regis W, *om.* E. **grigorii pronati** : *om.* H. *fin.* + dagoleiphi B, dagelephi R.

St. Mary Magdalene appears in Oengus on this day, and a gloss states that it is "the feast of her conversion to Christ."

Guntramn, king of Burgundy, died in 593. Gregory of Tours was his friend, and perhaps for that reason was mentioned here in T.

March 29.

liberii, teucri medicii, iuliae, ordinatio grigorii grigorii nazareni: *om.* H. **uictorini** : uicturini BW. **dolae** : R, dori W. **iulianae iuliani** : iulianae EW, iuliani B, + theodori (te- E, *om.* W) p(o)entalis iuliani HS. **achatiae** : acacie BW, achaiae E.

For the Ordination of Gregory (Thaumaturgus), see *D.C.B.* ii. 732b. See also Lawlor-Oulton, *Eus.*, ii. 221 f.

Oengus places Gregory of Nazianzus here, and his glossator makes the same confusion as T between Gregory of Nazianzus and Gregory the Illuminator of Armenia.

March 30.

domnini domnini : domni R. **pillo poli** : philopholi, fylipoli B, philopoli, philipuli E, phylopholi, filippoli W, filippoli R, philopoli S. **achaici tacaici** : acaci BWS, archaici E, iacaici R, + austasi niceci R. **liberi, lini, eufeniae, benedicti** : *om.* H. **pallatini** : palatini H. **uictoris**

marcellini : *om*. E.   **satuli** : satulli BW, *om*. E.   **crusis** : *om*. E.
agathoniae : agatonię (agad- E -thomę W) H.
Pillo poli may be a town named Philippopolis.
The Acts of Achatius (Ruinart, p. 152, Gebhardt, p. 115) state that his
examination took place on March 29, in the reign of Decius.
For *austasi niceci* see April 2.
Auriliani is a place-name (Orleans).

March 31.

    annisii : anesi H, + ambrosi R.   **teodoli** : diodoli H.   **pauli uictoris,
mariae eufemiae, iohannis** : *om*. H.   **protidae** : porti BWS.   **corneliae** :
cornilie H, + ualeriae H, + uuandoni ansberti uulframni W.   **abdae** :
S, *om*. E.
For *ambrosi* see April 1.
R has *natali vii uirginum martirum*. H has only four female martyrs.
T has six : *protidae   . abdae*.

April 1.

    mariae : R, *om*. BW.   **agapae** : agapis E, acapis, agapae S.   **erennae,
herenei** : herenei (-nę B) H, hereni, herenei S.   **maii, brigitae, ambrosii** :
om. H.   **ingenianae, ingeniani** : ingenianae (-ni E) H.   **partini** : parteni E.
pantenei : parteni (-emi E) H.   **uictoris** : uictoris (*ter*) H.   **alaxandri** :
alexandri BW.   **secundi bis** : secundi H.   **zefani** : stephani (-nae E) H.
dionisi : diunisi B.   **pantini paterni** : panteri (-theri E) H.
    St. Mary is on this day in Oengus, but the glosses connect it with her
visit to Elizabeth, not as T with her nativity.
    Syr. has Agape and Chionia on April 2 at Thessalonica, and their
passion (Ruinart p. 392) agrees. But H here places their martyrdom in
Heraclea. See, however, April 5.
    Ambrose of Milan died in the night between April 4 and 5, 397, and he
is commemorated on April 4 in BS. R places him on March 31.

April 2.

    amphiani : amfiani E, amifani R.   **proculi** (*bis*) : proculi H.   **satuli** :
satulli BW.   **teodoli** : theodoli H.   **ciriacii** : cyriaci BE.   **agathopi** :
agathopidiae E, agathophi W.   **proculae** : *om*. E.   **ciricae** : quiriaci BW,
ciriacae E.   **procliuiae, amisiani dioscori** : *om*. H.   **marcisii mastisii** :
mastissi B, mastesi E, mastisi W.   **puplii** : publi BW.   **orbani** : urbani W.
agapitis bis : agapitis (-etis E) H.   **dionisii** (*bis*) : dionisi EW, diunisi B.
gomisii : zonisi H.   **nicae** : niceti BRS, nici E, niceci W.   **austasii** :
om. BW.   **gordiani** : gortoniani BE.
    Eus. *M.P.* 4 has a martyr named Amphianus on 2 April 306. But he
was not an African, and he suffered at Caesarea. Cp. note on March 24.
    BW indicate that there was a group of martyrs : *marcellini satulli saturnini
quiriaci reginae proculae et aliorum iiii*. E has the same sequence, omitting
reginae proculae. R has *proculae reginae et aliorum iiii*. Assuming that
reginae is a title, rather than a personal name, we may regard the first four
names in H as the *alii iiii* and Procula the leader. T has all the names, but
one is displaced (Satulus), and others are intruders (Teodolus and Agathopus).
T also has *uiii* instead of *iiii*, and has severed *reginae proculae* from *ciriacii*.
    Macidoniae is a place-name.
    Nicetius Archbishop of Lyons died in 573. Austasius is the abbot
Eusthasius, successor of St. Columbanus at Luxovium (B. Krusch, *Jonae
vitae sanctorum*, p. 240). They are commemorated in R March 30.

April 3.

    benigni bis : benigni, benigne BE.   **agathae, meri, meriti** : agate
mereti B, agathę, meriti W, agâthae, merii S, agathemeri E.   **sinnidiae** :

om. **B. teosiae** : theodosie (theu- B) H, + donati H. **cresti** . christi B, chresti E, chiristi W, + aresti *etc.* H. **euagristi** : euagaristi E, ugaristi R. *om.* BW. **amphiani** : + agape chioniae B, + patricii H. **pauli** , **puplii** . . . **palatini** : *om.* H.

BEW have two martyrs, *euageri* and *benigni* (-*ne*) at Tomi, both at the beginning and the end of the present list. T notes the fact by the word *bis* after *benigni*.

Syr. has Chrestus and Pappus, who suffered in the city of Tomi, the capital of Scythia Minor. We infer that *tomae* was a place-name, and that Syciana (B), Sicilia (E), Sicia (W) and perhaps Sinnidia (ET) are attempts to write Scythia.

The names *agathae* and *meri* are fused together in E (*agathemeri*). There is a similar fusion of Euagrius and Crestus in T (*euagristi*) and R (*uagaristi*).

Of the nine names which are here omitted in H, seven re-appear in T April 4. Puplius is found in TH April 2 and Palatinus in H April 4.

April 4.

teodoli : theodoli H. **agathopi** : agathoni EW, agathopili S. **urbani** : orbani H. **successiae** : successi BW. **iulianae** : iuliani BW, + palatini H, + ambrosi BS. **quintiliani** : + publii (pup- E) H.

Syr. April 4 has Theodulus and Agathopus.

Instead of *successi iuliani* (April 3) we have here *successiae iulianae.*

April 5.

marciani (*bis*) : marciane BW, mariani S. **nicanoris, nicandri, nicanoris** : nicanoris H. **apollonii** (*bis*) : apolloni H. **herennae**: herenae (-rae B) H. **agape** : agamae E, + liciae (lu- E) H. **pauli** : plauti ER, plauii S, *om.* BW. **hireni** : irenis ER, *om.* BW. **traci** : taraci H. **probi** (*bis*): probi BW, *om.* E. **anfiani** : amfiani ES, *om.* B. **andronici** : antronici B. **karuli, babilli, fatuelis** : H.

Syr. has here Claudianus and Didymus, Alexandrian martyrs. H has Claudianus in Nicomedia and Didymus in Alexandria.

For Tarachus and Probus see May 13 and Oct. 11.

Gorman has Marcianus, Nicandrus, Fatuel, Claudianus, Apollonius, Irene and Amphianus. *Drum.* has Licia and Amplianus.

Chionia, Ireni and Agape are out of place. See April 1.

Scetha is Scythia.

April 6.

herensi berenei : berenei B, herenei EWS, hireni R, + hymnari B, imari E, himnari W. **firmi** : sirmi E. **quartilae** : quartille H. **ciriacii** : quiriaci BW, kyriaci E. **moysi** : morsi E. **rufinae** : rosinae E, rofinę, W. **successiae** : successi H. **florentii, florentini** : florentini H. **geminiani** : germiniani B. **epifani** : epyfani B, epefani W. **serapionis** : serafionis BW. **teodori** : theodori (theu- B) H. **romani bis** : romani, romane (*bis*) H. **gaii** : gagi H. **donati** : donati BE, donatę, donati W. **uictoris** : uictori E. **xixti** : sixti (*bis*) B, syxti (*bis*) E, xisti, xysti W. **timothei** : thimothei W, + diogenis (-ginis E) H. **ciri** : quiriace BW, cyriacae E. **zefani, ambrosii**: *om.* H. *fin.* + clusi timothei (thi- W) machariae martiae (margae E marthae W) maximę (*om.* E), herenei (hir- E -ni W), ammoni (-nis E, *om.* W) summistę (iuni mis- E suminis- W) apricii (par- W) uictoris marinae teguliani (eg- B) H.

Syr. April 6 states that Irenaeus, the bishop, suffered in the city of Sirmium and Cyriace at Nicomedia. Here Irenaeus is represented by *herenei* (EWS) ; Sirmium by *sirmi* (E), changed into *firmi* by the other authorities, and regarded as a personal name ; and Cyriace by *ciriacii*. For Irenaeus see Gebhardt, p. 162, and Ruinart, p. 404.

Xixtus is Pope Sixtus I.

TALLAGHT. L

April 7.

eleusii (*bis*) : eleusi H. **pelussi philosii** : pelusi BWS, peleusi E, pelosi R. **ciriacis** : R, cyriacis E, cyriaci S, *om.* BW. **dioginis** : diogenis H. **macariae** : machariae H. **capricae** : copricae BW. **firmani** : *om.* H. *Siriae, libiae, superioris* are place-names : Syria and Libya superior. *Syr.* has the presbyter Peleusius at Alexandria.

April 8.

connexi : conexi (-ci W) H, cornexi S. **ianuarii** : RS, *om.* BW. **macarii micarii maiori** : machari HRS. **concesii, concessae** : concessi WS, concessae BR, concessae concessi E. **saluatoris** : solutoris H. **maximae bis** : maximae H, maximi S. **pinnari** : pmari W. **ammoni** . S, *om.* W. **regani** : *om.* H. **timothei** : timori (thi- W -ris S) HS.

Ianuarius appears in Oengus April 8. *Syr.* has Maxima and Timotheus (not Timorius) at Antioch on the same day. It is probable therefore that Timotheus is correct, in spite of the fact that HS place Timorius in Africa. Cp. notes on March 24, April 2.

April 9.

uii uirgines : RS, u. uirgines EW. **dimetri** : demetri BE, dimitri W. **hilarii** (*bis*) : heracli B, helari S, hilari EW. **macharii** : mari H. **fortunati** : furtunati H. **donati** : *om.* E. **saturi, quadrati** : *om.* H. **uirginum u** : vii uirginum canonicarum (-corum E) H. **piloti** : poliucti (-icti W) H.

Syr. April 9 : " At Sirmium Demetrius."
Dedici is not a personal name : it has its origin in *dedicatio oraturii* (BW). *Simmimonis* is a corruption of Sirmium.
For *piloti   remanel* see Oengus : " The triumph of seven innocent holy virgins . whose blood it is that does not perish on the fair feast of Quadratus."
Donatus is apparently misplaced in BW before *et uii uirginum*. He is omitted in E, and appears after *uirginum septem* in S. In T he follows *aliorum uii*. These " other seven " may be the virgins. Thus we suggest that the correct reading is " *Fortunati et uii uirginum canonicarum   donati."*

April 10.

apollonii : appolloni BE, + granii H. **ilarii** : helari (hil- E) H. **saturnini** : *om.* W. **pinnadi, pinnadii** : pennadi B, pinnadi E, *om.* W. **teodori** (*bis*) : theodori BE, *om.* W, + gaviani E. **donatae** : donati BW. **concessae** : concessi BW, + domnini W. **successae** : successi B, *om.* W. **mariae** : *om.* H. **marcelne** : marcellę BE, *om.* W. **gagiani** : gaiani ES, *om.* W. *fin.* + syagrii S.
Syr. has " In Alexandria Apollonius."
Repensi diaconi is probably a corruption of *Dacia Ripensi* (S). *Tracia* (BE) might easily be confused with *dacia*, and *dacia* with *diac.*
It is possible that *gagiani* (TB), *gaiani* (ES), *granii* (*H*) and *gaviani* (E) are various spellings of one name.
Domnini (W) and *syagrii* (S) belong to April 11.

April 11.

hilarii maximi : *om.* W. **concessi** (*bis*) : concessi *om.* W. **dominni** : domnini BE, *om.* W. **petri iohannis mariae, teclae, ruphi** : *om.* H. **fortunatae, fortunati** : furtunati BW, fortunatae E, + donati (-tae E) H. **domitionis** : dominionis BE, domionis W. **eustorgii** : eostorgi E. **nestoris** : *om.* W. **filonis** : filoni BW, filonti E, + ceremoniae siagri (sy- W) H. **patricii** : + leonis papę, B.

Syr. April 11 says that Domnion suffered at Salona, which T calls Salonia. See also *Anal. Boll.* xviii. 399.
Dalmathae and *dalmathi* are corruptions of Dalmatia.
Gorman has Pope Leo here.

April 12.

isaac : isac W. **agothonis** : agatonis (-ni W) H. **musculae** : mustilę W. **noueliae** : nouellae BE, *om.* W, + ianuariae (-ri E) siluani muciani BE. **puplii** : publii BW. **mauri** : + hertule *etc.* H. **proclinae, celsi, annodi zefani** : *om.* H. **cipriani** : cypriani B, *om.* W.

B has more than a hundred personal names on this day. T has only 21. They are the Pope Julius, four martyrs at Pergamum, four (out of seven) at Capua, nine of a long list under the heading *alibi*, and three who are omitted in H. The remaining names of H are neglected in the collation above.

Julius died on 12 April 352. In T the Pope is removed from his original place to the head of the list, leaving the note of his deposition. It probably ran, " In uia Aurelia procliua (*proclinae* T) miliario iii in coemeterio Calepodii ad Callistum " (cp. B). Hence the seeming personal names *proclinae calepodi.*

April 13.

eucarpiae : eucapi BS, eucarpi E, eucapię W. **bassae** : passe BW. **parurae, leonitidis** : *om.* H. **castonicae, agathonicae** : azatonicae (ag- B) H. **pauli** : pauli (*bis*) H. **karuli** : catuli BS, caruli EW. **ianuariae** : ianuarii H. **policarpi** : pulicarpi B. **arobi** : aro W.

Agathonice, Paulus and Karulus are Pergamene martyrs (Eus. *H.E.* iv. 15, 48), whose names are curiously mangled. The correct names are Carpus, Papylus and Agathonice (Eus., H.E. iv. 15, 48, Gebhardt, p. 13). Carpus is called Cyrillus (*Syr.* Ap. 13), Carulus and Catulus (above). Papylus is called Paulus (*Syr.*, H March 12 and above), Papias (*Chron. Pasch.*, p. 481) and Papirius (Rufinus, *H.E.* iv. 15, 48, Gorman Ap. 13). Agathonice appears as Agatonius (H March 12) and Azatonice (above). The three suffered c. 170 (Lawlor-Oulton, *Eus.* ii. 137).

Accoli is a title : acolyte.
For *calipodi* see April 12.

April 14.

tiburtii (*bis*) : tiburtii (tiuor- W) H. **marciae** : marciae (*bis*) H. **corneliae** : corniliae (*bis*) H. **fortunatae, donati, ualenti** . *om.* H. **dominae** : domninae B. **maximi bis** : maximiani, maximi E, + decimę BW, docimi, deceniae E, + appolloni E, neapollonis R, appolonii S. **ciriaci** : quiriaci BW, cyriaci E. **prontii bis** : frontini (*ter*) B, frontini, frontoni (*bis*) E, fruntinę, frontuni W. **canditoris** : conditoris H. **produci** : prosduci BW, producti E, + landiberti W. **liurni** : liorni B, uurni W. **archilai** : arcilai BE. **foebi** : fevi E, *om.* BW. **simfronii** : simproni BR, simphroni, simproni E, sinproni W. **ualenti** : ualentini H. **optati** : optati (*bis*) H. **saturnini** : saturnini (*bis*) BE saturnini, saturni W.

For Tiburtius, Valerianus and Maximus see *Acta. s. Caeciliae* (Surius, vi. 505) and *Liber Pontificalis*, i. 509, ii. 55 f.

Apati, romae pretextati are the remains of " Romae uia Appia in cimiterio Praetextati " (B).

Probably neither *dioclitiani* nor *tituli* was the name of a saint or martyr. See R, as amended (*in titulo ciriaci iuxta* [*thermas*] *diocletianas*), and *Ricemarch*, p. 72. For the word *titulus* see *D.C.A.* ii. 1966.

April 15.

mossitis : mosętis B, mositis EW. **archilaii** . arcilai BE, archelai W, + comati (-tis E) H. **cipriani** : cypriani BW, + uironicę H. **lotae tertiae, leonidis** : *om.* H. **dionicae** : dioninę B, dominae E, deoninę W,

L 2

+ octauię H. **potamicae** : potamię BH, pomiae E. **predentii** : prodenti
BW, praditi E, + arcilai (arch- W) potami lupei (-perci E, -berci W)
apomidi (-odimi B -odemi W) H. **dioginis diac.**: diogenis diac. H, +
prosdoci (-uci E, prusduci W) uironicę (-niaę W) H. **felicis** : felicis (*bis*) BW.
marciani bis : marciani martiani W. **fortunati** · furnati W. **luciani** :
+ georgii (-giae E gi- W) germani (*om.* E) H.

    Lotae tertiae leonidis appear in H Ap. 16. TH have the group of martyrs
felicis   luciani on both April 15 and 16.

April 16.

    carisae : R, carissi (*bis*) H, + lotae (lu- B) leonedis (-idis E) tertie
(-ciae W) H. **christianae** : + gallae (ca- B) H. **calistae** : calisti (-esti
B) H. **teodorae** : theodorae (-osiae E) H. **gallidae, calliniae** : gallinie
(-nicę W) H. **niciae** : nicę H. **monicae** : moniciae (mun- B) H. **basiliae** :
basilii B. **leonidis** : leonedis (-ni- E) H. **uincentii** (*bis*) : uincentii BW:
caritonis, cantonis : caritonis B, cantoris E, caritoni W. **marciani bis** :
marciani H. **martirialis** : martialis E, *om.* BW. **antonii, eniani** :
antani E, aniani B, eniani W. **martialis** : marcialis H, + felicis fausti
felicis furtunati H. **siluani** : saluani B. **lucani** : luciani H, + goamali
(gom- E guam- W) parcilai (-ati B), micae gallieni, faustini luciani H.
calisti : calestę B caelesiae E calistę W.

    Syr. states that Leonidas and eight others suffered martyrdom at Corinth
on April 16. H gives their names as follows : *calisti carissi lotae leonidis tertiae
christianae calle (gallae) theodorae (-osiae) carissi*, nine in all. Eight of them
are in T April 15, 16.

    Lectoris is a title, and *cenobieris* (*colloliveris* ER) is probably a place

April 17.

    furtunati : fortunati E. **quinti** : *om.* W. **marciani** (*bis*) : marciani
H. **baruci** : barrucci B, barucci E. **mapolicii** : mappalici H. **galli** : +
theodore iuliani maceoni (meceonis E -ni W) H. **uictoricii** : uicturici BW.
hermoginis : R, hermogenis BW, ermogenis S. **iacobi** : *om.* H.

    Hermoginis ministri is misplaced. See H : *Petri diaconi et* (*om.* E) *herin.
ministri petri*, i.e., Peter the deacon, and Peter's minister Hermogenes. *Her-
mogenis* occurs, again out of place, among the Irish group April 16.

April 18.

    paterni : parteni H. **uictoricii** : uicturici BW. **calocerii** : coloceri
BW, + febi proculi apolloni (app- E) furtunati (for- E) crispini expediti
mappalici uicturini (tor- E) gagi H. **pampi lycii, pamphili** . pampyli
B, pampilici E, pamphyli W, pamphili S. **iuliani** : *om.* H. **micionis** :
imicionis B. **hermoginis** : hermogenis B, hermonis W. **turini mumi** :
turemuni (-rim- E) H. **sirici** : syrici W. **prisciani** . + eleutheri (eleo-
B -teri E) anthię (-teae E -tiae W) H.

    It seems that there are several inaccuracies in this list. *Syr.* April 18
states that Septimus and Hermogenes suffered martyrdom at Salona. The
alibi before Hermogenes in H is therefore incorrect. Parthenius and Calo-
cerus are also commemorated on May 19 here and in H, on Ap. 18 only *Rom.*
Several, if not all, of the nine names *febi . . . gagi* in H, omitted in T,
belong to April 19. *Furtunati, expediti* and *gagi* are found there; and *Carth.*
April 19 records Mappalicus.

    For Paternus and Calocerius see May 19.

April 19.

    hermoginis . hermogenis (*bis*) (-inis E) H. **aristonici** : aristonici
(*bis*) H, + furtunati H. **zefani, allicionis exsuperi** : *om.* H. **gagi** : gagi
(*bis*) H. **galatae** : galathe B. **rufi** : rufi (*bis*) H. **donati** : donati
(*bis*) H, + uitalis B, + sericiani (*bis*) B, sericiani, serciani W. **elladii** :

helladi B, heladii W. **ilarii** : hilaui (-ari E) H. **liberi** : calcolis heris B, cauco liberi (-bri E) EW, calco liueris R.

Militinae arminiae is Melitene in Armenia. *Liberi* is not a personal name, but a corruption of the place-name Caucoliberis.

Syr. April 19 has Rufus.

H on this day has six doublets, though T has none. This is partly explained by the fact that H has two distinct documents headed Melitene. Each has *gagi, aristonici, rufi.*

April 20.

heradii, aradi : aradi ERS, *om.* BW. **acceti, accessi, acciei** : araiaci BW, taccei E, + seruiani B, seruani W. **siluani** : saluaniani BW. **fortunati** : furtunati BW. **iohannis bis** : iohannis H. **gemnae bis** : gemmę (*bis*) B, gemmae E, gemę, geminę W. **comiliae corniliae** : comiliae, cornilii (-nilię W) BW, corneliae E. **fortunatae** : furtunatus W, *om.* B. **papiae** : + siluiani BW, silvani E. **mariae, maximi** : *om.* H. **orati** : honorati E. **ciriacii** : araiaci B, asaiaci E, aiaraci W. **meriani** : martini BW. *fin.* + senesii S.

There is here one place-name : Rome.

Oengus April 20 has Herodius, and in a gloss (April 19) Heradius. Martinus eps. appears in the Irish group.

April 21.

cessari : carcere BW. **silui uitalis** : salui uitatis E. **mariae, eugenii, petri pauli** : *om.* H. **fortunatae** : furtunatae H, furtunati RS. **papiae** : *om.* W, + felicis BE. **tiburtii** : tibertii B. **cesari** : cessari E, cęsarii W, + amphelici (-llici B appe- E) HS.

Cessari is an error. See W "in carcere requiescentes," and *Ch. Ch. Mart.*

April 22.

pilippi : philippi B, philipi E, filippi W. **gaii** : gagi BW. **tubiani** : turdiani H. **basillae** : basiliae (bass- B) H. **felicis, rogati** : *om.* H. **leonidis** : leonedis B. **epipodi** : eppepodi (epe- E) H, eppodi S. **ciriaci** : quiriaci (syr- E, ciaci W) H. **primoli** : primuli E. **mucae parmeni lucae elimae** : muci, parmeni luci elimas E, *om.* BW, + crisoli E.

Papiae and *caulisti* are corrupt and misplaced. See B " In cimiterio Calesti . . . Gagi papae."

Gerapuli is an error for Hierapolis, which should have been before Philip the apostle. See Eus. *H.E.* v. 24. 2.

April 23.

catuli, catulini : catulini H. **saturnini** (*bis*) : saturnini H, + georgii BS. **felicis** : felicis (*bis*) H. **theoni, theonae** : theone (theu- E) H. **chori, cori** : chori BW, cori E. **teodori** : theodori H. **uictori** (*bis*) : uicturini (uicto- E) H. **mariae, iuberii, ranastini agripini iohannis zefani** : *om.* H. **nabori** : nauori BW. **saluni** : saloni E, + ualeri ursi BW. **uictori** (*tert.*) : uicturi W. **uitalis** : + theodori B, theodone (-rae E, -nę W) H.

T has only the names under the heading *In Africa* in H. Accordingly the collation neglects the name under Rome, Alexandria, and Valentia.

S has Georgius at Rome. He appears in TBE, April 24, 25.

April 24.

georgii : georgae E, *om.* W. **fortunati** : fortuni B, furtuni E. **felicis secundi** (*bis*) : felicis secundi H. **coronae, carionae** : coronae H. **rofinae:** rufinae BE. **naboriae:** nabori (namb- E) H. **mariae, ualerii, ursi clioni, uitalis, lauri, zephani iohannis, barthoci** : *om.* H. **sedrac**

(sid- BW) **misac abdinago** (abden- B): *om.* E. **militi bis** : melliti R, *om.* H. **saturnini** (*bis*): saturnini H. **siluani, silui, silutani:** siluiani (*bis*) B, siluani EW. **liberalis** (*bis*) : liberalis H. **meturi, meturii** : meturi H. **tomini, tommodi, tonicisi** : toniti BW, tumnini E. **baradii, barachi :** barachi H. **floriani, florii** : floriani BW, floriani (flori) E, + theonis H. **fortuni** : furtuni EW. **fusci** : fuscini (fusci) E. **germani** : serani B, serari W, serani (gerani) E. **zotici:** zoticę BW, goticae (zotici) E. **firmani** : feriani B, tibiriani E, firiani W. **mammetis** : mauenti BW, auenti (mauenti) E. *fin.* + ananias *etc.*

E has two lists of Alexandrian martyrs, nearly alike. They are treated in the collation as one, variant names being noted by brackets. T omits Africans in H, and they are neglected.

Ualerii, uitalis and *ursi* are borrowed from H April 23. *Silui, mariae, zefani, uitalis* and *iohannis* appear in T April 23 and 24.

Ch. Ch. Mart. has Mellitus as a confessor in Britain. He died 24 April 624 (Bede, *H.E.* ii. 7).

For Georgius see *D.C.B.* ii. 645 ff.

April 25.

marci euang. : S, *om.* H. **hermoginis** : hermogenis BW. **memfi** : hermemphi BW, memphi E. **geurgii** : georgii BE, *om.* W. **nobilis** : novellis E, nubilis W. **calistae** : calisti E. **marciae** : marci E, marcę W. **fortunati** : furtunati H.

April 26.

cirilli : aureli B, aurili W, ircilli R, cyrilli S. **etuniae** : eutimiae E, eutemię R, *om.* BW, + primitiui ER, + aureli E. **leonidis:** leonedis W. **uictoricii** : uicturi (-rini E) H. **siricii** : syrici W. **uictoris** : uicturis E. **simplicis** : symplici W. **pollionis** : pullionis BW. **kalendini** : calendini H. **apollionis, apollonii** : apolloni B, appolloni E, apulloni W. **marciani** : marciane H, + felicissime ethimie (ti- E, aethe- W) marciani H. **laetissimi** : lictissimi (lit- E) H. **ructi leonis** : *om.* H. *fin.* + simie germani felicie euasie (-assiae E) gemelline (-eli- E -ini W) H, + cleti B.

Of the names in H omitted here in T four are found in April 27 : *feliciae, gemellinae, germani* and *timiae.*

April 27.

alaxandri, teodoli, militanae brigitoniae, mediae, senori assani anathasii : *om.* H. **euentii** : euantiae B, euancię W, *om.* E. **castori** : castoris E. **anchimi, antimi** : anchimi B, antimi ERS, oncimi W. **zenoni, senoni** . zenoni (zetn- W) H. **generi, genesi:** genosi B, generi E, genesi W. **zefani** : stefani (steph- W) H. **sodalis** : sodali E. **antonii antonini :** antonini BRS, antoni E, authonimi W. **maurimi** : marini BW, maurini E. **cutici, euticii** : eutici H. **elipidii** : hilpidi (*bis*) BW, hilpidi, helpidi E. **epei** eppei W. **hirudini** : husandi (us- E) H. **priami** : priani H. **hermetis** : hermitis EW. **hermogini** . hermogenis (-gin- E) H. **mariae** : marciani H. **germanae** : germani H. **liphandiae** : libandiae E, *om.* BW. **laetissimae** : legissime BW. **gemellinae** : gemmelinae B, gemerlinae E, gemellini W. *fin.* + uictorini (-ur- W) nicofori dioscori serapionis papie anthimii (*om.* EW) thimie (ti- E, thunicę W) mauriatti genonsi (gennosi E, genosi W) sodalis (sot- E) H.

Alexander was known to Oengus and Gorman as an abbot (or chief) of Rome.

Mediae is probably a truncation of *nicomediae.*

Assani may have been an Irishman. See Gorman April 27.

Anthimus (*anchimi*), Bishop of Nicomedia suffered in the persecution of Diocletian, apparently in 303 (Eus., *H.E.* viii. 6. 6 ; 13. 1. See Lawlor-Oulton, *Eus.* ii. 272). He is commemorated in *Syr.* April 24.

Syr. May 3 mentions Helpidius and Hermogenes, martyrs in Melitene. HRS have here two martyrs : H states that they suffered "in civitate Armeniae Militane," and RS "in Melito." It is clear that they are the same persons, and that they were transferred from May 3 to April 27 (*i.e.*, v non. Maii to v kal. Maii). It is also evident that *militanae* (T) is not a personal name, but the city of Melitene misplaced.

April 28.

egressio noe de arca : B, *om.* EW, + uitalis BRS. **cristifori, augustini, tomae erasmi, iuliani celsii eueni :** *om.* H. **uictorini, uictorinae** : uicturini (-tor- B) H. **eufrodisii** : afrodisi H. **tabilli** : tiballi (tu- B) H. **pilippi cari bis** : car[. .]lippi B, carippi E, carilippi W. **uictoris** . uictorini (-nae E -ur- W) H. **agapi :** + euseui (-ebi E)) H. **niciae** : nicee B, nicae E. **luciani** : lucani E, + euseci (-ici E -ebi W eutici S) H. **eunuchii** : eunici B, eunuci W. **donati** ; + mauroli (-rini W) lucani (-ati W) H. **mauilii** : manili BW, mannilli E.

Oengus has the passion of Christopher on this day.

Pilippi cari (*carlippi*) is an error for Charilampus, a presbyter who suffered on this day at Nicomedia (*Syr.*).

The *Passio s. Pollionis* (Ruinart, p. 404) states that Pollio suffered on April 27. A Pollio is also mentioned on April 26 (TH). The *Passio* tells us that the martyrdom took place at Cibalae in Pannonia. Though TH obviously regarded *tiballi* as a personal name it is a corruption of the name of that city.

Lictoris is probably not a name but a title, *lectoris*. H styles Agapus a lector. Gorman has on this day Augustinus and Vitalis.

April 29.

prosodoci : prostoci B, prosduci WS, prosdoci E, + valentini prudenti H. **marciasii** : marcialis H. **sabbati** : sabati W. **codñi** : eodomoni BW, codomani E. **nonnae** : *om.* H. **matrinae** : meturinę B, metronae E, metorinę W, + macculi (-lini B) H. **tigusti, augusti** : augusti (ag- EW) H. **uictorini** (*bis*) : uicturini (-tor- E) H. **maulini** : manili H.

We have here three clauses in H which have no connection with T. They are therefore neglected in the collation. Their headings are *Item, Africa* and *Alexandria* (*sec.*).

Syr. April 29 and H call Germanus a presbyter. T calls him a deacon. *Theusii* (TE) is an error for Tusciae. See BW.

T makes *bononiae* a personal name, by adding to it *et aliorum lxxxiii.* But it is clearly the name of Bononia (Bologne) misplaced.

April 30.

affrodisii : affrodi (afr- E) H, efrodisi R, frodisi S. **quirini papae** : quirini epi. (mart. B) HRS. **dorothae** : dorothei H, + rodiciani (*bis*) H. **terentii** : terentii (*bis*) H. **martini ter** : martini, marini H. **uictorii** : uicturi E, uiatoris WS. **claudii** (*bis*) : claudii H. **orimenti, clementis** : clementis BW, orimenti, clementis E. **onoragi** : honorati H. **dagarii** : dacari (dag- E dic- W) H. **lucini** : luciani W, + telesfori (-fosi B -isfor W), primosi H. **saturnini** : + emeliani H.

The collation has here to do with a dozen names at the beginning, and another at the end, of the list of H. We may call them A and C. Between them there are about fifty names, of which only one resembles a name in our list : *affrodi* (see above). But though *affrodisii* (T), *efrodisi* (R) and *frodisi* (S) have the appearance of personal names, there is reason to believe that they are corruptions of a place-name. *Syr.* April 30 tells us that in Aphrodisia of Caria Diodotus and Rhodopianus were martyrs. Rhodopianus is surely our Rodicianus (C), and the heading of C is "In Frodiria." Frodiria is not unlike Aphrodisia, which is still closer to *affrodisii* (T).

Quirinus was buried at Rome according to H, and EWSR describe him as a bishop. The sequel may be guessed. A scribe dubbed the Roman bishop Pope. Next he was elevated, after the custom of T, to a high place in the list of the saints. Finally, after *papae* was inserted *et aliorum xxx*, and Papa became a personal name. There can be little doubt that he is the Quirinus, Bishop of Sisciae in Pannonia, who was put to death at Scarabaritia (Oeden-berg) on May 31 (*sic*). See Ruinart, p. 497.

In *Carth.* April 30 we find " martyris Claud[ii]."

The heading of A is Alexandria and that of the second clause C In Frodiria. But there are five names common to both. It is probable that some of them are misplaced.

May 1.

pilipi : philippi BW, pilippi E. **iacobi apostoli fratris domini** : iacobi, iacobi ap. BE, iacobi ap. WR, iacobi WS. **nicodimi, germani, petri renouati iohannis, zefani** . *om.* H. **eleutherii** : eleuteri E, heleotheri W. **alaxandri** : alexandri H. **felestiui** : pelesti BW, felisti E. **agapiti** : + mathei BE. **quintiniani** : quintiani H. **gaii** : gagi H. **apollonii** : appolloni E, + eufemi H. *fin.* + quinti . . . iustini H.

Frigiae is a place-name (Phrygia) misplaced. See B.

May 2.

saturnini (*bis*)   saturnini H. **hippoliti eupolitis** : eupolitis E, epolitis R, *om.* BW. **elpidii** : helpidi B, helpedi E, hilpidi W. **hermoginis:** hermogeni H, + germani celestini sanctine (scant- E) optati memori (memm-E) sanociani (ani E sciani W) H. **zefani, alaxandri mariae, transillae** : *om.* H. **celestini** : caelestini EW, + felicis H. **quintini** : acetini B, acettini E, caetini W. **belleci** : hellaci B, bellici E, bellapi W, bellaci S.

Syr. May 2 has " In Alexandria Saturnilus."

Helpidius and Hermogenis are misplaced here. See April 27.

Transillae may be a corruption of *translatio*. See W : *sanctinae . transia.*

May 3.

crucis christi inuentio : *om.* E, + hermogenis (-inis E) H, + iuuenalis B. **mariae u. conceptio, musae** : *om.* H. **euentii** . heuenti B, ebenti W, + alexandri (alax- E) H. **teodoli** : theodoli (-uli E) H. **ambrosii** : arboni H, + mariani H. **rufinae:** rufini BW, + furtunionis (-nonis E) furtunati (for- E) eusebii auiti H. **fortunati** : furtunati BW.

The Invention of the Cross and the Conception of St. Mary appear again at May 7.

The last sixteen names here in E belong to May 4, and they are not used in the present collation.

For Hermogenes see April 27.

Gorman has on this day Alexander and Theodorus (*sic*). He styles Alexander Pope.

May 4.

antherii, mariae romulae : *om.* H. **siluani** : + nestori furtunati (*om.* EW) mitton (-ni E) antonini corcodomi (-ced- W) H. **urbani bis** : urbani BE, *om.* W. **antoninae** : antonię W. **celestinae** : caelestini (cel-B) H, + felicis H. **romani** . + bellici marcialis (-ali B -ani E) H. **emetuni** : mittuni floriani petri H.

On this day three groups of forty martyrs are recorded : at Alexandria (BWS), in Africa (ER), and at Rome (T).

Antherius is identified in T as Pope Anterus. But he died on 3 January 236.

Syr. May 4 has " In Nicomediae Antoninus," disagreeing with HRS.

NOTES ON THE ROMAN CALENDAR 153

May 5.

ascensio, gallae, belli, marciasi, iohannis, zefani . *om.* H. **herennae** : herenae H. **felicissi** : felicissime H. **eutini, eutemi** : eutimi BERS, *om.* W. **grigorii** : gregorii H. **hilarii** : helari W. **petiui, petri** (*bis*) : petiui BW, petri E. **erennei** : herenei H, + peregrini H. **archilai** : archelai B. **necturi** : nectari H. **niceti** : + iuuiniani BW, iuliani E.

Syr. May 5 : " In Alexandria Euthymius (*eutemi* above) and Heros Bishop of Antioch.' The place of the martyrdom of Euthymius is not mentioned in BE. Heros does not appear in our manuscripts. He may be the successor of St. Ignatius (Eus. iii. 36.15, iv. 20).

Eutini et non iustinus is explained by a gloss on Oengus . " Eutimus et non Justini ut quidam codices habent."

Marciasi is borrowed from May 4. Marcialus is beside Mithunus in B May 4, but not there in T.

May 6.

mattei : mathei BES, *om.* W, + primi BE. **iacobi** (*bis*) : iacobi H. **iohannis fil. zachariae, mariae, brigitonae** : *om.* H. **mauriani** : mariani H. **heliodori** : eleodori E, hiliodori W. **concordii** : concordię W. **curice** : caricie BW, calriciae E. **ausidiae** : aufidie (aff- E) H. **iudith** : iuthid E. **acacae** : acute H. **faustinae** : + hilariani (hel- W) . . . magropi H. **uictoris** : uictoris (*ter*)H. **marcelli** : marcellini BE, *om.* W. **maximi** : *om.* W, + bafrobiti BE. **augustini** : acutiani B, agustiani E, *om.* W, + niceti B, nitici E. **ualeriani** : ualeri BWS.

On this day we have in H three clauses corresponding to the first twelve names in T. After them is a clause headed *Mediolani*. In it we find 79 names in BE, and in W 46 corresponding to the earlier names in the list. T has nine names, *curice* . . *felicis* corresponding to the first ten in H, and five corresponding to the last six in BE. B shows that T blunders here : " Acutiani. Niceti. cum aliis septuaginta. Item Gaiani cum aliis xx. Antisiodoro depos. s. Valeri episcopi." T omits Nicetus, and places *et aliorum lxxii* after *gaiani* instead after the ignored *niceti*. Moreover Valerianus is a martyr of Milan instead of Auxerre.

A gloss on Oengus reminds us that May 6 is the feast of St. John before the Latin Gate. Hence John's appearance in T. But he is the Baptist ! *Carth.* May 6 mentions Marinus (Maurianus T) and Jacobus.

May 7.

agnitio s. crucis : inuentio s. crucis ER, *om.* BW. **conceptio mariae, scolasticae, zefani felicitatis** : *om.* H. **afrodisti** : frodisi R, *om.* H. **macrobii** : + eutici B, cuthei E, eutheci W. **augustini** : agustini (*bis*) H. **pudentellae postellae** : potentellae (pud- E) H, + achaici ES, acaici R, + canti B. **allae** : *om.* BW. **septimnae** : septemine B, septimae E, *om.* W. **dextrae** : dextri BE, *om.* H. **rogatae** : rogati B, *om.* W. **maximi** : maximi (*bis*) H. **uicturi bis** : uictori (*bis*) B. **augustini** : agustini H. **gaginati** : gagianti BW, gaianti E. **frontoni** : fontoni B, furtuni E. **quinti** : quinte B. **priuatiani** : *om.* W. **arnesii** : arnisi B, *om.* W. **donati bis** : donati (*ter*) BE, *om.* W. **nauigii puluini** (-ueri BE) **octouiani** (octau- BE) **marini** : *om.* W. *fin.* + uictori mulieri placidi (*nomina lxvii*) H.

The list of W here is an abridgement ; and T has contact with only the first 33 names in BE.

Agnitio s. crucis and *conceptio mariae* are borrowed from May 3.

Syr. May 7 has " Flavius and four other martyrs." Apparently they were Flavius, Augustinus, and the three brothers, Marcellionus, Macrobius and Euticus. But if so, we must doubt the accuracy of BE and W.

For *ac(h)aici*, see May 8.

May 8.

maximi : maximi (*bis*) BE, + anthus B, anthosi E, authys W.   **cessi** (*bis*) : cesi B, *om*. EW.   **donati** (*bis*) : donati (-tae E) H.   **lucii** (*bis*) : luci H.   **saliuae, mariae, eupiae, sincliticae, dati, odroni, lurentii** : *om*. H. **secundilae** : secundolae W.   **marciae** : + agati H.   **daticae** : *om*. W, + gundoni B, guddini E.   **uictoriae** : uicturiae EW.   **stertitiae** : stertiae B, stercitae E, sterciȩ W.   **floridae** : floridi B, floridae (*bis*) E, floredȩ W. **ninae** : nenni B, *om*. W, + casti B, + gagi furi BE.   **flauiae iuliae** : *om*. W, + felicis BE.   **famosae** : famorie E, + honestae (-ti B) H, + nigri BE. **feliciae** : *om*. W.   **maximae** : + datiuȩ tuniani thidi (cutidi E) BE. **cutidi** : eutici H.   **fortunati**: furtunati H.   **saturnini**: saturnine B.   **tertuli**: + celestini (-ne W) faustine H.   **tamphi** : tampi H.   **rustici** : rusticae E, *om*. W.   **marciani** : martiani B, marcialis E, *om*. W.   **batizi** : baptici BW, battaci E.   **uictoriani** : uictoris BE, *om*. W.   **ianuarii** : *om*. E.   **capitis** : *om*. EW.

On this day B has nearly a hundred personal names. T has contact with only the first 53 of these names. E is in accord with B, and W abridges. The collation does not take account of the names in H after *faustine ianuarii*.

Syr. May 11 has Maximus at Constantinople. It would seem that the Maximus mentioned here is too early by three days. Moreover in ER May 7 we find Acaicus and in H May 8 Agatius. They are no doubt names of the same person, for each is connected with Constantinople. *Syr.* May 10 has " In Nicomedia Acacius the martyr." Nicomedia might be changed for Constantinople. We may assume that dates and places are incorrect in our authorities.

Odroni appears also in the Irish group.

Ch. Ch. Mart. may explain the genesis of the proper name *Capitis* (TB) It says : Victor " nouissime gloriosi martirii cursum *capitis* abscisione compleuit." Is it possible that *cessi* is a corruption of " *abscisione* " ?

May 9.

reuelatio michaelis, memmertius : *om*. H.   **tomae et iohannis et andreae** : *om*. EW.   **gindei, cendei** ; quindei BW, gindei ER.   **zenonis**: zenoni BW.   **affrodisii** : afrodisi (afra- B) H.   **effenici** : ephenici E, *om*. BW.   **timothei** : thimothei W.   **gordiani** : + primoli H.

For the manifestation of St. Michael see Oengus May 9 and *D.C.B.* ii. 1177.

Four of the names in this list appear on May 10.

For Mamertus, Bishop of Vienne, and his institution of the Rogation Days, see *D.C.B.* iii. 790. He died about 480.

May 10.

epimacis : ephimici B, ephimacis R, epymachi S.   **midoris, maioris** : midonis ER, maioris BWS.   **diutii** : datiui EW, *om*. B.   **teclae** : theclae E.   **furionis** : furtunionis (-tin- W) H.   **mariae, iusti, iacobi** . *om*. H. **lucellae**: bucelle B.   **probatae**: probati BS.   **mocae**: moece BW, mecae E. **quirilli** : cyrilli H.   **gindei** : cindis B, cendis E, cendeis W.   **dionini** : dionis (-ni- E) H.   **achaci** : acaci B, acaici E, *om*. W.   **crispionis** : cripionis E.   **affrondisii** : afrodisi BE, *om*. W.   **primitii** : priuati BE, *om*. W.

T has contact with the personal names in H under Rome, Axiopolis, Africa, and two under Tarsus. The rest of H are omitted in collation.

Five of the nine names under Africa appear also under Tarsus (BE).

Epimachus was a martyr earlier than Gordianus. Gordianus was buried in his tomb. See *AA.SS.* May ii. 553, *Analecta Boll.* i. 508.

Protextati is the cemetery of Praetextatus.

Justi, iacobi are one person, *iacobi iusti*, James the Just (Eus. *H.E* ii. 23. 4).

Syr. May 10 has Acacius in Nicomedia (cp. May 8), but here he is in Axiopolis.

May 11.

 iob, maii, inerti : *om.* H. **antimi** : antimi (*bis*) E. **dimetri** : demetri B, demitri W, + thadthei (tadh- E taddei W) nepotiani mamerti (mamm- B) H. **attici** (*bis*) : attici ER, *om.* BW. **montaniani, montani** : montaniani BRS, montani EW, + maiuli (-oli E) H. **iulii bis** : iulii H, + crispi W. **uicturini, uicturinis** : uicturini (uicto- E) H. **fortunati** : furtunati H. **comini**: commini W. **iulii** : + crispi, ianuarie H. **septimi primuli** : semtimi, primoli W. **marnili** : manili B, manili (*bis*) E, manile, manili W, + uictorie . . epemini nerei H.
 Oengus and *Drum.* have Job here, and *Ch. Ch. Mart.* on May 10.
 Maii, iulii bis (T) is an error. The correct text is *maiulii, iulii* (H).
 Carth. May 11 has Saint Maiulius.

May 12.

 pancrati : panradi W. **nerei** : nerci E. **aquilei** : achillei (-ilei E) H. **ciriaci** (*bis*) : cyriaci E, quiriaci RS, *om.* BW. **maximi** : ER, *om.* BW. **gratii** : gradi W. **pancratii** : prancati (prac- E) H. **rotheris** : sotheris B, roteris EW, + soteris H. **moisitis** : moysitis BW. **affroditi** : afroditi BW, afnoti E. **achilis** : acillis B, achillis W, + moireis (-rei E -sei W) H. **zefani** : *om.* H. **alaxandri** : *om.* B, alexandri W.
 Pancratius (St. Pancras), Quiriaca (*Cyriaci*) wife of Clemonius, and Sotheris (*Rotheris*), a virgin, suffered on 12 May, 304. See *Anal. Boll.* x. 53.

May 13.

 init. + martini B, + seruatii W. **andronici** : + uictoris H, + inuici aucti B, daveti E. **affrodissii** : afrosedi B, aprodisi E, afrodisi W. **sabini** (*bis*) : sabini (sau- W) H. **agripae** : agrippae H, + acris B, aeris E agcris W. **mariae, perpetuae, gerbassi**: *om.* H. **lucii** (*bis*): luci BW, lucinillae E. **credulae**: credule (-li) B, credolae (oritulae) E, cridule (creduli) W. **quirillae** : cyrille (cir-) B, cirillae E, cyrille W. **grissi** : gripfi B, grisi E, griffi W. **alaxandri** : *om.* BW, + gagi sebastiani (sab- W) marcelliani (-ini B) H.
 H has two lists of Alexandrian martyrs. When a name is identical in both it is counted as one in the collation. When there are different names, but evidently names of the same person, the differences are indicated in brackets.
 The Acts of Tarachus and Probus (Ruinart, p. 422) state that they were put to death on Oct. 11, and they are commemorated in T on that day as well as April 5 and here. See Ap. 5, Oct. 11 and *D.C.B.* iv. 781.
 Alexandri (TE) is a corruption of Alexandria. In T it is misplaced.

May 14.

 secundini : secundiani BW. **uictorini** : uicturiani (-ini E) H. **taraci, affronnidis, pali, eutherii** : *om.* H. **madiani** : medion BW, mediani E. **alaxandri** : alexandri BW, + proculi aframi H. **maximini** : maximi E, maximiani W. **adacti** : adaucti (*bis*) BW, adaviti (*bis*) E, + denegothie B, demecutiae E, + maximini BW, + adeodati H.
 T does not mention any of the names in H under Rome, Milan or Auvergne.
 Taraci and *affronnidis* appear in May 13. *Affronnidis* may be identical with *aframi*.
 Militis is probably misplaced. BW have *uictoris et militis*. E omits *militis*.
 According to the Acts of Victor and Corona (*AA.SS.* May iii. 266 : *Analecta Boll.* ii. 291) they suffered in Egypt. *Siria* (H) is probably an error for Cilicia, the native country of Victor. Victor and Corona appear in HR Feb. 20, while one recension of their Acts place them on April 24. See further *Ricemarch*, i. 87 (12 kal. Aug.)

May 15.

primus penticosti, populae, bamororae : *om.* H. **timothei** :
thimothei W. **rosulae** : R, *om.* H. **andrae, andreae** : andreae (-rei W)
H. **cotiae** : cotthie B, chottiae E, chotitidie W. **simplicii** : + prestabilis
H. **cirici**: cyrici H. **pauli**: pauli (*bis*) H. **dionisii**: dionise B, dionisiae
E, diunise W, + trici B, praetece W, tredici S. **minerui** : menerui BW.
eradii : heracli (-di E) H, + uictoris H.

May 16.

dioclitiani : diocliciani BW, + mengenis (-eni B) H. **florentii** (*bis*) :
florentii H. **aquilini bis** : aquilini, aquili BW, + peregrini primi (*om.* E)
fidali (-uli E -oli W) H. **uictorini** : uictoriani B, uicturini E, uicturiani W,
uicturianae S. **heradi** : eracli B, heracli W. **paulini bis** : paulini H.
menserini : menerimi B, menserimi E, meneremi W. **gaiani bis** : gaiani
(-ionio W) H. **uincentii** : uinanti W. **minerii** : meneri (meu- B) H.
pauli : pauli (*bis*) H. **minorgi** : monorgi BW. **auriani uicturiae,
basillae** : *om.* H. **ioueni** : iouini (inv- W) H. **herilii** : heracli B, herceli
E, hereli W. **niderni** : nideruni H.

Auriani is a corruption of Isauria, a district in Asia Minor. See in H *in
es auria* and in S *in isauria*. *Victuriae* which follows is a doublet with *Victorini*.

May 17.

andrionis : adrionis (at- R) ER, *om.* BW, + parteni B, paterni ER,
parthini W, partenis S. **basillae** : basilae ES, basilię W, basellae R.
basiae, adomnini, potomonis, hiemi, *om.* H. **caloceri gallicorii** :
caloceri BERS, galligori W. **liberii** : libi E. **pauli bis** : pauli H, +
peregrini B. **arthemi** : artemi H. **primi eponi** : primi BE, e pono W.
heracli : eracli E. **calori** : calcori (ga- E) H. *fin.* + calisti uincentii
felicis S.

Pope Liberius died in the autumn of 366. He is commemorated also on
Sept. 23, and on Aug. 27 in the Greek Menology.

For *Caloceri gallicorii* see May 19.

Between *liberi* and *pauli* is *adomnini* in T. In H *niuiduno* is between
liberi and *heracli pauli*. We may therefore suppose that *adomnini* is a corruption of a place-name : Niuidunum.

May 18.

marci : R, *om.* EW. **potomonis** : potamonis BERS, pantamoni W.
bostasii : S, bustasii (bas- E) H, hostasi R. **hortasii**: ortasi E. **sera-
pionis** : syrapionis E. **pantini** : panteri (-theri E) H. **dicorii**: dioscori
H. **palmi**: + pitigon (petecon W, petegondi E) cenron (-ni E, cesson W) H.
mariae, urbanae, zefani, michaelis : *om.* H. **lucianae** : locani E.
agnae : aeginę (eg- E) H. **hermoni** : hermon B, hermonis E, hermone W.
discori : dioscori H, + efuchi (euchi E) serapionis (sera ionis W) H. **panto-
moni** : patamon B, potamonis E, pactamon W, + panteri (-theri E) H.
luciosi : luciosae E. **pedecladi** : peteglondi (-ni E, petecl- W) H, + aran
B, dieranti E, aeran W, + datiui (*sec.*) H. **casii** : cassi BE, *fin.* + patri
etc. S.

Oengus has Marcus, and the gloss calls him Pope and Evangelist.
Syr. May 19 mentions Serapion and twelve other martyrs. Cp. H.

May 19.

urbani : urbani (*bis*) BW, urbani, urbanae E. **decii regis, decii** :
decii imperatoris H, decii regis R. **paterni proni** : paterni (*bis*) B, parteni,
paterni W, parteni, prenni E, patertiani R. **galli curii**: gallicorum B, galitori
W. **iudicii**: indici H. **urbanae bis**: urbanę (or- E) H, + romanae BW.
coloniae : colonicę H. **iuliae** : iulicae E. **sarrae, clorini florini,
fausti** : *om.* H. **selincii seleucii** . seleuci H. **dominici** : glonici B,

donici E, clonici W. **crescenti** : criscenti B. **areni bis** : areni H. **quinti** : quintuli E, + primuli (-oli W) salusti H. **fortunati** : furtunati BW, + duorum (*om.* E) donatoris (*bis* E) primi indicę (dicessi E) locustę (lucussae E, lugustę W) rogatę H. **emelii** : emili H. **basilii** : baseli B, + praetextate (pre- B) baselię (basiae E, -ilię W) partini (-thini B) H. **pullioli** : puliuchi (polio- E pulio- W) H. **pudentianae** : S, *om.* H.

The first seven names in T are an account of the martyrdom of Calocerus and Parthenius. These two are mentioned in April 18 and May 17. *Rom.* May 19 has " Partheni et Caloceri in Callisti Diocletiano ix et Maximiano viii." This proves that this day is correct. But it also shows that, in despite of THR and the Acts (*AA.SS.*, May iv. 302), the martyrdom did not take place under Decius, but under Diocletian in the year 304.

Sarrae may be a corruption of Caesarea. *Clorini florini* is a doublet.

Alaxandri is an error for *In Alexandria*. See BW.

Pudentianae is doubtless the virgin Potentiana, mentioned on this day in *Drum.* and *Ch. Ch. Mart.*

May 20.

marcellosae : marcelosae E. **uictoriae** : uictorii B, uicturii W. **basillae** : baseli B, basilae E, basilissę W. . . . .

August 2.

teothotae : theodotae (-the B) HS, theodoti R. **zefani ep.** : stefani (steph- W) H. **zefani diac.** : stephani BW, *om.* E. **luciani, pauli** : *om.* H. **nicetae** : niceti BW.

Theodota and her three (not seven as BW have it) children seem to have suffered on September 2. See *Acta s. Anastasiae* (*AA.SS.* Aug. i. 152) and *Syr.* Sept. 2.

Zefani epi. is Pope Stephanus l, who died in 257. See *D.C.B.* iv. 727.

Lucianus was not a martyr, but the person who revealed the relics of the proto-martyr ; and Paul may be a reminiscence of Acts vii. 58.

Musitaniae is an error for *Mauritaniae*, which is itself an error for Nicomedia (*Syr.* Sept. 2).

August 3.

inuentio corporis zefani stephani BW, stefani E. **hermelii, ermilii** : hermili H. **efronii, effronii** : eofroni (eu- E) H. **acellae** : *om.* E. **drogenis:** S, drogens B, dragens W, *om.* E. **zefani** (*sec.*) : sterani B, stefani E, stephani W. **nicodemii** : nicodimi E, nicomedi W, + abibon BW. **samuelis** : gamalielis (game- W) H. **iohannis** : *om.* H. **metrapolis** : metropoli BE, matrofili W.

Drogenes is called Diogenes in *AA.SS.*, Aug. i. 213.

Gorman and *Ch. Ch. Mart.* have Abibon.

Oengus has " John's metropolis " in accord with T.

August 4.

crescentionis : criscentionis (cre- E -tianę W) H. **sacinthi** sachinti BW, quinti E. **iustini** : iusti W, + herenti W, herenei S. **floriani** : S, *om.* H. **eracli:** heracli W, *om.* BE, + dassi sive bassi W bassi S. **isei** : RS, sege B, isaci E, seiae W, + bartholomei (-miae E)H. **philistinae mimi zefani** : *om.* H. **laurenti** : *om.* H.

AA.SS. Aug. 1, 318 has the group *iusti crescentionis sacinthi* in the form *crescentiano iusto et forte sachinto uel iacunto.* We may infer that *iusti* is an adjective.

Herenti, floriani, eracli, dassi, bassi, philistini, mimi appear also on T H Aug. 5.

Heremeti is not a personal name, but the title Hermit. See BW, " De heremo."

August 5.

herentii, irinei, irennei : hereni (-nti) B, hirenei E, hererenni W, irene R, hereni S. dassi, bassi, dasi : dassi (dassi sive bassi) B, dasi ER, dassi W, classi S. heraclii bis, aradi: heracli (er-) B, eracli ES, heracli W, eradi R, + dedicatio basilicae s. mariae BW. affri : afri EW, *om.* B. leonis, tethasii, donati : *om.* H. filistini : filistine B. osuualdi : S. osualdi E, *om.* BW. nimni : mimmii B, mimmini E, mimi W, memmii S.
The first three names in B are a duplicate of those under Axiopolis. The differences of spelling are indicated in brackets.
Afer was the uncle of Afra (Aug. 6), and they suffered at Augusta Vindelicorum (Augsburg). See *AA.SS.* Aug. ii. 37.
Cassianus was Bishop of Augustodunum (Autun). See *D.C.B.* i. 414 and *AA.SS.* Aug. ii. 66.
Augusti is a corruption of one of the cities mentioned above.
Oswald, King of Northumberland, was killed on 5 August 642. He appears in Oengus, Gorman, *Drum.* and *Ch. Ch. Mart.*

August 6.

sixti : syxti E, systi W, xisti S. felicis : felicissimi BERS. agapiti : agapitis E. laurentii : *om.* E. ypoliti : eppoliti BW, *om.* E. affrae (*bis*) : afrae H. mariae cirillae ueneriae, marci caliusti, cronani : *om.* H. faustini, pretextati : *om.* E. *fin.* + flauei R.
Rom. has " Xysti in Callisti et in Praetextati Agapiti Felicissimi." This indicates that Sixtus was buried in the cemetery of Callistus, and Agapitus and Felicissimus in the cemetery of Praetextatus. BWT regard Praetextatus as a martyr, and WT misplace the name, while B rightly has it before Felicissimus. Xystus II was martyred on 6 Aug. 258 (*D.C.B.* iv. 1197; *AA.SS.* Aug ii. 131).
Caliusti (*callisti*) is misplaced in T and is regarded as a martyr. See BW.
Affrae, ueneriae, faustini appear on August 7
Cronani is an Irish saint. See below, and Gorman August 7.

August 7.

septem fratrum . . . arcadii : *om.* H. sopronii : soffroni B, suffroni E, sumfroni W, sofroni R, sophronii S. donati : + quiriaci R. uastini : faustini H. ausenti : *om.* W, + carpefori B, carpofori S. affrae : afrae BE, *om.* W. ueneriae : ueneriae (*bis*) B.
For the seven sleepers at Ephesus see Gregorius Tur., *De Gloria Mart.*, cap. 94. The names here agree with his, except that Ianuarius takes the place of Martianus. The numeral clii here is an error for clu (see note p. 115). Gregory tells us that the " resurrection " took place under an emperor named Theodosius ; and the interval between the death of Decius (251) and the accession of Theodosius I, son of Arcadius (408) is 157 years. The note on p. 115 is only two years astray. Nevertheless the writer states that the awaking took place under Constantine son of Helena. The error is probably due to the fact that the list of the sleepers ended with Constantinus. Oengus Aug. 7 and his glossator had T before them.

August 8.

secundi (*bis*) : secundini secundi BW, secundi RS. seriani : seuueriani H. uictoriani: uicturine, uictoriani B, uictorini, uicturiani E, uicturiani W. albani bis: albani B, in albano, albani E, in albono R. ciriaci: cyriaci (*bis*) BW, cyriaci, cyriacitis E. crescentiani : criscentiani BW, + memmie BW, memiae E. smragdi : zmaragdi E. faustini : faustini (*bis*) B. eutiani : euticiani (-tiani B) H. iulianae : iuliane (*bis*) BE. trifoniae mariae · *om.* H. mecronae : metrodore (-tronae E) H, + leonidis

(-edis B) H. **agapae**: agapiae E. **choruntonis**: corinthionis B, corvitonis E, corithonis W. **corpofori** : carpofori BE, carpori W, carpoofori R. *Rom.* August 8 has " Secundi Carpofori Victorini et Seueriani Albano. Et Ostense . . . Cyriaci Largi Crescentiani Memmiae Julianetis et Ixmaracdi." From this statement we learn that nine personal names in TH are approximately correct. It also shows that *corpofori* (Carpofori) in T is misplaced. Moreover we find that *ostensi albani bis* are not three persons, but two places, Via Ostiensis (Rome) and Albanum (Albano in Italy) Cp. ER. *Largi crescentiani* appear also in August 9, under a different heading.

August 9.

antonii, fintinni : *om.* H. **firmi** : in sirmi E, in syrmio S. **permonii** : pergamo E. **crescentiani** : criscentiane BW, crescentionis E, + veriani marcelliani secundiani romani E. **tiberiani** : + anni BW. **teodori** : theodori H. **laudaici, iudaci** : laudici H. **policarpi** : pulicarpi B, pauli carpi E. **sixti** : sixti *(bis)* B, xysti E, syxti W, + agatopi H. **nemiodani** : nomidiane BW, nomediani E.

On this day only the first few lines of H correspond to T. Accordingly the collation goes no further than the name *agatopi*.
Fintinni is probably the name of an Irish saint.
The river Anio is beside Tiburti (Tivoli). Since *anni* appears in BW near *Tiburti* we may conclude that Tiburti is a place-name. In fact E describes it " Tiburti in Tuscia."
It is clear that *in sirmi* (E) and *in syrmio* (S) are derivatives of *in sirmio*. It is also obvious that either *firmi* (BW) or *in sirmio* is corrupt. But if we substitute *in sirmio* for *firmi* in BW we have *in oriente in sirmio*, which is impossible ; for Sirmium is in the west. Accordingly *firmi* is correct. Moreover the Acts of Firmus and Rusticus (*AA.SS.* Aug. ii. 419) tell us that these two suffered on August 9 at Verona ; and Verona is in the west. Hence it appears that Firmus and Rusticus are misplaced. Omitting them we have BW *In oriente permoni criscentiane*, E *Pergamo crescentionis*, and S *In oriente crescentiani*. The result is that *permoni* is not a personal name but a corruption of Pergamum, and that the true text is *In oriente pergamo criscentiane*.

August 10.

laurentii : + syriaci E. **zefani, perpetuae** *(bis)*, **petronillae, felicitatis, cassiani annae** : *om.* H. **crescentionis** : criscentionis BW. **arcarei** : arcanei E, archanarei W, + iacenti (iaci- E) ianuarii H. **quirilli** : cyrilli BW. **gemini** : S, gemmini B, zemni E, gemminę W. **crispinae** : crispini B. **menellae** : menniae E, memmiae S, *om.* BW. **iulianae** : *om.* BW, + zmaragdi E. **terentiae** : cerentiae E. **isiodorae** : sidore BW, sidonae E. **affrae** : afrae E, *om.* BW. **crescentiae** : criscentiae W. **portiani, pontiani** : pontiani H. **cresti** : cristi B, + euticie (-cii W) H. **ciriaci** : quiriaci BW, *om.* E. **cirici** : cyriacę H. **eugenii** : *om.* E. **pastoris** : + lucellae H. **largi** : ES, *om.* BW, + crescentiani E. **leocis** : leucyppi B, leocippiae E, leucippi W. **leocipi** : leucippi H. **seui** : + archanarei (arca- E) H.

Laurentius is commemorated in *Rom.* and *Carth.* on this day. He suffered martyrdom in 258.

ER, after the notice of Laurentius, have *et loco alio uirorum xi et uirginum xiii.* BW have merely *et alibi.* T has a similar note, but suppresses *loco alio,* thus implying that the twenty-four suffered in Rome. E, after *uirginum xiii,* repeats from August 8 *cyriaci largi crescentiani menniae iulianae zmaragdi.* T borrows, from that source, *minellae, iulianae, largi.* Moreover *ostensae affrae* (T) and its companion *in arieto afrae mil. vii vallis ostensae* (E) may be neglected as intruders. Afra has appeared already in HS August 7 ; here she is awkwardly placed in E between Laurentius and Felicissimus, without support from BWS. Ignoring these names we have four lists in TH from *criscentionis* to *mariae*.

BW have eleven masculine names, followed by thirteen, for the most part feminine. Here, no doubt, are the eleven men and the thirteen virgins. E omits two names. T omits six, and does not follow the sequence of H.

For Perpetua and Felicitas see Harris-Gifford, *Acts* of *Martyrdom of P. and F.*, 1890. The passion is commemorated in H March 6, 7, in *Rom.*, *Syr.* March 7. The Greek date is February 2. See also T Oct. 13.

T creates Ostensa a martyr, and, contrary to its wont, gives us a place-name.

August 11.

tiburti : tyburti B. **ciciliae** : caeciliae (ce- B) H. **mariae munisanae teclae, zefani, gairi** : *om.* H. **cornilii** : cornelii S, *om.* EW. **gauricii** : *om.* BE.

Munisanae may be a doublet with *susannae*, and *gairi* with *gauricit*

August 12.

macarii (*bis*) : machari H. **iuliani** (*bis*) : iuliani (*ter*) E. **crisanti** : crissanti B, cristini E, crissante W. **uinciae agnae, ciciliae, agathae, columbae, radicundis** : *om.* H. **clariani, clarinae** : clarinae E, *om.* BW. **dariae** : *om.* E, + claudi (cladii B), helarie (hilari E), iasonis mauri H. **eupuli** : eupoli (-pli E) H, + ueretie (-raciae E) H. **marci** ER, *om.* BW. *fin.* + octaue, sixti R.

August 13.

hipoliti, ipolissi . eppoliti B, hyppoliti E, epoliti W. **pontiani** : ponciani W. **antici** : anthiochi (-ci W) BW, antonini E, + anoci BW, antiochi E. **cornilii calisti** : calesti B, caelestis E, cornitii W, + cassiani H. *fin.* + radegunde, BWR, radegundis S, *om.* E.

There is here much confusion. *Rom.* has " Ypoliti in Tiburtina et Pontiani in Callisti." B agrees with this, but after *luciani* it has *calesti* for the second time, and the *et in foro cornilii*. E has *caelistis*, supposing it to be a personal name, and omitting *et in foro cornilii*. W omits *calisti et in foro*, and regards *cornilii* as the name of a martyr. Evidently T has two names of martyrs : *cornilii calisti*.

Queen Radegundis died on 13 August 587. See *D.C.B.* iv. 534. Cp. August 12.

August 14.

assumptio mariae, sinlaiae : *om.* H. **fortunati** . furtunati H. **dimetri** : demetri BE. **felicis** : felicis (*bis*) E. **fortunae** : furtunati B, furtunatae E, *om.* W. **bermiae** : hermiae B, beriniae E. **eracli** . heracli BW. **dissi parini** : parmi diss i BW, parmidissei E, + herme H. **posses-soris** : possessori W. **prosalm bis** : prosolmi (-lini E) prosalami H, + heracli (er- B) H. **uincentiae** : + eusebii tituli conditoris H, + prosolmi B, prosolini E.

Drum. and *Ch. Ch. Mart.* have here the Vigil of the Assumption. Gorman has Eusebius here.

August 15.

init. + adsumptio s. mariae BW(R)S. **stratonis** : strationis W. **ignati, tursi . . . geurgii** : *om.* H. **pilippi** . philippi (-ipi E) H, + euticiani (eutit- B) HS.

Syr. Aug. 15 has Philip and Antiochus.

For Straton, Philip and Eutychianus see *A A.SS.*, Aug. iii. 418 (August 17).

Ignatius, Tursus and Zefanus appear also on Aug. 16

August 17.

dissiae disiae BE, *om.* W. **romulae, eli, gallae iohani transillae, zefani** : *om.* H. **mammetae** : mammetis, mammite B, mammetis, mammetae E, mammitae W. **emilianae**: emeli H. **mammetis monachi** : mammae E. **desei** : dissei (-isei E) H.

Gorman has on this day Mammes, Transil and Johan.

August 18.

agapiti : agapti E. **panteni** : pilentiae (philan- B) H. **pontimi** : pontemi E. **martini** : BRS, *om.* EW. **palanciae** : philantiae, pilentię B, pilentiae lantiae EW. **scolasticae marciae, cristinae luciae, sincliticae, erennae, romani** : *om.* H. **mosae** : masse (mo- E) H. **candidae, candidi** : candedi BW, candidae E. **helianae** : heliante B. **amantiae** : amicie B, maciae E, amatie W. **talamae taianae** : tatianae E, *om.* BW. **potomi** : potonii W, + martyrii agapiti eziaci (-iae WB ziai E) H, + arnulfi E. **dasci bis** : dissei BW, disciae E.

Philantiae (*panteni*) is Philanthes of Amasia mentioned in *Syr.* August 18.

Carth. has Massa and Candida on the same day.

Pope Martin died on 16 September 655, and is therefore misplaced here.

August 19.

magni (*bis*) : magnae R, *om.* W. **silonis, filionis, philonis** : silonis BER, filionis WS. **quirilli** : cyrilli H. **gelasii** : zelasi (el- W) H. **timothei** : thimothei W. **pontoni, eogeniae, laurentii, zefani . . . pauli** : *om.* H. **rosini** : rufini (roff- W) HRS. **leontii** : + ferreoli B. **marcioani** : marciani BE, mariani WS. **teodotae** : theodoli (te- E) H. **gaddae**: gatte B, ganddae E. **s. crucis** : *om.* E. **fin.** + ualentiani leonti dioscori pisti arcii diomedis agatini zeli pamphili coloui B.

For Magnus see *AA.SS.* Aug. iii. 701.

Oswin, King of Deira, was murdered on 28 August 651.

The last three clauses of B Aug. 19 correspond to EW Aug. 20. Consequently each article of B is dated one day earlier than that of EW up to Aug. 27, when the scribe of B divided an article into two parts, dated respectively Aug. 26 and Aug. 27. From Aug. 28 onwards the articles of B and EW correspond.

August 20 (B 19).

iulii . . . angeli, mammetis, quintini, ualentionis, mathei, luxorii : *om.* H. **ualentini** : ualentiani B, ualeriani E, ualentini aniani W, ualentiniani S. **pampilii** : pamphili B, pampi E, pamphyli W. **coloni** : coloui B, colonicenip W, *om.* E. **maximi** : *om.* BE. **pistriardi** : pisti arcii H. **diomidis** : diomedis (dim- W) H, + agatini (-thini E) H. **fin.** + fileberti WR.

Syr. has Dioscorides on this day.

It is difficult to believe that " Pampilii episcopi cum clero suo " are tne famous twelve martyrs in the Diocletian persecution. For that Pamphilus was not a bishop, and he was put to death on February 16 (Eus. *M.P.* 7 ff., *Syr.* Feb.16).

Alexandri is a corruption of Alexandria.

Philibertus died about 684.

August 21 (B 20).

init. + iuli B. **uincentii** : + auguri (-ori E) eulodi (eo- B) ippoliti (op- W) H. **ualentiani, ualentini** : ualentini H. **quadrati** : quadrati (*bis*) E, quatrati (*bis*) B, quatrati W, + primi EW, + pisti (pri- E) H. **timothei** : *om.* H. **leontiani, leontii** : leonti H. **luxori** : luxuri (-ori E) H, + traiani H. **artosii** : ortosii B, artiui E, artorii W. **sotici** : zotici (zet- E) H, + agatangeli (zat- E, azatangli W) privati H.

TALLAGHT. M

Here we compare EW Aug. 21, with B Aug. 20, and the first clause of B Aug. 21.

T Aug. 20 has nine personal names which also appear in T Aug. 21.

Zoticus is mentioned in *Syr.* Aug. 21.

August 22 (B 21).

timothei : thimothii W, *hiat.* B. **expectiti** : epictiti H. **aprilis** : aprelis E. **felicis** (*bis*) : felicis H. **tasseusi, sedrac natani** : *om.* H. **meneruii** : *om.* BW. **emiliani** (*bis*) : emeliani H. **simfroniani** : simforiani (-phor- E sym- W) H. **pigrini** : peregrini ER, peregrinorum W, *om.* B. **martialis** : marcialis H. **nectiui, necturi**: nectari B, nectaris E, nectavi W, + seui H. **marcelli** : *om.* BW. **aurelii**: R, aurae BW. **ipoliti** : ippoliti E, *om.* BW. **medardi** : *om.* E.

Rom. and *Carth.* have Timotheus on Aug. 22.

For Symphorianus see Ruinart, p. 78.

August 23 (B 22).

fortunati : furtunati H. **hermoginis, ermoderi** : hermogenis BW, ermodori E. **sirti** : sixti (xis- W) H. **martialis** : marcialis H. **zefani, ciciliae mariae basillae, dn̄o arafranis** : *om.* H. **hermogeratis** : hermogerati H. **laurentii** (*bis*) : laurenti H. **abundi** : habundi E. **inocentii** : innocenti BW, innocentum, innocenti E. **mirendini** : merendini W. **ipoliti, munni, ypoli** : yppoliti qui dicitur nonnus BW, nunni ER. **ciriaci bis** : quiriaci (cyr- E) H. **archilaii** : archilei B, archelai E. **laudi, claudii** : claudi BE, *om.* W. **apollinaris** : appollinaris E, appolonaris W, *om.* B. **sidonii** (*bis*) : sidonii (-nodi E) H. **neonis**: *om.* W. **archei** : arcei E, *om.* BW. **domninae** : domninae BE, *om.* W, + mineruini (-rvi W) eleazari (eli- B, elez- E) H. **asteri** : *om.* W. *fin.* + sinforiani B.

Augusti is a corruption of Augustodunum, and *arafranis* of Arverna.

Archei is probably a duplicate of *Archilaii.* T has five other duplicates in this article.

August 24 (B 23).

zenoni, genobii, zenoui : genobi BW, zenoui E, zenonis R. **iulii, iunillae, magenoli** : *om.* H. **italicae** : *om.* W. **capitolini** : capitulini BW. **emeritae** : *om.* W. **genesi** : + patricii geldardi (geddordi E) H, + epadi B, eptati W. **partholomei** : vig. bartholomei B, *om.* EW. *fin.* + audoini WS.

Four names here are also on August 25. Their presence in this place is due to the use of a misdated article. See August 20.

Carth. has " Genesis mimi."

August 25 (B 24).

bartholomei : *om.* W. **eptati** : aptati E, *om.* W. **genesi** : genis E. **iulii** : + hermetis iusti pastoris H. **patricii, reuersinae, mariae italicae, iunillae zefani timothei, ioseph** *om.* H. **euticitis** : R, euticetis ES, *om.* BW. **eoticae** : euticae H, eutici S. **rufine** : rufini S. **iohannis** : iacobi fratris iohannis R, *om.* H.

August 26 (B 25).

quinti, cinti : quintini BW, quinti E. **zefani quarti, bassi meroni, celsi, rufini** : *om.* H. **maximiani** : maximiliani BW. **seueri** : seui H. **mercurii** : mercori E. **uictoris** : uictoris (*bis*) H. **coloceri bis, eleutheri** : eleuteri B, cleotheri E, eleutheri W. **basillae** : baseli W, *om.* E.

Bassi, basillae and *meroni, mercuri,* may be doublets.

August 27 (B 26, 27).

rufi, rufini : rufi ERS, rufini BW. **sabbati, sabasti** : sabbati ER, sabasti BWS. **felicis** : + aronti (ora- W) H. **zefani bis** : stefani (steph- B) H, + sulpicii B. **laurenti, dionisii, domni gauiniani castori mariae teodoriae, baluinae**: *om.* H. **sabiani, sauiani** : sabiniani BW, sauiani ER. **honorati** : honori E, honorini R. **tribuni** : + emannis (et manis E, et mannis W) H. **cesarii** (*bis*) : cessari E, cesarie R, caesarii S, + siagri BW, suacri E. **iohannae** : iohanne (-es B) H, + serapionis BW. **petri** : petro E. **basillae** : basileae E, + olti B, olii W.

B here divides a single article into two. The two correspond to EW 27. Rufus (not Rufinus) is correct. See *Analecta Boll.*, v. 329.
Syr. Aug. 27 has "Sabas the presbyter and Alexander."
Potenti is not a personal name, but the place, Potentia, at which four martyrs suffered on this day : Arontius, Honoratus, Fortunatus (=Felix above) and Sabinianus (= Sabianus). See *AA.SS.* Sept. i. 135.
Hermes appears also on August 28 (*q.v.*).
Clerici is apparently the title of Serapion. Since Serapion is omitted in T, "clericus" suggests a personal name.
Petrus, Johannes and Serapion were the sons of Tribunus and his wife Mannis.

August 28.

hermis hermetis : hermetis H. **zefani bis** : stefani (steph- B) H, + polei B, polici E, polieni W. **alexandri** : alaxandri E, + uiuiani H. **augustini** : agustini H, + iuliani bibiani (uiui- E uibi- W) H, + pelagii S. **fausti** : faustini E, *om.* BW. **excellentissimi laurenti ciriaci scribae basillae** : *om.* H.

Hermes appears in *Rom.* Aug. 28 : "Hermetis in Basillae Salaria vetere." The name of the companion of Hermes is here Basileus H.
Constantii is an error for the city of Constantinopolis.
St. Augustine, Bishop of Hippo, is commemorated on Aug. 29 in *Carth.* Basilla the virgin is misplaced from H Aug. 29.

August 29.

init. + sauinae RS. **helesei**: helisie B, *om.* E. **heli**: helie BW, *om.* E. **pauli bis** : pauli H. **felicis** : + candidę (-edi W) foricię (furinae E) adausię H. **zefani, concordiae mariae elizabeth coronae** *om.* H. **gemillinae** : gemellinae H. **basillae** : + nicę (-ci E -ceae W) H.

Natalis et aliorum dcccc is misplaced and corrupt. It comes from *natale s. iohannis . . . aliorum dcccc mar.* (BW).
The decollation of the Baptist at Sebaste (on the site of Samaria) is here in BW. TS have in view the later legend of the finding of his head at Emesa (Emisma T, Emissa S). See *D.C.A.* i. 883a.
Syr. Aug. 29 has Basilla.
For *Mariae elizabeth* see Dec. 18.

August 30.

init. + commodellę B. **agapae . . . herennae, eufemiae . . . cirillae, geurgii, paulini . . . iohannis** : *om.* H. **felicis** : *om.* W. **adauti** : adacti B, adauoti R, adaucti W.

The first seven names in T seem to indicate a group of female martyrs, and the last four may be the group in H, *gaudentiae uirg. cum aliis tribus.*
Felix is commemorated in *Carth.* Aug. 30.

August 31.

paulini lini : paulini H. **zefani, collociae mariae, marialitae fithionae humilianae, iohannis brigitoniae** : *om.* H. **iulianae** : iulię H. **italicae** : uitalice W, + antiquire (-ri W) . BW. **uincentii** :

M 2

uincentie B.   **uitalici** : italicae E, + eladi (ell- B) sirgi (se- E, sy- W) florentini (-ianae E) adcenie (*om.* EW) optati H.   **emiliani** : emilini B. **antinchi antiochi** : antinei BW, anthimei E, + maximi BW.
Triueris (Trèves) should have been before *paulini.*
Lini is a duplicate of the last four letters of *paulini.*

September 1.

ciciliae, tonsae musae mariae agnae, teclae, zefani, egidii laurentii, nausi iesu naue, gedeon, uincentii donati (*ter*): *om.* H.   **calistae:** caleste BE, + tasciae H.   **donatae** : *om.* E.   **fortunatae, fortunati** : furtunati H, + primi materni E.   **prisci** : prisci (*bis*) E.   **marci** : marciani W, *om.* E.   **torentiani** : terentiani (terr- E) H.   **euodii** : erodi E, euoti W.   **hermoginis** : hermogenis BW.   **felicis** (*sec.*) : *om.* E.   **constantini** : constanti ES, constansi R.   **feliciani** : RS, *om.* H.   **amansi** ; amausi H.   **uictor.i** : uictoris H, + lupus W.   *fin.* + uenerae S.

Iesu naue (Joshua son of Nun) and Gideon appear in a gloss on Oengus, Gorman, *Drum.*, and *Ch. Ch. Mart.*, Sept. 1.

Fortunatus, Donatus and Felix were three of a band of twelve brothers. They were buried on Aug. 29, but were commemorated on Sep. 1 (*AA.SS.* Sep. 1. 138).

Cleomannis is an error for the name of one of the districts in Gaul called Cenomani.

Tascia (Tuscus), Dubitatus and Ualentius appear also on Sept. 2 (H).

September 5.

taurini, tauri: taurini (*bis*) BES, taurini WR.   **herculini** : herculiani (-lani E) H, + aristusi (-osi W) BW, + eutici maximi E.   **zefani, mariae iuliae iulitae, quintiani torsi** : *om.* H.   **saturnini bis**: saturnini BE, *om.* W.   **saturnini** (*tert.*): saturninae H.   **memorati**: nemosati H, nemorati S.   **arapolini** : arapollini H, + ferrioli (-eoli B) H.   **ferrucionis**: ferrutionis W.   **nimpi** : R, nemfidi BW, nimpi, nimfidae E.

Rom. has here Acontius (*sic*) in Porto, Nonnus, Herculanus and Taurinus. None of the authorities have Nonnus.

Syr. has Nymphius.   Doubtless *nimpi* and *nimfidae* are corruptions of that name.

Quintiani torsi may be a confusion of *quinti anitorsi* (=*quinti arconti* H).

September 6.

eleutherii : eleuteri BE, eleotheri W.   **coditi** . cuttidi BE, cottidi W, guttidi S.   **zefani** : *om.* H.

This Eleutherus was an Abbot in Rome.   See Gregory, *Dial.* 4.

September 7.

init. + innocenti R.   **senoti, sinoti** : senoti BW, sinoti E, sinociae S. **festi** : fisti B.   **acuti** : agusti B.   **lauani, capudaci laurenti** : *om.* H. **anathasii** : amastasii H, + agustalis (*om.* W) euorti   chlodoaldis (-ova- E) regine (*om.* E) H.

Capudaci seems to be an error for Capua ciuitas.   Possibly *lauani* may be a corruption of Aureliani (Orleans).

September 8.

mariae : *om.* E, + timothei (thi- W) H.   **eulaliae anastasiae britoniae hirandinis, iohannis, zefani pampili neotini** : *om.* H.   **fausti** : fausti (*bis*) B.   **pii bis** : pii W.   **teophili** : theofili (-oli W) H.   **piotheri** : neotheri H.   **nemesis** : nemesi (nemm- B) H.   **ammoni, ammonis** : ammoni (*bis*) BE, ammoni W.   **petri** : petrini E.   **seuerini** : sauini (se- E) H. **dimetri** : demetri H. **dedimi** : didimi BW, dudini E. **nistori mistori** : mitisori (mito- E) H, + panei B, panemoti E, paneti W, + achillae (-ilae E) H. **orosei**: orusei H. **isiodori** : hysidori B, isidori E, hisidori W. **serapionis** (*sec.*) : *om.* W, + migete (-itiae E -ite W), H. **siluini** : siluiani B, silvini E, siluani W. **metri** : *om.* W. **orobionis** : arapionis B, aropionis W. **seueri** : seueri (*bis*) BW. *fin.* + adriani RS.

Syr. on Sept. 8 mentions Faustus a presbyter, Ammonius and twenty other martyrs ; and on Sept. 9 Siluanus.

On the names *nemesis* . . *ammonis* see note on Sept 10.

September 9.

hacunti, iacinti : iacenti (-inti E) H. **alexandri** : in alēx E. **tiburti**: tiburi E. **eleasi**: cleasi H, + ammoni BW. **fortunati**: furtunati H, + marci H. **liberati** : lebrati, *om.* E. **deusii geurgii damiani eugulfi cirici iohannis** : *om.* H. *fin.* + kerani S.

Rom. has Gorgonius on this day. Another Gorgonius is commemorated on March 11.

Ammonius appears at Sept. 8 (TH) and Sept 10 (H).

September 10.

euepiae : R, euplie BW, eufepiae E. **cursici** : cupsici H. **hisici** : hysici B, + alapon (-oni E) H. **siluasii** : siluani BW, + saluii B, + nemesi . . herosi H. **hielini, augusti nectari depletori mauriolioris zarii salui tursi zefani, iohannis pauli** : *om.* H. **dedimi** : didimi (du- E) H. **merefori, merosori** : meresori (meri- W) H, + panoepsi (-nopia E -nepsi W) . siluini H. **hilarii** : helari W, + doletatuli B, catuli E, doletatule ualentini (-nae E) H.

Dedimi merefori (*merosori*) is a remnant of a list of Alexandrian martyrs in H, beginning with *nemesi* and ending with *siluini* (or with *seueri*, as we shall see), seventeen in number (apart from such notes as *et aliorum viii*). Now *Syr.* has on this day commemorated " Nemesius the presbyter and seventeen others." In our list there are seventeen names, and at first sight they are names of the group of martyrs headed by Nemesius. But it has no less than six doublets : *nemesi nemesini, ammoni* twice, *herosi orosi, panoepsi panemoti, siluani siluini, niceti* twice. Obviously the list is corrupt. On the other hand there is a similar list at Sept. 8, from Nemesius to Severus, numbering seventeen names, agreeing with *Syr.* Moreover it has no doublets, and it includes all the names in the list of Sept. 10, if *migetae* and *niceti* are the same person. It seems therefore that the more correct list of the Alexandrian martyrs is misplaced under Sept. 8, and belongs to Sept. 10.

Depletori is a corruption. See Sept. 13.

Pope Hilary died 467.

September 11.

prothi : proti H. **iacinthi** : iacinti (-enti W) H. **eugeniae** : *om.* E. **siri** : syri W. **euleliae mariae musae, militiadis, petri iohannis tomae** : *om.* H. **basillae** : *om.* E, + ingenui BW. **ypoliti** : ippoliti (epo- W) H. **patientis** : patienti B, pacientis E, + regule maurilionis B. **donati** : donatae BE.

Rom. has " Proti et Iacinti in Basillae."

Gorman has Eulalia.

Basilla is the name of a cemetery.

Patiens, Bishop of Lyons, died *c.* 485 (*D.C.B.* iv, 199).

September 12.

timothei : RS, *om.* H. **epuli** : cupli B, eupli EW. **serapionis** : serapioni W. **petri** : proti BWRS, perti E. **ipoliti** : hippoliti B, ippoliti E, ypholiti W, + amenone B, ammoni E, ammone W. **sanctinae**: sanctini H,

mariae, transili, zefani iuliani laurentii celsi : *om*. H. herclii : eracli B,
heracli E, heracliae W. teophili : tiophile B, diofili E, *om*. W, + matronę H,
eusebii : + beati sacerdotis, euanti epi., euanti epi. B, sacerdotis epi.,
evanti epi. E, beati sacerdotis epi., beati epi. W.

September 13.

   felicissimi : felicis E, felicissi W. secundini, secundi : secundini
BW, secundi ERS, teodoli : theodoli BE, *om*. W. timothei : *om*. W.
litori, depletori, lodori : litori (*bis*) B, litori EW. marulionis : maurilionis
H. pectori, parmenii quinti, geurgi : *om*. H. beati : *om*. EW.   :.
   Agusti is a place-name—Augustodunum.
   Beati is probably not a personal name.
   Depletori (T) and *deplitori* (E) are blunders of *depos litori* (B). It is
possible that *pectori* is an error for *litori* or *nectari*.

September 14.

   cornelii : cornili BW. cipriani : + aurelii S. dionisii bis : dionisi
H. felicis : felicis *bis* E. honori : honorati B. dimetri : demetri B,
demetri, dimetri E, dimitri W. zetae : zettae E. mariae romulae,
iohannis petri zefani mathei : *om*. H. epartii : epanti E, eparci W. *fin*.
+ exaltatio s. crucis BW.
   Pope Cornelius died in 252.
   For the *Acta Cypriani* see Gebhardt, p. 124 ; and note *Rom*. and
Carth. Sept. 14.
   R has *apparatio s. crucis* instead of *exaltatio s.c. Epartii* may be an
error for *apparatio*.

September 15.

   ded. basil. mariae, epacti zefani, ioseph maglaconi mariae
sincliticae : *om*. H. cirini : cyrini H. serapionis leonti (*bis*) : sera-
pionis leonti H. seleuci : seleoci B. arthei · marcii B, artei E, arcii W.
ualerii : ualeri (*bis*) BW, faleri, valeri E, + cundiani E. cirionis : cyrionis
R, *om*. BW. merobi : macrobi E. stratoris : stratonis BER, stratori W.
pauli, paulini : pauli BW, paulini E, + ualeriani aplini (appini E, albini W)
H. gordiani : *om*. E. arcioni : archeon BW, *om*. E. constantii : +
apri B. nicodimi : nicondimi R, nicomedis S, *om*. H.
   Oengus and Gorman have the dedication of the basilica of Mary.
   Galitiae is an error for Galatia. Cp. E.
   Syr. has Serapion on Sept. 14 and Seleucus on Sept. 15.
   TH have a group of martyrs : *cirini serapionis leonti croci*, and BW call
them "three (*sic*) brothers." Elsewhere (*A A. SS*. Sept. iv. 14) they are
named Cronides, Leontius and Serapion. Obviously *cirini* and *croci* are corrup-
tions of Cronides. Note also *cirionis*.

September 16.

   init. + luciae S. felicis bis : felicis (*bis*) BE, felicis W. zefani,
iohannis (*bis*), mariae, romulae gallae : *om*. H. uiatoris : uictoris (*bis*)
BE, uictoris W. spepati : sperati H, + nauati (nou- E -iti W) corinthi
(-ti E) H. lolati : lopati (lov- E, lup- W) H. prisciani, prisizati : pris-
ciani BW, prisizani E. tussi : tyrsi H, + naboris B. salui : salti W.
papiae : pafies B, papias E, papiae, pafies W. secundae : secundae (*bis*)
BE. donatae : *om*. W. bessiae : bissie B, besiae E, *om*. W. generosae :
om. W. ciciliae : caeciliae (*bis* B) H. emerentianae merentianae :
emerentianitis (-natis W emerentiae E) H. eufemiae : + geminiani S.
   Carth. has Eufemia on this day.
   Emerentianitis in E is cut in two, one portion of the name preceding, and
the other following *eufemiae*.

September 17.

gordiani, dordiani : gurdiani (gor- B) , H. **magrini** : macrini BE. ,**constantii, constantiae** : constanti BW, constantiae ERS. **sanctini** : sanctini BW, sanctiae ER, + landeberti (-perti S, -teberti B, -diberti W) BWRS. **paulini** : pauli BW. **maronii** : macrobi (-pi B) H. **gaudiani** : ga diani W. **laurentii, paliosi petri mauricii, mariae trinsille**: *om.* H. **isici** : ysici B, husici E. **socratis** : *om.* W. **zefani** : stephani,B, stefani E, *om.* W. **eufemiae** : + saleosi EW, + seu posto B, stoporei E, sui portio W.

Gordiani magrini and *maronii gaudiani* seem to be a doublet in TH. *Calcidoni* is apparently a place-name (Chalcedon).

Gorman and *Ch. Ch. Mart.*, have Laurentius.

September 18.

trofimi : trophimi E. **sisti** : syxti (xis- W) H. **eustorgi, eutropii** : eustorgi W, eutropi BERS. **saturi bis** : satyri BW. **dimetri pallei** : demetri pallae E, *om.* BW. **nibi heli** : *om.* BW. **primadi** : parimadi E, *om.* BW. , **pauli, iuliani**: *om.* H. **castoris niceti ianuarii angi, paterni felicis** : E, *om.* BW. **medeti** : medethei E, medecii S, *om.* H.

The last twelve names in E on this day *pii* . . . *singoni*, with the exception of *paterni felicis*, have no connexion with T. They are therefore discarded in the collation.

Syr. has Oceanus on Sept. 18. But Castor appears in *Syr.* Sept. 19, and Ianuarius in *Carth.* Sept. 19. This suggests that the list *dimetri* . . *felicis*, without support, except from E, is misplaced. In fact ,on Sept. 19 we find in BW a list, without support from E, which includes every name in our list save *pauli* and *angi*. Pauli is probably a doublet with *pallei* ; and on Sept. 19 *aniceti* B, *ancii* W, correspond to *angi*.

For Trophimus see Sept. 20.

September 19.

dimetri: demetri BE. **aniceti, anci** (Irish group): aniceti BER, ancii W. **palei nilii**: *om.* E. **pari madieli**: parimadi helii B, pari madi helii W, *om.* E. **saturi** : saturnini S, *om.* E, + niceti BW. **trofi** : trophi B, trophy W, *om.* E. **ferili** . ferreoli B, ferioli WS, feaioli R, *om.* E, + iuliani BW. **militi** : mileti S, *om.* E. **iorgii** : trogi BW, *om.* E.

The list beginning with *pii* (BW) is disregarded in the collation. Cp. note on Sept. 18.

Diapoli is an error for *Neapoli.*

Peleus, Nilus, Patermuthius and Elijah were "perfected by fire" on 19 Sept. 310. (Eus. *M.P.* 13). The names are here sadly deformed. The martyrs suffered, not at Alexandria (BW), but at Phaeno.

September 20.

daromae : doromae BER, dormidoni W, doromi S. **constantiae** : constantiae *(bis)* H, + vig. mathei B. **priuatae priuati** : priuati H. **felicis** : felicis *(bis)* H, + ianuarii S. **dionisii** : *om.* W, + dorothei BS, dorothe W. **iohannis celsi** : *om.* H.

The Greek Acts of Trophimus *(AA.SS.* Sept. vi. 12) state that, with his companion Dorymedon, he suffered on Sept. 18 at Synnada. *Syr.* has Dorymedon at Synnada under Sept. 20. W has here "Sinada ciuit. nat. s. Dormidoni." It is possible therefore that *daromae* etc. are corruptions of Dorymedon. Trophimus does not appear in *Syr.* But under Sept. 18 he is mentioned as a martyr at Alexandria (BW) or Chalcedon (ERS). The date is that of the Acts.

September 21.

mattei: mathei (-ithei W) H. **eldoni, sedrac** . . . **clementis**: *om.* H.

September 22.

expueri : exsuperii (exu- EW) H.   **candidi** : candedi BW.   **uitalis :** + siluani BS, + siluestri B, + germani H.   **pantaleonis** . . . **ipocrati, mariae** . . . **erasmi** : *om.* H.   **basillae** : basilae E.

The scribe of T seldom deliberately tells us the place of a martyrdom. But in this place he mentions two, the city of Sacina above the river Rhone, and Necomedia.   *Sacina, Uelensi* seems to be a corrupt spelling of Acaunum Ualensium (St. Moritz in the Valais).   Cp. *ualensi loco agaunum* (B).   There the massacre of the Theban Legion took place.   According to the *Passio s. Mauricii* (Ruinart, p. 274) only the names of four martyrs were known: Mauricius, Exsuperius, Candidus and Victor.   But TH mention Innocentius and Vitalis.

Rom. has " Basillae Salaria uetere," with the date 22 Sept. 304. Oengus has Pantaleo.

September 23.

sosii : sossi E, sosi R, *om.* BW. *Carth.* has *Sossi.*   *Euasnit* is explained by W : " Tecle que aroma igne deposita *euasit* " etc.

For Thecla see Gebhardt 215.

September 24.

siri, mariae, elizabeth secundae, siluani zefani silurini, iohannis, petri lini cornilii : *om.* H.   **martialis** : marcialis BW, maleialis E, + uictoris H.   **tuitsi** . tyrsi H.   **uictoriae** (*bis*) : uictoriae BW, *om.* E, + desiderii B.   **faustinae** : + ualeriẹ celerinẹ (-ni E -ianẹ W) donatulẹ (-tillae E) luciosẹ H.   **crizofori** : cristofori laurenti H.   **marci** : *om.* E.   **stragili** : gargili H.   **liberi** . ERS, *om.* BW.   **nobilis** : *om.* E.   **priscillae** : R, *om.* H.

Priscillae was probably the name of the cemetery in which Pope Liberius was buried.   The death of Liberius is commemorated on both September 23 and 24.   The latter date seems to be correct (Lightfoot, *Apostolic Fathers,* I. i. 299 f.).

Elizabeth may have been mentioned in a note on the Conception of the Baptist known to the scribe of T.

Peter and Popes Linus and Cornelius are out of place here.   Cornelius is commemorated on Sept. 14, Peter and Linus Dec. 22.

September 25.

bardoniani : barduniani BW, + marci WS.   **carpi eucarpi** : eucarpi (*bis* B) H.   **eusebii senatoris** : E, *om.* BW.   **zefani pauli timothei titi** : *om.* H.   *fin.* + luxuri migeni nabroti faustini appollinaris E, + marci W.

Eight names above (five of E) appear in Sept. 26.

September 26.

senatoris faustini : *om.* E, + apollonaris (app- W) BW.   **luxurii** : luxorii BW, *om.* E.   **migni** : migigni BW, *om.* E.   **zefani, cirici iohannis** : *om.* H.   **nabartii** : naporti B, nabori W, naborti S.

Rom. has " Eusebii in Callisti " in Sept. 26.   This seems to show that the following names in E are misplaced under Sept. 25.

September 27.

timothei : thimothei W.   **cosmae** : cosinae W.   **damiani** : + antimi S, + leontii S, legonti B, + eutropii S.   **eleuterii** : eleutheri W.   **andronici** : andronaci E, + romani E.   **florentiani** : florentini W.   **iohannis celsii laurentii** : *om.* H.

Cosmas, Damianus, Anthimus, Leontius and Eutropius were brothers (S) See *D.C.B.* i. 691 ; *AA.SS.* Sept. vii. 469.

September 28.

marcialis : + leontii S. **laurientiae** : laurentino B, laurenti W, + iuuiniani B. **uictoriae** : uicturiae W. **luciosae** : luciẹ W, + emili (-eli B) gagili (-eli E) H. **mariae, scolasticae teothosae, cristinae, sincliticae, zefani**: *om*. H. **longiosae** : longese (-gae E) H, + secundae E. **candidae** : *om*. E. **ualeriae** : uariae W, + celerine BW. **uictoriae** : uicturiae E, *om*. W. **gurgelli** : gurgilii (-eli E, -uli W) H. **fausti** : faustini H. **placidi** : placedi W.

None of the names under Rome, Auxerre or Genoa in H appear in T. We therefore discard them. We have to do with a single group of African martyrs. R dispatches it with the words " Marcialis et aliorum xx." The same words head the list in E. And again "et aliorum xx" appears after *placidi* in TH. We expect that the list should have 21 names. Actually T has 22 names (or 21 if *scolasticae* is not a personal name, but a title), while H has about the same number. But these lists of T and H do not agree. T has 6 (5) names which are not in H, and H has 3 (4) which are not in T. Sixteen names are in both T and H.

Secundae (E) may be an error for *candidae*.

Leontii (S) is doubtless borrowed from Sept. 27.

September 29.

euticii, euteci : eutici H. **sosii** : possesi E. **ampuli** : anbuti B, ambodi E, ambuti W, + salutari E. **heracliae** : eracliae BW, in eracla ES. **eugeniae mariae, humilianae teothotae, zefani, iohannis, geurgii, martini, patricii ciricii** : *om*. H. **traciae** *(bis)* : traciae BW, *om*. E. **celidoni** : celedoni (cael- W) H. **iamputiani ambodi** : ampuni B, ampli E, ambuni W. **paluti** : plauti BE, *om*. W.

Syr. has two persons named Eutychius, a bishop and a martyr. T therefore is right in commemorating two, Euticius and Eutecius against all our other authorities.

Heracliae may be an error for Heraclea. See ERS. Possibly *heracliae, traciae* is a corruption of Heracleia Trachinia (see BW).

Salutari (E) is probably a corruption of *via salaria* (B).

For St. Michael see *D.C.A.* ii. 1177.

September 30.

ieronimi : hieronimi (her- B) H. **antonini** : BRS, antoni EW. **licasti** : casti BS, (in) mesoli casti ER, *om*. W. **celsii, zefani, iohannis, honorii noe mariae** : *om*. H. **fictoris** : uictoris H. **desidei, desiderii** : desiderii BE, desiderii *(bis)* S, *om*. W.

Evidently T attaches the last syllable of *mesoli* to *casti*, omitting *meso*. *Mesoli* is a place-name (E). It is probably identical with Massyli in Numidia (Smith, *Dict. of Greek and Latin Geography*, ii. 453).

October 1.

lucae ev. aduentus reliquiarum, petri, iohannes, pauli, basillae basilissae, transillae, musae eugeniae brigitoniae baluinae geurgii, ciricii, autisii laurentii, doctoris : *om*. H. **crescentii** : criscenti H. **euagri**: euacri B. **denegotiae** : denegothiae W. **faustini** *(bis)* : faustini H. **alexandri** : alaxandri E. **eupropii** : eoppi, coppi B, eutropi E, eoprobi, copraepi W. **zefani** dedic. ecclesie s. stephani B, *om*. EW, + digne H. **remedii** : remigii B, + uedasti WR, + amanti R. **pignae** : digne BW, pigrae E. **catiae** : gottiae B, cotiae E, gotthiae W. **gotiae** : cotie *(bis)* BE, *om*. W, + passi BW. **christi** : cristi B, charisti E.

A gloss on Oengus states that the relics mentioned here were brought to Armagh. One tradition held that their final resting was at Armagh, another that they were deposited at Tallaght.

Remigius died about 530.

A glossator on Oengus rightly states that Germanus was Bishop of Auxerre. He died on 31 July 448, and was buried on Oct. 1.   See *D.C.B.* ii. 654.

It seems that *digne* (*pignae, pigrae*) *gotiae* (*catiae*) and *denegotiae* are various spellings of the same name, though B scatters them under two place-names. *Autisii* is a place-name : Autisiodorum. *Baluinae* is probably the name of a cemetery. See Oct. 4.

October 2.

euliter : eleuteri (-theri W) H, + liodiceri R, leodegarii S.   **primici, primi** : primi H.   **aurilli, cirilli** : quirilli BWS, quirini E.   **epetini, pitini** : pitini BW, epetini E.   **eusebii** (*bis*) : eusebi H.   **secundiani** : secundiani (*bis*) H.   **martini** : *om.* H.   **pantaleonis** : ponti leonis, placionis (plat- W) leonti BW, pantaleonis, platonis leonti E, pontii leonis S.

October 3.

candidae : R, candidi S, *hiat.* W.   **teuthotae, teodosti** : teoctisti BS, teotisti E, thugeni W, theotisti R.   **marcianillae, marciani, marcelliani** : marcelliani S, marciani R, *om.* BW, + uictoris H.   **felicis** (*bis*) : felicis H. **amboni** : amponi H.   **geni, celsii** : *om.* H.   **leodargi** : leudegarii B, *om.* EW.   **spargi** : separgi B, gapargi E, sapargi W.   **marci** . RS, *om.* BW. Leodegarius was murdered in 678 (*D.C.B.* iii. 684).

October 4.

marci : *om.* EW.   **marsini** : marsi H.   **marciani** : marcelli E, **dassi** : dasii EW.   **audacti** : adaucti BW, adauti, + carusi B, marusi W, + restituti BW.   **baluinae** : albine B, balbinae E, *om.* W, + marcellini B, marcelli E.   **iunillae leonillae heuualach bis** : *om.* H.

Marcus was an Egyptian. See B.

October 5.

placidi : *om.* E.   **euticii et al. xxx** : euti et al. xxx W, euticii et al. viii ERS.   **baraci** : barici H.   **firmati** : + flauiane (-inae E) H. **uictorini** : uicturini EW, + fausti H.   **quintini, zefani** : *om.* H.   **pelagii** : pilagi E.   **apollinaris** : appollonaris BW, appollinaris E.

For the Acts of Placidus, his brothers Eutychius and Victorinus, his sister Flauia, Donatus, Firmatus, Faustus and thirty others at Messana in Sicily, see *AA.SS.* Oct. iii. 114.   But Donatus does not appear here, and Flauiana suffered in Gaul.

Valenaci is a corruption of Valentia in Gaul.

October 6.

init. + marcelli H.   **casti** : casti (*bis*) BW.   **emelii** : emili (*bis*) B.   **saturnini** (*bis*) : saturnini W.   **zefani, teodorae mariae concordiae** : *om.* H. **felicis** : fedis B, fidis WS.   **fausti** . faustini BWS, *om.* E.   **marcialis** : *om.* E.   **baluinae** : balbinae E.

October 7.

mattei . mathei E, *om.* BW.   **carti** : quarti H.   **figii baricii** : sirgi [. . .] B, sigibarci E, syrgi W, sergi et bachi, sargi S.   **augusti** : agusti H.   **dionisii ianuarii** : *om.* BW, + faustini E.   **zefani iohannis, mariae, coronae iuliae rusticae, martini laurentii bis martini, iosippi rustici celsii murici** : *om.* H.   **marcialis priuati** : *om.* BW.   **tutillae** : tullie BE, *om.* W.   **pelagiae, eracli iuliani** : *om.* BW.   **apulei** : apullei R, *om.* H. *fin.* + columbani R.

Rom. Oct. 7 has " Marcus in Balbinac." This Pope appears on Oct. 6. All the names marked here omitted by BW, but having support from E, including *faustini*, appear in BW Oct. 8, and T there repeats all except

ianuarii. *Syr.* Oct. 8 has Pelagia under Antioch, and thus proves that they are misplaced here. See also E Oct. 8.
Rusticus is mentioned in BW Oct. 9, and in E Oct. 8.

October 8.

fausti : faustini H. **eusebii** (*bis*) : eusebii ERS, *om.* BW. **eraçli** : + candidi E, + tituli sui E, contituli sui R. **diodari** : diodori E, *om.* BW. **pilagiae** : pelagiae H. **chionae agapae herennae, iohannis** : *om.* H. **attici** : *om.* BW. **luduli** : lugduli E, *om.* BW. **iulii** : *om.* BW, + **gereon** affreniae dionisi E. **septimi** : *bm.* BW: dionisii: diunisi B; + ianuari BW. **eliuter rustici** : eleuteri rustici ER, *om.* BW. **marcillieni** : marcellini E, *om.* BW. **genuini** : *om.* BW. **nubii** : nuvii E, *om.* BW, + priminae E. **probii** : *om.* BW, + andronaci faruulfi E. **tracii** : taraci E, *om.* BW. **martialis priuatis** : marcialis (mart- E) priuati E.

Syr. Oct. 8 has Pelagia, who has support from H, and *Syr.* Oct. 9 Diodorus, who is supported by E only. Here there are 20 names without support from BW. All but three are in BW Oct. 9, though only eight of them appear in T Oct. 9. There are also here three place-names (E): Rome, Phrygia and Agrippina (Cologne). Two of them are also in BW Oct. 9. It is clear that all these are misplaced in this day.

October 9.

eusebii : *om.* BW. **eraclii** : eradi E, *om.* BW. **dionisii** : dionisi (*bis*) ES. **diodori** : diudori W. **attici** : caiti E, + quintisi . . . taraci E. **secundae** : *om.* BW, + salsae E. **mariae laudae lucidae eufemiae cirillae petri, pauli parisaci quintini, iuliani antonii** . *om.* H. **buti** : buttoli B, budduli W, *om.* E. **duoli** : luddoli BW, *om.* E. **septimi** : septimae E. **iulii** : *om.* E. **acripini** : agripini BW, agripinae E, + gereon BS, + afre BW. **eleutri** : eleutheri BW, *om.* E, + dionisii ep. BW, + rustici . . probi BW. **antonici** : andronici H.

Syr. has Diodorus on this day. We have here in T *eusebii eraclii dionisii, secundae salsae* without support from BW. They appear also in TH Oct. 10. The scribe of T suppresses *rustici . . . probi* BW, which are in TE Oct. 8 ; and the long list *quintisi . . . iocundi* in E Oct. 9.

Attici (*cauti*) appears in BW Oct. 10.

Gereon and Afra (Affrenia) are mentioned in E Oct. 8 and R Oct. 10.

If we glance at the first few lines of B on this day, and place beside them a passage of T, omitting some unsupported names, we shall discover some places. B : "In Laudicie frigie ciuitate   In Gall. ciuitate colonie Agripini." T : "Frigiae (. . .) Laudi Lucidae (. .) Acripini." Here we have Phrygia, a corruption of Laodicea, and Coloni i Agrippina (Cologne). A fourth place-name is Parisius (Paris).

Pauli parisaci is probably Paul the Pharisee.

October 10.

dionisii : + septimę B, septimi WS. **zefani fusti, marthae trifoniae perpetuae pauli ianuarii** : *om.* H. **diodoris** : clidoni B, *om.* EW. **salsae** : + geriani R, + cauti *etc.* BW.

T suppresses the list of names beginning with *cauti quintasi* in BW. Quintasius is mentioned in *Carth.* Oct. 10.

T has *eusebii eracli dionisii diodoris secundae*, and *pauli* in both Oct. 9 and Oct. 10.

October 11.

taci, danais : tanasi BW, taraci ERS. **probi** : ERS, *om.* BW. **andrioni, andoci** : andronici ERS, *om.* BW. **placidi** : placedi W. **fausti,** **faustini** : fausti H. **iohannis celsii, antoni uenusti petri, quintini** **quinti** : *om.* H. **uincentii, uenantii** : uenanti W, *om.* BE.

The *Acta ss. Tarachi Probi et Andronici* (Ruinart, p. 422 and *AA.SS.*
Oct. v. 566) give us the correct names of the first three persons mentioned
above and the date of their martyrdom (Oct. 11). BW give Tarachus the title
presbyter (*presbit.*, *prbi.*) : an error for *probi*. See Ap. 5, May 13.
Taraci probi andronici, eracli appear in BW Oct. 10.

October 12.

hedisti : edisti BW. **heustasii euasii** : eustasi BW, eustati E.
zefani, mariae petronillae, pauli, laurentii **mamedisti, secundi** : *om.*
H. **prosiriae** : proseriae BE. **eucharisti** : eucaristi BE. **fortunatae**
fortunati : furtunati BW, fortunatae, furtunati E. **celesti** : calesti
BW, caelesti E. **pilionis** : opilionis B, opinionis WS, + fecei E. **donati**
burri : burri (bo- R) donati (bo- R) ER, *om.* BW.

Two place-names : Syria and Biturices.
Laurentii mamedisti is an error for "uia Laurentina Edisti."

October 13.

marcelli ep., marci ep. : marcelli (*bis* E) H. **martialis, marciae** :
marcialis ERS, marciae BW. **fausti** : fausti (*bis*) H, fausti, faustini S.
andrae, andriani : adriani BWS, adriae ER. **musae proseriae perpetuae**
felicitatis mariae, munesanae, agripiani, simplicii probi aciriani
rusti : *om.* H. **achanusti** : athanasii H.

Syr. Oct. 13 has "In Chalcedon Adrias the bishop."
For the Acts of Faustus, Januarius and Martialis see Ruinart, p. 535
and *AA.SS.* Oct. vi. 193.
Fausti, andriani and *probi* are in T Oct. 11, as also are *marcelli* and
marcialis.
Proceria and *mariae* are in T Oct. 12.
For Perpetua and Felicitas see note on Aug. 10.
Aciriani is probably a corruption of Andrianus.

October 14.

calisti celesti : calesti B, calisti E, caelesti W. **calapotii, mogemoc-**
ineicaill, prociui: *om.* H. **saturi**: saturi (*bis*) H, + placidi H, + domni E.
lupili, luppi : lupi (*bis*) H, + auriliae (-eli E) H. **ampodi** : + modesti
H. **saturnini** : + simplici H. **paulini** : *om.* BW. *fin.* + fortunatae S.
Calapotii is a cemetery : "In cimiterio Calepodi" (BW).
Rom. Oct. 14 has "Callisti in uia Aurelia miliario iii."
Oengus has here Paulinus, a bishop.
Mogemocineicaill is apparently a corruption of Mocholmoc Insi Cain,
which would be a pet form of Colum, who is in the Irish list.

October 15.

cecae : careae S, *om.* BW. **sussi** : sossii S, *om.* BW. **lupi** : lupilie B,
luplili W, lubuli R, lupuli S, *om.* E. **mirei aufichi** : minei aufidi E, *om.*
BW. **saturnini**: S, *om.* BW, + ambrosii luciani S. **nerei**: *om.* BW.
zefani agripini patricii donaetae, mariae brigitoniae saetaminae
tommeni : *om.* H. **fortunatae** : furtunatae W, *om.* E.
Maurorum is the only name which has support from H. Six names
supported by E appear also on Oct. 16. *Lupi* and *fortunatae* have support
from BW, but without support from E. Evidently a scribe placed E Oct. 16
immediately after the short article in Oct. 15 (not noting the date) ; and then,
discovering his mistake, transferred *cereae* (*cecae*) to Oct. 16. Cp. Oct. 9, 10.
Agripini is a place-name (see EWR). Apparently *patricii* is a corruption
for the city of Patrias (see R).
The Mauri, according to *Ch. Ch. Mart.*, are the martyrs of the Theban
Legion.
Donaetae may be a repetition of (*for*)*tunatae.*

October 16.

caere : caecrae B, cereae E, cecrae W. **leudgari martini, iohannis zefani mariae heraclae, transillae, michaelis** : *om.* H. **siasii** : sussi BW, *om.* E. **meri** : merei BW, *om.* E, + aufidi BWS, + uicturiae nobilitanae mariani galli S. **saturni** : saturnini BW, *om.* E, + nerei BWS, ambrosii + lucẹ B.
For *leudgari* see Oct. 3. For Ambrosius and Lucas see S Oct. 15.

October 17.

nicodimi alexandrini : nicomedia alexandri BW, in alaxandria nicomedis RS, in alāx nicodimis nicom̄ alaxandri E, + nini H. **nobilitani** : S, in belitani E, mobilitanae W, + mariani (-nẹ W) H. **zefani, agnae, mariae, marialitae, petrassii, laurentii** : *om.* H. **ueneriae, uenerei** : ueneri H. **uictoriae** : uictorii (*bis*) B, uictoris, uictoriae E, uicturiae (*bis*) W, + basillae (bassilae E) H, + luce B. **mammae** : memmae BE, + zitiani B, zidiari E, yziciani W, + primae H. **donatae**: donati, donate H, + seuere H. **lucitini, accintini** : luci cittini BW, luci et tinni E, lucii S. **rusticiani** : rustitiani B, + seruiliani H. **ianuarii** : + mustuli (-oli W) H. **crescentii** : criscentiani (cres- E, -ciani W) H. **rufiani** : rufiniani H. **uel hic honor michaelis** : *om.* H.
There seems to be some confusion in the beginning of THRS here. BW have *nicomedia alexandri*, while RS have *alexandria nicodimis*. One of these may be right and the other wrong. E has both. T has two personal names, *nicodimi alexandrini*, inclining to BW. *Alexandrini* (T) may be an error for *alexandri nini*.
For *michaelis* see Oct. 16.

October 18.

lucae : lucae (*bis*) BW. **pilippi** : filip E, philippi RS, *om.* BW. **luci**: luci (*bis*) E. **uictorini**: uictorinẹ W, *om.* E. **petri, teclae mariae fithioniae uictoriae ciciliae eunuchei, pauli simfroniani, trifoniae**: *om.* H. **ianuarii** (*bis*) : ianuarii HS. **bressei, beresepiae** : beresi epi. H. **uictricis**: uitricis W. **leucii** : *om.* E. **agnae** : agnetis B, agnitis W. **uictorici** : gituri E, uicturici W, **uictoris** : + dasi (-silae E) H. **martialis** : marcialis H. **euticis** : eutecis W, euticetis S.
Carth. Oct. 18 has "Leuci et Victurici."
Potioli is a place-name (Puteoli).

October 19.

austini, austeri, asperi : asteri BE, austeri W, asperi R. **susii** : sussi H. **festi** : festi (*bis*) E. **ianuarii** : *om.* E. **prosodociae** : prosdoci (-ciae E) H, prosduci S. **nicae mariae** : nicematris B, nicae matris EWR, nicae S. **humilianae, agathae ozi, iohannis, tomae, celsii** : *om.* H. **domnae** : domne W, *om.* BE. **nectasiae, eustasiae** : ej[us]tasie B, et tassiae ER, *om.* W, + asti busti H. **pelagiae** : + columbani W. **beronici** : berononici B. **euthicitis** : eutici E, euticetis RS, *om.* BW, + acutii S.
Neapuli, puteolis are place-names.

October 20.

eutici : euticis W. **promicei** . promaci H. **dassi** : dasi BW, *om.* E, + zosimi H. **ianuarii** (*bis*): ianuarii (*bis*), ianuarie B, ianuariae (*bis*) E, ianuari, ianuarianẹ W, ianuarii RS. **suscemi suscimi, sisinni** : sussimi (*bis*) B, sisinni E, sussimi W, susimi S. **luci** : lucẹ W. **marcelli** : marcellini H. **iohannis, muriae** (*bis*) **zefani, iulianae dariae marialitae** : *om.* H. **caprassii** : caprasi H. **dorothae** : dorotae E, dorothei S.
Syr. Oct. 20 has Eutychius, giving the correct spelling of Euticius.

October 21.

dasciometis dasi : dasci ometis B, dasciometis E, dasi W, dasci (dassi S) cometis RS. **euteci**: eutici (*bis* B -cis W) H. **zomei**: zotici (zoth- W) H. **gagi** : gai ER. **modesti** : modesti (*bis*) BW. **desei** : dissei BE, disei W, + afrigis BW, apricis E. **maceri** : matheri BW. **macarii** : machari (*bis* B) H. **diciei** : dicei BW, *om.* E, + proculi (*bis*) festi BW. **iusti** : iusti (*bis*) BW. **iohannis, zefani, geurgii** : *om.* H. **beati** : + uictoris (uiat- E) H.

Syr. has Desius (*dasi*), Gaius (*gagi*) and Zoticus (*zomei*). For their Acts see *Analecta Bollandiana*, xx. 246.

October 22.

mattei, tomae : *om.* H. **pilippi** : philippi (-ipi B phy- W) H. **hermetis, hermae bermae** : hermetis BW, hermae ES, hermedis R. **seueri** : seueri (*bis*) BE, seueri, seuerini R. **leugadi, eugathi** : leogadi B, leogathi E, leugati W, leucadii S.

Syr. has " in Hadrianopolis of Thracia Philippus, the bishop and martyr, and Hermes." The *Passio s. Philippi* (Ruinart, p. 409, *AA.SS.* Oct. ix. 545) mentions Severus, a presbyter, and Hermes, a deacon, as " discipuli " of the bishop, Philip.

October 23.

ciciliae, seusepi : *om.* H. **seuersi** : seuresi W, *om.* B.

Syr. has Severus and Dorotheus.

Oengus (gloss) states that Longinus pierced the Lord's side. See March 15.

October 24.

iohannis, securi (*bis*), **zefani, kari epolei, iuliae mariae, iulitae ciciliae** : *om.* H. **paperi** : papiri ERS. **flauiani, flauianae** : flauiani (*bis*) BE, flauiani, flauini W. **uictoris** : uictorie (-urie W) H. **euagri** : R, eucariẹ B, eugari E, eutheri W, theocharii S. **uictoris** (*sec.*) : uictoris (*bis*) B, uictori, uictoris E.

Frigiae, herapoli represent Hierapolis in Phrygia.

Claudianus, according to *Syr.*, suffered on Oct. 25 at Hierapolis. TH have Oct. 25 two martyrs named Claudianus, but neither had any connexion with Phrygia.

October 25.

flauani : flauiani H. **gauani sauini** : gauini ES, sauini BW, gabeni R. **saturi** : *om.* E. **uitalis** : + sanctonis uibiani W. **paperi, sapiri** : papiri H. **neonis, quinti bonifati** : *om.* H. **eucharisti** : chari H. **crispiani** : crispini H, + crispiniani BWS, crispiani E.

Syr. Oct. 25 has Claudianus at Hierapolis.

October 26.

marciani : + flori (fori W) H. **cedi, martini zefani danielis** : *om.* H. **titi** : tuti BWS. **eraclidae** : heraclidae ER, eracli W, **eracliae** S, + flori H, + siggerāni B.

Syr. has Silvanus and Marcianus. Silvanus does not appear here in THRS; and Marcianus suffered at Antioch, not at Nicomedia as HRS place him. The *Acta Luciani et Marciani* (Ruinart 164 ; *AA.SS.* Oct. xi. 817) give the date of their martyrdom, but do not mention its place.

For *marciani cedi* perhaps we should read *Marci Aniceti* or *Anacleti*.

October 27.

gaii (*bis*) : gagi H. **eumini, euminiae** : cumini, cuminie B, eomeni E, eumini, euminiẹ W, eumini R, eumenii S. **noconi** : chononis B, canonis, noconi E, noconi W, cononis R. **leogi, longi** : longi BW, logi E. **metrobi, medroti** : metropi BS, metrobi EW, metrubi R. **marciani** : mariae W, mariani S. **eulaliae insolae anastasiae, silini, cerionis, petri, celsii** : *om.* H. **uicti** : uieti H. **proti** : poti W. **comini** : commini W. *fin.* uig. apost. simonis et indae B, + mariniani cristani dariae S .

Syr. has "In Eumenia, a city of Phrygia, Thrase[as], Polycarpus, G[aius] and eight others." Evidently *eumini, cumini*, etc., are not personal names but the city of Eumenia. *Tarsi* is probably an ill-spelling of Thraseas. It may be observed that the groups of Phrygians in B, E and W include eight names, corresponding with the "eight others" of *Syr.*

October 28.

cannanei : cananei BW, *om.* E. **tathei** : iudae zelotis BW, iudae E. **samaridi, marandi** : smaracdi B, zmaragdi E, marandi W, smaragdi RS. **sufroni, suffroniani, infiani** : suffroni BR, sofrori E, suffronisiani W, sofronii S. **amantii, ammaranti** : amaranti H. **cinti** (*bis*) : quinti H. **iohannis pauli zefani, cirillae hirundinis, bonifatii cartatae** : *om.* H. **archilai** : arcelladi BW, archeladi E. **marinae** : marianae H.

In BRS after *suffroni* is *in suanis* (*si-* B) a city of Persia. W connects the place-name with the personal name, and thus creates *suffronisiani.* T omits *is* and gives us *suffroniani. Infiani* is corruption of *in sianis.*
Cartatae is probably a corruption of *Carthagine,* misplaced.
Pope Bonifacius II was buried 17 Oct. 532 (*D.C.B.* i. 329).

October 29.

sacincti : sacinti B, sacinoti E, iacincti, sacinoti S. **uictoris, uitalis, taimthinae** : *om.* H. **lucii, luciani** : lucini W, lucii, lucini S.
Carth. Oct. 29 has "Sancti Feliciani et Vagensium."

October 30.

calendionis : calendini ERS. **marcialis** : marciani BE, + maximi BE. **marciali** : marci H. **teophili** : tiofili BW, theofili E. **luciani** : + uictoris H. **lucae** (*bis*) : lucae (-ciae E) H. **orbani** : urbani EW. **atici** : attici H. **romulae mariae emilianae, marcelli, mundani butini** . *om.* H. **firmae** : + hermetis H. **marci** : marciani H, + nazari H. **gerbassi protassi** : geruasi (gerb- E) protasi H.
Syr. Oct. 30 has Calandion at Nicomedia. TH have him also on Oct. 31.

October 31.

quintini : + ianuarii H. **rogati** : rogatiani BE, *om.* W. **uincentii** : *om.* W. **dagon**i : diaconi B, dogoni E, daconi W. **siluani bis** : silviani silvani E. **calendionis** : kalendionis (cal- W) (*bis*) H, + bonefacie (boni- W) H. **felicissimi** : felicissime BW. **donati** (*bis*) : donati W, + romani H. **rusticiani** : rusticiani (*bis*) E, rustiani W, *om.* B. **fortunati** : furtunati B, furtunati, fortunati E, furtunati (*bis*) W. **mammi** : mimmi BW, mimi E. **angelari** : angelafi H. **nundini bis** : nundinis E. **zefani, mariae, celsi, germani teophili marci felicis cirilli quinti** : *om.* H. **ualerii** : + uincenti (uic- B) H. **gallae, gallicae** : gallicae (sa- E) H. **agapi** : agapie B, agapitae, agapini E, agapitẹ R, + uictorie (*bis* E) H. **petri** : petri (*bis*) B, + marcoti (macracoti E) mammari H. **crescentis** : criscentis BE, *om.* W, + alterni uictorini BE. **uigilanti** : uigelanti B, *om.* E. **pilippi** : philippi (-ipi E) H. *fin.* + uigilia s. benigni B.
For Calendon see Oct. 30. Twelve names are common to Oct. 30 and 31 in T.

December 17.

init. + uictoris EWRS. **uictoriae**: uicturiae W. **uictoriani**: uicturiani EWS, + iudichaili R. **carti** : quarti (E)WS. **simplicis** : simplici (E)WS. **amponii** : ampamovi (E)W. **octori** : tuturi (E) ottori W.
From Dec. 17-24 we are deprived of B.
On this day E has only two names. But E Oct. 18 has a list corresponding to WS, including the two in E 17.
Carth. has Felix, Honorata and others on this day.
Judicaelus, a Breton, died on 17 December 658 (*D.C.B.* iii. 467).

December 18.

basiliani : baseliani S. **tarsi, saluatoris iuliani teodini, celsii, cresti . . . teucri, martini, saluatio mariae** : *om.* EWRS. **teotecti** : teotiecni E, theoni W, theotecni R, teocteni S. **cinti** : quinti EWS, + donati uicturiae dioscori E. **simplicii** : + ampamovi felicis vincenti tuturi E. **pompini** : pomponii S, *om.* E. **pauli** : *om.* E. **uictoris** : *om.* W, + uictoriani adiutoris quarti honorati E.
Nineteen names in this article are also found in T Dec. 19. The list beginning with *aritife* in W Dec. 18, is not counted in this collation. It will be used in the next article.

December 19.

secundini (*bis*) **zosimus** : secundi zosimus EWRS, *om.* (W). **ciriaci** : cyriaci ES, caeriaci W, quiriaci R. **uictoriae bis** : uictoriae, uicturicae, uicturiae E, uicturiae (*bis*) (W) *om.* W. **iulianae mariae brigitoniae marialitae, zefani celsii, petri, mariae magdalenae et elizabeth** : *om.* EW(W)RS. **spinae** : pinnae E, *om.* W, + privatolae (-ulae (W)) caeciliae E (W). **anathasii** : anastasi W, *om.* E (W). **grigorii crisanti** : *om.* E(W), + dari WS. **teotini** . theoticni E. theoni (W), *om.* W. **cinti** : quinti E (W), *om.* W. **simplici** : *om.* W. **pomponi** : pommori E, pompini (W), *om.* W. **pauli** (*bis*) : pauli W (W), + aritifi E, aritife (W). **cresci** (-sti (W)) **digni datuli feliciani** : E (W), *om.* W, + moisetis E, moysitis (W). **rogatiani martirii** (-tyri E -thyri (W)) **honorati** (*bis*) : horati honorati (W), *om.* W, + evasi (W), + **priuati** : *om.* W. **tintii** : tinni E (W), *om.* W, + salutoris E, saluatoris (W). **siti uicturi** : siti teturi (W), *om.* W, + uicturici E (W), **ciciliani** : caeciliani E, caeliani (W), *om.* W, + semtimini (septimi E) . quintulae E (W). **saturnini** : + caecilianae E (W). **famonis** : nani famonis E, namfamonis (W), *om.* W. **felicis uincentii aresci** (-ti E (W)) **musci** : *om.* W, + siddini EW(W), + adiutoris . . papisci E(W). **saturi** : *om.* W. **uictoris** : uicturis (W), *om.* W + afrae uictoris E (W). **uictorini** : uictoriņę (W), *om.* W. **basiliani** : bassiliani E, basiliani (*bis*) (W), *om.* W, + honorati (*tert.*) E.
W between brackets is W 18. It is parallel with E 19.
There are 19 names common to Dec. 18, 19. All of them (ap rt from Maria and Elizabeth) are in E. They have support from WRS in Dec. 18 and not from Dec. 19. They probably belong to Dec. 18.
Magdalenae is a slip. See Dec. 18 and Luke 1. 40.

December 20.

ignatii : *om.* W, + athanasi E. **uictoriae agathae, ciciliae, anastasiae, basii innocentii, cinti** : *om.* EW. **refrini** : zephirini E, zeferini WR, caprini S. **anastasii** : *om.* W, + siddini E. **liberi** : liberati WS, *om.* E. **bontiani** : pontiani R, pontentiani S, *om.* EW. **zosimi pauli secundi** : *om.* W, + cyriaci E. **beati grigorii, criscantii darii** : *om.* W.
Eight names are common to T Dec. 19, 20.
Bithaniae is a place : Bithynia.
For Pope Zephyrinus see *D.C.B.* iv. 1215.
For Pontianus and Anastasius see *Anal. Boll.* xxix. 416.

December 21.

tomae : thomae EWRS, + passi W, + innocenti uicturiae WS.
iohannis : *om.* W, + festi ER, + iuli zepherini E. **sereni zefani celsi,
dimetri bis iononati iohannis mathei** : *om.* EW. **teclae** : *om.* WRS,
+ ronidicodiae liberatis E, + zosimi ES, + auruli (-ili W -elli S) EWS, + basai
victoriae E, + secundi (-dae W) zosimi seriaci (si- W) EW. **focci** : foci
ES, foce W. **flori** : florenti S, + honorati EWS.

According to the earliest tradition Thomas was the apostle of Parthia
and Bartholomew that of India. See Eusebius and Rufinus, *H.E.* iii. 1. 1,
v. 10. 10. For the meaning of India see Lawlor-Oulton ii. 164.

December 22.

init. + basiliae ES, basilei W. **felicis** : felicis (*bis*) EW. **fisti apolloni
eugeni, eugeniae eulaliae decimi** : *om.* EW. **arizo** : aristoni EW.
teodosiae : theodosiae (teud- S) EWS, + didimi EW. **honori** : honorati
W. **dimetri** : demetri WS.

Flori, dimetri and *honorati* are in Dec. 21.

December 23.

**felicis, uictorini, dimetri honori, florii arizoni, zefani, transillae,
musae romulae mariae abrahae, teli, pauli, sanctorum africae** : *om.*
EW. **eurasti** : evaristi EW. **celsi** : sisti EW. **uictoris bis** : uictoris W,
+ titiani (tic- W) EWS, + eliti E, cliti W. **iohannis** : + festi E, felicis W.
felicis (*bis*) : felicis EW. **eleutherii** : eleuteri E. **cornelii** : cornili WS.
euaristi : EW, + metelli EWS. **colnilii** : cornili EW. **triani** : atriani E.
traiani WS. **siriani** : + baselini (-illini W) niceti EW. **paulini** : pulli
EW, + anicleti (anincliti W) sopatri EW. **saturnini** : + eufrosini EW.
cartulae : castulae W. **celesti** : caelesti EW. **petri loni** : petri apoš,
lini E, petri apolloni W. **sicti** : syxti (*bis*) E, xisti syxti W. **solani** : +
eutaristili (euch- W) basilini (-imi W) EW. **zeferini** : zephirini E.
gallini : galliti W. **abilionis** : appolinis E, apolloni W, + egeni (eug-
E) EWS.

Peter appears both here and Dec. 24. *Syr.* has him on Dec. 24.
Petri loni (T) and *petri apollini* (W) are obviously corruptions of *petri
apoš lini* (E). Linus was the successor of the apostles Peter and Paul.
EW do not mention Paul here; but T has him, and in T Dec. 24 the two
apostles appear side by side. *Pauli abilionis* (T), no doubt, is a corruption
of *pauli apoš lini.*

In T we find five names common to Dec. 22, 23; and a sixth if *apolloni*
and *abilionis* are a doublet.

December 24.

luciani : luciae S. **zefani geurgii, petri laurentii, ciricii celsii** :
om. EWS. **metrobii** : metropi S. **genoti** : zenoti WS. **teothini** :
theutini E, teutini W, tiutini S. **timisti** : tomisti W, + drusi (du- W)
donati EWS.

NOTES ON THE BRUSSELS ABSTRACT

Bibl. Royale No. 5100-4

'Only the principal variants are recorded. The readings of LL are in thick type.

Jan. 1.

Incipit martira Oeng*us* mc. Oibleain 7 Maolruain íc. *add. as title.*

Colman m. Echdach : *under Jan. 5.*

The explanation is, that the entry for Jan. 1 in Br. is written across the page, Jan. 5 occurring at top of col. 2. In making a fair copy of his first draft of the "Seanleabar," O'Clery inadvertently took the name Colman m. Echdach standing at the end of Jan. 1, as belonging to Jan. 5 immediately underneath, and there inserted it, preceded by 7 " et," to couple it with Mac Óge of that day.

Jan. 3.

Fintani : *om.* **Cilline m.h. Colla** . *at end of entry.* **dunud** : ionad nominatur : + locus.

Jan. 4.

Maelan Enaig : *comes after* Aediui. **Fiadnatan** : Fidnatan.

Jan. 5.

o Loch Meilchi : *om.* ; *interlined* LL. **Tamlachta** : Tamlachtan.

Jan. 6.

o Airiud Ind(aich) *etc.* : o Airiud si*n* lacherclach. **Tulilatha ab.** . Tuililatha uir. ab. Chilli Dara.

A line has been skipped after *la*, evidently by O'Clery, as the arrangement in LL does not lend itself to an omission of the kind. *sin* is an error for Indaich. Read with LL, Lassar Cherclach.

Jan. 7.

Modici : Modichu. **Ingena Fergnae** lnghen Fergnai, *corr* inghena *in marg. by another hand.*

Jan. 8.

Erc(n)at : *om.* **N(echt)an** . Nechtan an n͞e͞r. **Sarani,** *etc.* : *follows* Nechtan.

The omission of Ercnat, which is only partly traceable in LL, would show that the page was at this point already much faded when the " Seanleabar " was transcribed. Nechtan is now almost illegible. The true reading is Nechtan Neir. Oengus has : Nechtan ner (neir, nair) de Albae. AU 679 has " Dormitatio Nectain Neir " ; *Neir* is om. in Chron. Scottorum obit, A.D. 675. *Ner* in poetry is a rare epithet, used of a celebrated person or ruler, and is generally misunderstood. It means " boar " or powerful animal ; cp. Cormac's Glossary, ed. O'Donovan-Stokes, p. 122 ; ed. Meyer, No. 968.

Jan. 9.

Finani : *comes after* Lomchon. **7 Baetini** . 7 *om.* **To** ( ) : *om.*

Jan. 10.

Tommine comarbae ( ) : Tomini Arda Macha, *following* Maelodran.
There is some retracing here in LL and this name now resembles Tomini,
with dropped *i*. But the true reading would seem to be Tommine or
Tommini. The letters following, illegible to the Facsimilist, look like *co*,
and above the line *marb*. The scholiast of Gorman has " comarbae Patraicc,"
and he apparently consulted LL. Cp. Jan. 12 *infra*.

Jan. 11.

Carthinisii . Carthinisa, + *in marg., seemingly by Colgan* : Amadeus
seu Ama-Iesu.

Jan. 12.

Faelani sancti : F. episcopi. **Baithene ab.** .i. mac Brenaind⟩ :
Baitine mc. Nemainn ab. **Baith** : + Ban*naig* (*and similarly O*). ⟨ o Chill
Airiss ⟩ *om.*
Nemainn is a misreading of Brenaind. The small initial *b* is somewhat
widely separated from *r* by the projecting letter of the line below, and so was
overlooked by the " Seanleabar " scribe, who misread the name as Nemaind
(Todd, as m̅c̅ o nemaind). Gorman (gl.) has Nemnainn, which would show
that the glosses there are derived, in part, from LL ; for there is re-inking
in this portion of the page, and the lower part of the bow of *b* (a*b̄*), standing
over *e*, has the appearance almost of an *m*-stroke (⁀). Hence Nemnainn in
the scholia to Gorman.
o Chill Airiss is interlined, and partly effaced, hence perhaps its omission
by the " Seanleabar " scribe.

Jan. 13.

o **Dergderc** (*infra lin.*) : *om.* **Teochonnae** : Doconnae

Jan. 14.

7 Baetain Mc. Lugei : 7 *om.* **Latharnis 7** : *om.*
Br. has a marginal note, seemingly by Colgan, on Baetan : uel Buadanus
et idem et Mac Luige. Gorman (G) has *Baetan mor mac Lugei*. gl. *.i. eps. Insi
Moire*, " i.e. bp. of Inis Mór," and also has Lugbe as a separate commemora-
tion. Apparently therefore Sancti Lugbei should be read for sancti Lugei,
and Inis Mór, interlined, should go with Baetán.
Latharnis was evidently omitted through homoeoteleuton with Itharnais.

Jan. 15.

Diarmait presb. : Diarmait presbi.
In LL the bold shaft of *f* in Feli (brought forward from the line above)
is in close contact with the cross-stroke of *b*, causing it to look almost like
b̄i. Hence the above misreading on the part of the " Seanleabar " scribe.

Jan. 16.

Laebdercc : lethderc. **Iarloga** : *precedes* Dianach. **Fursei** : Fursa.

Jan. 17.

m. Ethechtaig i Cúil Chorra : *om.* **In Clarenech** : In *om.* **Sanctae
Micae** : *precedes* Molasse. **depositio** : *om.*
A whole line has evidently been skipped, as the omission of *In* before
Clarenech shows. The disposition of the text in LL does not lend itself to
such a lapse, consequently O'Clery must have been at fault.

N 2

Jan. 20.

i **Lath Chain** : o Lath Cain. **Duib Dligid** : Duib Diligid.
In the former, Br. repeats the error of LL. Read *Lathrach*.

Jan. 21.

m. Laich : mc. L ac*h* (*sic*) ; *with* Laoich *interlined by another hand.*
Here Br. repeats the error of LL. Read *Cellaich*.

Jan. 22.

.i. : *om.* **Lonan find** : Lonan fan*n* ; *with* fion*n* *interlined by another
hand.*
In LL, *fi* of fi*nd*, owing to the length of the horizontal stroke, resembles
fa. Hence the misreading fa*nd* in the " Seanleabar " (O'Cl. fan*n*).

Jan. 29.

Mochonna : M̄c̄. Con*n*a. **Blatha uirg.** : *om.*

Mar. 12.

Maele : Mel.

Mar. 13.

Conchend m. Lucennain : m. Lucennain *om.*
Colman ⟨bdic⟩ : uel hic Colman ⟨bdic⟩.
In LL Conchend ends the line, and meic Lucennáin is carried on to the
space left blank on the preceding line, and so was accordingly overlooked by
the " Seanleabar " scribe.
Colman of Clúain Tibrinne also occurs Mar. 9, hence '' uel hic,'' but the
meaning of '' bdíc '' is not clear

Mar. 15.

Trenech : Trenach de*r*g. **Tiu** : Tui.
In LL de*r*g is immediately over Trenech, but under Diu- (Diucaill). In
GDO(n) it is the epithet of Diucaill. Trenech does not occur elsewhere as a
name.
For *Tiu*, the gloss on G and D have *Tri hingena Eltin* " the three daughters
of Eltin,'' and such is the reading of T^1. But Tiu occurs as a proper name,
though masculine ; cp. Rawl. B. 502, 89 *g* (LL 349 *f*, LB 16 *e*).

Mar. 16.

no **Clúana Mo[i]r** (*interl.* LL) : *om.* **Curitani sancti** : sancti *om.*
Tuama : cuánda Tuama.

Mar. 17.

Patricii epi. : *add. from Roman list supra.* **Ruimni** : Ruimi. **Nasci** :
Nasar. **Conchend** : *add. at end.*
In LL *nasci* is written small below the line ; the final *i*, which is joined
to *c* and dropped, caused it to be misread as the symbol for a*r*.
Conchend, omitted elsewhere, has obviously intruded from Mar. 13, which
was probably on a line with Mar. 17, in the " Seanleabar,'' therefore it must
be an error of O'Clery's.

Mar. 18.

Ericbirt : Ericb*r*ict. **Coemain sci.** : Caemani ep.

Mar. 19.

Auxilinus : *om., but added by another hana.*

Mar. 20.

Muccin : Muiccini. **Dirthaigi** : Turthaig*h*i.

Mar. 21.

Ennae Áirni meic Ainmire : *sic.*
Br. here repeats error of LL. Ainmere, King of Fir Arda, was the grandfather of Enna, i.e., his mother's father ; so for *meic* should be read *hui.*

Mar. 22.

Deeid : *Con*feidh, *with* maleo Deedi *alongside in another hand.* **Lilchaig** : i lLilchaich.
ɔ*feid* is a misreading of *deeid.* In LL the *d* is rather open, and could be mistaken for ɔ (= con) ; the *e*, unlike the one following, has no rounded base, and approximates to a short-stemmed *f*, for which it was carelessly mistaken by the scribe of the " Seanleabar."

Mar. 23.

Monan : monachi ; monaige legendum, *add. alongside in another hand.*
Ingen Feradaig : Inghena F. **Feda** : Fedo.
Here *monachi* is an extension of monā LL, which may stand for Mona*nn*, gen. sg. of Monu (GD), but the place remains unidentified.

Mar. 26.

Cilliani . . . ł Mochelloc : Cilliani *and* ł (uel) *om.* **Molocga** ⟨.i. **Lilchaig**⟩ : Moloco Lilcaich ; .i. (= id est) *om.* **Garban Achid** : Achid *om.* **Dairind** : *sic*, + si *add. by another hand.*
Cillian has been rejected for Mochelloc, which occurs in Ôengus. Where a variant is given, as above, the " Seanleabar " scribe generally accepts it as a correction. Cp. Ap. 6, 9. Cilleni, interlined at the end of the article, is in Br. also. There seems to be some confusion in regard to these two names ; cp. the notes in Fél. Ôeng.
In LL Achid is somewhat distant from Garban, and is immediately over the Achid of the next entry, hence no doubt its omission. Br. repeats the error of LL in writing *Dairind* for *Dairindsi.*

Mar. 29.

Lumnain : Lum*m*ain. **Ethni** : .i. (= id est) *add. before* Ethni. **Lassar. Algasach** : *occur at end of entry* ; uirg. *added after* Lassar.
A line was passed over at first.

Mar. 30.

Ballni : Balna. **Cassan** : Casad. **Ferguis** : Fergusa. **Sancti Colmani** : *repeated.*
Casad is a misreading.

April 1.

o Thamlactain Bairchi : *is attached to* Aedan laech.
In LL it begins in marg. and is continued under *Aedan laech.* The scribe of the " Seanleabar " regarded it as applying to Aedan.

April 4.

Tigernach ep. : epi*scopus om.* ; *interlined LL.* **Eois** : Eoais.

April 5.

Antiosi ep. : *om.*

April 6.

Aedeai ⟨ı⟩ : *om.* Aidech *adopted*.

April 7.

o Daire : *om.* **Finani** ... **in oculis eius fuit ista obliquitas**
F. . . . obliquitas fuit in oculis eius.

April 8.

m. h. Duibni = mc. h. Suibne. **m. Fergusa** : mc. mc. Fergusa.

In LL the small initial *d* of *Duibṁ* occurs just under a full stop at end of Timothei. on the line above, which combines to give it the appearance of *S*. Hence the error of the " Seanleabar " scribe.

April 9.

m. h. Echdach *corr.* **Elich** . mc. h. Eachdach.

In LL Ech-dach, which is partly interlined, is lightly stroked through, and Elich written before *-dach.* It is impossible to say whether the cancellation was made by the scribe of LL or not. The omission of Elich by the " Seanleabar " scribe would point to the alteration having been made posterior to him, were it not that he more than once chooses a single reading when offered two ; cp. Mar. 26, Ap. 6, 9, Aug. 13. Echach Éle is, however, a population group, according to MacNeill (Early Irish Population Groups, §111) and so Echdach ·or Echach Éle may be the true reading, and that intended by the LL scribe. Elich is apparently in his hand.

April 11.

Frossaig : Frosaisaig. **Mael Dalua** : Mael Dalad.

April 16.

Hermogenis : *om.*

April 17.

nomen fontis : *om.* **id est** (symbol 12) : *om.*

The names of the community of Eig are omitted ; quorum nomina in maiore libro scribsimus. In LL *nomen fontis* is interlined, and unobtrusive, hence its omission.

April 18.

Eugeni ep. : in LL is placed in marg. just before *Cogitosi*, at which point it is incorporated in the Brussels MS.

April 20.

Communis sollemnitas, *etc.* *om.*

April 21.

Maele Rubi aƀ : Maolrubach. **Bretan** : Brét.

In LL aƀ is pressed in at end of line, running on to preceding word, and being not unlike ac*h*, gave rise to the above misreading.

April 22.

m. h. in Baird : i*n* om.

April 23.

Macc Óge 7 : *om.* **Soairlech** Soardlech. **isind Ednean** : ind Edhnén. **7 Deitche 7 Rian** : Dechthe 7 Mían*n*.

April 24.

    Ecbrichti : Echtbrichti. **Cichmaig[e]** : Cichmaige. **meic Coelbad :** *om.* **Lugaid presb.** : Lucc*aidh* sac. **Meicc Baetain** : M*eic*c Bec : ain, *letter after* c *corr. and obscure* ; *above the line in another hand*, Baotain.

April 26.

    Beccain Clúana : Béccani Clúana aird.
    Becain of Clúain Aird is May 26, whence no doubt *aird* of Br. was taken.

April 28.

    maccu Tratho : m̄c̄. cutrito.
    Tr*atho* LL is below the line, very small, and lends itself to the misreading Tr*ito*, the superior *a* resembling an *i*.

April 29.

    .i. Cilli . i Cill. **Luccraid Cilli Luccraide** : *om.* **Enani. Ega :** Enani. Aego.
    Luccraid *etc.* is omitted through homoeoteleuton with *Muscraige*, line above.

April 30.

    ut alii : ut quidam.

May 1.

    Gobnini : Gaibnidi. **m. Mael śnechtai** : mc. Maile Snecta, *and attached to* Oseni. **Banbain ep.** : *occurs after* Mancheni. **Aedgein Fobair :** *occurs after* Braccani.
    In LL the *o* of Gobnini is elongated, and could be mistaken for *a*. m. Mael Śnechtai is interlined in LL and is partly over Oseni, hence the above error in the " Seanleabar." Further, Banbain and Aedgein Fobair, placed in marg. in LL, have been incorporated into the text of the " Seanleabar " at the points opposite which they occur.

May 2.

    Nechtain *etc.* : + .i. i Fid Conailli " i.e. in Fid Conailli." **Cuansae :** Cuamsie. [*sic*]

May 3.

    Condlaed ⟨Roncend prius⟩ : Roncend. Connlai. *After* **Neccain** *are added* Fergusa, C*o*ncraid, Donna*n*.

May 4.

    .i. : *om.*

May 5.

    Euchbrit . Euctbrict.

May 6.

    Echin : Ethin.
    In LL Ec*h*in resembles Et*h*in. Hence error in " Seanleabar."

May 7.

    .i. : *om.* **Mochuaróc** : Mocholmoc, *with* Mociaroc *add. above by another hand*, (?) *Colgan's*.

May 8.
Commani, etc. : *om*

May 9.
Dracon : Dreman. **Santan cendmar** : San⟨c⟩tan, c *add. above line*,
Cendmar : *om., interlined* LL.

May 10.
.XCI° *etc.* : .XC° anno . . lᵐᵒ anno, et mensibus tribus, et decimo [*sic*]
diebus. **Cormaic** : Conmaic. **Lemnae** : Lemmae. .i. : *om*.

May 11.
Coemgini : + G*linne* da Locha. **Findnaige** . Finnmaighi. **infirmus**
hifīr. **Loegaire** : Lag*uiri*. **ro chomarc** : ro imcomaircc. **rasossed** .
roseisedh. **nîba** [*in marg.*] : nirbat.
Cóemgen of Glenn dá Locha is commemorated on June 3. The above
addition to the " Seanleabar " has no authority.

May 12.
Herc Nasa .i. i Tilaig Léis⟩ : Erc i Maig Léis. Nasci.

May 13.
Dublittrech Find : Dublitir. et.
There is some confusion here. Dublitter's day is May 15, where he
properly appears in both MSS. and in Gorman. In the latter his epithet is
in dagfind " the good and fair." In Br. (" Seanleabar ") the scribe broke off,
perhaps suspecting an error. *et* could not be a misreading of *find*, which is
clear. *Find* may be a suspension of Findglasi.

May 15.
Airechair : Airechtair. **la h. Liathán** . *om.* **Tochonne ep.** : *om*
Dublitri : Dublitir. **Comman mac Dimmae** : *precedes* **Cainnech.**
Two lines have been skipped.

May 16.
Bregbesach filii Bron*aig* : Bregboesach filii Bron*dii*.

May 17.
Dromma Feise : *om*.
In LL Dromma Enaig 7 Dromma Feise are *in marg.*, Enaig being written
above Dromma, and the second place name below, which would account for
its omission by the scribe of the " Seanleabar."

Aug. 1.
m. Riaguil : ⊣ .i. (i.e.). **Insi me*ic* Lugein** . me*ic om.* **Airdne**
⟨ꝉ **Ernaide**⟩ : ꝉ *om*. **Móri** : Móir.
In LL ꝉ, interlined, has the appearance of an aspiration mark, hence its
omission.

Aug. 2.
Cuallacta . Cuanꝉ.

Aug. 3.
Clúana Tarbfethi. Limmid : *sic*.
The error of LL is repeated. Read *Fethlimmid*

Aug. 5.

Br. has : Deest quintus dies videndus in alio codice, *in another hand, seemingly Colgan's.* •

Aug. 5.

i Cill : Cillī.

Aug. 7.

Senain : Senani, *add. man. al.* **Darii dōr** : Dari dór, *precedes* Temnani. Here what is evidently an error in LL is repeated in the " Seanleabar," viz., Darii dōr, for Darii uir., who is commemorated on the following day.

Aug. 8.

.lxxx. anno : *om.* **eius** : suae. **quieuit** : *qui symbol as in LL, but with cross-stroke.* **Curchach** : Curcach, *recte.* **filli Nessani** : mc. Nesain. In LL the *qui* symbol is traversed by the accent on *bó* underneath, which accounts for the cross-stroke in Br., as if it were the Irish *air* symbol.

Aug. 9.

presb. : sac. **Ciarain** : *follows* Cethri mc. Ercain. **Udnochtain** : Udnochtad. **quiescunt** : *om. ; below line LL.*

Aug. 10.

Udnochtan : *add. before* Mael Ruain. No justification for this, which may be an error of O'Clery's.

Aug. 11.

Mael : Maeile. **Etractae** : Etra*h*tae, *corr. man. al.* Etractae. **Banbnatan** *follows* **Toidiliae** : Todile.

Aug. 12.

Murchad : Murcadh, *with* Muiredha*h* potius *add. above line by later hand.* Gorman has *Muiredach,* so also D, and the note in the Franciscan copy of Fél. Ōeng. Neither name can be identified.

Aug. 13.

Dianlama : Diailama. **Caetren ⟨↑⟩** : *om.* The " Seanleabar " follows LL in attaching Dianlama to Brigit. Both G and D have Clúain Hai, treating Dianlama as a proper name, viz., Dianland. The name does not appear elsewhere, nor can Clúain Dianlama or Clúain Hai be identified. The " Seanleabar " adopts the interlined variant Carthind, and rejects Caetren. Cp. Ap. 9.

Aug. 15.

Colmain o Achud : *om.*

Aug. 16.

et sancti Conani : *om.* Could be mistaken by a careless scribe for a pendant to the preceding line, and hence overlooked.

Aug. 23.

Aird : Arda.

Aug. 25.

    Imgain : i Maigin.

Aug. 27.

    m. h. in Baird : in *om.*

Aug. 30.

    Muadan Aricail Muadán : *is under Aug.* 29.

It is difficult to explain this misplacing of Muadán, except as an error of homoeocatarcta. In LL it follows *Cronan*, and the last line in Aug. 29 begins with *Coronae*. At this point Cronan may have caught the eye of the " Seanleabar " scribe, or O'Clery's. Both G and D follow LL.

Aug. 31.

    Colum Cuile *add. at end*.

For this there is no authority. Perhaps a marginal variant of Colman Cuile, Aug. 18, has intruded ?

Sep. 1.

    Br. has here two notes, one perhaps by Colgan, remarking on the great confusion in the days of this month down to the 23rd, and the omission of the 19th and 20th.

Sep. 4.

    i n Ard Brecain : *om.*, *also* **7 soror eius**, *etc.*, *marg. inf.* .i. *om. after*
Comgelli.   **Fiachrach** : *om.*

Sep. 5.

    ⟨†⟩: *om.* **Elacho** : Elacha, *inserted after* **Eolog anchoritae.** **Scuili** : suili.

Here the confusion of LL is repeated : Elacho and Eolach being by-forms of Eolang. The two points under *Elacho* have been taken by the scribe of the " Seanleabar " to indicate the transference of that name to the space under *Eolog*, where there are also two points. In Fél. Óeng (*O*) four MSS. have Eolach, only one (LB) Eolang. Cp. LL 353ª 26 : Eolang i nAthbi Bolg i mMuscraige Mittini.

Sep. 6.

    Coluim ⟨.i. Crossaire⟩ ó Russ. idem 7 : Colum o Ros nossaire .i.

In LL *.i.* is somewhat removed from *Crossaire*, and is traversed by a border, of which it looks a part, hence it was overlooked by the scribe of the " Seanleabar " who took Crossaire as a continuation, *supra lin.* Russ. Nossaire must be a misreading of O'Clery's, LL being perfectly clear.

Sep. 7.

    The error of LL with regard to the omission of *Toite Inse* is repeated.

Sep. 9.

    et Fer da Chrich : *precedes* Findbarr ; et *om.*

Sep. 10.

    Finnio : Einnio. **Findbair Maigi** . Finnbarr mac Bindi. **Bennchair** : *om.* ; *added below line LL.*

In LL *F* of Finnio is unmistakable. ɫ mc. Buidi is written under Senach Gairb, and over Maigi. It was thus mistaken by the scribe of the " Seanleabar " for a variant of Maigi, which he did not understand, and was adopted by him, *Buidi* being easily misread *Bindi*, which it resembles.

Sep. 12.

    m. Nad Fraich : .i. mc. Nat Fraich.

Sep. 13.

    presb. sac.

Sep. 14.

    Coeman Brecc ic Ross Ech. i Cailli Follommuin . Ingena Coluim i Cremthannaib : Colman Brec ic Ross Ech. Inghena [ ] i cCailli Follomon. Colum i Crémtannaibh. **Mael Tolaig**, *etc.* : *om.*

    In LL there is a stop after *Ech*, and *i.Cailli Follammuin*, which forms the next line, being slightly smaller, was mistaken by the " Seanleabar " scribe for a gloss on *Ingena* underneath. Reading *Colum i Cremthannaib* as a separate commemoration, and being at a loss to complete *Inghena*, he left a space. This was reproduced by O'Clery. *Choluim* was then added by another hand, seemingly Colgan's, with the note : *forte Colum de quibus Marian.* 13 *Sep.*

Sep. 15.

    Clúana Mor : Clúana Moir, i *subscr.* **Fata** : Foda. **Meic Taidc** : *om.* In LL *Mor* is frequently written for *Moir* after the gen. *Clúana.* The subscript *i* in *Br.* would appear to have been added as an afterthought. Cp. Oct. 8.

Sep. 16.

    in Hí Coluim Chille : *om.* **Critain** : *om.*

Sep. 17.

    Broccain .i. : i.. *om.* **Riaguil Muccinsi** . Riacc innsi, *under following day.*

    Riacc is a misreading of *mucc*, which in LL might be misread *riucc.* The transposition is no doubt due to O'Clery in copying his first transcript. Cp. Jan. 1, Oct. 10, 16, 22. The omission of Riaguil, which is quite clear in LL, is hard to explain.

Sep. 18.

    Dedicatio basilicae Martini . *om.*

    This entry, together with *Gemmae uir.*, is out of place, but the latter is in Br. also.

Sep. 19.

    presb. : sac. *After* **Comgell uir.** *are added* : Fergus Cruithnech. Faendelach. Saran mc. Trenaich, *with note by another hand, perhaps Colgan's :* Desunt hic 20 et 21.

    For Fergus, see Sep. 8 ; Fáendelach, Sep. 18 ; and Sarán, Sep. 21.

Sep. 20.

    Aedain : *om.*

    In LL Aedain is out of place, being the last name in the Roman list, and likewise no doubt in the "Seanleabar," hence its omission by O'Clery.

Sep. 21.

    Saran m. Tigernain m. Móinaig : *entered under Sep.* 19 *as* Saran mc. Trenaich.

    In marg. LL, and rather inconspicuous, hence its omission in the first place. The misreading Trenaich can hardly be due to the " Seanleabar " scribe.

Sep. 22.

m. Ernini : *om.*
This day is headed .XU. Kl, following LL, though 22 *in marg.* At end
is written : .XIIII. kl.   XIII. kl.   XII. kl.   XI. kl.   X. kl.   IX kł.
Adomnani, *etc.* By the above device Br., or it may be the " Seanleabar,"
seeks to re-adjust the error in the dates in LL.

Sep. 23.

Sarani : Ciarani.
The error must be due to O'Clery, misreading a sloping capital *S* as *Ci*,
i.e. C + dropped *i.* LL has a small long *s.*

Sep. 28.

Finnio : *om.* **Lucraid** : Lucnaid. **Gildae** : *om.* **Iunilli** .i. : .i. *om.*

Sep. 29.

Meic Ieir ep. : ep. *om.*

Sep. 30.

Rothan: Ronan *corr.* Rodan. **Airmer:** Airmera. **Loegaire,** *etc.. om.*

Oct. 1.

Doithnennaig : Doithnemnaig. **Columbae abb. Benchair frater
Cassain** : Colmán mc. Duach frater Cassain.
Colmán mac Dúach is under Feb. 3. There seems no justification for
his name being substituted here. LL is quite clear.

Oct. 2.

ł **Omne** : *om.*

Oct. 4.

ep. : et. **Senain** : Senach.

Oct. 5.

Hibernensium : *om.* **quas** : s̄s̄. **Da Locha** : *comes after* congre-
gauit. **Duib** : *as in LL., comes before* Baethellaig. **Abna** : Olma.
The error of LL as to Duib dá Locha is repeated. In LL the bow of *b*
in *Abna* is blotted, and it was evidently misread by the " Seanleabar " scribe
as *lm.* The Facsimilist misread it *Alna.*

Oct. 6.

Fir da Chrich : .i. *add.*

Oct. 7.

Colmani sauch : *add. by another hand.* **Comgilli** : Comgilla.

Oct. 8.

Mochritoc : Moelifitrigh.
A strange substitution. The name has passed from here doubtless into
D, which has Maelchriotóg for Mochritoc.

Oct. 9.

Clúana Mór : Clúana Moir.

Oct. 10.

Sillani ab. : ab. *om.* **Sennan ep.** : *is under Oct. 11.*
The misplacing of Sennan may be explained by Br. being an abstract.
The last name in Oct. 10, when the Roman names were eliminated, would be
contiguous to the first Irish names of the following day. O'Clery made the
mistake in re-copying his first draft. Cp. Jan. 1, Sep. 17, Oct. 16, 22.

Oct. 11.

Cainnig .m. Daland : Cainnig mc. h. Dal*and*.
Br. has here corrected LL.

Oct. 12.

Berchan : .i. (i.e.) *prefixed.* **Noeden** : Noende.
A correction of LL, in which Berchan is entered as a separate com-
memoration.

Oct. 13.

om. *There is a note in another hand, perhaps Colgan's,* " deest dies 13."
The omission is probably due to O'Clery, whose eye was misled by the
Latin form of the last name, *Comgani,* and so he passed over the two Irish
names.

Oct. 15.

Sci. Tommeni : *om.* **Fintianae,** *etc. om. For the rest the order is* :
Natiuitas Colmani, Boíthine, Cuani, Maele Cosni, Cronae u., Cormani.,
Galmae, 7 soror Ultain.
The disarrangement is due to the scribe of the " Seanleabar," who mis-
took Sci. Tommeni for a Roman saint, as in LL he is seemingly the last in
that group. The symbol ¶ being to the right instead of the left was over-
looked. He then passed to *Natiuitas,* which is prominent. Later on, dis-
covering his error he went back, omitting, however, Fintianae.

Oct. 16.

xuiii . xuii. *recte.*
Lucinnani ab. *om.* **Taicthig** : *expuncted.*
Eogan Lis Moir : *is under Oct. 17.*
Lucinnani, also om. GD, was apparently regarded as a foreign name.
Eogan (end of col. LL) was in error transferred to beginning of the following
day, from O'Clery's first draft of the abstract. Cp. Jan. 1, Sep. 17, Oct. 10, 22.
The dates are correct in Br. from this point to the end of the month, with
the exception of 18, 19, 27, where LL is followed.

Oct. 17.

Nóinachi ab. . *om.*

Oct. 18.

m. Coirtgid : .i. mc. Cortgid.

Oct. 19.

Cronan Tomma Gréni. Crinan Cule Lagin : Crinan Droma igin.
Cronan Cule Lugdidh. **Magniu** : *comes between the above.*
LL is quite clear, so the confusion must have arisen in transcribing the
" Seanleabar."

Oct. 20.

Tomma Gréni . Droma Greine.

Oct. 21.

Mc. h. Gairb, *etc.,* *om.*   **Sillan magister** : *om.*
Fintan ⟨.i. mc. **Tuchain**⟩ : Fintan mc. Tul*chain* .i. Munna.
fuerunt : faciunt.
Lasrani. Commani . . . Lasrian 7 Comain 7c̄a. Aliorum nomina
scribsi in magno (*scl.* libro].
Mael Aithgeain : Maelanaigh, *corr.* atgein, *later hand.*
In LL the initial of Fintan is larger than those of the first two names,
which in comparison would appear to belong to the Roman group. Appar-
ently the " Seanleabar " scribe followed LL in this respect, and hence their
omission by O'Clery, misled also no doubt by the Latin epithet of Sillan, viz.,
magister.

Oct. 22.

Sarani : + cule coll̃, *expuncted.*
Cule Colla goes with Dalbach, Oct. 23, and duly appears there in Br.
It crept in here from O'Clery's first draft, for the existence of which it furnishes
additional evidence : cp. Jan. 1, Sep. 17, Oct. 10, 16.

Oct. 23.

Doidnain . Toidnáin. **Mael** : Maele. **Laidcinn** : Laidcend. Colcai*n*
added.
There is no authority for Colcai*n*.

Oct. 26.

Britonia : Brita*n*nia. **et Darbellin** : et *om.*
Another hand, seemingly Colgan's, has interlined *Cail* after Darbellin,
and added a note on Cell Maignend : " *potius i Cill na n-ingen,*" which is the
reading of O(n)GD.
Br. retains the faulty *.uii.* of LL, corrected however *supra lin.* to *iiii.* by
another hand, seemingly Colgan's.

Oct. 27.

presb. i lLetracha : sac. Lettracha. **Rectini craibdech. Colmain** :
om.
The two last-named occupy two lines in LL. The omission may be due
to O'Clery.

Oct. 30.

m. h. Gualae : .i. (id est) *prefixed.* i lLaind **Mocholmóc ata** :
Mocholmóc ata *om.*
Br. breaks off at *Laind.* The following note in the hand of Michael
O'Clery occupies two lines at the foot of the page, shaved by the binder, so
that only the upper portions of the letters are left in the second line : *ni juarus
an cuid ele don martarlaic san seanleabar i cCill Dara* 22 A ( ). " I did not find
the rest of the Martyrology in the old book in Kildare 22 A(pril ?)."
After *i lLaind* another hand, seemingly Colgan's, takes up the pen, and
completing October, passes to Dec. 17, and thence to the end. He gives his
authority *A san leabar mor so sios,* " From the Big Book what follows." He
omitted, however, to finish the entry of Oct. 30 relating to Mocholmóc, *viz.,*
Mocholmóc atá, but proceeded at once to *Airnich meic Echin.*

INDEX OF PLACES (Roman Calendar).

Nividunum, Adomnini, May 17 ; *Nyon, Switzerland.*
Nola, Nolanae urbis, Aug. 31 ; *Nola, in Campania.*

Ostensa vallis, Ostensae, Aug. 10.

Paneas, Panes, Jan. 24 ; *Caesarea Philippi.*
Parisii, Parisilis, Jan. 3, Oct. 9.
Patras, Patricii, Oct. 15.
Pergamum, Permonii, Aug. 9.
Perusia, Pero-, Jan. 29 ; *Perugia.*
Philippopolis, Pillo Poli, Mar. 30.
Phoenicia, Fen-, Aug. 29.
Phrygia, Frig-, May 1, Oct. 8, 9, 24.
Pictaui, Jan. 13 ; *Poitiers.*
Potentia, Potenti, Aug. 27 ; *Potenza.*
Puteoli, Putiolis, Potioli, Jan. 25, Oct. 18, 19; *Pozzuoli.*

Ratiaria, Retiaria, Dec. 31 ; *Arzar Palanca, on the Danube.*
Rauenna, Rauiani, Raumani, Jan. 25.
Redones, Redontii, Jan. 6 ; *Rennes.*
Repensi, *see* Dacia.
Retiaria, *see* Ratiaria.
Rhodanus, Ro-, Sep. 22 ; *the Rhone.*
Roma, Jan. 18, 21, Mar. 12, Ap. 14, 20, Aug. 6, 10, Sep. 14, Oct. 8, 16, 26, Dec. 23.
—— Basilicae Mariae, dedicatio, Sep. 15.
—— Cathedra Petri, Jan. 18.
—— [Cymiterium] Aproniani, Approm-, Dec. 25.
—— —— Balbinae, Baluinae, Aug. 27, Oct. 1, 4, 6.
—— —— Basillae, Sep. 11.
- —— —— Calepodi, Calip-, Calapotii, Ap. 12, 13, Oct. 14.

Roma [Cymiterium] Calesti, Callisti, Caliusti, Caulisti, Clisti, Jan. 10, 16, 20, Ap. 22, Aug. 6.
—— —— Pretextati, Prot-, Ap. 14, May 10, Aug. 6.
—— —— Priscillae, Jan. 16, 18, Sep. 24, Dec. 31.
—— [Via] Appia, Apati, Ap. 14.
—— [Via] Laurentina, Laurentii, Oct. 12.
—— Via Ostiensi, Ostensi, in via Ostensi, Aug. 8, 22.
—— [Via Salaria Vetus], Salutari Veterae, Jan. 23.
—— [Thermae] Diocletianae (-itiani), Ap. 14.

Sacina, *see* Acaunum.
Salona, Saloniae, Ap. 11 ; *capital of Dalmatia.*
Sarrae, *see* Caesarea.
Scythia, Scetha, Ap. 5.
Sirmium, Firmi (?) Ap. 6, Aug. 9, Simmimonis, Ap. 9.
Smyrna, Spirnae, Mar. 12.
Suanis, Infiani, Oct. 28 ; *a city of Persia.*
Syria, Siriae, Ap. 7, Oct. 12.

Tabilli, *see* Cibala.
Tarracona, Tara-, Jan. 20.
Thebais, Teb-Jan. 17.
Theusii, *see* Tuscia.
Thracia, Traciae, Sep. 29 (2).
Tiburti, Aug. 9 ; *Tivoli.*
Ticina urbs, Oct. 16.
Tomi, Tomae, Ap. 3 ; *Tomisvar.*
Treveris, Tri-, Jan. 29, Aug. 31 ; *Trèves.*
Turones, Turoni, Dec. 30 ; *Tours.*
Tuscia, Theusii, Ap. 29.

Valentia Galliae, Valenaci, Oct. 5.

INDEX OF PERSONS (Roman Calendar).

Christus, Iesus, Dominus—*contd.*
circumcisio, Jan. 1.
crucifixus et conceptus est, Mar. 25.
eductio ex Egipto, Jan. 11.
epifania, Jan. 6.
initium predicationis, May 1.
inuentio crucis, May 3, 12.
natiuitas, Dec. 25.
resurrectio, Mar. 27.
Christus, Oct. 1.
Cicilia, *see* Caecilia.
Cicilianus, *see* Caecilianus.
Cint-, *see* Quint-.
Cionus, *see* Chionus.
Cip-, *see* Cyp-.
Cir-, *see* Cyr-.
Clarina (+ Clariani), Aug. 12.
Claudia, Jan. 2.
Claudianus, Ap. 5, Oct. 24, 25 (2).
Claudio, Caudio, Jan. 3.
Claudius, Mar. 20, 21, Ap. 30 (2), Aug. 23 (+ Laudi).
Cleasus, Eleasus (+ Deusii), Sep. 9.
Clematus, Jan. 23.
Clemens, Jan. 20, Ap. 30, Sep. 21.
Cleomannis, *see* Index of Places: Cenomani.
Clericus, Jan. 7, 14†, Aug. 27†, *see* Index of Places : Heraclea.
Cletus, Dec. 30.
Clionus, Ap. 24.
Clistus, *see* Callistus.
Clonicus, *see* Dominicus.
Clorinus, *see* Florinus.
Codomonus (Codñi), Ap. 29.
Collectius, Collegus, Mar. 18, 19.
Collocia, Aug. 31.
Colnilius, *see* Cornelius.
Colocerus, Aug. 26 *bis.*
Colonica, Coloniae, May 19.
Colonus, Aug. 20.
Colotus, Mar. 18 (2).
Columba, Aug. 12.
Comilia, *see* Cornelia.
Cominus, May 11, Oct. 27.
Commodus, Mar. 20.
Concessa, Ap. 8, 10.
Concessus, Mar. 12, Ap. 8, 9, 11 (2).
Concordia, Aug. 29, Oct. 6.
Concordius, May 6.
Conditor, Canditor, Ap. 14.
Connexus, Ap. 8.
Constantia, Sep. 17, 20.
Constantina, Jan. 29.
Constantinus, Jan. 29, Aug. 7, Sep. 1.
Constantius, Jan. 3, Sep. 15, 17, Aug. 28. *See also* Index of Places : Constantinopolis.
Contius, Mar. 22.

Corintho, Chorunto, Aug. 8.
Cornelia, Cornilia, Mar. 31, Ap. 14, 20 (+ Comilia).
Cornelius, Colnilius Cornilius, Cornolius, Jan. 23, Aug. 11, 13, 15, Sep. 14, 24, Dec. 23, 31.
Corona, Jan. 1†, 13, Ap. 24 (+ Carionae), May 14, Aug. 29, Oct. 7.
Coroticus, *see* Caroticus.
Corpoforus, *see* Carpoforus.
Corus, *see* Chorus.
Cosmas, Sep. 27.
Cotia, May 15.
Cotidius, *see* Eutychius.
Credula, May 13.
Crescens, Oct. 31, Dec. 29.
Crescentia, Aug. 10, Oct. 1.
Crescentianus, Aug. 8, 9.
Crescentio, Aug. 4, 10.
Crescentius, May 19, Oct. 1, 17.
Crestus, Crescus, Ap. 3, Aug. 10, Dec. 18, 19.
Crisantius, Aug. 12, Dec. 19, 20.
Crisconius, Jan. 15.
Crisothelus, Mar. 20.
Crispianus, Oct. 25.
Crispina, Aug. 10.
Crispion, May 10.
Cristiforus, Crizoforus, *see* Christophorus.
Cristina, Aug. 18, Sep. 28.
Cronanus, Aug. 6 ; a doublet of Irish Crónan out of place.
Cronides, Crocus, Sep. 15.
Crucessius, Jan. 14.
Crusis, Mar. 30.
Curiaca, *see* Cyriaca.
Curica, *see* Caricia.
Curius, May 19.
Cursicus, Sep. 10.
Cuticus, Cutidius, *see* Eutychius.
Cymminus, Jan. 13.
Cyprianus, Ciprianus, Ap. 12, 15, Sep. 14.
Cyriaca, Ciriaca, Cirica Curiaca, Mar. 16, 17, Ap. 2.
Cyriaces, Ciriaces, Ap. 7.
Cyriacus, Ciriacus, Jan. 3, 11, 12, 13, 20 (2), 21, Ap. 2, 6, 14, 20, 22, May 12 (2), Aug. 8, 10, 23 *bis*, 28, Dec. 19, 25.
Cyricus, Ciricus, May 15, Aug. 10, 15, 30, Sep. 9, 21, 26, 29, Oct. 1, Dec. 24.
Cyrilla, Cirilla, Quirilla, May 13, Aug. 6, 30, Oct. 9, 28.
Cyrillus, Cirillus, Quirillus, Mar. 20, 21, Ap. 26, May 9, 10, Aug. 10, 19, Oct. 2 (+ Aurillus), 31.

Cyrinus, Cirinus, Sep. 15.
Cyrio, Cirio, Sep. 15.
Cyrus, Cirus, Ap. 6.

Dactilus, *see* Datulus.
Dagarius, Ap. 30.
Dagonus, Oct. 31.
Dalmathi, Dalmathae, *see* Index of Places.
Damianus, Sep. 9, 27.
Danais, *see* Tanasus.
Daniel, Oct. 26.
Daria, Aug. 12, Oct. 20.
Darius, Dec. 20.
Daroma, Sep. 20.
Dascus, Aug. 18 *bis*.
Dascus Omes, Dasciomes, Oct. 21 (+ Dasi).
Dasius, Dassius, Aug. 5, Oct. 4, 20, 21.
Datica, May 8.
Datiuus, Diutius, Jan. 26, Mar. 14, May 10, 18, Dec. 25.
Datulus, Dactilus, Dec. 18, 19.
Datus, Jan. 21, 24, 27, May 8, Dec. 31.
Decimus, Dec. 22.
Decius, May 19 (2), Aug. 7, Oct. 18.
Decronus, Mar. 22, 23.
Dedalus, *see* Didalus.
Dedicus, Ap. 9† ; = dedicatio.
Dedimus, *see* Didymus.
Defensor, Oct. 17.
Demetrius, Dimetrius, Ap. 9, May 11, Aug. 14, Sep. 8, 14, 18, 19, Dec. 21 *bis*, 22, 23, 29.
Denegothia, Denegotiae, Oct. 1.
Deoclatus, Jan. 7.
Depletorus, Sep. 10, 13 ; corruption : deṗ (depositio) Litori, *see* Litorus.
Deseus, *see* Disseus.
Desiderius, Sep. 7, 30 (+ Desideus), Oct. 19.
Deusius, Sep. 9, *see* Cleasus.
Dextra, May 7.
Diacii, Jan. 21† ; = diaconorum.
Diaconus, Jan. 14†. *See also* Index of Places : Dacia.
Diapoli, *see* Index of Places : Neapolis.
Dicieus, Oct. 21.
Dicorius, *see* Dioscorus.
Didalus, Dedalus, Jan. 18.
Didymus, Didimus, Dedimus, Ap. 5, Sep. 8, 10.
Digna, Pigna, Oct. 1.
Dignus, May 15, Dec. 18, 19.
Dimetrius, *see* Demetrius.

Diocletianus, Dioclitianus, ·May 16.
See *also* Index of Places : Roma : Thermae Diocletianae.
Diodorus, Diodarus, Oct. 8, 9, 10, 27.
Diogenes, Mar. 26, Ap. 7, 15.
Diomedes, Diomides, Aug. 8, 20, 21.
Diona, Mar. 14 (2).
Dionina, Dionica, Ap. 15.
Dioninus, May 10.
Dionysius, Dionisius, Mar. 14 *bis*, 16 *bis*, 17, 18, 19, 23, Ap. 1, 2 (2), May 15, Aug. 7, 27, Sep. 14 *bis*, 20, Oct. 7, 8, 9, 10, Dec. 26.
Diopus (2), *see* Index of Places : Diospolis.
Dioscorus, Discorus, Dioscri, Ap. 2, May 18 (+ Dicorius), Aug. 20 *bis*, Dec. 17.
Disseus, Dissus, Deseus, Aug 14, 17 ; Oct. 21 (+ Dicicei).
Dissia, Aug. 17.
Diutius, *see* Datiuus.
Dm̄o, Aug. 23.
Doctor, Oct. 1.
Dola, Mar. 29.
Domicius, Dec. 29.
Domina, Domna, Ap. 14, Aug. 23, Oct. 19.
Dominicus, Clonicus, May 19.
Dominnus, Domition, Ap. 11.
Domnus, Dominus, Mar. 20, 21, 30, Ap. 11, 18, Aug. 17.
Donaeta, Oct. 15.
Donata, Mar. 12, Ap. 10, 12, 20, Aug. 8, Sep. 1, 16, 18, Oct. 17, Dec. 31.
Donatianus, Aug. 6.
Donatus, Jan. 11, 25, 27, Mar. 27, Ap. 6, 9, 14, 17, 18, 19, 20, 24 (3), 28, May 7 *bis*, 8 (2), Aug. 5, 7, Sep. 1 (3), 5, 9, 11, Oct. 1, 12, 30, 31 (2), Dec. 17, 28, 30, 31.
Dordianus, *see* Gordinaus
Dormientes (vii) in Effeso, Aug. 7.
Dorostolus. Dorozolus, Dec. 25, 26.
Dorotha, Ap. 30, Oct. 20.
Dorotheus, Dorothus, Mar. 12, 28, Oct. 23.
Dorozolus, *see* Dorostolus.
Dotus, Mar. 27.
Dreconus, Mar. 22, 23.
Drogenes, Aug. 3.
Dubitatus, Sep. 1.
Dula, Mar. 25.
Duno, Jan. 1, *see* Index of Places : Augustodunum.
Dunus, Mar. 12.
Duolus, Oct. 9.

Ebicianus, Jan. 11, 12.

Hacuntus, *see* Iacintus.
Hedistus, Oct. 12 (+ Mamedistus ?).
Helapus, *see* Elasippus.
Heleseus, Aug. 29.
Heliana, Aug. 18.
Helias, Heli, Eli, Elias, Aug. 17, 28, Sep. 18, Dec. 25, 26.   In Sep. 19 Eli is wrongly attached to the corrupt *Pari Madi :* see Patermuthius.
Heliodorus, May 6.
Helius, Mar. 26.
Heracla, Oct. **20**.
Heraclia, *see* Index of Places.
Heraclida, Eraclida, Oct. 26.
Heraclius, Aradius, Eraclius, Herclius, Herilius, Heradius, Eradius, Jan. 1, 12, Ap. 20, May 15, 16, 17, Aug. 4, 5 *bis* (+ Aradi), 14, Sep. 12, Oct. 7, 8, 9, 10, 11.
Herapoli, *see* Index of Places.
Herculianus, Herculinus, Sep. 5.
Heremetus, Aug. 4†.
Hereneus, Herensus, *see* Irenaeus.
Herenna, *see* Irene.
Herentius, Aug. 5.
Herilius, *see* Heraclius.
Herinipus, Sep. 22.
Herisus, Erisinus, Jan. 2, 13.
Hermes, Ermes, Jan. 1 (2), 4, 21 (+Hermis), 22, 24, Mar. 26, Ap. 27, Aug. 27, 28 (+ Hermis), Oct. 18, 22 (+Hermae, + Bermae), Dec. 31.
Hermilius, Hermelius, Ermilius, Aug. 3.
Hermogenes, Hermogines, Ermoderus, Ap. 17, 18, 19, 25, (Hermogini) 27, May 2, Aug. 23, Sep. 1 ; p. 106.
Hermogeratus (–tis), Aug. 23.
Hermologus, Sep. 22.
Hermon, Hermonus, May 18.
Herolus, May 15.
Heustasius, *see* Eustasius.
Heuualach, Oct. 4 *bis*.
Hielinus, Sep. 10.
Hiemus, May 17.
Hieronymus, Ieronimus, Sep. 30.
Hilaria, Dec. 31.
Hilarius, Ilarius, Jan. 3, 27, Mar. 12, 16, 17, Ap. 9 (2), 10, 11, 19, May 5.
Hilarius epi. Pictauis, Jan. 13,
Hilarius papa, Sep. 10.
Hippocratus, Ipocratus, Sep. 22.
Hippolytus, Hippolitus, Hipolitus, Ipolitus, Ypolitus, Jan. 29, May 2 (+ Eupolitis), Aug. 6, 13 (+ Ipolissus), Aug. 20, 23 (+ Ypoli), Sep. 11, 12.

Hirenus, *see* Irenaeus.
Hirudinus, Hirundo, *see* Husandus.
Hisicus, Sep. 10.
Hispanus, Jan. 19.
Honis, Mar. 22.
Honoratus, Jan. 1, 16, 18, 19, 21, 27, 29, Ap. 26, (Onoragus) 30, Aug. 27, Dec. 17, 19 (2), 21, 29, 30.
Honorius, Jan. 5, 6, 16, Mar. 18, Ap. 5, Sep. 14, 30, Dec. 22, 23.
Hortasius, May 18.
Hortinsus, Hortensus, Jan. 11.
Hortisianus, Jan. 17.
Humiliana, Aug. 31, Sep. 29, Oct. 19, Hursinia, Mar. 14.
Husandus, Hirudinus, Hirundo, Ap. 27, Aug. 16, Sep. 8, Oct. 28.

Iacintus, Iacinthus, Sep. 9 (+ Hacuntus), Sep. 11.
Iacobus, Mar. 14, 22, Ap. 17, May 6, (2). Apostolus, Dec. 27. Apostolus et frater Domini, Mar. 15, May 1. Frater Domini, Mar. 25. Justus, May 10. Ordinatio, Dec. 27.
Iamputianus, Sep. 29 ; confusion of Ampulus or Ambodus, *q.v.*
Ianuaria, Jan. 5, 6, Ap. 13, Dec. 25.
Ianuarius, Ianarius, Jan. 5, 9, 11, 13, 14, 19, 22 *bis*, Mar. 13, 17, 19, Ap. 8, 17, 18, May 8, 10, 14, 15, Aug. 7, Sep. 7, 18, 19, 29, Oct. 1, 6, 7, 10, 11, 13, 17, 18 (2), 19, 20 (2), 27, 30 (3), Dec. 28.
Ieiunarius, Jan. 7, 8.
Iemsolius, Ierolius, Mar. 18.
Ierenus, *see* Irenaeus.
Ieronimus, *see* Hieronymus.
Iesu Naue, Sep. 1.
Ignatius, Aug. 15, 16 (2), Dec. 20, 25.
Ilarius, *see* Hilarius.
Indicus, Iudicius, May 19.
Inertus, May 11.
Infantes occisae, Dec. 28.
Infiani, *see* Index of Places : Suanis.
Infirmus, Jan. 28.
Ingeniana, Ap. 1.
Ingenianus, Ap. 1.
Ingenua, Mar. 14, 15.
Ingenula, Jan 17.
Ingenuus, Jan. 11, 13, Mar. 18, 19, Sep. 5.
Innocentia, Aug. 10.
Innocentius, Inocentius, Mar. 12, 14, 15, Aug. 23, Sep. 22, Dec. 20.
Insola, Oct. 27.
Ioannes, *see* Johannes.
Iob, May 11.
Iocundus, Iocundidus, Jan. 5, 6, 8.

Iohanna mil., Aug. 27.
Iohannes, Mar. 12, 31, Ap. 11, 20 *bis*, 23, 24, May 1, 5, 8, 12, Aug. 7, 15, (Iohani) 17, 25, 30, 31, Sep. 8, 9, 10, 11, 14, 16 (2), 20, 21, 24, 26, 27, 29, 30, Oct. 1, 7, 8, 11, 16, 19, 20, 21 24, 28, Dec. 21 (2), 23.
Iohannes apostolus, May 9.
Iohannes Baptista, May 6, Aug. 29, Sep. 24.
Iohannes metrapolis, Aug. 3.
Iohannis, apostoli et euang., assumptio, Dec. 27.
Iononatus, Dec. 21.
Iorgius, Sep. 19.
Ioseph, Mar. 20, 24, Aug. 25, 30 *bis*, Sep. 15.
Ioseph sponsus Mariae, Mar. 19.
Iosephus, Iosepus, Iosippus, Mar. 19, 20, 21 (2), 22, Oct. 7.
Iouanus, Iouianus, Iouenus, Mar. 12, 16, May 16.
Ipocratus, *see* Hippocratus.
Ipolissus, Ipolitus, *see* Hippolytus.
Irenaeus, Hereneus, Herensus, Hirenus, Erenneus, Irineus, Ierenus, Mar. 26, Ap. 1, 5, 6 (+ Bereneus), May 5, Aug. 5 (+ Irenneus).
Irene, Erenna, Herenna, Ap. 1, 5, May 5, Aug. 18, 30, Oct. 8.
Isaac, Ap. 12, 26, immolatio, Mar. 25.
Iseus, Aug. 4.
Isicus, Sep. 17.
Isiodora, *see* Sidora.
Isiodorus, Sep. 8.
Italica, Aug. 24, 25, 31.
Iuberius, Ap. 23.
Iudacus, Aug. 9.
Iudicius, *see* Indicus.
Iudith, May 6.
Iulia, Mar. 29, May 8, 19, Aug. 16, Sep. 5, Oct. 7, 24.
Iuliana, Jan. 27, Mar. 29, Ap. 4, Aug. 8, 10, 14, 31, Oct. 20, Dec. 19.
Iulianus, Jan. 6, 26, 27, Mar. 16, 23, 29, Ap. 2, 3, 12, 18, 28, Aug. 9. 12 (2), 19, 20, 21, 25, 31, Sep. 12, 18, 21, 24, Oct. 7, 8, 9, 31, Dec. 18, 25, 26.
Iulita, Aug. 16, Sep. 5, Oct. 24.
Iulius, Jan. 6, 19, 22, Ap. 26, May 11 *bis*, Aug. 20, 24, 25, Oct. 8, 9, Dec. 20.
Iulius eps. Romae, Ap. 12.
Iunilla, Jan. 17, Aug. 24, 25, Oct. 4.
Iunius, Mar. 25, Dec. 25.
Iusta, Aug. 31.
Iustinus, May 5, Aug. 4.

Iustus, May 10†, Aug. 4, Oct. 14, 21, 24.

Kalendinus, *see* Calendinus.
Karulus, *see* Carulus.
Karus, *see* Carus.

Laetissima, Ap. 27.
Laetissimus, *see* Lictissimus.
Largus, Mar. 17 (2), Aug. 8, 9, 10.
Lauani, *see* Index of Places : Aureliani.
Laucius, Jan. 15.
Laudae, *see* Index of Places : Laodicaea.
Laudicus, Laudaicus, Aug. 9.
Laudus, *see* Claudius.
Laurentia, Sep. 28.
Laurentius, Mar. 23, (Lur-) May 8, Aug. 4, 6, 10, 15, 19, 23 (2), 27, 28, Sep. 1, 7, 12, 17, 27, Oct. 1, 7 *bis*, 17, Dec. 24. *See also* Index of Places : Roma : Via Laurentii.
Laurus, Ap. 24.
Lazarus, Jan. 19.
Lea, Sep. 28.
Lectoris, Lictoris, Ap. 16†, 28† : = lector.
Leo, Ap. 22, 26, Aug. 5.
Leocipus, Leocis, *see* Leucippus.
Leocus, Jan. 27.
Leodegarius, Leodargus, Leudgarus, Oct. 3, 16.
Leodotius, Leodocius, Jan. 25.
Leogus, *see* Longus.
Leonides, Leonitides, Ap. 13, 15, 16, 22, 26.
Leonilla, Jan. 17, Oct. 4.
Leontius, Leotinus, Jan. 20 *bis*, 21, Mar. 20, Aug. 19, 20, 21 (+ Leontianus), Sep. 15 (2).
Leucippus (2), Leocis Leocipus, Aug. 10.
Leucius, Leusius, Jan. 1, 17, 18, Oct. 18.
Leudgarus, *seee* Leodegarius.
Leugathus, Leugadus, Oct. 22 (+ Eugathus).
Leusius, *see* Leucius.
Libandia, Liphandia, Ap. 27.
Liberalis, Ap. 24 (2).
Liberatus, Sep. 9.
Liberius, Mar. 29, 30, Ap. 19, May 17, Sep. 23, 24, Dec. 20. *See also* Index of Places : Caucoliberis.
Libia, *see* Index of Places.
Libosus, Librosus, Dec. 29.
Licasti, Sep. 30, a confusion of "*in Mesoli Casti,*" *see* Castus, and Index of Places, *s.v.* Massyli

Mereforus, see Merosori.
Merentiana, see Emerentiana.
Merianus, Ap. 20.
Meritus, see Merus.
Merobius, Sep. 15.
Meronus, Aug. 26.
Merosorus, Sep. 10 (+ Mereforus).
Merus, Ap. 3 (+ Meritus), Oct. 16.
Mesalanus, see Miselianus.
Messor, Ap. 15.
Messurianus, Messorinus, Misurianus,
Jan. 27, 28 (2).
Metellus, Jan. 24.
Metrus, Sep. 8.
Metrapolis, Aug. 3†.
Metrobius, Oct. 27 (+ Medrotus),
Dec. 24.
Metrodora, Mecrona, Aug. 8.
Meturus, Ap. 24 (2), 30.
Mica, Micca, see Mucius.
Micarius, see Macarius.
Micea, Miceta, Jan. 18.
Michaea, Michia, Jan. 15.
Michael, May 18.
Michael, archangeli reuelatio, May
9 ; dedicatio basilicae, Sep. 29 ;
honor Oct. 16, 17.
Micio, Ap. 18.
Midor, see Maior.
Migdonus, Mar. 12.
Mignus, Migignus, Sept. 26.
Miles, May 8†(?) ; = miles ; militis
et al. xliii, Jan. 1.
Milisa, Mar. 16.
Militana, Militina, see Index of
Places.
Militiades, Melciades. Jan. 10, Sep. 11.
Militus, Ap. 24 bis, Sep. 19.
Mimmus, Mammus, Oct. 31.
Mimus, Aug. 4.
Minerius, May 16, 17.
Mineruus, Meneruus, May 15, Aug. 22.
Mineus, Mireus, Oct. 15.
Minister, Ap. 17†.
Minorgius, May 16.
Minucius, Jan. 23.
Minus, see Guntramnus.
Mirendinus, Aug. 23.
Mireus, see Mineus.
Miria, see Misia.
Mirtha, Mirti, Jan. 10.
Misac, Ap. 24.
Miselianus, Mesalanus, Jan. 17.
Misia, Mar. 27 (+ Miria).
Missor, Jan. 14.
Mistorus, see Mitisorus.
Mistrianus, Jan. 17.
Mitisorus, Mistorus (+ Nistorus),
Sep. 8.

Mittunus, Emetunus, May 4.
Moca, see Moeca.
Moderata, Ap. 6.
Modesta, Mar. 13.
Modestinus, Mar. 13.
Modestus, Jan. 11, 12, Ap. 6, Oct. 21.
Moeca, Moca, May 10.
Mogemocineicaill (?), Oct. 14 =
perhaps Mocholmóc, an Irish saint,
inserted out of place.
Moisitis, May 12.
Molendion, Jan. 19.
Moleus, Mar. 24 (doublet with
Timolaus).
Momatia, Mar. 21.
Monachus, Mar. 21.
Monica, Ap. 16.
Montanianus, May 11.
Montanus, Mar. 26, May 11.
Mosa, see Massa.
Moscentus, Muscentus, Jan. 12.
Mosetis, Mossitis, Ap. 15.
Moyseus, Jan. 18.
Moysus, Ap. 6.
Muca, Ap. 22.
Mucius, Muccus, Municus, Micca,
Mica, Jan. 17.
Mumus, see Turemunus.
Mundanus, Oct. 30.
Mundus factus est, Mar. 25.
Munesana, Munisana, Aug. 11†, Oct.
13†.
Municipus, Jan. 22.
Municus, see Mucius.
Munnus, see Nonnus.
Muria, Oct. 20 (2).
Muricus, Oct. 7.
Muridanus, Mar. 12.
Musa, see Massa.
Muscentus, see Moscentus.
Muscius, Dec. 19.
Muscula, Ap. 12.
Musitania, see Index of Places :
Mauritania.
Mussurus, Jan. 24.

Naborius, Nabor, Naboria, Mar. 14,
Ap. 23, 24.
Nabortus, Nabartius, Sep. 26.
Namfamo, Famonis, Dec. 19.
Narcissus, Narcisus, Jan. 1, 3.
Nascussus, see Marcusius.
Natalis, Jan. 1†, Aug. 29† ; natale,
see notes.
Natanus, Aug. 22.
Naue, (Iesu Naue), Sep. 1.
Nauigius, May 7.
Nausus, Sep. 1.
Nazarius, Aug. 8.

Polyeuctus, Pilotus, Poliucatus, Pulliolus, Jan. 7, Ap. 9, May 19.
Pomerus, Poemus, Mar. 19, 20.
Pompinus, Pomponus, Dec. 18, 19.
Pontianus, Bontianus, Aug. 10 (+ Portianus), 13, Dec. 20, 31.
Pontimus, Aug. 18.
Pontonus, Pontomus, Aug. 18, 19.
Popula, May 15.
Portianus, *see* Pontianus.
Possessor, Jan. 2, 3, 9, 10, Aug. 14.
Postella, *see* Potentella.
Potamia, Potamica, Ap. 15.
Potamo, Potomo, May 17, 18 (+ Pantomonus).
Potentella, Pudentella, Postella, May 7.
Potenti, *see* Index of Places, *s.v.* Potentia.
Potioli, *see* Index of Places : Puteolis.
Potomus, Aug. 18.
Predentius, *see* Prodentus.
Pretextatus, *see* Index of Places : Roma : Cymiterium Pretextati.
Priamus, Ap. 27.
Prima, Jan. 3.
Primadius, *see* Patermuthius.
Primianus, Jan. 1 (+ Priminianus), Dec. 29.
Primicus, *see* Primus.
Primitius, *see* Priuatus.
Primitiuus, Jan. 22.
Primolus, Primulus, Ap. 22, May 11.
Primus, Jan. 3, 19, 21, 27, May 17, Aug. 9, 26, Oct. 1, 2 (+ Primicus), 25.
Priscaria, *see* Picaria.
Priscianus, Ap. 18, Sep. 16 (+ Prisizatus), Oct. 12.
Priscilla, Jan. 18, Sep. 24, Dec. 31, *see* Index of Places : Roma : Cymiterium Priscillae.
Priscus, Jan. 1, Sep. 1, 28, Oct. 1.
Prisizatus, *see* Priscianus.
Priuata, May 2, Sep. 20.
Priuata, Sep. 20.
Priuatianus, May 7.
Priuatus, Primitius, Priuatis, May 10, Oct. 7, 8, Dec. 18, 19.
Probata, May 10.
Probatus, Dec. 28.
Probus, Ap. 5 (2), May 13, Sep. 27, Oct. 8, 11†, 13.
Processa, May 8.
Processus, Jan. 27.
Prociuus, Oct. 14.
Proclina, Ap. 12†, 15.
Procliuia, Ap. 2.
TALLAGHT.

Procula, Ap. 2.
Proculus, Ap. 2 (2), 14, May 1, Oct. 19.
Prodentus, Predentius, Ap. 15.
Producus, *see* Prosducus.
Promacus, Promiceus, Oct. 20.
Pronatus, Mar. 28.
Prontius, *see* Frontinus.
Pronus, May 19.
Prosalm, Aug. 14 *bis.*
Prosdocia, Prosodocia, Oct. 19.
Prosducus, Producus, Prosoducus, Ap. 14, 29.
Proseria, Prosiria, Oct. 12, 13.
Protasius, Protassius, Oct. 30.
Protextatus, *see* Index of Places : Roma : Cymiterium Pretextati.
Protida, Mar. 31.
Protus, Prothus, Sep. 11, Oct. 27.
Publianus, Puplianus, Jan. 24, 25.
Publicanus, Jan. 27.
Publius, Puplius, Jan. 19, 21, 27, Ap. 2, 3, 14.
Pudentella, *see* Potentella.
Pudentiana, May 19.
Puer, Jan 3†, Oct. 21, 30.
Pulliolus, *see* Polyeuctus.
Puluinus, May 7.
Pupl-, *see* Publ-.
Puteolis, *see* Index of Places.

Quadratus, Ap. 9, Aug. 20, 21.
Quartilla, Quartila, Quartilda, Mar. 18, 19, 20, Ap. 6.
Quartinus, Mar. 18.
Quartus, Cartus, Ap. 12, May 10, 14, Aug. 26. Oct. 7, Dec. 17.
Quinta, May 7.
Quintasius, Oct. 17.
Quintianus, Cintianus, Ap. 1, May 1, Sep. 5, Dec. 31 (2). *See also* Anitorsus.
Quintilianus, Jan 22, Ap. 3, 4.
Quintillus, Jan. 27, Mar. 20.
Quintinianus, May 1.
Quintinus, Jan. 21, May 2, Aug. 15, 19, 20, 30, Oct. 5, 9, 11, 31.
Quintus, Cintus, Jan. 4, 9, 10, 11, 12 (?), 19, Mar. 19, 20, Ap. 5, 17, May 7, 10, 19, Aug. 10, 26, Sep. 5, 13, Oct. 11, 25, 28 (2), 29, 30, 31, Dec. 17, 18, 19, 20. *See* Sep. 5, note.
Quirilla, *see* Cyrilla.
Quirillus, *see* Cyrillus
Quirinus, Mar. 12, Ap. 30.

Raba, Mar. 14.
Radicundis, Radegundis, Aug. 12.

P

Scholastica, Scolastica, May 7, Aug. 18, Sep. 28†.
Sconisius, Jan. 18.
Scriba, Aug. 28.
Sebastianus, Sabastianus, Jan. 6, 19, 20.
Secunda, Jan. 27, May 8, Sep. 16, 24, Oct. 9, 10, 31.
Secundianus, May 6, Oct. 2.
Secundila, Secundola, May 8, Sep. 24.
Secundinus, May 14, Aug. 8, Sep. 13, Dec. 19 (2).
Secundulus, Mar. 24.
Secundus, Jan. 5, 13, 19, 21, 23, 25, 26, 27, 28, Mar. 22, 23, Ap. 1 *bis*, 6, 24 (2), Aug. 8 (2), Sep. 13, Oct. 12, Dec. 20, 29.
Securus, Oct. 24 (2), Dec. 30.
Secutor, Ap. 13.
Sedrac, Ap. 24, Aug. 22, Sep. 21.
Sefa ( ), Jan. 11, = (?) Stephanus, *q.v.*
Seleucus, Mar. 24, May 19 (+ Selincius), Sep. 15.
Semion, *see* Simeon.
Senator, Sep. 25, 26.
Seno, *see* Zeno.
Senonus, *see* Zenonus.
Senorus, *see* Zenonus.
Senotius, Sep. 7 (+ Sinotius).
Separgus, Spargus, Oct. 3.
Septem fratres dormientes in Effeso, Aug. 7, p. 114.
Septimna, May 7.
Septimus, Ap. 18, May 11, Oct. 8, 9.
Sequens, Dec. 31.
Serapion, Mar. 20, 21 *bis*, 22, 26, Ap. 6, May 18, Aug. 7, 28, Sep. 8 (2) 11, 12, 15 (2).
Serenus, Jan. 5, Mar. 16 *bis* (+ Sirenus), Dec. 21, (Rereneus) 30.
Serianus, *see* Seuerianus.
Serotina, Dec. 31.
Seruulus, Seruulius, Jan. 21, Mar. 18, 19.
Seuerianus, Serianus, Jan. 23, Aug. 8.
Seuerinus, Sep. 8.
Seuersus, Oct. 23.
Seuerus, Jan. 1, 11, Aug. 26, Sep. 8, Oct. 22, 23, 24, Dec. 30.
Seusepus, Oct. 23.
Seuus, Aug. 10, 21.
Sextus, *see* Sixtus.
Siasius, *see* Susius.
Sictus, *see* Sixtus.
Sido, *see* Sodo.
Sidonius, Aug. 23 (2).
Sidora, Isiodora, Aug. 10.

Sigibarcus, Figius Baricius, Oct. 7.
Silinus, Oct. 27.
Silo, Aug. 19.
Siluanus, Mar. 12, Ap. 15, 16, 20, 24 (+ Silutanus), 30, May 4, Aug. 31, (Siluinus) Sep. 8, (Siluasius) Sep. 10, Sep. 24, Oct. 31 *bis*.
Siluasius, *see* Siluanus.
Siluester, Dec. 31.
Siluinus, *see* Siluanus.
Siluius, Mar. 13, 15, Ap. 21, 23, 24.
Silurinus, Sep. 24.
Silutanus, *see* Siluanus.
Simeon, Semion, Jan. 5 *bis*.
Simf-, *see* Symph-.
Simmimonis, *see* Index of Places : Sirmium.
Simon, Oct. 28.
Simplicius, Simplicis, Ap. 26, May 15, Oct. 13, Dec. 17, 18, 19.
Sinclitica, May 8, Aug. 18, Sep. 15, 28.
Sinforus, Jan. 6.
Sinlaia, Aug. 14.
Sinnidia, Ap. 3.
Sinotus, *see* Senotius.
Sión, Jan. 7.
Sircionus, *see* Siridonus.
Sirenus, *see* Serenus.
Siria, *see* Index of Places.
Sirianus, Dec. 23.
Siricius, Ap. 18, 26.
Siridonus, Esiridonus, Sircionus, Siritionus, Jan. 2.
Sirtus, *see* Sixtus.
Sirus, Sep. 11, 12, 24.
Sisinnius, Sep. 1, Oct. 20.
Sistus, *see* Sixtus.
Situs, Satus, Dec. 18, 19.
Sixtus, (Xixtus) Ap. 6, Aug. 9, (Sirtus) 23, (Sistus) Sep. 18, (Sictus) Dec. 23, (Sixtus) 31 (+ Sextus).
Sixtus ep. in Roma, Aug. 6
Smaragdus, Samaridus, Smragdus, Mar. 12, Aug. 8, Oct. 28 (+ Marandus).
Socrates, Sep. 17.
Socratus, Oct. 17.
Sodalis, Ap. 27.
Sodo, Sado (+ Sido), Jan. 25, Sep. 22.
Solanus, Dec. 23.
Solutor, Ap. 6.
Solutus, Ap. 23.
Sophronius, Sopronius, Aug. 7.
Sorentius, Mar. 20.
Sosius, *see* Susius.
Soticus, *see* Zoticus.
Spargus, *see* Separgus.

P 2

INDEX OF PLACES (Irish Calendar).

Abaind Lorgaid, p. 104 ; near Kells.
Abla, Sep. 12 ; Colmani epi. Ablae.
Achad, Aug. 15.
Achad (Abal, G), Mar. 26 ; perhaps Aghowle, bar. of Shilelagh, co. Wicklow.
Achad Bó, Sep. 5 ; Aghabo, bar. of Upper Ossory, Queen's co.
Achad Cinn (G), Cathub of, Ap. 6 ; al. Achad na Cille, Aughnakeely, townl. near Kilconway, co. Antrim.
Achad Conaire, Aug. 9 ; Achonry, near Ballaghadereen, co. Sligo.
Achad Coraind, June 8 ; Killoran, near Ballymote, bar. of Corann, co. Sligo.
Achad Dubthaig in Mag Lí (G), Gúaire Bec of, Jan. 9, 22 ; Achadowey, bar. of Coleraine, co. Derry.
Achad Duma (G), Taeda of, Jan. 31.
Achad Farcha (G), Rónán Find of, Dec. 23 ; in bar. of Slaney, co. Meath.
Achad Ferta, Jan. 14.
Achad Findnaige (Findnichae, O(n) ; Achad Findich, on the brink of the Dothra, G), May 11, i e., on the Dodder, in S. co. Dublin.
Achad Fota, Jan. 6.
Achad (Gobra, G), Feb. 22.
Achad Lurchair, Dec. 23 ; Aghalurcher, co. Fermanagh (Hogan).
Achad Mór, Aug. 30.
Achad na Cró, June 12.
Achad Úr, Mar. 19 ; Freshford, bar. Crannagh, co. Kilkenny.
Ailbe, Sept. 11, 25 ; probably Clonalvy, or Moynalvy, co. Meath.
Ailech, June 10 ; Elagh, or Greenan Elly, bar. of Inishowen, co. Donegal.
Airbre, in Uí Cennselaig, July 10 ; in co. Wexford.
Airdne, Mar. 8, May 30.
Airdne Cáemáin, June 7, also June 12 ; Ardcavan, bar. of Shelmalier, co. Wexford.
Airdne Dairinse, Mar. 26, May 30 ; in co. Wexford (? Hogan).
Airdoni, see Erdam.

Airec (O), Manchéne of, Jan. 2 ; a river near Disert meicc Cuilinn, in Laigis, Queen's co.
Airecul (Aricul, G), May 15.
Airecul Múadáin, Aug. 30 ; Errigal, co. Monaghan.
Aired Boinne, July 6.
Aired Chassáin, see Ard Chassáin.
Aired Drochait (Rind D., G), Feb. 22.
Aired (Fota, G), July 2.
Aired Indaich, Jan. 6.
Aired (Locha Con, G), Ap. 8 ; Errew, par. of Crossmolina, co. Mayo.
Aired Muilt, Loch Eirne, Feb. 28 ; church in diocese of Clogher, co. Tyrone (Hogan).
Aired Suird, Feb. 23 ; probably Swords, co. Dublin.
Airene, Sep. 16, Critan of, = Mochritóc Airene, Rawl. B. 502, 94a 10, LL. 368e ; on the Dodder, co. Dublin. Cp. May 11.
Airther Achaid, Sep. 30.
Airther Maige, in Túath Ratha (G), Díarmait of, Jan. 16 ; Armoy, in Toorah, co. Fermanagh.
Alba, June 20 ; Scotland.
Árann, gen. Áirni (Árne, O ; Áru, gen. Arand, G), Mar. 21, Dec. 31, dat. Áraind, May 11 ; island of Aranmore, in Galway Bay.
Árasnae, Mar. 19.
Ard, gen. na hArda, Feb. 23 ; the Ards, of which there are several.
Ard Achad in Tethba (G), Mel of, Feb. 6 ; Ardagh, co. Longford.
Ard Bó, Feb. 21 ; Arboe, par. and townl. in bar. of Dungannon, co. Tyrone.
Ard Breccáin, Sep. 4 ; Ardbraccan, near Navan, co. Meath.
Ard Caín, Sep. 8.
Ard Carna, Mar. 7 ; Ardcarne, near Boyle, co. Roscommon.
Ard Chassáin (Eired, i.e., Aired, Cassáin, G), Jan. 28.
Ard Cruinn, July 11.
Ard Fota, see Aired Fota.
Ardgal, see Clúain Acuir, Ráith mac Stíalláin.

Ard Leccaig in Mag Ene, Dec. 19;
near Ess Ruaid (D), *i.e.*, Assaroe
or Ballyshannon, co. Donegal.
Ard Lonáin, Dec. 18.
Ard Macha, Jan. 10, May 24, July 1,
Aug. 24; Armagh.
Ard meic Nasca (O G), Lasrián of,
Oct. 25; on the brink of Loch
Laig in Ulster (On), Holywood, co.
Down.
Ard Mór, July 24; Ardmore, co.
Waterford.
Ard Sratha, Aug. 23; Ardstraw,
near Strabane, co. Tyrone.
Ard Trea, July 8; Artrea, bar. of
Upper Dungannon, co. Tyrone.
Ard Ulad, May 29; the Ards, co.
Down.
Armag, gen. Armaige (Anmaige, G),
Ap. 22.
Áth Blair (G), Condmach of, July 9.
Ath Clíath (G), Síatal of, Feb. 12;
Dublin.
Áth Egais, June 1.
Áth Ferna, Feb. 11; either Ferns,
co. Wexford, or Aghafarnan, in
bar. of Lr. Kells, co. Meath.
Áth Innich (A. ind eich, G), July 23.
Áth Liacc, Feb. 7; Athleague, on the
Suck, co. Roscommon.
Áth Omna, Aug. 31.
Áth Siláin (A. Blair, G), July 9.
Áth Truim, Feb. 17, Oct. 11; Trim,
co. Meath.

Bairnech (LL, 353 *a* 31, OnG) in
Muscraige Mittine, Gobnat of,
Feb. 11: Ballyvourney, in W.
Muskerry, co. Cork.
Ballna, gen. Ballni (Balla, G), Mar.
30; in bar. of Carra, or Burris-
carra, co. Mayo.
Becc-ére (G), Ibar of, Ap. 23; Beg-
gery Island, in Wexford Har-
bour.
Belach (G), Jan. 1.
Belach Dúin, June 14; Castlekieran,
near Kells, co. Meath.
Belach Febrat (G), Lachtán of, Mar.
19; pass over the Ballyhoura
Hills, border of Cork and Limerick
(Hogan).
Belach Féle, Jan. 15.
Bennchor, Feb. 28, Ap. 8 21, 22, 26,
May 10, 16, June 11 12, Aug. 1,
22, Sep. 10, 11, Oct. 1, 27; Bangor,
co. Down.
Berba, *see* Ross Glassi, the River
Barrow, in Leinster.

Berrech (G), Crunnmáel of, June 22,
p. 114; in Fotharta, in Leinster.
Biror, May 9; Birr, King's co.
Both Conais, Sep. 4; in Inishowen,
co. Donegal.
Both Domnaig, May 3; Bodoney,
bar. of Strabane, co. Tyrone.
Bréchmag, Sep. 30; Breaffy, bar. of
Carra, co. Mayo.
Brega, *see* Mag Locha.
Breifne, *see* Cúil Rúscach.
Bretain, Ap. 21; Britain, Britons.
Brí Ele, *see* Crúachan Brig Éle.
Brí Molt, July 16; perhaps Brey-
molt, now Primult, King's co.
(Hogan).
Brug Lóeg (B. Long, G), July 15.

Cáelchad (Cáolachadh, G), Aug. 20;
there are Keelagh in Derry and
Cavan, and Keelaghy in Fer-
managh (Hogan).
Caill Insi Ailche, Dec. 21.
Caille Follamain, Sep. 14; Killalon,
a large parish in the north-west of
co. Meath (Walsh).
Cairpre, Coirbre (?), Jan. 7.
Cairpre húa Cíarda (G), Máel Aith-
gen of, June 6; Carbury, co. Kil-
dare.
Caisel (Caisel Irróe of Uí Fíachrach
Múaide, G), June 8; Killaspug-
brone, near Sligo.
Cammachad, Mar. 31; Cammagh,
bar. of Carrigallen, co. Leitrim
(? Hogan).
Camus, Cammas, gen. Camsa, Oct.
30; on the Bann, near Coleraine,
co. Derry.
Carn Furbaide, Mar. 6; Carn townl.
bar. of Abbeyshrule, co. Longford.
Cassán Linne *i.e.* Linn Dúachaill,
Linn Úachaille (G), May 30; river
near Dundalk, probably Anna-
gassan.
Cathair Meic Conaich, Mar. 26; near
Lismore.
Cell Abbáin, Abbán of, Mar. 16, Oct.
27; Killabban, bar. of Bally-
adams, Queen's co. (Stokes).
Cell Achaid, Mar. 26, June 25;
Killeigh, near Tullamore, King's
co.
Cell Achid, Ap. 28; Killaha, bar. of
Magunehy, co. Kerry (Hogan).
Cell Achid (Droma Senáin, G), Dec.
24.
Cell Áedáin, in Ulaid (G), Áed of,
Ap. 1; prob. in co. Down

Cell Afféin (G), Affíne of, June 3 ; near Glendalough, co. Wicklow.

Cell Aíne (Ané MS.), in Slíab Breg, Mar. 9 ; in co. Louth.

Cell Aird, Mar. 14 ; Killard, near Kilrush, co. Clare.

Cell Aird (Coill Aird, G) in Uí Ercáin (Uí Garrchon On G), dat. i cCill Aird, July 3 ; i n-iarthur Lagen O (R'), 'in west of Leinster,' in co. Wicklow.

Cell Airiss, Jan. 12 ; Killarush townl., near Kanturk, co. Cork.

Cell Airthir, Oct. 24.

Cell Alaid, Aug. 12 ; Killala, co. Mayo.

Cell Arcalgach, Aug. 20 ; on the brink of Loch Lébenn (G), now Loch Lene, in co. Westmeath.

Cell Ausailli (CC), Auxilius of, Sep. 16 ; Killosshy, near Naas, co. Kildare.

Cell Barrfhind (G), Barrfhind of, May 21 ; Kilbarron, bar. of Tirhugh, co. Donegal.

Cell Becc, gen. Cilli Bicci, Feb. 21.

Cell Biccsige (G), Bigsech of, June 28 ; Kilbixy, bar. of Moygoish, co. Westmeath.

Cell Chéli Chríst (G), Mar. 3 ; in Uí Dunchada, Leinster.

Cell Chóelbad (G), Coelba of, Aug. 21 ; north of Kells.

Cell Chúaca, in Coirpre Úa Cíarda (G D), Cúacha of, Jan. 8 ; Kilcock, co. Kildare.

Cell Cobraind, May 3 ; Kilcorney, co. Cork (Hogan).

Cell Coíne (Cóeme G), Ap. 4.

Cell Colmai, May 5.

Cell Comarthae, May 19.

Cell Cúle, Mar. 9, June 11 (Coill Cola, G), July 4 ; Kilcooley, near Tulsk, co. Roscommon.

Cell Culinn, June 11 ; Jan. 28 (G) ; Old Kilcullen, co. Kildare.

Cell Cunga, Ap. 11.

Cell Curcaine, July 21.

Cell Dáelen, Mar. 23.

Cell dá Les, May 9 ; now Templelusk, bar. of Arklow, co. Wicklow (Ronan, Journ. R.S.A.I. LVII. 108).

Cell dá Lúa, in Dál Cais (G), Flannán of, Dec. 18 ; Killaloe, co. Clare.

Cell Dara, May 3 ; Kildare.

Cell Delga, Jan. 31 ; Kildalkey, bar. of Lune, co. Meath.

Cell Delgraige (Elgraige, G), Dec. 13, p. 101 ; in the termon of Kells, co. Meath.

Cell Draignech in Uí Dróna (G), Erníne of, Aug. 18 ; Kildreenagh, bar. of Idrone, co. Carlow.

Cell Droichit (G), Imchad of, Sep. 25 ; in the Ards, co. Down (Hogan).

Cell Duma Gluind, dat. i cill Duma Gluind, Dec. 26 ; Kilglinn, co. Meath.

Cell Eae (Ae G), Dec. 22.

Cell Elge (G), Trían of, Mar. 22 ; in Connacht.

Cell Éo, June 30.

Cell Findche of Áth Duirn in Osraige (G), Finnech of, Feb. 2 ; Killinny, in bar. and par. of Kells, co. Meath.

Cell Findmaige, Ap. 29 ; in bar. of Arklow, co. Wicklow.

Cell Fortcheirn in Uí Dróna (G), Fortchern of, Feb. 17, Oct. 11 ; in bar. of Idrone, co. Carlow.

Cell Gabra (Gobrai G), June 24 ; perhaps Kilgory, p. of Kilnoe, co. Clare, or Kilgory, par. of Killabban, Queen's co. (Hogan).

Cell Gíalláin, in Huí Muiridaig, p. 116 ; in Castledermot deanery, diocese of Dublin.

Cell Glassi, Aug. 6 ; par. of Kilglass, bar. of Moydow and of Ardagh, co. Longford.

Cell Gobuil, June 5 ; between Assaroe (Ballyshannon) and Donegal, D.

Cell Ilin (G), Áedán of, Jan. 1 ; north of Faughard, co. Louth.

Cell ind Ailithir, p. 112 ; in Garumna Island, co. Galway.

Cell Ingen Léníne, (GDOn), Mar. 6 ; Killiney, co. Dublin.

Cell Lomchon (G), Lomchú of, Jan. 9 ; in Ulster.

Cell Lucinni, Aug. 4 ; al. Kill Lochin, par. in diocese of Elphin (Colgan), or Killucan, in Westmeath (Walsh).

Cell meic Dúach (G), Colman of, Feb. 3 ; Kilmacduagh, bar. of Kiltartan, co. Galway.

Cell Lucraide, Ap. 29.

Cell Máelchétair (G), Máel Céthair of, May 14 ; Kilmalkedar, bar. of Corkaguiny, co. Kerry.

Cell Maignenn, Oct. 19, 26, Dec. 18 ; Kilmainham, near Dublin.

Cell (na, G) Manach, July 31 ; Kilnamanagh, co. Kilkenny.

Cell (na, *G*) Manach, Dec. 31 ; Kilmanagh, par. of Tallaght, co. Dublin (Hogan).

Cell Már, *see* Cell Mór.

Cell Modúit in Uí Maine, Feb. 10 ; perhaps Killamude, bar. of Tiaquin, near Mountbellew, co. Galway (Hogan).

Cell Molassi, Jan. 17 ; Kilmolash, near Lismore, co. Waterford.

Cell Móna (*G*), Polán of ; Kilmona, par. of Rahugh, bar. of Moycashel, Westmeath.

Cell Mór (úa Nialláin *G*), Ap. 4 ; in bar. of O'Neilland W., co. Armagh.

Cell Mór, May 25, Aug. 3 ; Kilmore, near Monaghan.

Cell Mór Díthruib, Aug. 9 ; Kilmore, co. Roscommon.

Cell Moshílóic in Uí Cennselaig (*G*), July 13 ; Kilmichaelogue par., Gorey, co Wexford.

Cell Múadáin in Slíab Choirpre, p. 112 ; Kilvoydan townl., near Corofin, co. Clare.

Cell Mu(i)ne, Mar. 1 ; Menevia, now St. David's, Pembrokeshire.

Cell na nIngen (*OnG*), Darbellinn of Oct. 26 ; Killininny, in par. of Tallaght, co. Dublin.

Cell Naíle (*G*), Nóele of, Jan. 27 ; Kinawley, co. Fermanagh.

Cell Rathnaite (*C*. Rait *G*, Raith *D*), Aug. 9 ; Kilraghts, townl. and par. in co. Antrim (Hogan).

Cell Róa, Ap. 15 ; Killroe, in Tirawley, co. Mayo.

Cell Rois, Jan. 28 ; Kilrush, co. Clare.

Cell Rúaid, Oct. 16 ; par. of Kilroot, Lr. Belfast, co. Antrim.

Cell Saile, in Crích Conaill (*G*), Aug. 11, Etracht of ; Kilsally, par. of Ballyclog, Tyrone (? Hogan).

Cell Scíre (*G*), Scíre of, Mar. 24 ; Kilskeer, in bar. of Upper Kells, co. Meath.

Cell Segain, Jan. 21 ; perhaps = Cell Segéne, now Kilsaney, an old church and burial ground in Ardbracken par., w. of Navan (Walsh).

Cell Talten, May 18 ; Teltown, co. Meath.

Cell Tarsna, Jan. 20 ; Kiltrasna townl., par. of Killashandra, co. Cavan, or Killeany, co. Galway (Hogan).

Cell Túama (or Tóma), Mar. 16 ; Kiltoom, bar. of Fore, Westmeath.

Cell úa Maigech (*G*), Senach of, Feb. 11 ; perh. Killimy, in par. of Coolbanagher, Queen's co. (Hogan).

Cell Uinchi in Conailli, May 2 ; Kilanny townl. and par. near Dundalk, co. Louth, or Killuny, co. Armagh (Hogan).

Cennanus, Aug. 21 (*G*), Kells, co. Meath.

Cenn Cláir (Dísert Cinn Clair, *G*), June 29 ; Kinclare, various.

Cenn Etig (*G*), Fínán of, Ap. 7 ; Kinnity, bar. of Ballybrit, King's co.

Cenn Garad, Mar. 1, Aug. 10 ; Kingarth, in Bute.

Cenn Locha, Mar. 8, p. 116.

Cenn Locha Sílenn, Coitchenn and Critán of, p. 116.

Cenn Sáile, July 9 ; Kensale, near Malahide, co. Dublin.

Cenn Sáile, Feb. 26 ; Kinsale, co. Cork.

Cera, May 30 ; bar. of Carra, co. Mayo.

Clochar, Feb. 2 and June 29 (*G*) ; there are many Clochars, here probably Clogher, co. Tyrone.

Clochar Bainne, Mar. 4, Clúain Bainb (*G D*) which may be near Cloonbony House, in par. of Rathcline, co. Longford (Hogan).

Clúain, Ap. 26, July 19 ; = Clúain moccu Nóis, Jan. 20 (*D*), Mar. 1 (*D*), Ap. 6 (*D*).

Clúain Acuir, Sep. 30 ; in Ardgal (*G*), *i.e.* in E. Meath.

Clúain Áeda Aithmet, in Luigne (*GD*), Níad of, June 5 ; (?) Clooneagh townl. in co. Sligo (Hogan).

Clúain (Haí *G*), Brigit of, Aug. 13.

Clúain (Airb *G*), o Chluanaib, May 17.

Clúain Airbelaig, Sep. 4 ; Cloonnarrell townl., co. Donegal (Hogan).

Clúain Aird, May 26 ; i cClúain Aird mo Bhecócc i Muscraighe Breoghain *G*, Kilpeacan, bar. of Clanwilliam, co. Tipperary.

Clúain Airdne (*sic G*, Cuairne *LL*), Sep. 30.

Clúain Airthir (Lúi Airthir *G*, Lui Erthir *On*), Sep. 24 ; Magheracloone, co. Monaghan.

Clúain Andobor (C. an dobor, Hogan), Aug. 30, near Killeigh, bar. of Geashill, King's co.

Clúain Arathair, Ap. 25.

Clúain Bairenn (G), Cairech Dergáin of, Feb. 9 ; Cloonburren, co. Roscommon.

Clúain Bráin, Mãy 1 ; near Louth (Colgan).

Clúain Brónaig, Dec. 19 ; Clonbroney, co. Longford.

[Clúain, GOn] Bruchais, May 1 ; near the river Flesk, co. Kerry (Stokes).

Clúain Caa, Oct. 3.

Clúain Caí, May 24 ; in Eoganacht of Caisel (Cashel), co. Tipperary.

Clúain Caichni, May 10 ; near the river Barrow (Hogan).

Clúain Caín, Feb. 7, Ap. 26, May 11, June 6, July 25 (Cactne G, Caichtne D), Aug. 1 ; Clonkeen ; there are several, probably that in co. Louth (Hogan).

Clúain Caín Finnabrach (G), Aedán of, Jan. 1.

Clúain Cairpthe, Feb. 15 ; Kilbarry, par. of Termonbarry, co. Roscommon.

Clúain Catha, July 16 ; Cloncha, bar. of Inishowen, co. Donegal.

Clúain Conaire, Sep. 16, Dec. 18 ; Cloncurry, co. Kildare.

Clúain Connaid in Cuircne (G), Comgán of, Oct. 13 ; in Westmeath.

Clúain Credail (G), Íta of, Jan. 15 ; Killeedy, bar. of Glenquin, co. Limerick.

Clúain Crúich, May 16 ; (?) Concrew, par. and tl. co. Limerick (Hogan).

Clúain Cúallachta, Aug. 2.

Clúain Cullaig (Collaing G), Dec. 19 ; Cloone, co. Leitrim (Stokes).

Clúain dá Acra, in the Cechair (G) Sárán of, Sep. 21.

Clúain dá Andobair, p. 98.

Clúain Dabóetóc (G), July 22 ; Clondavaddog, 9 m. north of Ramelton, co. Donegal.

Clúain Daetcain, July 13 ; C. Daithgen D, C. Deochra, *i.e.* in Uí Dega in Uí Cennselaig, or in C. da Aithgeid, O(n) in Uí Dega : in bar. of Gorey, co. Wexford. *See* Cell Moshflóic.

Clúain dá Fhiach, Dec. 23, in Cíannachta of Glenn Geimin in Ulster (D), now Keenaght, co. Derry.

Clúain Daim, in Uí Echach Ulad (G), Mochommóc of, Dec. 26 ; par. of Clonduff, diocese of Dromore.

Clúain Dalláin (G), Conall of, Ap. 2 ; near Snám Ech, in Uí Echach of Ulster : Clonallan, near Newry, co. Down.

Clúain Dartada, Feb. 12 ; in old diocese of Glendalough.

Clúain Deochra, Jan. 11 ; Clondara, par. of Killashee, co. Longford. Cp. Clúain Daetcain.

Clúain Díanláma, Brigit of, Aug. 13 ; Clúain Haí (GD).

Clúain Dobtha, Mar. 3.

Clúain Dolcáin, Aug. 6 ; Clondalkin, near Dublin.

Clúain Ech, Ap. 28.

Clúain Eidnech, Feb. 17, 21 ; Clonenagh, Queen's co.

Clúain Emain, June 4, July 1 ; Cloonowen, near Athlone.

Clúain Eóis, Ap. 4, p. 102 ; Clones, co. Monaghan.

Clúain Eorainne (Eossáin, G), Sep. 8.

Clúain Escrach, Mar. 18 ; Cloonascrach, bar. of Clonmacnoon, near Ballinasloe, or Cloonascrach, bar. of Dunmore, near Tuam (Hogan).

Clúain Etchéin, July 24.

Clúain Ferta (Brénainn), May 16 ; Feb. 21 (G) ; Clonfert, co. Galway.

Clúain Ferta Molúa, Aug. 4, Dec. 23 ; Jan. 12 (G) ; Clonfertmulloe, bar. of Upper Ossory, Queen's co.

Clúain Fidnaige (Find Aighne G), Sep. 28.

Clúain Find, June 28.

Clúain Fobair, Aug. 6 ; Cloonfore ; there are several.

Clúain Fota (in Fir Bile G), Ainmire of, Sep. 15 ; Feb. 11, Etchen of (G) ; Clonfad, bar. of Farbil, co. Westmeath.

Clúain Fota, Mar. 11 (Fine, in Fir Tulach, G), Senach of, Aug. 21 ; Clonfad al. Clonfadforan, in bar. of Fartullagh, co. Westmeath (Hogan).

Clúain Géise, Ap. 25, p. 112 ; seems Clongesh, near Longford (Hogan).

Clúain Grenaich, Jan. 18.

Clúain Hí, Mar. 19 ; Cloonee ; there are several.

Clúain Iraird, Feb. 9, 11, Aug. 21 ; Clonard, co. Meath.

Clúain Laíg, Mar. 24 ; Clonleigh, near Lifford, co. Donegal.

Clúain Lothor or Lothur, Mar. 8, Aug. 8 ; par. of Clonlogher, near Manorhamilton, co. Leitrim.

Clúain Már, Dec. 18, 24, Cumméne of = Clúain Mór Moédóic, *q.v.*

Clúain meic Féicc, June 5.
Clúain Máeláin, Mar. 20 ; perhaps Cloonmealane, par. of Kilmanar, bar. of Magunihy, co. Kerry.
Clúain Mind, Ap. 19 ; (?) Clonmin, par. of Galloon, co. Fermanagh (Hogan).
Clúain moccu Noís, June 13 ; Clonmacnois, King's co. See also Clúain, above.
Clúain Móescna, in Fir Mide, i.e. in Fir Tulach, Jan. 9, July 16, Aug. 26, p. 114 ; in bar. of Fartullagh, co. Westmeath.
Clúain Mór (of Fir Arda, G), Ossíne of, Jan. 1 ; Clonmore, bar. of Ferrard, co. Louth.
Clúain Mór (Moédóic), Feb. 8, Mar. 16, Ap. 11, May 23, July 2, Sep. 15, Oct. 9, Dec. 18 ; Clonmore, near Hacketstown, co. Carlow.
Clúain Mór, in Uí Failgi, Jan. 16 ; in Offaly, King's co.
Clúain Railgech, Aug. 6 ; perhaps Cloonrallagh, near Longford (Hogan).
Clúain Ráithe (Raitte, Br.), June 19 ; Clonraw, co. Cavan, or Clonrah in King's co. (Stokes).
Clúain Sasta, Ap. 30, Aug. 4 ; Clonsast, par. in bar. of Coolestown, King's co.
Clúain Tarb, Aug. 3 ; Clontarf, near Dublin.
Clúain Tibrinne. Mar. 9, 13, Oct. 24 ; Clontivrin, near Clones, co. Monaghan.
Clúain Tiprat, June 13 ; Clontibret, bar. of Cremorne, co. Monaghan.
Clúain Uinsenn (Usend, Br.), June 2 ; (?) Clooninshin, par. of Meelick, co Mayo (Hogan).
Clúana, May 17 (dat. ó Chlúain Airb, G).
Cobran, June 21.
Coirbre, see Cairpre.
Comrar, gen. Comraire, Sep. 25 ; Colman Comraire oc Usniuch, LL. 372 d 60 ; now Conry, near Hill of Uisneach, Westmeath.
Conailli, dat. pl. i Conaillib, May 2 ; = Conaille Muirthemne, part of co. Louth.
Condere (G), Tochonna of, May 15 ; par. and diocese, co. Antrim.
Congbál Glinne Súilige in Cenél Conaill (G), Fíachra of ; Conwal, bar. of Kilmacrenan, co. Donegal.

Connachta, Mar. 30, Ap. 16 ; Connaught.
Conmaicne (G D), Tochumracht of, June 11 ; co-extensive with present diocese of Ardagh, co. Leitrim and co. Longford.
Corcach, Jan. 14, Mar. 17, May 21, Sep. 25, 26 ; Cork.
Corco Duibne (G), Fínán of, Ap. 7 ; Corcaguiny, co. Kerry.
Corco Moga, p. 112 ; in Connacht.
Corco Trí, of the Lugni of Connacht, Oct. 12 ; bar. of Leyney and Corran, co. Sligo.
Corco Solgoinn Crúaich, p. 126.
Cráeb Laisre, Jan. 1 ; near Clonmacnois, King's co.
Craíbech, gen. Craibige (Crébicce, G), Jan. 15, dat. o Chraebaig (Crebhicc, G), Mar. 3 ; there are several Creevaghs, perh. that in the par. of Clonmacnois, King's co. (Stokes).
Cremchaill, May 31 ; Cranfield, co. Antrim (Reeves), but there are several.
Cremthanna, dat. pl. i Cremthannaib Mar. 21, Sep. 14.
Crích Maini, July 10 ; between River Suck and the Shannon (O'Donovan) ; or in Tethba in Westmeath and co. Longford (Walsh).
Crochán, Aug. 3 ; perh. near Westcove, co. Kerry.
Crúachan Maige Abna, Oct. 5 ; Crohane, bar. of Slieveardagh, co. Tipperary.
Crúachan Bríg Éle (G), Mac-Caille of, Ap. 25 ; Croghan, near Philipstown, King's co.
Cúairne, Jan. 13, Sep. 30 ; Clúain Airdne G.
Cúil, gen. Cúle, Aug. 18 ; various places of the name.
Cúil Bennchair in Lurg, on the brink of Loch Eirne (G), Lugech of, Oct. 6 ; Banagher, par. of Devenish, co. Fermanagh (Hogan).
Cúil Cíchmaige (Clúain C., G), Ap. 24.
Cúil Collainge, Oct. 23. Cp. LL. 374c 44.
Cúil Corra, Jan. 17 ; Coolarn, near Galtrim co. Meath (Stokes).
Cúil Crema, Jan. 8 ; perhaps Coolcraff, par. of Abbeylara, co. Longford (Stokes).
Cúil Lagin (Lugdidh, Br., Conlaing, G, Connlaigh, On), Oct. 19.
Cúil Maine (G), deacon Áed of, Aug. 31 ; Collooney, near Sligo

Cúil Rúscach, Feb. 12 ; somewhere in Breifne, *i.e.* counties Cavan and Leitrim.

Cúil Sachaille, Aug. 1 ; now Taney, formerly Saeoyle, nr. Dundrum, co. Dublin (O'Reilly, R.S.A.I. Journ. xxxii, p. 381).

Cullenn, dat. Cullind, Jan. 14 ; near Cork.

Cunga, Ap. 17, June 8 ; Cong, co. Mayo.

Daire, Mar. 8, Ap. 7, May 3, July 31 ; Derry.

Daire (Dachonna, *G*) la Ultu, Ap. 12 ; in Ulster.

Daire Bruchaisi, Mar. 29 ; Derry-brughis, al. Killyman, co. Armagh.

Daire Caecháin, in Dál Riada, *GD*, Colman of, Jan. 1 ; Derrykeighan par. in d. of Connor.

Daire Cáelainne (Chailainne, *Br.*), June 19 ; al. Termonn C., near Castlerea, co. Roscommon.

Daire Eidnech, Oct. 6 ; in Eoganacht Caisil, *i.e.* Tipperary ; al. Daire na Flann, *see* Corconutan, Index of Persons.

Daire In*gine* Aillén, in Ard Ulad, May 29 ; Derry, a townl. in par of Ballyphilip, co Down.

Daire Lúráin, Oct. 29 ; Derryloran, co. Tyrone.

Daire Melle, Mar. 31 ; on border of Loch Melvin, co. Leitrim.

Daire Mór, May 20, July 31 ; Derrymore or Kilcolman, King's co.

Daire na Flann, in the Eoganacht of Caisel (*G*), Fer dá chrích of, Oct. 6 ; Derrynavlan, near Killenaule, co. Tipperary.

Dairinis of Máel Anfaid (oc Lios Mór Mochuda, *G*), Jan. 31, Mar. 8, Aug. 14 ; Molana, an island on the Blackwater, near Youghal.

Dairinis, *see* Airdne Dairinse.

Dairinis Cétnae, Ap. 15.

Dál Ríada (*G*), Jan. 1 ; the north-eastern part of co. Antrim.

Daminis, Sep. 12 ; Devenish, in Loch Erne.

Dartraige (*G*), *see* Druim Ailche.

Dartraige Coninse, June 15 ; bar. of Dartry, co. Monaghan.

Dergderc, Jan. 13 ; Loch Derg, on the Shannon, between Killaloe and Portumna.

Dergne, Dec. 23; Delgany, co. Wicklow.

Dermag, Ap. 19, June 21 ; Durrow, King's co.

Dermag úa nDúach (*G*), Fintan Máel-dub of, Oct. 20 ; Durrow, Queen's co.

Derthach, dat. ó Durthach, May 18, ó Derthaig, Sep. 30.

Déssi, Feb. 10 ; the Decies, co. Waterford.

Díamair, July 24, dat. ó Damair (*sic*), Oct. 24 ; Diamor, co. Meath.

Dísert, Feb. 2.

Dísert Cinn Clair (*G*), *see* Cenn Clair.

Dísert (Díarmata, *G*), June 21 ; Tristledermot, or Castledermot, co. Kildare.

Dísert Fulartaig in Uí Failgi (*G*), Fulartach of, Mar. 29 ; Dysart, bar. of Carbury, co. Kildare.

Dísert meic Ciluirn i lLaigis (*G*), Man-chéne of, Jan. 2 ; in Leix, Queen's co.

Dísert Máele Tuile (*G*), Máel Tuile of, July 30 ; Dysart, W. of Loch Ennell, co. Westmeath.

Dísert Con Lóchae i Curchibh (i Curcne *OnG*), July 11 ; Curcne is in the bar. of Kilkenny W., co. Westmeath.

Dísert Tola (*G*), Tola of, Mar. 30 ; Dysert O'Dea, co. Clare.

Domnach, Feb. 28, Oct. 29 ; perhaps Donagh, par. and townl. in co. Monaghan (Hogan), but there are several.

Domnach Aires, Sep. 30.

Domnach Brocc, Sep. 30 ; Donny-brook, near Dublin.

Domnach Clíabra, June 9.

Domnach Imlech, June 19 ; was in deanery of Balimor, diocese of Dublin, near Balicumin ; now Burgage, Blessington (Ronan, Journ. R.S.A.I. lx. 70).

Domnach Mór (mc. Laithbe i Mug-dornaib, *G*), May 20, May 27 ; Donaghmore, near Slane, co. Wexford.

Domnach Mór Áelmaige, Aug. 23 ; Donaghmore townl., bar. Droma-haire, co. Leitrim.

Domnach Mór Liphi, Dec. 31.

Domnach Mór Maige Coba (Dam-hairne *G*), Sep. 17 ; Donaghmore par. in Upper Iveagh, co. Down. Mag Damairne is now Maghera-morne, near Larne, co. Antrim.

Domnach Mór Maige Imchlair (*G*), Colum of, June 4, Sep. 6 ; formerly Ros Glanda, *which see*.

Domnach Mór Maige Lúadat, Oct. 27 ; Donaghmore, bar. of Salt, co. Kildare.

Dorn, Feb. 2. Finnech Duirn of Cell Findchi of Áth Duirn in Osraige ; Dornbuide, a hill in Mag Raigne, *G*.

Dothra (*G*), Findech of, May 11 ; the river Dodder, co. Dublin.

Druim (*OnG*), Sáergus of, May 30 ; Drumbeg par., co. Down (Reeves) ; probably near Killinny, par. of Kells, co. Kilkenny (Hogan).

Druim Ailche, Jan. 4 ; Drumully townl. and par., co. Fermanagh.

Druim Airbelaig, Jan. 15 ; Drumreilly townl. and par., co. Leitrim.

Druim Bairr, Jan. 16 ; perhaps Drumbarna on Lough Erne, par. of Magheraculmoney, bar. of Lurg, co. Fermanagh.

Druim Bertach, Feb. 18.

Druim Bidc, Jan. 17.

Druim Bó, July 24, Aug. 10 ; perhaps par. of Drumbo, near Lisburn, co. Down (Hogan).

Druim Bricci, June 17 ; Drumbrick, several townlands of the name.

Druim Bróon, Sep. 25, perhaps Drumbrone townl. in Farney, co. Monaghan.

Druim Clíab (*G*), Tarannán of, Jan. 12 ; perhaps Drumcliff, co. Sligo.

Druim Crema, Feb. 6.

Druim Culinn, May 3, 21 ; Drumcullen, bar. of Eglish, King's co.

Druim dá Dart, May 22.

Druim dá Dartraith Locha (or Hola), seven nuns of, p. 116.

Druim Dairbrech, Ap. 3 ; near the Slaney, in co. Wexford.

Druim Dresna (Dresa *G*), Feb. 18.

Druim Druith, Jan. 12.

Druim Enaig, May 17.

Druim Faindle (D. Níad *G*), Sep. 14 ; Druim Níad is in Ulster, (?) Drumneth townl., par. of Magherally, co. Down (Hogan).

Druim Feise (Fess *G*), May 17.

Druim Ferdaim (*sic Br.*) = Druim Fertáin (*GOn*), Mar. 5 ; in Carbury, co. Kildare ; perhaps Dunfiert (Hogan).

Druim Ferta Mugaine, Colmán of, p. 116 ; in Offaly.

Druim Fhota (gen. Drommíota *MS*, Dromaata *G*, Dromatto *D*). Ap. 24.

Druim Ing (Druim Ing húa Segain *O*) Oct 10 ; Dromin, near Dunshaughlin, co. Meath (Stokes).

Druim Laidcinn, Mar. 9.

Druim Lara, Mar. 7 ; Drumlara (several).

Druim Lethglaise (*G*), Fergus of, Mar. 30 ; Downpatrick.

Druim Liacc (*G*), Lasriu of, Oct. 25.

Druim Licce, Feb. 9 ; Drumleek, co. Louth.

Druim Lommáin (*G*), Corc of, Feb. 4 ; several of the name.

Druim moccu Blai (mc. Ublai *TG*), gen. Droma mc. Blae), Mar. 9 ; in baronies of Upper and Lower Slane, co. Meath (Hogan).

Druim Mór, Jan. 16 ; Dromore. Domnach Mór Maige Ene (*G*), which is Kildoney, in par. of Kilbarron, near River Erne, co. Donegal.

Druim Mór (Mocholmóc of), June 7 ; Dromore, in bar. of Iveagh, co. Down.

Druim Neóid (*D*), Finán of, Feb. 13.

Druim Níad, see Druim Faindle.

Druim Ráithe, Aug. 9, 19 ; Drumrath, near Athlone, co. Westmeath.

Druim Ráithe, Mar. 6 ; perhaps Drumrat, bar. of Corran, co. Sligo, cp. AU, 1017 n. (Stokes).

Druim Samraid, July 22 ; Drumsawry, or Summerbank, Loughcrew, co. Meath.

Druim Snechta, Sep. 4 ; Drumsnat, near Monaghan.

Druim Tuirc, gen. Dromma Tuircc, Dec. 26 ; probably Drumturc, townl. in co. Monaghan.

Druim Uisseóit (*G*), Uisseóit of, July 28.

Druinn, dat., Feb. 4 ; Druim Lommain, *G*.

Dubad, Dec. 17 ; Dowth, on the Boyne, co. Meath.

Dún Blésci, Jan. 3 ; Doon, bar. of Coonagh, co. Limerick.

Dún dá Én, i Fidbaid Dáil Araide (*G*), Ercnat of, Jan. 8 ; Duneane in the Feevagh, bar. of Toome, co. Antrim.

Dún Gemin, in Cíannachta of Glenn Gemin (*G*), Jan. 8.

Dún Mór, in Uí Bríúin Cúalann (*G*), Sillán of, July 21.

Durmag, *see* Dermag.

Durthach, *see* Derthach.

Echdruim, gen. Echdromma, Ap. 11, Dec. 19 ; Aughrim, several.

Echdruim (Breccáin, *G*), May 7 ; Aughrim townl., in par. of Kilkcel, co. Down.

Echfhorad, Ap. 11 ; Aghara, bar. of Cuircne, co. Longford (Hogan).

Ech-inis (*G*), Cáelán of, Sep. 25 ; Aughinis, near Ramelton, co. Donegal.

Eidnén, dat. isind Ednean, Ap. 23 ; near Duleek, co. Meath.

Eig, gen. Ega, Jan. 12, Ap. 17, 29, 30, gen. Aego, Ap. 10 ; the island of Eig, off the coast of Inverness.

Eirne, three pilgrims of, p. 116.

Enach, Jan. 4 ; Annagh (many).

Enach Ard, Jan. 6 ; Annaghard (several).

Enach Ceir (Eir *G*), May 19 ; Annagher, par. of Clonoe, co. Tyrone (? Hogan).

Enach Dirmaige, July 6.

Enach Elti, Dec. 26 ; Annahilt, near Lisburn, co. Antrim.

Enach Lóeg, Sep. 9 ; = Enach Liac (Hogan), Annalec townl., near Thomastown, co. Kilkenny.

Eoganacht of Caisel (*G*), Fintan Máeldub of, Oct. 20 ; Cashel, co. Tipperary.

Erdam, Ap. 8, Airdoni (Erdoim *G*), Feb. 8.

Ernaide, in Muscraige Mitine, Feb. 11 ; in Muskerry W., co. Cork.

Ernaide, Mochonna of, Jan. 25.

Ernaide, Ness of, p. 108.

Ess mac nEirc, Mar. 8 ; now Assylin, near Boyle, co. Roscommon.

Ess Rúaid, Mar. 8 ; Assaroe, at Ballyshannon, co. Donegal.

Etardruim, June 4 ; several.

Familia Munnu, *see* Tech Munnu.

[Faithche] (Foighdhi, *G* ; Faithche Rawl. B. 502, 92 *g* ; Faidche *LL* 367 *d*) ; Ciaran of, Mar. 8 ; Faheeran townl., par. of Kilcoursey, King's co.

Fathan Becc (*G*), Colman of, July 8 ; Lower Fahan, in Inishowen, co. Donegal.

Fathan Muru (*G*), Cillíne of, Jan. 3 ; Fahan, par. of Upper Fahan, in Inishowen, co. Donegal.

Fergnaide (Forgnaige, *Br.*), Dec. 18 ; Forgney, near Ballymahon, co. Longford (Hogan).

Ferna, Jan. 31, June 22 ; Ferns, co. Wexford.

Fert Scéithe, in Muscraige Tri Maige, Jan. 1, Sep. 6 ; Ardskeagh, bar. of Fermoy, co. Cork.

Fid Chuilend, Aug. 8 ; Feighcullen, near Hill of Allen, co. Kildare.

Fid. Dúin, Mar. 23, May 18, Aug. 13, Oct. 1 ; Fiddown, co. Kildare.

Findabair Aba (*G*), Nechtain of, May 2 ; Fennor, on the Boyne, near Slane in Meath.

Findchell, dat. i Findchill, Jan. 25, but doubtful if a place ; is name of a person *GD*, F. of Slíab Gúaire.

Findmag in Fotharta (*G*), Moshacru of, Mar. 3 ; in Uí Cennselaig, near Cnamros, co. Wexford.

Findglaiss, Jan. 21, 27, May 15, Sep. 24 ; Finglas, near Dublin.

Fir Mide, p. 114 ; people of East and West Meath.

Fir Tulach, p. 44 ; bar. of Fartullagh, co. Westmeath.

Fobar, Jan. 20, 28, Feb. 5, May 1, June 10 ; Fore, co. Westmeath.

Fochard, gen. Fochairde Murthemni, Sep. 4, p. 102 ; Faughart, near Dundalk, co. Louth.

Foth(a)irbe Líatháin, Ap. 23.

Fotharta (*G*), Moshacru of, Mar. 3 ; bar. of Forth, co. Wexford.

Fotharta Mára (*LL* 353 *b*, *G*) Lugáed of, May 12 ; near the three Rosses, co. Sligo.

Gabal Liúin, July 28 ; Galloon par., end of Upper Loch Erne, co. Fermanagh.

Gáilinne, of the Ulaid, Oct. 30 ; .i. tuath i nUltaib (*On*).

Galam, gen. Galma, Jan. 1, dat. Galaum Lagen, Sep. 4 ; (?) Gallow, par. in co. Meath (Hogan).

Garmna i n-iarthur Chonnacht, p. 112 ; Garumna Island, co. Galway.

Gilldae, Finnio of, Sep. 28 ; perh. Gillea, now Gill Abbey, nr. Cork (Hogan).

Glas Nóiden, Oct. 12 ; Glasnevin, near Dublin.

Glenn, Feb. 3 ; perhaps the Glens of Antrim.

Glenn Esa (Aesa *G*), Feb. 26.

Glenn dá Locha, Jan. 8, 11, Feb. 10, Ap. 22, May 3, June 3, Oct. 7 ; Glendalough, co. Wicklow.

Glenn Faidli, Dec. 29 ; Gleneely, bar. of Newcastle, co. Wicklow.

Glenn Medóin, Feb. 18 ; Clonmethan, Balrothery, co. Dublin (Hogan).

Glenn Móna, Feb. 12 ; (?) Vale of the Glennamony river, co. Mayo (Hogan).

Glenn Munire, July 21 ; Glenmunder, Little Bray, co. Wicklow (Ronan, Journ. R.S.A.I., lx. 69).

Glenn Sechis (G), Brónach of, Ap. 2 ; Kilbroney, co. Down.

Glenn Uissen, Jan. 27, Feb. 27, July 8 ; Killeshin, bar. Slievemargy, near town of Carlow.

Glestingberg, i.e. Glestonia, p. 110 ; Glastonbury.

Gobol, Jan. 25 ; in King's co. (Hogan).

Gort Cirb, Aug. 6 ; (?) Gortgrib, par. Knockbreda, near Belfast.

Granaret, dat. Granarit, Jan. 24 ; Granard, co. Longford.

Gulban Guirt moccu Gairb, July 30 ; Bennbulbin, co. Sligo.

Í, Coluim Chille, gen. Íae, Jan. 11, Feb. 24, May 25, Aug. 12, Sep. 16, Oct. 27, Oct. 28 ; Iona.

Imgan, Imdain (G), Aug. 25.

Imdúal, Mar. 28 ; (?) Imdel townl.. par. Drumballyrony, co. Down (Hogan).

Imlech Bren(aind) (?), June 15, Miliuc i nDartraige Coininnsi O(n)G, i.e. bar. of Dartry, co. Monaghan.

Imlech Broccada (G), Broccaid of, July 9 ; Emlagh, near Westport, co. Mayo.

Imlech Cassáin in Cúalnge, Sep. 11 ; Emlagh, co. Louth.

Imlech Fíaich, in Fir Cúl Breg (G), Bécgán of, Ap. 5 ; Emlagh, bar. Lr. Kells, co. Meath.

Imlech (= Imlech Ibair), gen. Imlig Sep. 10, again gen. Imlecha, Sep. 12, Dec. 30 ; Emly, co. Tipperary.

Inber Becce, July 17 ; Bangor Bay, co. Down (Hogan).

Inber Colptha, June 16 ; mouth of the Boyne, at Drogheda, co. Meath.

Inber Doíle, Sep. 13 ; Ennereilly, bar. Arklow, co. Wicklow.

Inber Melgi, Jan. 27.

Inber [Nóele] (cell Nóile, G), Jan. 27 ; Inver, bar. of Banagh, co. Donegal.

Inis Ailche, Dec. 21.

Inis Aingín, Jan. 7 ; Inishinneen, or Hare Island, on Lough Ree, co. Westmeath.

Inis Baíthín (G), Fidmune of, May 16 ; Baíthíne of, May 22 ; Inis-boyne, bar. of Arklow, co. Wicklow.

Inis Bó Finne, Aug. 8 ; Inisbofin, off coast of Mayo.

Inis Caíl, May 22 ; Inishkeel, near Glenties, co. Donegal.

Inis Caín, Jan. 10, Ap. 13 ; Inishkeen ; several, doubtful which.

Inis Caín (on Loch Méilge G), Oct. 14 ; Iniskeen, bar. of Rosclogher, co. Leitrim.

Inis Caín (of Daig), Aug. 18 ; Iniskeen par. in Louth and Monaghan.

Inis Cathaig, Mar. 7 ; Inishcathy, or Scattery Island, in the Shannon, near Kilrush, co. Clare.

Inis Causcraid (or Caumscraid), I. Causcraidh, July 22, I. Caumscraidh, July 29 ; Inch or Inishcourcy, near Downpatrick.

Inis Celtra, May 24, July 29, p. 118 ; Holy Island, Lough Derg, co. Galway.

Inis Clothrann, Jan. 10 ; Inis-cloghran or Quaker's Island, in Lough Ree, co. Longford.

Inis Crainn, May 20.

Inis Détna (Sétna, G), Mar. 16.

Inis Doigre (G), Talla of, Aug. 11 ; Inishterry, an island in river Boyle, co. Roscommon.

Inis Domle (Teimle, On), Jan. 30, Mar. 3, July 4 ; Little Island, on the Suir, near Waterford.

Inis Dúine, Oct. 1 ; Inchydoney, in Clonakilty Bay, co. Cork.

Inis Éndaim, July 23 ; Inishenagh, in Lough Ree, near Lanesborough.

Inis Eogain (G), Modíchu of, Dec. 18 ; Inishowen pen., co. Donegal.

Inis Faithlenn on Loch Léin (G), Fínán of, Mar. 16 ; Inisfallen, on Lr. Lake, Killarney.

Inis Liacc (G), Cúan of, Oct. 29.

Inis Locha Cré, May 15 ; Loch Cré, Sep. 7 ; Monahincha, near Roscrea, co. Tipperary.

Inis Locha Cróni, Jan. 27 ; perhaps Loch Croan, bar. of Athlone, co. Roscommon (Hogan, s.v. Loch Cróine).

Inis (moccu Cuinn G), Feb. 7 ; Inchiquin, Lough Corrib, co. Galway.

Inis maccu Dartada (G), Cummíne of, May 21.

Inis Mac nErnín (G), Sep. 22 ; Inchmacnerin, Lough Key, co. Roscommon.

Inis mac Nessáin'(On), Nessan's sons of, Mar. 15, Ireland's Eye, near Howth.

Inis meic Lugein (mc. Ualaing, G) Aug. 1 ; Inis meic Ualaing, according to Hennessy, is Inish Bofin in Lough Ree.

Inis Medcóit, Aug. 31 ; Lindisfarne.

Inis Menóc, Mar. 20 ; perhaps the islet south of Lindisfarne (Stokes).

Inis Mór, Jan. 14, 15, July 23, Aug. 1 ; (several).

Inis Mór, in Uí Maic Caille in Uí Líatháin, May 15 ; Great Island, Queenstown.

Inis Muredaig, Aug. 12 ; Inishmurray, off the coast of Sligo

Inis Pátraicc (G), Conna Cúairne of, Jan. 13 ; Inishpatrick, near Skerries, co. Dublin.

Inis Pích, Ap. 7 ; Inis Picht G.

Inis Sam, on Loch Erni, Jan. 18 ; = Inis Maige Sam, now Inishmacsaint, in Lough Erne, co. Fermanagh.

[Inis] Toitae, on Loch Echach, Sep. 7 ; on Loch Bec in Uí Tuirtre (G). Inistoide, in Loch Beg, near Toome Bridge, above Lough Neagh, co. Antrim.

Inis Úachtair, Dec. 21, 23, also Mar. 5, G ; island in Lough Sheelin, co. Cavan.

Irard, Feb. 8 ; o Irard, i nUíb Drona, i lLaignib (On) ; now Ullard, in Idrone, co. Carlow.

Irnaide, Oct. 13 ; perhaps Urney, par. near Strabane (Hogan).

Laigin, Sep. 4, etc. ; Leinstermen, Leinster.

Lann, Sep. 17, 18 ; perhaps Lynn, par. in co. Westmeath.

Lann Bechaire in Fine Gall (G), Lochéne of, Jan. 20 ; at Breemore, near Balbriggan, co. Dublin.

Lann Elo, Sep. 26 ; Lynally, near Tullamore.

Lann Lere (G), Furodrán of, June 18 ; Móenach of, Oct. 17 ; Dunleer, bar. of Ardeer, co. Louth.

Lann Mocholmóc, Oct. 20 ; now Magheralin (Machaire Lainne), near Moira, co. Down.

TALLAGHT.

Lann Rónáin (corr. from Ruadáin. Br.), May 22 ; now Magheralin, co. Down.

Lann Tuirriu (Turu, GO), May 28 ; (?) Lantaur townl., co. Monaghan (Hogan).

Lath(rach) Caín, Jan. 20 ; perhaps Laragh, in S. Leinster, Dublin, Kildare, and Wicklow (Hogan).

Lecan Midi, June 28, Dec. 29 ; Leckan, in co. Westmeath.

Lemchaill, Jan. 13, Feb. 21, Ap. 22, Oct. 25 ; Lowhill, Queen's co., but there are several.

Lemmag, Feb. 10, 19.

Lene, July 29.

Lés (G), Baíthíne of, Oct. 15.

Lessan in Slíab Callann (G), Sáran of, Sep. 21 ; Lissan, bar. of Loughinsholin, co. Derry.

Less Gabáil (G), Áed of, Jan. 25 ; Lisgool, on Loch Erne, co. Fermanagh.

Less Mór, Jan. 16, moccu Beonna, Jan. 22, Feb. 4, 9, 20, Ap. 17, May 14, 21, June 1, July 19, Oct. 16, Dec. 21, 29 ; Lismore, co. Waterford.

Less Mór, June 25 ; i nAlbain (O), i.e. in Scotland, an island in Argyleshire, between Lorne and Morvern (Reeves).

Lethduma, Mar. 30.

Lethet Corcaige (?), Sep. 30.

Lethglenn, Feb. 23, Ap. 18 ; Old Leighlin, co. Carlow.

Lettir, gen. Lettrach, Ap. 25 ; several.

Lettracha Odráin (in Muscraige Tíre OnG), Oct. 2, 27 ; Latteragh, bar. Upper Ormond, co. Tipperary.

Líathdruim, Feb. 8, May 16 ; Leitrim (several).

Líath (Mancháin, G), Jan. 24 ; Lemanaghan, King's co.

Líath Mór [Mocháemóc], Mar. 13 ; Líath, July 12 ; Leamakevoge, bar. of Eliogarty, co. Tipperary.

Líathros, Ap. 30 ; in Conailli Murthemni (GOn), i.e. co. Louth.

Lilchach, Mar. 12, 21, 26 ; al. Lully now Lulliamore or Lullymore townl., N. Kildare (Hogan).

Linn Dúachail, Mar. 30, see Cassán Linne.

Liphechar, Jan. 7.

Loch Bec in Uí Tuirtre (G), Toite of Inis Toite, Sep. 7 ; Lough Beg, north of Toome, in Derry and Antrim.

Q

Loch B[r]icrenn, in Uí Echach Ulad, Oct. 26 ; Lough Brickland, bar. of Upper Iveagh, co. Down.

Loch Con, Sep. 30 ; in co. Mayo.

Loch Cré (Inis Locha Cré, *G*), Sep. 7 ; now a bog (Monahincha), near Roscrea, co. Tipperary.

Loch Cúan, Aug. 6 ; Strangford Lough.

Loch nEchach, Sep 7 : Lough Neagh, in Ulster.

Loch Echin, May 6

Loch rne, Jan. 18, Feb. 28 ; Lough Erne, co. Fermanagh.

Loch Geirg, Jan. 1 ; now Lough Derg, co. Donegal.

Loch Laíg (*G*), Colmán of, Oct. 16, Nasce of, Oct. 25 ; Belfast Lough.

Loch mac Nina (L. mac Nen *G*, L. mac Neill *O*(*F*), Ap. 13 ; Lough Macneane, on the borders of Cavan, Leitrim, and Fermanagh.

Loch Melge, Meilchi, Jan. 5, Melge (*Br.*), July 17 ; Lough Melvin, in Leitrim, and Fermanagh.

Loch Munremair, Feb. 6 ; Lough Ramor, co Cavan.

Loch Ré, Jan. 1 ; Lough Ree, on the Shannon.

Loch Silenn (*G*), Carthach of, Mar. 5 ; Lough Sheelin, co. Cavan.

Loch Techet, Ap. 4 ; now Lough Gara, co. Sligo.

Loch Uane, June 12, p. 116 ; Lough Ooney, near Smithborough, co. Monaghan (Hogan).

Loch Uair, Feb. 7 ; now Lough Owel, co. Westmeath.

Lorg, i Lurg (*G*), Lugech of, Oct. 6 ; bar. of Lurg, co. Fermanagh.

Lothra (gen. sg.), Ap. 15 ; Lorrha, bar. of Lr. Ormond, co. Tipperary.

Lúa, June 2, note ; region along river Lee in Muskerrylin, co. Cork (Hogan).

Lúachair, gen. Lúachra, June 17 ; June 22 ; a district partly in bar. of Magunihy, co. Limerick, and in co. Cork.

Lugmad, Lugbad, Mar. 24, gen. Lugmaid, Aug. 19 ; Louth.

Luí Airthir (*G*), *see* Clúain Airthir.

Luigne Connacht, Oct. 12, also Nía of (*G*), June 5 ; bar. of Leyney, co. Sligo.

Lusca, Sep. 5 ; Lusk, co. Dublin.

Máethail, gen. Máethla, Feb. 14 ; Mohill, co. Leitrim.

Mag nAbna, Oct. 5 ; Mowney, bar. Lr. Ormond, co. Tipperary.

Mag Arnaide (*G*), Abbán of, Mar. 16, Oct. 27 ; Moyarney, near Newross, co. Wexford.

Mag Ascad (*G*), Cíar of, Jan. 5, Oct. 16 ; in Muskerry, co. Cork.

·Mag Bile, Jan. 2, Feb. 3, 11, Ap. 29, May 3, 31, July 27, Aug. 7, 25, Sep. 9 ; Maigi, Sep. 10, Oct. 1, 21 ; Movilla, co. Down.

Mag Coba, Sep. 17 ; in bar, of Upper Iveagh, co. Down.

Mag Damairne (*G*) for Mag Coba, above ; Magheramorne, co. Antrim.

Mag Duma, May 23 ; Moydow, co. Longford.

Mag Ene, Dec. 20 ; Moy, or Moygenny, a plain in S. Donegal.

Mag Éo, Mar. 12, 27, Oct. 20 ; Mayo.

Mag Éo (in Dál Cais, *G*), May 21 ; Maynoe, co. Clare.

Mag Escat (Ascad *G*), Cíar of, Jan. 5, Oct. 16 (*G*) ; in Muscraige Tíre (*O* n), in diocese of Killaloe, Lr. Ormond.

Mag Géise, *see* Clúain Géise.

Mag Liphi, Jan. 2, Mar. 9 ; plain of the Liffey, co. Kildare.

Mag Locha, in Brega, *i.e.* in Ros Éo, Ap. 10 ; = Mag Lacha, par. of Rathmoylon, between Trim and Enfield (Walsh).

Mag Locha, Sep. 24 ; Cainnech's daughters of ; perhaps same as above.

Mag Lúadat, Oct. 27 ; Maynooth, co. Kildare.

Mag Mennota, Feb. 22 ; Mag me*ic* Dodon, *G*.

Mag Níad, Jan. 16 ; in Túath Rátha, *G*, *i.e.* Tooraa, bar. Magheraboy, co. Fermanagh.

Mag Ratha, Dec. 27 ; Moyrath (several).

Mag Trea, Trega, Briunsech of, May 29 (*G*), p. 112 ; now Moytra, a plain in co. Longford (Stokes).

Maigen, gen. Maigni, dat. Magin, Maigin, Jan. 29, Mar. 4, Ap. 18, May 22 ; now Moyne, of which there are many.

Mainistir, Ap. 18 ; Monasterboice, co. Louth.

Mairge, Mairge ó Tig Scuithin, May 23 ; seems Slíab Mairge, now bar. of Slievemargie, Queen's co., which formerly included Tech Scuithin, now Tiscoffin, co. Kilkenny.

Menna Tíre, in Uí Méith, Jan. 26 ; now bar. of Monaghan, co. Monaghan (Hogan).

Methus Truim (Ethais Cromm, *G*), Jan. 24 ; Mostrim, now Edgeworthstown, co. Longford.

Mide, Oct. 27 ; Meath.

Midísel, Sep. 6, dat. Midísiul, Sep. 22 ; Meeshal, in Magourney par., Cork ; also Myshall par., co. Carlow.

Míliuc, dat., June 15, note ; in bar. of Dartry, co. Monaghan.

Míliuc, dat., Dec. 18.

Min, Min Drochat, gen. Mena, Mena Drochait (*OG*), Molaisse or Laisrén of, Sep. 16 ; river, townl. of Mundrehid, near Borris - in - Ossory, Queen's co.

Móethail Broccáin (*G*), Broccán of, July 8 ; Mothel, co. Waterford.

Móin Máeláin, Feb. 7.

Móin Miláin, Mar. 9, in Meath, near Lickblaw (Lecc Bladma).

Móin Mór (*GOn*), Gobnat of Bairnech in Móin Mór, Feb. 11 ; in bar. of Muskerry, co. Cork.

Móna, Feb. 18 ; in Scotland.

Monu, gen. Monan, Mar. 23.

Muccinis, May 12, Sep. 17, Oct. 16 ; Muckinish, Lough Derg, in the Shannon.

Mucnam (*G*), Máel Dóid of, May 13 ; Mucknoe, near Castleblayney, co. Monaghan.

Mulenn, gen. Colman Mulind, Jan. 9.

Mungarit, July 26 ; Mungret Abbey, near Limerick.

Muriab, Feb. 18 ; = Moreb, *i.e.* Moray, in Scotland.

Murmag, Mar. 31.

Muscraige Breogain (*G*), Bécán of, May 26 ; bar. of Clanwilliam, co. Tipperary. *See* Clúain Aird.

Muscraige Mitine, Feb. 11 ; bar. of W. Muskerry, co. Cork.

Muscraige Tíre, Odrán of, Oct. 2, 27 ; bar. of Upper and Lower Ormond, co. Tipperary.

Muscraige Trí Maige, Sep. 6 ; bar. of Orrery, co. Cork.

Nóendruim, Jan. 31, June 23 ; now Mahee Island, Strangford Lough.

Núachongbáil Réid Bairend, Jan. 19 ; Noughaval par., co. Longford.

Ossraige ; Ossory.

Partraige, June 26 ; proinntighe, *G*.

Ráith, gen. Ratha, May 19.

Ráith Aidme, Sep. 30 ; Ráith Aidhne in Dál Araide, *G*.

Ráith Blathmeic, in Dál Cais, Onchú of, July 9, 14 ; Rath Church, bar. of Inchiquin, co. Clare.

Ráith Derthaige, gen. Dirthaigi, Mar. 20 ; in Offaly.

Ráith Colptha (*G*), Tassach of, Ap. 14 ; Raholp, co. Down.

Ráith Eich in Raichnech (*G*), Ossíné's daughters of, May 3.

Raith Érenn, *see* Srath Érenn.

Ráith Lamraige, Feb. 11.

Ráith Liphthen (Liphiten, *Br.*), June 10 ; in Fir Cell in Midhe, *G* ; Rathline al. Rathlihen, Frankford, King's co., or in bar. of Balliboy, King's co.

Ráith (mac Stíalláin in Ardgal, *G*), Stíallán's sons of, Oct. 27 ; in East Meath (Hogan).

Ráith Maige (*G*), Ciarán of, Oct. 8.

Ráith Móentich, Feb. 5.

Ráith Murbuilg, Domongart of, Mar. 24 ; on Sleive Donard, co. Down.

Ráith na nEpscop, Feb. 16 ; Rathaspick, co. Wexford (Hogan).

Ráith Noí in Uí Garrchon, Aug. 18 ; Rathnew, co. Wicklow.

Ráith Ossáin (*G*), Feb. 17 ; near west gate of Trim (Colgan).

Rathan, Raithen (*G*), Constantín of, Mar. 11 ; Carthach of, May 14 ; Fidmune of, May 16 ; Fidairle of, Oct. 1 ; Rahen, near Tullamore, King's co.

Rechru, dat. Rechraind, June 16 ; either Rathlin island, off Ballycastle, co. Antrim, or Lambay island, off Howth, co. Dublin.

Ros Ailithir, Aug. 14 ; Roscarbery, co. Cork.

Ros Airthir, on Loch Erne (*G*), Findche of, Jan. 1 ; Rossory, near Enniskillen.

Ros (Aiss, in Inis, *G*), Dec. 21.

Ros Bennchair, June 29 ; Rossmanagher, near Quin Abbey, co. Clare.

Ros Branduib, Sep. 26 ; Rossbran townl., Kildare, and Queen's co. (Hogan).

Ros (Comáin, *G*), gen. in Rois, Dec. 26 ; Roscommon.

Ros Cré, Ap. 28, Dec. 19 ; Roscrea, co. Tipperary.

Ros Cruthnecháin, Dec. 18.

Q 2

Ros Cumulca, Jan. 9.

Ros Dela (in Mag Locha, in Mide, On), Aug. 24 ; Rosdalla, par. of Durrow, co. Westmeath (O'Donovan, Walsh).

Ros Ech, in Caille Follamain, Sep. . 14 ; Russagh, or Clonabreany, now comprised in par. of Diamor, bar. of Fore, co. Meath (Cogan).

Ros Éo, Ap. 10, see Mag Locha, in Brega, i.e. in Ros Éo.

Ros Fachtna, Feb. 13 ; Ros Raithe, G.

Ros [Glanda], Sep. 6 ; Ros Glanda G, aft. Domnach Mór Maige Imchlair, now Donaghmore, co. Tyrone.

Ros Glas(s)i, Dec. 22 ; for bru Berbha, G, on the bank of the Barrow ; Rosglas al. Monasterevan, Queen's co.

Ros Ingite, Dec. 23.

Ros mac nÁeda, i.e. at Snám Luthair, Loch Eirne, p. 116, see Snám Luthair.

Ros Mind Bairend, Mar. 16 ; Rosmarkin, diocese of Ross, Scotland (Hogan).

Ros Mór, Jan. 30 ; in Uí Dega (G) ; Rosminogue, near Gorey, co. Wexford.

Ros Raithe (G), Crúachnat of, Feb. 13.

Ros na Seanchae (Enche, G), Jan. 31 ; (?) Rossena townl., Queen's co. (Hogan).

Ros Tuirc, Sep. 17 ; in Mag Raigni (G), i.e. in Ossory.

Rúimen, gen. Ruimni, Mar. 17 ; Ruim, D, perhaps Island of Rum, Hebrides (Stokes).

Rúscach, Aug. 20 ; Rooskagh, bar. of Moycashel, co. Westmeath.

Rúscach, gen. Rúscaigi, Oct. 18 ; Dec. 20 (Br.) ; in Cúalnge (G) ; Rooskey, co. Louth.

Rúscach, dat. Roscaig (MS. Aroscaig), Dec. 30.

Saiger, Mar. 5 ; Seirkieran, near Birr, King's co.

Sailbec, Jan. 13, (G) ; (?) townl. of Sallow or Selloo, co. Kildare (Hogan).

Saxo, Ap. 21, July 21 ; a Saxon, i.e. Englishman.

Scelec, Ap. 28 ; = Scelec Micheil, the Greater Skellig, a rock island, off the coast of Kerry.

Senbotha Fola, Oct. 27 ; in Uí Cennselaig (G), now Templeshanbo, in diocese of Ferns, co. Wexford.

Senchoimét, June 24.

Senchua (G), Alténe of, Jan. 11 ; now Shancoe, bar. of Tirerril, co. Sligo.

Senduma, May 23.

Sentreib, dat., May 31 ; perhaps Santry, near Dublin.

Sláne, May 31 ; Slane, co. Meath.

Slébte, Feb. 7, Oct. 12 ; Sletty, near town of Carlow.

Slíab Bladma, July 20 ; Slieve Bloom mountains, on borders of King's and Queen's counties.

Slíab Breg, Mar. 9 ; Slieve Brey, between Mellifont and Dundalk, co. Louth.

Slíab Calann, Sárán of, Sep. 21 ; Slieve Gallion, in par. of Lissane, co. Derry.

Slíab Culinn, July 6 ; Slieve Gullion, co. Armagh.

Slíab Eblinne, May 4 ; the Slieve Phelim mountains, N. of co. Limerick.

Slíab Gúairi, Jan. 25 ; Oct. 13 (G), Finnsech of ; Slieve Gory, co. Cavan.

Slíab Liacc, July 30 ; Slieve League, co. Donegal, W.

Slíab Mairge (G), Scothíne of, Jan. 2 ; Slievemargie, Queen's co.

Slige, Feb. 17.

Snám Ech (G), see Clúain Dalláin ; Carlingford Lough.

Snám Luthair, May 27 ; perhaps Slanore townl., near Lough Oughter, co. Cavan (Hogan).

Sord, gen. Suird, Mar. 16 ; Swords, co. Dublin.

Srath Érenn, Srath Irenn, Feb. 14 (Br.), Srath Eret (sic) i nAlbain, June 20 (Br.), Ráith Erenn (G), Srath Érenn (On) ; now Dundurn, par. of Comrie, Perthshire (Reeves) ; near St. Fillan's, at E. end of Loch Earn (Skene, cit. Hogan, s.v. Ráith Erend).

Srath Eret, see Srath Érenn.

Taliucht dat., June 19, o Thobucht, G.

Tamlachta, Jan. 5, 28, Feb. 10, 25, July 7, Aug. 10, Sep. 6 ; Tallaght, near Dublin.

Tamlachta, in Boirche, Ap. 1, Oct. 18 (i mBairche, G) ; in the townl. of Lisnacree, bar. of Mourne, co. Down (Reeves).

Tamlachta Findloga (*G*), Findlug of, Jan. 3 ; in the Cíannachta of Glenn Gemin ; bar. of Keenacht, co. Derry.

Tamlachta Glíad, Feb. 4 ; in Glenn Ríge, *G* ; now Ballymore Rectory, in diocese of Armagh (Reeves).

Tamlachta Umail, by Loch Bricrenn, dat. Tamlachtain, Oct. 26 ; in. bar. of Upper Iveagh, co. Down.

Tamnach, dat. Tamnaigh, June 14, Cummán of Cell Chuimne in Tamnacha (*G*) ; Kilkevna, bar. of Gallen, co. Mayo.

Tamnach (Buada, *G*), July 21 ; (?) Tonnaboy townl., co. Fermanagh (Hogan).

Tech Aireráin i mMidi, Oct. 27 ; al. Tech Airennáin, Erennáin, now Tifarnan or Tyfernan, co. Meath.

Tech Baíthín (*G*), Baíthíne of, Feb. 19 ; Taghboyne, par. of Church-town, co. Westmeath.

Tech Bretan (Dún Tige Bretan, *G*), Jan. 7 ; Tibradden townl. in par. of Cruagh, co. Dublin.

Tech Colláin (Connáin, *G*), June 29 ; Stackallan, co. Meath.

Tech Eóin (*G*), Eoan of, Aug. 17 ; now St. John's Point, in par. of Rathmullan, co. Down.

Tech [Ernáin], Jan. 17.

Tech Ingen Choluimm in Cremthainn (*G*), Sep. 14.

Tech Ingen mBaiti beside Sord (*On*) Eithne and Sodelb of, Mar. 29 ; Swords, near Dublin.

Tech Lúta, in Fotharta Mara (*LL*, 353 *b*, *G*), Lugáed of, May 12.

Tech Máel Aithgen in Coirpre húa Cíarda (*G*), Máel Aithgen of, June 6 ; bar. Carbury, co. Kildare.

Tech Meic Findchon (Findcáin, *G*), May 8.

Tech Mochúa in Laigis (*G*), *see* Mochúa, Dec. 24 ; Timahoe, Queen's co.

Tech Mofhinna (*G*), Cíarán of, Oct. 8.

Tech Munnu (Mófhinnu), familia of, Oct. 21 ; Taghmon, bar. of She-maliere, W., co. Wexford.

Tech na mBretan i Termond Cennansa (*O* n), Darbellin of, Oct. 26 ; in the glebe-land of Kells.

Tech na Comairce, May 28 ; Tegna-gomark, in the par. of Clonleigh, co. Donegal.

Tech na Manach, Oct. 29.

Tech Ríagla (*G*), Ríaguil of Mucinis, Sep. 17 ; Stagreel, par. of Tirella, co. Down.

Tech Scuithín, Jan. 2 (*On*), May 23 ; Tiscoffin, co. Kilkenny.

Tech Tacru (= To-Sacru), Mar. 3, Tassagard, now Saggart, near Tallaght, co. Dublin.

Tech Taláin, May 27 ; Tehallan, co. Monaghan.

Tech Túa, Dec. 22 ; Taghadoe, near Maynooth, co. Kildare.

Tech Úa nGortig, July 19.

Telach Léis, May 12 ; Telach Lis, *OnG*. in Uí Echach Ulad, *O* ; now Tullylish, bar. of Iveagh, co. Down.

Telach Ólaind, *see* Telach Úaland.

Telach Úaland, dat. ó Thilaig (Tholaigh *G*) Úaland, Jan. 23, Tulach na Lann, *On* ; ó Tilaig (Thulaigh, *G*) Olaind, Aug. 7.

Teni (?), oteni *Br.*, July 25.

Terga, gen. Thergaidh *Br.* (Ten-gaidh *G*), July 19.

Tethba (*G*), *see* Ard Achad in Tethba.

Tipra Fachtna, Feb. 13, May 18 ; Tibraghny, bar. of Iverk, co. Kilkenny.

Tipra Oss (T Rois Rain, *G*), July 27.

Tír Aeda, Súaibsech of (*G*), Jan. 9 ; bar. of Tirhugh, S.W. co. Donegal (Hogan).

Tír dá Chráeb, Jan. 31 ; Teerna-creeve, par. of Castletownkindalen, co. Westmeath.

Tír dá Glas, May 1, 24, 26 ; Terry-glas, co. Tipperary.

Tír Oenaig, Feb. 19.

Tír Rois, June 13.

Toitae, gen., Sep. 7, *see* Inis Toitae.

Torach (*G*), Ernán of, Aug. 17 ; Tory Island, off Donegal.

Trelec (*G*), Mobéccu of, May 29 ; Trillick, co. Tyrone

Túaim Átha, o Thuaim Athi (Atha *G*), Mar. 7 ; perhaps Tooma, bar. of Mohill, co. Leitrim (Stokes).

Túaim dá Úalann (*G*), Ferdomnach of, June 10 ; Tuam, co. Galway.

Túaim Dracon, May 9 ; Toomregan par. in co. Cavan.

Túaim Gréni, Oct. 19, 20 ; Toom-graney, bar. of Upper Tullagh, co. Clare.

Túaim Muscraige, Ap. 29 ; Tomes, bar. of W. Muskerry, co. Cork.

Túaim Nóa, July 5 ; Tumna, bar. of Boyle, co. Roscommon.

Tugnid, gen. Tugneda, Aug. 21, perh. Tynan, co. Armagh (Reeves).

Tuilén, May 16; o Thuilen hi fail Cenansa na rrig, O (n), i.e. Dulane, near Kells, co. Meath.

Tulach, gen. Tulcha, May 20; Tulach Fortceirn (G), Torannán of, June 12; Tullow, co. Carlow.

Tulach Carpait, dat. o Thulaig Carpait i mMenna Tiri i nUíb Meith, Jan. 26; Tullycorbet, co. Monaghan.

Tulach Min Molaga (G), Lochéne of, Jan. 20; near Mitchelstown, co. Cork.

Úachtar Achaid (in Cenél Lúacháin, G), July 7; perhaps Oughteragh, bar. of Carrigallen, co. Leitrim (Reeves).

Úamag, dat. o hUamaig, July 5, Br., hó Hummigh (G), which Stokes (p. 404) takes as 'Huammach's descendant.'

Úarán (G), Ternóc of, Jan. 30; Oran, co. Roscommon.

Uí Cennselaig, July 10; in co. Wexford.

Uí Díarmata, in Connacht, Ap. 16; in Corcamroe, co. Galway.

Uí Echach Ulad, Feb. 18, Oct. 26; now bar. of Iveagh, co. Down.

Uí Ercáin (Uí Garrchon, OnG), July 3; in Leinster.

Uí Fidgeinte (G), Curifíne of, July 20; in co. Limerick.

Uí Garrchon, Feb. 18, July 3, note, Aug. 18; in Leinster, co. Wicklow.

Uí Líatháin, May 15; comprised baronies of Barrymore and Kinnataloon, co. Cork.

Uí Maic Caille, May 15; bar. of Imokilly, co. Cork.

Uí Méith, Jan. 26; bar. of Monaghan, co. Monaghan.

Uí Segáin, Oct. 10, note; north of Ardbraccan, co. Meath.

Uí Senaig, of Corco Solgoinn Crúaich, p. 126.

Ulaid, acc. pl., Ultu, Ap. 12, gen. pl. Ulad, Sep. 29; Ulstermen, Ulster.

INDEX OF PERSONS (Irish Calendar).

Áedlug, saint, gen. Áedlugha, Feb. 26.
—— of Ard Chassáin, Jan. 28 ; Aired Chassáin, *GD.*
Aengus, *see* Óengus.
Affíne, June 3 ; of Cell Afféin, *GD.*
[Agna], one of the three nuns of Druim dá Dart, May 22 ; *sic GD.*
Áicclech, gen. Aicclig, Aug. 14.
Aignech, see moccu Aignich.
Ailbe, bp. of Imlech [Ibair], Sep. 10, 12, 30. His true day is Sep. 12.
—— cruimther ' presb.,' Jan. 30.
Ailbictus, gen. Ailbicti, of familia Mundu, Oct. 21.
Ailchú, gen. Ailchon, of Eig, Ap. 17.
Ailerán, Dec. 29 ; lector of Clúain Eraírd, *G* ; Erearán, *D.*
Ailgne, Aeilgnei, May 11.
Ailgniad, Mar. 8.
Ailill, gen. Ailello, Ailella :
—— s. of Ségíne, June 25.
—— bp., of Clúain Emain, July 1 ; of Ard Macha, *GD.*
—— bp., Jan 13 ; of Ard Macha, *GD.*
Ailill, three daughters of, Aug. 9.
—— sons of, Jan. 16.
—— f. of Cúangus, Mar. 13.
Ailither, bp., of Achad, Sep. 30 ; a gl. on Corcán, *G.*
—— of Clúain Géise, Ap. 25.
—— of Muccinis, May 12 ; cp. p. 112.
—— of familia Mundu, Oct. 21.
—— abb., Jan. 7.
Ailithir, dá ailithir déc, ' twelve pilgrims,' of Inis Uachtair, Dec. 23.
Aillén (Ailleain *MS.*), f. of Cuman, May 29.
Ailténe, of familia Mundu, Oct. 21.
Ainbthíne, d. of Máel Dúin, p. 116.
Ainmere, gen. Ainmerech, of Ailech, June 10.
—— of Clúain Fota, Sep. 15.
Ainmere, gen. Ainmire, s. of Rónán, Mar. 21. *See* note, p. 181.
Airbertach, f. of Carthach, Mar. 26.
Airchinnech, f. of Findgan, Oct. 24.
Airechar, f. of Sárán, May 15.
Airechtach, of Inis Mór, Jan. 15.
Airennán, Airendán.
—— moccu Foduib, Feb. 1.
—— bp., of Tamlachta, Feb. 10.
—— from Tech Airennáin, Oct. 27.
—— Jan. 5.
Airennán, f. of Fínán, Feb. 12.
Airerán, sapiens et abb. of Tamlachta after Máel Rúain, Aug. 11.

Airetán, of familia Mundu, Oct. 21.
Airgenán, of familia Mundu, Oct. 21.
Airmedach, abb. of Cráeb Laisre, Jan. 1.
—— Airmidach, from Cunga, June 8.
Airmer Craíbdech ' the pious,' from Bréchmag, Sep. 30 ; Airinne, *D.*
Airnech, s. of Echen, Oct. 30 ; Ernach, *OGD* ; gl. *i.e.* mac Iairnd ' son of Iron ' . . . and in Dún dá Én in Fidbaid Dál Araide is he, *O* (*L*).
Aithechán, of [Inber] Colptha, June 16 ; Aithcáin, *GD.*
Aithgen, gen. Aithgin of Both [Domnaig], May 3 ; om. *GD.* Aithgne, Rawl. B. 502, 89 (pedigree) ; *i.e.* Cormac, *LB.* 14 *e.*
—— bp., of Mag Bile, Sep. 9 ; Mael Aithchein, *G,* Mael Aithgein, *D.*
Aithmet, of Clochar, Feb. 2 ; bp., *GD.*
Alténe, of familia Mundu, Oct. 21.
—— Jan. 11 ; Elténe s. of Máelán, from Senchua, *G.*
Amalgaid (Umalgaid, *MS.*), s. of Eochaid, June 9.
—— Jan. 22.
Amarma, conjux regis Gothorum, July 8.
Amla, see moccu Amla.
Ana, in Clúain Grenaich, Jan. 18, p. 116.
Ancus, Anci, Sep. 19.
Anfudán, bp., of Glenn dá Locha, Jan. 11.
—— (3) of familia Mundu, Oct. 21.
—— of Ros Cré, Dec. 19.
—— Dec. 23 ; of Ros Ingite, *GD.*
—— Anfodan, Sep. 16.
† Antiosus, ep. Ap. 5.
Araide, f. of Cummíne, July 29.
Arconi, gen., of familia Mundu, Oct. 21 ; Arconus (?) = Archú, gen. Archon.
Artgeni, gen., of familia Mundu, Oct. 21 ; Artgenus (?) = Artgein.
Arun, bp., of Clúain Caín, Aug. 1.
Augustín, of Bennchor, Oct. 28.
Auxilius, (Auxilinus) Mar. 19 ; Sep. 16 ; bp. and brother of St. Patrick, p. 100.

Baán, Ap. 27.
Báetán, s. of Colmán, Feb. 5.
—— bp., s. of Lugeus, Jan. 14 ; of Inis Mór, *GD.*
—— bp., of Clúain [moccu Noís], Mar. 1 ; moccu Corbmaic, *GD.*

Boetius or Bregbesach, s. of Brónach, May 16 ; *i.e.* Buite of Mainister Buite, whose true day is Dec. 7, *OGD.*

Boga, d. of Comgall, Jan. 22.

Boíthíne, *see* Báethéne.

Bolcán, in Cell Chúle, July 4.

Braccán, bp., May 1.

Bran Bec ' the Little,' from Clóenad, May 18.

Bran, s. of Conall, K. of Leinster, p. 126.

Brandub, of familia Muñdu, Oct. 21.

—— bp., June 3, 13 ; s. of Máenach,*D.*

—— Feb. 6 ; from Loch Munremair, *GD.*

—— p. 116.

Brecc Féle, of Belach Féle, Jan. 15.

—— gen. Bricc, Oct. 16 ; epithet of Coemgen, *GD.*

Brecc, f. of Áed, Feb. 28, May 4.

—— f. of Fulartach, Dec. 21.

Breccán, s. of Dímmán, in Cell Mór Díthruib, Aug. 9.

—— of [Clúain] Catha, July 16.

—— of Echdruim, May 7.

—— abb. of Mag Bile, Ap. 29.

—— of familia Mundu, Oct. 21.

—— Oct. 12.

Bregbesach, *see* Boetius.

Bregdae, f. of Cillíne, Dec. 28.

Brélach, s. of Fidchellach, Feb. 17.

Brénaind, Brendinus.

—— of Biror, May 9 ; his true day is Nov. 29.

—— of Clúain Ferta, May 16.

—— Egressio familiae Brendini, Mar. 22.

—— Jan. 9.

Brénaind, f. of Báethéne, Jan. 12.

Bresal, from Derthach, May 18, Sep. 30 ; 17th abb. of Í.

Bresal, s., of Díarmait, p. 102 ff.

Briccéne, of familia Mundu, Oct. 21.

Brig (Brige), of Coirpre, Jan. 7.

Brigit, d. of Dímmán, May 21.

—— d. of Domma (Droma *MS.*), Feb. 7, (Doma) in Mag Liphi, Mar. 9.

—— of Clúain Díanlama, Aug. 13 ; Diailama, *Br.,* Clúana Hai *GD,* where Dianland (*sic*) is a n. pr.

—— of Móin Miláin, Mar. 9.

—— saint, Feb. 1 ; of Cell Dara.

—— Sep. 30.

Brion, ancestor of Ernéne, Sep. 27.

Brittán, of Ráith, May 19.

Briunsech, virg. (Brun*n*seci *MS.*) May 29 ; d. of Crimthann, from Mag Trea, *GD.*

Broccaid, July 9 ; of Imlech Broccada, *GD.*

Broccán, s. of Énna, Jan. 1.

—— s. of Lugaid, Aug. 14 ; occad, *G.*

—— of Clúain meic (Féicc, *G*), June 5.

·—— of Imgan, Aug. 25.

—— of familia Mundu, Oct. 21.

—— of Ros Tuirc, Sep. 17.

—— scríbnid ' scribe,' July 8 ; of Móethail Broccáin, *G.*

—— Ap. 9, Ap. 11, June 27.

Brocéne, of familia Mundu, Oct. 21.

Broednea, *see* Findbarr, of Cell Cunga.

Bróen, bp., of Caisel, June 8 ; from Caisel Irróe of Uí Fíachrach Muaide, *GD.*

Brónach, virg., gen. Brónchi, Ap. 2 ; from Glenn Sechis, *OG,* Cell S., *D.*

Brónach, f. of Boetius (*i.e.* Buite), May 16.

Bronchén, of Lethet Corcaige, Sep. 30.

Búachaill, gen. Búachalla, f. of Ríaguil, Ap. 13.

Buadge, July 31, perhaps in error for Tamnach Buada, *GD.*

Budgocthéne, of familia Mundu, Oct. 21.

Búgno, Briton, Ap. 21.

Buide, f. of Senach Garb, Sep. 10.

Buite, *see* Boetius.

Bute, f. of Columb, Mar. 25.

Ca, see moccu Cae.

Cada, of Druim Tuirc, Dec. 26 ; Cota, *GD.*

Cáernán, Jan. 31.

Cáetren, see Caírthenn.

Cáe—, *see* also Caí—, Cóe—.

Cetené (gen. Cateni *MS.*), of familia Mundu, Oct. 21 ; Cetenus (Colgan).

Cail, *see* Senchaid, from Dubad.

Caílann, gen. Caílainne, of Daire Cáelainne, June 19, p. 108.

Caílchú, of Clúain Airthir, gen. Cailchon, Sep. 25 ; of Lúi A., *GD.*

Cailleacha, na teora, ' the three nuns,' of Druim dá Dart, May 22, *i.e.* Agna, Cassin, Luigsech (*G*) ; ' seven,' p. 116.

Ca|i]mmíne, Mar. 25, p. 118 ; of Inis Celtra, *GO* (n).

Caínchomrac, of Cenn Cláir, June 29 ; of Dísert Cinn Cláir, *GD.*

Cainchomrac, of Inis Éndaim, July 23.

Cainer, d. of Cruthnechán, Jan. 28 ; of Cell Culinn, LL 353 b 10.

Cainnech, m. [= moccu] Dalann, Oct. 11 ; abb. of Achad Bó, *GD.*

—— of Airecul, May 15.

—— presb., Jan. 31.

—— Jan. 23.

Cainnech, daughters of, from Mag Locha, Sep. 24.

—— *see* moccu Cainchi.

Cairech Dergáin, Feb. 9 ; virg. of Clúain Boirenn, *GD.* Cp. Óeng.², 70 ff.

Cairell (Cairił *MS.*), of Eig, Ap. 17.

—— of familia Mundu, Oct. 21.

—— (Carilla), in Tír Rois, June 13.

Cairell, f. of Daig, Aug. 18.

Caírlan, bp., Mar. 24.

—— Mar. 23.

Cairland, f. of Eoán, Aug. 17.

Cairnech, from Tuilén, May 16 ; a Briton from Cornwall, *O* (n).

—— *See* also Carnech.

Ca(i)rpre, bp., of Mag Bile, May 3.

—— Cromm 'the Bent,' Carpre Cruinn, Mar. 6 ; bp. of Clúain maccu Nois, *G* ; s. of Feradach, *D.*

Cairpre, daughters of, Jan. 15, Aug. 15.

Caírthenn (Carthinisius), bp., Jan. 11 ; Orthinis, *GD.*

Caírthend or Caetren, f. of Moloca, Aug. 13.

—— f. of Trea, Aug. 3.

Caisín, of Senduma, May 22 ; one of the three nuns of Druim dá Dart, *GD.*

Caite, p. 108.

Caitte, f. of Ultán, Ap. 4.

Calb, bp., of Tulach Carpait, Jan. 26.

Camal, *see* Mochamal.

Cammóc, *see* Mochammóc.

Canan, s. of Corae, Mar. 20 ; Conan, s. of Coree, *GD.*

Cantán, of familia Mundu, Oct. 21.

Caradíc, May 19.

Caramnán, July 20.

Carilla, *see* Cairell.

Caritán, of Druim Lara, Mar. 7.

Carnán, daughter of, Ap. 24 ; Cairnán, *G*, Caornán, *D.*

Carnech, bp., gen. Carnig, Mar. 28 ; s. of Sárán, *G*, Cairnech, *D.*

Carthach, s. of Airbertach, Mar. 26 ; bp., *G.*

—— s. of Óengus, of Druim Ferdaim, Mar. 5 ; also of Inis Úachtar, *G.*

Carthach, *i.e.* Mochutu, of Les Mór, May 14.

Carthinisius, *see* Caírthenn.

Cass, of Bennchor, Ap. 26.

—— of Lethglenn, Feb. 23 ; Ernín Cas, *GD.*

Cass, f. of Dímma, May 12.

Cassán, s. of Nemán, Mar. 1.

—— of Domnach Mór, June 4.

—— of Clúain Ráithe, June 19, 20. *GD.*

—— of Imdúal, Mar. 28.

Catha, crumther 'presbyter,' s. of Óengus, in Clúain Eorainne, Sep. 8.

Cathbad, July 1.

Cathbad, daughters of, in Aired, July 2 ; of Aired Fhoda, *GD.*

—— f. of Colmán, Sep. 22.

—— sons of, from Miliuc, Dec. 18 ; of Imblech, *GD.*

Cathboth, Sep. 16 ; Cathbad, *GD.*

Cathchán, of Ráith Derthaige, Mar. 20 ; bp. *GD.*

Cathub, bp., Ap. 6 ; s. of Fergus, of Achad Cinn, *GD.*

—— bp., Ap. 8 ; *om. D.*

Caurnán, of Clúain Ech, Ap. 28 ; Cáernan, *GD.*

—— Bec, 'the Little,' Jan. 6.

Celba, Aug. 21 ; Cóelba from Cell Chóelbad, N. of Cennanus, *G.*

Céle Críst, Mar. 3 ; from Cell Céle Críst, in Uí Dúnchada, in Laigin, *GD.*

Celianus Scottus, saint and mart., July 8 ; *i.e.* Céle clérech, who suffered at Würzburg along with Áed and Tadg, *GD.*

Cellach, s. of Dúnchad, July 18.

—— deacon, *i.e.* the Saxon, in Glenn dá Locha , Oct. 7.

—— of familia Mundu, Oct. 21.

[*Cel*]*lach* f. of Flann, Jan. 21.

Cellachán, of Clúain Tiprat, Sep. 24.

Cellán, s. of Fínán, June 17.

—— húa Fíachrach, May 1 ; bp., *GD.*

—— presb., Oct. 8.

Cellóc, *see* Mochellóc.

Cenannán, Mar. 26.

Cenn Fáelad, abb. of Bennchor, Ap. 8.

Cenn Fáelad, f. of Dúnchad, May 25.

Céra (Caerae), from Ráith Móentich, Feb. 5.

—— saint, virg., Feb. 8.

—— saint, Sep. 9.

Cerclach, Jan. 6 ; (?) epithet of Digdi 'Circular,' Stokes, *G*, p. 340.

Cethech, St. Patrick's bishop, gen. Cethig, June 16.

Cianán, abb., Feb. 25.

Ciar, d. of Dub Réa, Jan. 5, gen. Céire, Oct. 16, where gl. mother of the children of Dub, in Mag Ascad, G. Ceir Ascad .i. nomen campi, LL. 353a 31, in Aired, ib. 353b 40.

Ciara, see moccu Ciara.

Ciarán, s. of Áed, Jan. 5.
—— s. of Colgu, May 19.
—— mac in tsáer, 'son of the wright,' Sep. 9; i.e. of Clúain maccu Noís.
—— húa Mesa, of Ard Fota, Feb. 24; GD have Héise of Aired Foda, Ciarán of Uaim; entry corrupt.
—— of Belach Dúin, June 14.
—— in Cell Mór Díthruib, Aug. 9.
—— of Clúain Sasta, Ap. 30.
—— of Eig, Ap. 17.
—— of Ros Cumulca, Jan. 9.
—— of Saiger, Mar. 5.
—— from Tech Úa nGortig, July 19.
—— (Quiarani), i.e. Mochúaróc, May 7; Ciaróc of Echdruim Breccáin, GD.
—— saint, Feb. 25; om. GD.
—— Mar. 8; gl. Foighdi, GD; cp. Ciarán Faithche, Rawl. B. 502, p. 92 g.
—— Oct. 8; of Ráith Maige and Tech Mofinna, GD; abb., D.

Ciarán, f. of Lappán, Feb. 11.

Cilchíne, of familia Mundu, Oct. 21.

Cilléne, Cillíne:
—— s. of Lubnán, Ap. 14.
—— moccu Colla, Jan. 3; abb. of Faithne Mura, GD.
—— (3) of familia Mundu, Oct. 21.
—— abb. of , July 3; Cillíne Droichteach, 'pontifex,' G.
—— of Inis Doimle, Mar. 3.
—— of Lilcach, Mar. 12
—— saint, Ap. 19, Oct. 22.
—— abb., Jan. 8.
—— bp., from Tech Táláin, May 27.
—— Jan. 16, Mar. 26.

Cillián, s. of Doidnán, Oct. 23.
—— or Mochellóc, s. of Tulodrán, from Cathair Meic Conaich, Mar. 26; Cilléin, G, Cillén, D.
—— s. of Bregdae, Dec. 28.

Cinne, sac., Feb. 1; virg. GD.

Clárainech, of Clúain Caín, June 6.
—— (Clarenech) of Druim Bidg, Jan. 17.
—— clárenig, na trí, i.e. Báethéne, Ségéne, and Crónán, Jan. 29.

Clothach, gen. Clothaig, saint, May 3, perhaps only an epithet 'famous' for Conlaed, who precedes in G, Stokes; Clothaighi, Br.

Clothrann, of Inis Duine, gen. Cloth-rainne, Oct. 1; virg., d. of Conall, GD.

Cobarchar, of Gulban Guirt moccu Gairb, July 30.

Cobba, d. of Báetán, Jan. 18; Coppa, GD.

Cobrán (Coibran), of Clúain, July 19.
—— of Clúain Cúallachta, Aug. 2.
—— of Eig, Ap. 17.
—— (2) of familia Mundu, Oct. 21.

Cocca, June 6.

Cócha, of Ros Bennchair, June 29.

Cocnat, p. 108.

Cóe, see Mochóe.

[Cóel, Cáel], d. of Mac Íeir, Oct. 26, name om. through homoeoteleuton, but in OGD; of Cell na nIngen, GD.
—— cruimther 'presbyter,' of Cell Mór, May 25.
—— Ochtra, Feb. 17; om. G, etc.
—— (Cail) idem et Senchaid from Dubad, q.v.

Cóelán, Cáelan:
—— of Daire Cáelainne, June 19.
—— of Inis Celtra, July 29.
—— of Tech na Manach, Oct. 29
—— Dachoe, June 30; om. GD.
—— Sep. 25; of Ech-inis, GD.
—— (Colain), July 25.
—— see Mochóe.

Cóelbad, sons of (?), Ap. 24.

Cóemán, Coímán, Cáemán.
—— of Airdne Cóemáin, June 7; i.e. Santlethan, June 12.
—— of familia Mundu, Oct. 21.
—— of Ros Cruthnecháin, Dec. 18.
—— of Mag Mennota, Feb. 22; of Mag mc. Dodon, GD.
—— Brecc, at Ros Ech, Sep. 14.
—— saint, Mar. 18, Oct. 16.
—— Aug. 14; s. of Daigre, GD.
—— Mar. 14, Sep. 16.

Cóemán, f. of Erníne, Jan. 11.
—— f. of Rétach, June 10.

Cóeme, see Mochóeme.

Cóemell, p. 108.

Cóemgen, abb. of Glenn dá Locha, June 3.
—— abb., May 11.
—— Oct. 16; C. Brecc, GD.

Cóemnat, of Cúil Cíchmaige, Ap. 24.
—— gen. Coímnatán, Sep. 23; Cóemnat, G, Comnat, D.

Cóemóc, see Mochóemóc.
Cóemsa (Caimsae), virg., Feb. 25 ;
from Tamlachta, G.
Cóeti, Oct. 24 ; Caeti ep., G ; of Í.
Cogitosus, sapiens, Ap. 18 ; Cogitois,
G ; om. D.
Coibsenach, bp., Oct. 16.
Coílman (Coilmani), of familia Mundu,
Oct. 21.
Coíne, of Cell Coíne, Ap. 4 ; Cóeme,
of Cell Cóemhe, GD.
Coip, d. of Carnán, Ap. 24 ; p. 108.
Coirtged, f. of Colmán, Oct. 18.
Coitchenn, of Cenn Locha Sílenn, p.
116.
Colba, sons of, Ap. 24 ; Caelba, G.
Colbrand, f. of Tetgall, Ap. 16.
Colchán, f. of Rígnach, p. 116.
Colgu moccu Dunechda, Feb. 20 ; of
Clúain maccu Noís.
Colgu, f. of Táed, gen. Colgan, Jan.
31.
—— f. of Cíarán, May 19.
Colla, see moccu Colla.
—— see Mocholla.
Colmaid, f. of Dagán, gen. Colmada,
Sep. 13.
—— f. of Molibba, Jan. 8.
Colmán, s. of Andgen, July 14.
—— s. of Báeth, in Druim Ráithe,
Aug. 9.
—— s. of Cathbad, of Midísil, Sep.
22.
—— s. of Coirtged, Oct. 18.
—— s. of Corardán, of Imlech Brēn.,
June 15 ; s. of Corodran, of Miliuc,
GD.
—— s. of Crónán, July 11.
—— s of Dairchell, Dec. 27.
—— s. of Daráne, from Daire Mór,
July 31 ; bp., s. of Óengus, G.
—— s. of Dui, Feb. 3 ; of Cell meic
Dúach, GD. Also Oct. 1, Br.
—— s. of Eochaid, Jan. 1, p. 116.
—— s. of Fuidicán, Oct. 24.
—— s. of Lenín, Oct. 15.
—— s. of Lúachán, June 14, 17.
—— s. of Míce, June 18.
—— s. of Róe, from Rechru, June 16.
—— moccu Arti, see Mocholmóc, of
Druim Mór.
—— moccu Laígsi, May 15 ; of
Tulach meic Comgaill, D.
—— moccu Telluib, Feb. 8 ; bp., G.
—— descendant of Fíachra, in Sen-
botha Fola, Oct. 28 ; Oct. 27, GD.
—— Sep. 16 ; descendant of Lonán,
G.
—— bp., of Abla (?), Sep. 12.

Colmán, from Achad, Aug. 15.
—— bp., of Ailbe, Sep. 11.
—— of Ard Bó, Feb. 21.
—— in Áth Truim, Feb. 17.
—— of Cammachad, Mar. 31.
—— i.e. Gúaire, in Cell Aird in Uí
Ercain, July 3 ; of Caill Ard in Uí
Garrchon, GD.
—— of Cell Rúaid, Oct. 16.
—— of [Clúain] Bruchais, July 12.
—— of Clúain dá Fhíach, Dec. 23.
—— of Clúain Tibrinne, Mar. 9, Mar.
13 ; Mar. 10 only, GD.
—— of Comrar, Sep. 25, s. of Bronach,
d. of Milchú, LL 372d 60.
—— of Cúil, Aug. 18.
—— of Daire Mór, May 20.
—— of Druim Ferta, p. 116.
—— of Eig (2), Ap. 17.
—— of Gabal Liúin, July 28 ; Com-
gall, GD.
—— bp., of Inis Bó Finne, Aug. 8.
—— of Lann Elo, Sep. 26, Oct. 3.
—— of Linn Dúachail, Mar. 30.
—— of Loch Echin, May 6.
—— from Loch Munremair, Feb. 6 ;
Colum, GD.
—— of Midísel, see Colum, from Ros
[Glanda], Sep. 6. Cp. Colum, s. of
Cathbad, Sep. 26.
—— Mulind. of Mulenn (?) or ' of the
Mill,' Jan. 1 ; from Daire Cáecháin
in Dál Ríada, GD ; son of
Conaill s. of Caiss, etc. Rawl. B.
502, 89 h.
—— (10) of familia Mundu, Oct. 21.
—— in Muriab, Feb. 18.
—— of Partraige, June 26 ; Proinn-
tige, GD.
—— of Ros Branduib, Sep. 26.
—— from Tamlachta Gliad, Feb. 4 ;
Cíaran, GD.
—— Stelláin, of Tír dá Glas, May 26.
—— of Túaim Gréne, Oct. 20.
—— Bán, ' the White,' Oct. 19.
—— Cerr, from Dergderc, Jan. 13 ;
of Sailbecc GD ; in Clúain Ruiss
on the brink of Loch Dergderc,
LL 366 g.
—— Cerr, Mar. 8 ; cp. Jan. 13.
—— Crón, ' the Yellow or Swarthy,'
May 21.
—— Find, ' the Fair,' Ap. 4.
—— Imrama ' of the Voyage,' July
8 ; from Athan Becc (i.e. Fathan)
in Inis Eogain, GD.
—— Infirmus (?), Mar. 5.
—— Lobor ' the Leper,' in Mag Éo,
May 21.

Conamail, Oct. 8.
Conán, of Eig, Jan. 12.
—— (2) of familia Mundu, Oct. 21.
—— saint, Aug. 16.
—— Feb. 17, Ap. 26, Oct. 28.
Conandil, of Ess Rúaid, gen. Conanla, Mar. 8.
Conbesach, of familia Mundu, Oct. 21.
Conbrán, of familia Mundu, Oct. 21.
Conbrat, gen. Conbruit, of familia Mundu, Oct. 21.
Conchend, s. of Lucennán, Mar. 13.
—— Conchand, from Cáelchad, Aug. 20; Concand, gl. *i.e.* Coinchend from Cáolachad, *GD.* Cp. following entry.
—— of Cell Achid, Ap. 28 ; *om.* D na Conchind, (pl.) *G*, as if including Christopher Dog-head, who suffered under Decius, also commemorated on this day, *supra.* To him alone the notes in Fél. Óengusso (*O*) refer.
Conchille, of familia Mundu, Oct. 21.
Conchobar, see moccu Conchobair.
Conchraid, gen. Conc[h]rada, Mar. 3.
Cond, see moccu Cuinn.
Condla, bp., May 10.
Condláed, formerly Roncend, of Cell Dara, May 3.
Condmach, of Áth Siláin, July 9 ; Áth Blair, *GD.*
Condóc (Condoci), of familia Mundu, Oct. 21.
Condorchon, of familia Mundu, Oct. 21 ; (?) gen. of Condorchú.
Congal, gen. Congaile, of Eig, Ap. 17.
Congal, f. of Guirminni, gen. Congaili, Feb. 22.
Congnathe, of familia Mundu, Oct. 21.
Conich, s. of Lúachanán, Sep. 23 ; Conaing, *GD.*
Coníne, Feb. 12.
Coningen, *i.e.* Cúach, of Cell Findmaige, Ap. 29.
Conlae, bp., from Roscach, Dec. 30.
Conmáel (Conmaili), of familia Mundu, Oct. 21.
Conmind, of Eig, Ap. 17.
Conn, see moccu Cuinn.
Conna, saint, Sep. 30 ; Mochonna, of Cluain Airdne, *GD.*
—— virg., Mar. 3.
—— see also Mochonna, Teochonna, Tochonna, Tochunne.
Connán, bp., from Tech Colláin, June 29.
Connath, abb. of Daire, gen. Connathi, Ap. 12 ; Conna, *GD.*

Connidi (gen.), of Eig, Ap. 17.
Connrach, cruimther, ' presb.,' Feb. 23.
Conocán, of familia Mundu, Oct. 21.
Constantín Briton, s. of Fergus, Mar. 11, abb. of Raithen Mochuta, *GD.*
Copán, f. of Fintain, Sep. 27.
Cora, gen. Corae, f. of Canan, Mar. 20 ; Corre, *GD.*
Corán, of Eig, Ap. 17.
—— of familia Mundu, Oct. 21.
Corardán, f. of Colmán, June 15.
Corc, crumther ' presbyter,' of Cell Mór, Ap. 4.
Corc, of Druinn, Feb. 4 ; of Druim Lommáin, *GD.*
Corcán, Jan. 7 ; bp. *GD*, where two are mentioned.
Corconutan, Dec. 23 ; *om.* *GD*, which have a saint of this name under Nov. 3, of Daire Eidnech *G*, of Daire na Flann, *D.*
Coritan, in Cell Mór Díthruib, Aug. 9 ; *om. G*, Curitan, *D.*
Cormac, descendant of Líathán, June 8, abb. of Durmag and bp. ; an anchorite also, *G* ; also June 21 *recte.*
—— in Achad Findnaige, May 11.
—— crumther, ' presbyter,' in Árann, May 11 ; *om. GD.*
—— of Both Domnaig, see Aithgen.
—— bp., Feb. 17, of Áth Truim.
—— bp., Jan. 7.
—— May 10 ; is f. of Áed, *GD.*
—— see moccu Cormaic.
Cormán, of Galam, Oct. 15 ; Cormac, *GD.*
Corodne, July 24 ; Crodne, *GD.*
Corpnata, July 17 ; Craebnat, virg., *GD.*
Cóta, from Druinn, Feb. 4.
Craine (?), p. 108.
Creber, Sep. 30 ; *om. GD.*
Cremthand, of Mag Duma, May 23.
Cresíne, f. of Erníne or Ernóc, Aug. 18.
Crimthann, f. of Briunsech, *GD*, May 29.
—— f. of Feidlimid, Aug. 28.
Crínán, of Cúil Lagin, Oct. 19.
Cristán, from Teni (?), July 25 ; Critan *GD.*
Critán, s. of Dáire, Feb. 7.
—— s. of Illadon, May 11 (*bis*), *i.e.* Mochrítóc.

Cú Lóchae, son of, *i.e.* Falbe, July 11.
Cucalíne, of Eig, Ap. 17.
Cúige, son of, Sep. 19.
Cuilén, bp., in Lemchaill, Ap. 22.
Cu[i]mnech, gen. Cumnig, Mar. 14.
Cuint, at Snám Luthair, May 27 ; *om. GD.*
Cúla, mother of Becgán, Ap. 5.
Cumma, of familia Mundu, Oct. 21.
—— *see* Mochumma.
Cum(m)an, virg., d. of Alleán, in Ard Ulad, gen. Cumne, May 29.
—— d. of Maine, in Aired Boinne, July 6.
—— of Glenn Móna, Feb. 12 ; Cumméin *GD.*
—— Becc ' the Little,' from Tamnach, June 14.
Cumman, mother of Mochta, Mar. 24 ; of Caimíne, Mar. 25.
Cummeán (Cumeane), bp., Feb. 17.
Cumméne, Cummíne :
—— s. of Araide, July 29.
—— s. of Báetán, May 19.
—— s. of Dub, from Druim Druith, Jan. 12.
—— Find ' the Fair,' s. of Fíachna, abb. of Í, Feb. 24 ; *i.e.* Cummeneus Albus.
—— s. of Lugaid, May 21 ; of Inis maccu Dartada, *GD.*
—— of Clúain Már, Dec. 18 ; Cuimin *GD* ; also Dec. 24 ; Cumméin Cróbán ' death-pale,' *G.*
—— abb. of Damoirne, Sep. 17 ; of Bennchor, *GD.*
—— abb. of Druim Bó, Aug. 10.
—— Comméin, abb. of Druim Snechta, Sep. 4 ; Cuimméin, *GD.*
—— (2) of Eig, Ap. 17.
—— (3) of familia Mundu, Oct. 21.
—— June 1, Aug. 14, Aug. 22.
Cúóc, of familia Mundu, Oct. 21.
—— *see also* Mochúóc.
Cuppa, of Cenn Locha, p. 116.
Curcach (Curchach), of Clúain Lothur, Mar. 8, Aug. 8.
Curcan, of Cell Curcaine, gen. Curcaine, July 21 ; Curcach of Cell Curcaige, *D.*
Curennán in Ros, Dec. 21 ; Currin of Ros Aiss in Inis, *GD*, Dec. 22.
Curifíne, July 20 ; Curbín craíbdech, in Uí Fidgeinte, in Munster, *GD.*
Curitán, saint, bp., abb. of Ros Mind Bairend, Mar. 16.
Cutbrict (Cutbeirt *G*), Saxon = Cuthbert, in Inis Menóc, Mar. 20.

TALLAGHT.

Dabóetóc, Dabeoodóc (*MS.*), July 22 ; of Clúain dá Báetóc, *G* ; Dabhaotócc, *D.*
Daborchú, gen. Daborchon, of familia Mundu, Oct. 21.
Dabreccóc, of Túaim Dracon, May 9 ; Dabriccín, *GD.*
Dachonna (= Conna), ɔ. of Odrán, Feb. 17.
Dadnán, bp. of Cell Cunga, Ap. 11.
Dafinna, s. of Declán, June 9.
Dagán, presb., s. of Colmaid, of Inber Doíle, Sep. 13.
—— bp., Mar. 12.
Dagán, brother of Molibba, Jan. 8.
Daig, s. of Cairell, of Inis Caín, Aug. 18, p. 126.
—— s. of Nemnall, gen. Dego, Feb. 19.
Daigre, from Clúain Acuir, Sep. 30.
Daigre, f. of Beógaes (= Beógna), abb. of Bennchor, Aug. 22.
Dairchell, of Glenn dá Locha, gen. Dairchella, May 3 ; bp., *GD.*
—— of familia Mundu, Oct. 21.
Dairchell, f. of Colmán, Dec. 27.
Dáire, saint (Darii), Feb. 13.
—— (Darii dör, *sic*), Aug. 7 ; *om. GD.*
—— virg., Aug. 8.
—— Dec. 20.
Dáire, three sons of, Feb. 7, p. 116.
Dalbach, of Cúil Collainge, Oct. 23.
Dallán, s. of Forgall, from Maigen, Jan. 29 ; the author of *Amra Choluimb Chille.*
Dal(l)ann, see moccu Dalann.
Daloe, of Tech Bretan, Jan. 7
Damnat, of Slíab Betha, June 13.
Daniél, bp., of Bennchor, Sep. 11.
—— (Dainel), of Tulach, May 20.
—— bp., Feb. 18.
Dara, f. of Falbe, or Máel Dóid, June 29 ; Derbdara, *GD.*
Daráne, m. of Colmán, from Daire Mór, July 31 ; his mother's sister *O* (n).
Darbellin, d. of Mac Íeir, of Cell Maignenn, Oct. 26 ; Darbile *G*, of Cell na nIngen, *OGD*, or in Tech na mBretan, Kells, *O* (n).
Darbile, d. of Muiredach, p. 116.
Darerca, saint, Sep. 9 ; Dererce, *G.*
—— virg., Jan. 15 ; d. of Cairbre, *D.*
—— virg., Mar. 23.
—— (Dererca), Mar. 22 ; sister of St. Patrick, *GD.*
—— *see* Moninne.
Darinill, d. of Mac Íeir, of Cell Maignenn, Oct. 26.

R

Darluga, virg., from Lemmag, Feb. 10 ; Derluga, D.

Dartinne, virg., in Cell Aird, July 3.

Dauid, of Cell Mune, Mar. 1.

Decell, son of, Jan. 1.

Dechonen, of Clúain Arathair, Ap. 25 ; Deocain Nenn G, Mend, D. Cp. Dechoin Nem, LL 366 d.

Declán of Ard Mór, July 24.

Declán, f. of Molasse, Aug. 12.

—— f. of Dafinna, June 9.

—— f. of Lugidon, Jan. 6.

Deed, gen. Deeid, f. of Trian, Mar. 22.

Degitge, Mar. 22.

Deitche, Ap. 23.

Demmán, of Eig (2), Ap. 17.

Denach, of Inis Détna, Mar. 16 ; Denecc of Inis Sétna, GD.

Deon (Deoni), of familia Mundu, Oct. 21.

Derbfiled, p. 108.

Dererca, see Darerca.

Dergán, f. of Mochota of Druim, Sep. 9.

Derlugach, Feb. 1, abbess of Kildare after Brigit, G.

Dermór, d. of Maine, in Aired Boinne, July 6.

Deuraith, Jan. 13.

Díanach, bp., of Druim Mór, Jan. 16 ; of Domnach Mór Maige Ene, GD.

—— bp., Jan. 6 ; om. GD.

Díanlam (?), gen. Díanlama, Brigit Clúana Díanláma, Aug. 13 : but Dianland, Díanlann, is commemorated as a saint, GD.

Díarmait, s. of Eochaid, from Aired Indaich, Jan. 6, p. 116 ; a bishop, GD.

—— s. of Lucrad, from Clúain Fidnaige, Sep. 28 ; bp., of Clúain Find Aigne, GD.

—— s. of Mechar, Jan. 16, bp., of Airther Maige, in Túath Ratha, GD.

—— from the Dísert, June 21 ; Dísert Díarmata, GD.

—— of Glenn Uissen, July 8.

—— of Inis Clothrann, gen. Dermoto, Jan. 10.

—— (2) of familia Mundu, Oct. 21.

—— bp., Ap. 24.

—— presb., Jan. 15.

—— Oct. 12, Dec. 20.

Díarmait, f. of Comgell, July 7.

—— s. of Cerball, K. of Ossory, p. 101 ff.

Díbléne, saint, Diblini, Jan. 14.

Díchu, see Modíchu.

Dícuill, of Clúain Brain, gen. Dicollo, May 1.

—— gen. Dicollo (4), of familia Mundu, Oct. 21.

Dida, virg., June 3 ; om. G, etc.

Digde cerclach ' the Circular,' Jan. 6 ; Cerclach is a separate name in GD.

—— virg., Ap. 25.

Dímma, s. of Cass, May 12.

—— Dub ' the Black,' Jan. 6 ; bp. of Condere, GD, see note in D.

—— of familia Mundu, Oct. 21.

—— gen. Dimae, Jan. 7 ; om: GD.

—— Mar. 9, Mar. 22.

Dímma, f. of Commán, May 15, July 15.

—— (Doma MS.), f. of Mocholla, May 25.

Dímmán, of Inis Caín, Jan. 10.

—— June 27.

Dímmán, four sons of, in Cell Mór Díthruib, Aug. 9.

—— f. of Brigit, May 21.

Dímmóc, see Modímmóc.

Dínertach, of Clúain Mór, gen. Dínertaig, Oct. 9.

Dinil, mac in tsaír ' son of the wright,' Aug. 14.

Diogéne (?) (Diogeni) ; of familia Mundu, Oct. 21.

Diraith (Dirathi), of familia Mundu, Oct. 21.

Discrét (Discreti), of familia Mundu, Oct. 21.

Diucaill, s. of Máeldub, in Aired Muilt, at Loch Erne, Feb. 28 ; Dichuill GD.

—— s. of Nemán, Dec. 25.

—— Derg ' the Red,' s. of Nessan, Mar. 15.

—— of Achad na Cró, June 12.

Diuir, of Enach Ceir, May 19 ; Enach Éir, GD.

Diuréne, Oct. 6

Dobí (= Mobí), of Inis Cúscraid, July 22.

Doborchú, f. of Mochommóc, June 17.

—— see also Daborchú.

Docáem, bp., Jan. 31.

Dochumma (= Mochumma), of Nóendruim, Jan. 31.

Doidnán, f. of Cillián, Oct. 23.

Doíthnennach, of Fid Dúin, Oct. 1.

Doma, f. of Brigit, Feb. 7 (Droma), Mar. 9.

Domdachán, of familia Mundu, Oct. 21.

Domma, see Modomma.

Eochu, gen. Echach, f. of Lugaid, Mar. 24.
Eodus, the seven sons of, from Maigen, May 22, p. 116.
Eogan, bp., of Ard Sratha, Aug. 23.
—— of Less Mór, Oct. 16.
—— ep. and sapiens, of Mag Cremchaill, May 31 ; of Mag Bile, *GD*, *recte*.
—— sapiens, May 28.
Eogan, three sons of, May 19.
—— f. of Ernán, Jan. 1.
—— f. of Suibne, Jan. 19.
—— *see* Mac Táil, June 11.
—— *see also* Eugene.
Eoganán, s. of Óengus, in Ard Leccaig, Dec. 19 ; Dec. 20, *GD*.
Eolang, Eolach, Elacho anchorite of Achad Bó, Sep. 5 ; more correctly in Athbi Bolg in Muscraige Míttini, Plummer, BNE, II, 325.
Epscoip 'bishops,' *see* Secht n-epscoip.
Erc, bp., from Domnach Mór Maige Coba, Sep. 17 ; Maige Damairne, *GD*.
—— bp., of Domnach Mór Maige Lúadat, Oct. 27.
—— bp., of Sláne, p. 124.
—— (Herc) Nasci, 'of the tie,' in Telach Léis, May 12.
—— bp., Oct. 2.
Erc, sons of, from Dermag, Ap. 19.
Ercán, son of, July 15.
—— four sons of, Aug. 9.
Ercnat, Jan. 8 ; of Dún dá Én, in the Fidbaid, in Dál Araide, *GD O*(n).
Ercón (Erconi), of familia Mundu, Oct. 21.
Ereclach, Mar. 3.
Erednat, virg., gen. Erednaton, Ap. 10.
Ericbert, Saxon (= Hereberht), Mar. 18 ; Erbericht, *G*.
Ernán, s. of Áed, May 16, Ernain, p. 116.
—— s. of Eogan, Jan. 1 ; *om. G*, nephew of Columcille, *D*.
—— of Eig, Ap. 17.
—— Aug. 17 ; of Torach, *D*.
—— Jan. 17.
Erne, of Clúain Railgech, Aug. 6 ; Ernín, *GD*, Aug. 5.
Ernéne, Erníne, Ernín :
—— s. of Cóemán, Jan. 11.
—— s. of Cresíne from Ráith Noí, Aug. 18 ; from Cell Draignech in Uí Dróna *G* ; Ernóc, *O*.

Ernéne, (= Febair) d. of Airchinnech, Feb. 28.
—— descendant of Bríon, Sep 27
—— of Clúain Deochra, Jan. 11.
—— of Clúain Find, June 28.
—— May 30 ; of Cremchaill *GD*, May 31.
—— (2) of Eig, Ap. 17.
—— of Lethglenn, Feb. 23.
—— (2) of familia Mundu, Oct. 21.
—— from Ros Ingite, Dec. 23.
—— bp., Jan. 26, Ap. 12.
—— May 12.
Ernine, three daughters of, July 6.
—— sons of, Sep. 22 ; of Inis Mac nErnín, *GD* ; *om. Br*.
Ernóc, *see* Mernóc, Ternóc.
Etáin, virg., of Túaim Nóa, July 5.
Etchen (Etchani), bp., Feb. 11, of Clúain Fota in Fir Bile in Mide, *GD*.
Etchii, gen., June 3 ; *om. G, etc.* ; no doubt = Eutici (June 4) *G* and Mart. Rom., out of place here, along with Zefani which follows.
Ethechtach, f. of Ultán, Jan. 17.
Ethern, bp., from Domnach Mór, May 27.
Ethne, d. of Baite, Mar. 29 ; of Tech Ingen mBaite, beside Sord, *O*.
—— d. of Maine, in Aired Boinne, July 6.
—— Feb. 26.
Etracht, virg., Aug. 11 ; Athracht d. of Tigernach, from Cell Saile, in Crích Conaill, *GD*.
Euchaid, *see* Eochaid, Jan. 1.
Euchbirt (= Eadbert), Saxon, May 5 ; succeeded Cuthbert as bp. of Lindisfarne in 688.
Eugéne, bp., Eugan *G*, Eogan *D*, Ap 18.
—— of familia Mundu (*bis*), Oct. 21.
—— (Eugenii), saint, Mar. 15.
—— peregrinus, Dec. 26.
Eulang, Dec. 29, Eolang from Lecan Midi, *GD*.

Fachtna, s. of Mongach, from Ros Ailithir, Aug. 14 ; bp. and abb. o Dairinis Máelanfaid in Uí Ceinn selaig, *GD* ; abb. of Mainisdrecl Maíle Anfaid, *O* (n).
—— from Cráebach, Mar. 3.
—— bp., from Núachongbail, Jan 19.
Fachtna, f. of Midu, Feb. 17.
Fáelán, s. of Áed, Mar. 31.

Fergus, from Úamag, July 5; hó Hummigh, GD.
—— saint, July 19.
—— bp., gen. Ferguis, Mar. 30; of Druim Lethglaise, GD.
—— Jan. 20, Mar. 23, 24, Ap. 27, July 24.
Fergus, seven daughters of, in Inis Celtra, gen. Fergasa, May 24.
—— of the Picts, f. of Constantín, Mar. 11.
—— f. of Rónán, Ap. 9.
Fergusán, of Eig, Ap. 17.
Fétháed, gen. Féthaido, Mar. 31.
Fethchú, bp., gen. Fethchon, July 23.
Fethgna, saint, Feb. 12.
Fethlimmid of Cell Már, Aug. 3.
Fethlug, Dec. 19; Faethleg, G; Faoithleglan, D, under Dec. 20.
Fíac, in Slébte, Oct. 12.
Fíacha, see Moffacha.
Fíachna, s. of Feradach, f. of Cummíne, Feb. 24.
—— of familia Mundu, Oct. 21.
—— Mar. 30, Ap. 29.
Fíachna, ancestor of Áedán, Jan. 1.
Fíachra Cáel, 'the Slender,' of Clúain Caín, July 25.
—— abb., of Iraird, Feb. 8; also of Congbál Glinne Suilige in Cenél Conaill, GD.
—— in Slébte, Oct. 12.
—— bp., gen. Fiachraich, Sep. 28.
—— July 25, Sep. 4.
Fíachra, ancestor of Cellán, May 1.
—— ancestor of Colmán, Oct. 28.
—— Fechtnach, descendant of Túathal Techtmar, p. 118.
Fíadabair, of Úachtar Achaid, July 7.
Fíadal, abb. of Cell Achid, gen. Fíadaili, Dec. 24.
Fíadnat, virg., gen. Fíadnatan, Jan. 4.
Fíatach, see moccu Fíatach.
Fidairle, descendant of Súanach, Oct. 1; abb. of Rathen, G.
Fidbothach, of familia Mundu, Oct. 21.
Fidchellach, Feb. 17; om. GD; (?) dittogr. of following entry.
Fidchellach, f. of Brélach, Feb. 17.
Fidmune, descendant of Súanach, May 16; anch. of Rathen and from Inis Báithin, GD.
Finán, s. of Airennán, Feb. 12.
—— of Eig, Ap. 17.
—— (2) of familia Mundu, Oct. 21.
—— Lobor 'the Leper,' of Sord or of Clúain Mór, Mar. 16; also in Inis Faithlenn on Loch Léin, G.

Finán Camm, 'the Squint-eyed,' Ap. 7; of Cenn Etig and Slíab Bladma, GD, and of Fir Cell, LL. 353a 36.
—— the Saxon, Jan. 9.
—— saint, Feb. 13; of Druim Neóid, D.
—— bp., Jan. 8; of Rímid, GD.
—— Oct. 4; s. of Fergna, GD.
Finán, f. of Cellán, June 17.
Finchad, bp., May 16.
Findbarr, i.e. Broednea, of Cell Cunga, Sep. 9.
—— of Corcach, May 21.
—— abb. of Inis Doimle, July 4; s. of Áed of Áth Clíath, GD.
—— of Mag [Bile], Sep. 10.
—— of familia Mundu, Oct. 21.
—— sac., July 25.
Findbarr, f. of Commán, July 29.
Findbeó, of Inber Melgi, Jan. 27.
Findchadán, of the Ard, Feb. 23.
Findchán, bp., of Druim Enaig and Druim Feise, May 17.
—— of Eig, Ap. 17.
—— of familia Mundu, Oct. 21.
—— bp., p. 116.
—— aircisiremh 'the much tortured,' Mar. 11.
—— June 4, Oct. 29.
Findchán, f. of Sillán, Aug. 25.
Findcell, virg., gen. Finceille, Ap. 24.
—— (?) i.e. moccu Greccae, Jan. 25.
Findche, of Loch Rí, Jan. 1; Fainche Garb, 'the Rough,' from Ros Airthir, on Loch Erne, GD.
Findchritán, of Craíbech, Jan. 15.
Findchú, gen. Findchon, of Eig, Ap. 17.
Findech of Dorn, gen. Finnchi, Feb. 2; bp., of Cell Finnche, of Áth Duirn in Osraige, GD.
—— of familia Mundu, Oct. 21.
—— virg., of Slíab Gúaire, gen. Findche, Jan. 25.
Findgan, s. of Airchinnech, Oct. 24.
Findlug, of Dún Blésci, gen. Findlugo, Jan. 3; of Tamlachta Findloga in the Cíannachta of Glenn Gemin, GDO (n).
—— June 5, in Cell Gobuil; from Clúain maic Féice, GD.
—— May 11.
Fingaille (Findgailli), of familia Mundu, Oct. 21.
Fingen, s. of Odrán Febla, Feb. 5.
Finnach, f. of Baíthéne, May 22.
Finnán, of familia Mundu, Oct. 21.
Finnén, May 17.

Finni, crumther 'presbyter,' of Druim Licce, Feb. 9.

Finnia (Finniaui), Mar. 2, Sep. 27.

—— (Uinniauii senis), Dec 29

Finnián, of Mag Bile or of Clúain Iraird, Feb. 11 ; his day is Dec. 12 ; Finnia of Mag Bile, *GD*.

Finnio moccu Fiatach, Sep. 10 ; = Findbarr (*O*), Findian (*G*), Finnén (*D*), of Mag Bile, also under Feb. 11 *supra*.

—— of Árann, Dec. 31 ; *om. GD*.

—— Sep. 28, *read* of Gilldae. Cp. *O(n)*.

Finnsech, virg., of the Irnaide, gen. Finnsige, Oct. 31 ; of Slíab Gúari in Gailenga, *GD*.

—— Feb. 17 ; *om. GD*.

Fínóc, *see* Moffnóc.

Fintain, s. of Copán, gen. Fintanne, Sep. 27.

Fintan, s. of Eochaid Belach, Jan. 1, p. 116.

—— s. of Toichthech, Jan. 1.

—— s. of Tulchan, Oct. 21, *i.e.* Mundu of Tech Munnu, pedigree p. 122.

—— of Achad, Mar. 26, *om. GD*.

—— of Ard Caín, Sep. 8.

—— of Clúain Caín, May 11.

—— sac., of Clúain Caín, Feb. 7.

—— of Clúain Cruich, May 16 ; *om. GD*.

—— abb., of Clúain Eidnech, Feb. 17.

—— of Druim Ing, Oct. 10.

—— Jan. 3 ; of Dún Blésce in Munster, *GD* ; brother of Findlug, *q.v.*

—— Corach, *i.e.* in Lemchaill or in Clúain Eidnech, Feb. 21 ; bp., of Clúain Ferta Brénainn, *GD*.

—— Máeldub, Oct. 20 ; of the Eoganacht of Caisel, and at Dermag Úa nDúach, in northern Osraige, *G*.

—— os psalmorum, Mar. 27, p. 116 ; F. Bél na psalm, *GD*.

—— abb., Sep. 19 ; s. of Áed Finnlíath, *D*.

—— abb., Oct. 9 ; s. of Tal, *D*.

—— May 10 ; *om. GD*.

—— Oct. 1.

Fintan, f. of Lassar, Mar. 23.

Fintiana, saint, virg., Oct. 15 ; Fintína, *G*, *om. D*.

Firlan, descendant of Fáelán, Feb. 28 ; *om. GD*.

Flann (Fland), s. of Fairchellach, Dec. 21.

Flann (Fland), s. of Laich (*sic*), abb. of Findglaiss, Jan. 21 ; *read* Cellaich, *i.e.* Cellach, AU. 812.

—— Find, of Cullenn, Jan. 14.

—— of Inber Becce, July 17 ; Flann Becc, *GD*.

—— Ap. 20

Flann, f. of Bláithmec, July 24.

Flannán, s. of Tairdelbach, Dec. 18 ; confessor, from Cell dá Lúa in Dál Caiss, *GD*.

—— of Cell Ard, Mar. 14.

Fodub, *see* moccu Foduib.

Foilend, Mar. 3 ; d. of Áed and sister of Colga of Cell Colgan, *D*.

†Foim (*sic*), June 2 = (?) Forondán of Lúa, *OGD*.

Foindelach, Sep. 18.

Foirtheith, gen Foirthetho, Aug. 17.

Follamon, s. of Nath Fraích, July 31 ; s. of Oengus, s. of Nath Fraích, *G*.

Fonere, of Domnach, Oct. 29 ; Foenir *G*, Faoinir *D*.

Forannán, s. of Áed, Feb. 15.

—— of Cell Eae, Dec. 22.

—— (?) June 2.

Forcellach, of Fobar, June 10.

Forgall, f. of Dallán, Jan. 29.

Forirthech, Oct. 5 ; Fortech, *G*, Fortrach, *D*.

Fortchern, Feb. 17 ; also Oct. 11 (*recte*) ; of Cell Fortcheirn in Uí Dróna, *G*.

Fráech, crumthir, 'presbyter,' from Clúain Cullaig, Dec. 19 ; Dec. 20, *G*.

Frossach, anchorite, gen. Frossaig, Ap. 11.

Fuidbech, s. of Illadan, Feb. 4 ; of Cillín, *GD*.

—— July 6 ; *om. GD*.

Fuilén, of Druim Fota, Ap. 24.

Fuinechta, Dec. 19.

Fulartach, s. of Brec, Mar. 29 ; bp. of Clúain Eraird, and from Dísert Fulartaig in Uí Failgi, *GD*, s. of Brecc, s. of Scandal, Dec. 21.

Fullenn, of Áth Innich, July 23 ; Áth ind eich, *GD*.

Fursa (Fursei), Jan. 16 ; abb. of Lagny ; his brother Fáelán, Oct. 31.

Furudrán, s. of Máenán, June 18 ; of Land Lere, *G*.

—— of familia Mundu, Oct. 21.

—— in Lann Tuirriu, May 28.

—— saint, July 28.

—— bp., July 26.

—— Ap. 27 ; *om. GD*.

Matóc, pilgrim, Ap. 25 ; brother of Sanctán, and s. of Deichter, d. of Muiredach Muinderg, King of the Ulaid, *D*.

Mechar, f. of Díarmait, Jan. 16.

Méche, f. of Scíath; Sep. 6.

Medóc, *see* Momedóc.

Medrán, bp., June 6, also June 8. His day is June 8 (*O*), where he is moccu Macthéne of Daire meic Marga (in *LB*. note).

Mel, bp., Feb. 6 ; of Ard Achad in Tethba, *GD*.

Mella, of Clúain Hí, Mar. 19.

—— of Daire Melle, Mar. 31.

—— Mar. 9 ; *om. GD*.

Mellán moccu Cuinn, of Inis, Feb. 7.

—— de Britonia, in Uí Echach Ulad, Oct. 26.

—— Oct. 28 ; *om. GD*.

—— bp., p. 116.

Mellán, f. of Crónán, Feb. 10.

Mellián, in Cell Rois, Jan. 28 ; Meallán *D Br.*, Accobran *G O(n)*.

Ménni, gen., of familia Mundu, Oct. 21 ; (?) = Móenne.

Mernóc, Dec. 23 ; s. of Decel, and of Cuman, sister of Colum Cille, *D*.

Mesa (?), ancestor of Cíarán, Feb. 24.

Metán, from Túaim Átha, Mar. 7.

Míadnat, of Aired Drochait, Feb. 22 ; Midabair, of Rind Droichit, *GD*.

Míannach, s. of Failbe, July 18.

—— Ap. 23 ; of the Ednén, *GD*.

Mica, of Airdne or Ernaide, Aug. 1.

—— saint, Jan. 17.

Míce (Micii), f. of Colmán, June 18.

Midabair, p. 116. *See* also Midnat.

Midgna, f. of Midúi, *i.e.* Momedóc, Mar. 23.

Midgus, s. of Erc, of Cell Talten, May 18.

—— saint, gen. Midgussa, Ap. 10.

Midnat, of Cell Lucinni, Aug. 4, p. 108.

Midu, s. of Fachtna, Feb. 17.

Midúi, s. of Midgna, *see* Momedóc.

Mind, *see* moccu Mind ; Muind, *BB*, *Rawl*.

Mingor, daughters of, June 25 ; daughter, *D*.

Miuchbrit (Miuchbriti), of familia Mundu, Oct. 21.

Mobéccu, May 29 ; in Trelec, *GD*.

Mobéóc, Oct. 28 ; Mobéccóc, *GD*.

Mobí Cláirenech, 'table-faced,' of Domnach Brocc, Sep. 30.

.—— —— s. of Beoáed, of Corco Thrí of the Lugni of Connacht, *i.e.* Berchán, abb. of Glass Noíden, Oct. 12.

moccu Aignich, Ultán, Mar. 14.

moccu Amla, Mocholmóc, July 19.

moccu in Baird (= Longobardi), Nechtán, Ap. 22.

—— —— Usaille, Aug. 27.

moccu Beonna, Mocholmóc, Jan. 22.

moccu Birn, Nem, June 14.

—— ——- Tomméne, June 12.

moccu Cáe, Ecca, Jan. 20.

moccu Cainchi, Féchíne, Feb. 19 ; moccu Cuinge, p. 116.

moccu Cíara, Lucell, Mar. 21.

moccu Cill, Cainnech, Jan. 31.

moccu Colla, Cillíne, Jan. 3.

moccu Conchobair, Ultán, Sep. 4.

moccu Cormaic, Abbán, Mar. 16, Oct. 28.

—— —— Mofhíacha, Dec. 27.

moccu Cuinn, Áedán, Oct. 9.

—— —— Mellán, Feb. 7.

moccu Dalann, Cainnech, Oct. 11.

moccu Duib, Neman, Sep. 13.

moccu Duibni, Áedán, Ap. 8.

moccu Dunechda, Colgu, Feb. 20.

moccu Elich, Áedach, Ap. 9.

moccu Fíatach, Finnio, Sep. 10.

moccu Foduib, Airénnán, Feb. 1 ; Oidaib, *G*, Oidib, *D*.

moccu Gaile, Mocholmóc, Oct. 30.

Moccu Gairb, abb. of Mag Bile, Oct. 21.

Moccu Greccae, in Findchell, Jan. 25. *See* Notes.

moccu Gúalae, Mocholmóc, Oct. 30.

moccu Laígsi, Colmán, May 15.

—— —— Óenu, Jan. 20.

moccu Loígde, Crónán, July 18.

moccu Lugair, Molasse, Sep. 16.

moccu Lugbe, Féchín, Dec. 28.

moccu Machthéni, Murchú, June 8. Cp. Medran, June 6, 8.

moccu Mind, Mosinu, Feb. 28.

moccu Nechte, Molasse, Jan. 19.

moccu Nessi, Cruimther, June 9.

moccu Ochae, Molúa, Aug. 4.

moccu Roída, Túa, Dec. 22.

moccu Telluib, Colmán, Feb. 8.

moccu Temne, Commán, Feb. 27.

moccu (*maccu*) Tratho, Luchthigern, Ap. 28.

Mochamal, May 16.

Mochammóc, of Inis Caín, Ap. 13.

Mochellóc, from Telach Úalann, Jan. 23.

—— Mar. 7, Dec. 23.

—— *see* Cillín, s. of Tulodrán, *i.e.* from Cathair Meic Conaich, Mar. 26.

Mocnopa, Jan. 23 ; Mochuppa, *GD*.

both GD have ' abb. of Í or from
Tech Aireráin in Mide,' and D
adds ' of the race of Conall Gulbain
s. of Níall.' Under Oct. 27 O (n), the
three localities are mentioned, and
in addition, ' or he is in Gair meic
Moga, an island in Corco Duibne,'
i.e. Garinis, co. Kerry. The name
is repeated under Oct. 26 in GD.
In O he is under Oct. 27 only.
Odrán of Tír Óenaig, Feb. 19.
—— saint, Mar. 6.
—— bp., May 8 ; om. G.
—— sac., May 16 ; s. of Béoáed,
  GD.
—— Sep. 10.
Odrán, f. of Dachonna, Feb. 17.
—— Febla, f. of Fingen, Feb. 5.
Oebleán, of familia Mundu, Oct. 21.
Óebnat Find, ' the Fair,' from Ros na
  Seanchae, Jan. 31.
Óengus, bp., grandson of Oíbleán,
  Mar. 11.
—— of familia Mundu, Oct. 21.
—— bp., of Ráith na nEpscop, Feb.
  15.
—— Feb. 18 ; bp. of Druim Ratha,
  D.
Óengus, f. of Carthach, Mar. 5.
—— f. of Catha, Sep. 8.
—— f. of Conall, Sep. 9.
—— f. of Eoganán, Dec. 17.
—— f. of Fergus, Feb. 15.
—— f. of Lugáed, May 12.
—— f. of Mochúa, Dec. 23.
—— f. of Mothríanóc, Feb. 2.
—— daughters of, Feb. 23.
Óenu moccu Laígsi, abb. of Clúain,
  Jan. 20 ; om. G.
Oíbleán, grandf. of Óengus, Mar 11.
Oilleóc, of Clúain Etchéin (?), July 24 ;
  (?) = Mobéoc GD.
Oiséne, bp., July 22.
—— (Ossino), of Tergad, July 19 ;
  Tengad, GD.
Olbe, s. of Lussén, Aug. 1.
Olcán, bp., Feb. 20.
Omne, see Onme.
Onchú, gen. Onchon, July 9, also s.
  of Blaithmec, July 14. His day
  is July 9, O, where in the note to
  F he is of Ráith Blaithmic in
  Upper Dál Cais.
—— i.e. Húa ind écis, ' grandson of
  the poet,' Feb. 8 ; mac ind éicis,
  Oct. 5.
Onme (i.e. simul) vel Omne (i.e.
  Gíallán ' little hostage '), Oct. 2,
  p. 116.

TALLAGHT

Orcán, of familia Mundu, Oct. 21.
Ossán, bp., Feb. 17.
—— in Áth Truim, Feb. 17.
Osséne, Ossíne, Osséin :
—— of Clúain Mór, Jan. 1 ; s. of
  Cellach of Clúain Mór Fer nArda,
  GD.
—— (2) of familia Mundu, Oct. 21.
—— of Terga, July 19 ; Tengad, GD.
—— May 1, July 22.
Ossíne, daughters of, May 3 ; of
  ⸰ Ráith Eich, in Raichnech, G.
Ossu, f. of Echbritan, May 27.

Papán, in Sentreib, July 31 ; a son
  of Óengus, s. of Nath Fráech, G.
Pátraic (Patricius), bp., Mar. 17 ;
  baptism of [Sinell s. of Finchad],
  see Fél. Óeng.,² p. 113 n.. Ap. 5 ;
  ordination of, Ap. 6 ; successor of,
  Jan. 10.
—— Hostiarius and abb. of Ard
  Macha, Aug. 24.
—— abb. and bp., of Ros Dela, Aug.
  24.
Petar, gen. Petair, June 4, om. D ;
  Patrocus, G.
[Pilip] nóebepscop, ' a holy bishop '
  from Clochar Bainne, Mar. 4 ;
  Pilip of Clúain Bainb, GD.
Polán, May 21 ; of Cell Móna, GD.

Rathnat, of Cell Rathnaite, Aug. 9 ;
  of Cell Raith, GD, Aug. 5.
Reat, deacon, Mar. 3.
Rectaire, of Eig, Ap. 17.
Rectíne craíbdech ' the devout,' Oct.
  27.
Rethach, s. of Cóemán ; Rétach,
  June 10 ; Rethech, G.
Rethe, son of, Oct. 3.
Ríagán, crumther ' presbyter,' Aug.
  9 ; Rigan, G.
Ríagol, f. of Columb, Aug. 1 ;
  Riangal, GD.
Ríaguil, s. of Búachaill, Ap. 13 ;
  Riachuill mac ua B., G.
—— of Bennchor, June 11 ; Reguil,
  GD.
—— of Muccinis, Sep. 17, Oct. 16 ;
  of Tech Ríagla, in Leth Cathail,
  GD. Under both days in O also.
  Probably different persons.
Rían, in Fothirbe Líatháin, Ap. 23 ;
  om. GD.
Richell, virg., gen. Ricille, May 19 ;
  d. of Athracht, D.
Rignach, d. of Feradach, gen. Rig-
  naige, Dec. 18.

S

S

Su(i)bne, abb. of Í, Jan. 11 ; s. of Cuitre, *GD*.
—— s. of Eogan, Jan. 19.
—— bp., from Cobran, June 21.
—— of the Scelec, Ap. 28.
—— saint, Sep. 27.
—— abb., June 22 ; of Í, *GD*.
—— Oct. 28.
Suignán, of familia Mundu, Oct. 21.

Tadc, mart., July 8 ; suffered at Würzburg, along with Áed and Celianus, *GD*.
Tadc, the sons of, Sep. 15.
Táde, f. of Comgall, July 24 ; Tádén, *G ; om. D*.
Táed, s. of Colgu, gen. Taeda, Jan. 31 ; Táedóc, of Achad Duma, *GD*.
Taicthech, gen. Taicthig, Oct. 16.
Tairchar, the sons of, of Loch Mac Nen, Ap. 13 ; Terchor, *GD*.
Tairdelbach, f. of Flannán, Dec. 18.
Tal, son of, Oct. 9.
Talarag, the sons of, Sep. 8 ; Talarc, *GD*.
Talmach, saint, Mar. 14.
Tarannán, abb. of Bennchor, June 12 ; and from Tulach Fortceirn in Laigin and from Druim Clíab in Cairpre, *GD*.
Tassach, saint, Ap. 14 ; bp. of Ráith Cholptha, *GD*.
Teldub, see moccu Thelluib.
Temnán, of Linn Dúachail, Aug. 7 ; Linn Uachaille, *GD*.
Temne, see moccu Temne.
Temneán (Temmiani *MS.*), mon., Aug. 17 ; Temnán, *G*, Temnén, *O*.
Temnióc, *see* Mothemnióc.
Teochonna, of Cúairne, Jan. 13 ; Teo same as Do ' Thy ' ; Conna Chuairne, *G, i.e.* tuilledh anma ' an addition of a name,' from Inis Pátraic ; Mochonna *O*(*n*)*D*.
Teóra cailleacha ' the three nuns,' of Druim dá Dart, May 22 ; *i.e.* Agna, Cassin, and Luigsech, *G*.
Ternóc of Clúain Mór, July 2.
—— anchorite, Feb. 8 ; to the west of the river Berba, *GD*.
—— Jan. 30 ; of Úarán, *GD*.
—— Feb. 28.
—— p. 116.
—— *see* Mac Rethi.
Tetgall, s. of Colbrand, Ap. 11.
Tíaman, of Aired Suird, Feb. 23 ; Tián, *GD*.
Tián, f. of Máel Tuile, Oct. 23.

Tigernach, of Aired, Ap. 8 ; Tigernán, of Aired Locha Con, *G*.
—— bp., of Clúain Eois, Ap. 4 ; p. 102.
—— bp., Mar. 17
Tigernán, f. of Sárán, Sep. 21.
Tipraite, of Mag Ratha, Dec. 27.
Tiu ingen Eltíne, Mar. 15 ; cp. p. 180.
Tiugmach, bp., July 7 ; Trigmech, *GD*.
Tobia, Jan. 1.
Tochonna, bp., May 15 ; of Condere, *GD*.
—— (Tochunni), Sep. 6.
Tochumracht, virg., June 11, of Conmaicne, *GD*.
Toichthech, of familia Mundu, Oct. 21.
Toichthech, f. of Fintan, Jan. 1.
Toidilia, Aug. 11 ; Talla, uirg., from Inis Daigre, *G*.
[Toite], of Inis Toite on Loch Echach, Sep. 7 ; on Loch Bec in Uí Tuirtre, *GD*.
Tóla, bp., Mar. 30 ; of Dísert Tola, *GD*.
Toliac, saint, Dec. 17 ; Moliac, *OGD*.
Tomma, of Bennchor, Ap. 22.
Tommán, July 26 ; of Mungarit, *OGD*.
—— bp., Mar. 18.
Tomméne, successor of Patrick at Armagh, Jan. 10.
—— moccu Birn, pilgrim, of Loch Úane, June 12 ; *om. GD*.
—— saint, Oct. 15.
Tora, *see* Mothora.
Torannán, *see* Tarannán.
Torman, Mar. 10 ; gl. sons of Torman, s. of Cruaiden, *GD*.
Torptha, July 16.
Tosa (Tosai), of Druim Laidcinn, Mar. 9.
Totholán, June 17.
Tratho, see moccu Tratho.
Trea, d. of Caírthend, Aug. 3 ; of Ard Trea, *GD*.
—— of Ard Trea, July 8 ; virg. *GD*, no place given.
Trenech, Mar. 15.
Trénlug, the descendant of, gen. aui Trenloco, anchorita, June 3 ; ua Trianlugo, *G*.
Trénoc, *see* Mothríanóc.
Trian, gen. Tréno, s. of Deed, Mar. 22 ; from Cell Elge, *GD*.
—— saint, of Cell Daelen, gen. Treno, Mar. 23 ; *om. GD*.

ADDENDUM.

At the moment of going to press another copy of the obscure marginal poem printed on p. 92 ff. has unexpectedly come to light. It is preserved in a MS. of the 14th century, which the National Library of Ireland has just acquired, along with others, from the Phillipps Collection at Cheltenham, where it bore the press-mark 7022. It is a small vellum. numbering 78 leaves, formerly No. 10 in the collection of Edward O'Reilly (see his *Irish Writers*, p. ci), and written for the most part by Adam O'Cianan, d. 1373. The poem occurs on folio 24*a* 16, but is in another hand. It enables us to restore several passages illegible in LL., and to correct a few misreadings of our own and of the Facsimilist. The readings are as follows :—

Stanza 1. (*a*) *Auguist tair*, 'in the East,' and so LL. ; (*b*) *genair Crist ar druim domain*, 'Christ was born on the ridge of the world' ; (*c*) *na ceann*, 'of the heads,' a cheville for *cen fell* LL. ; (*d*) *cuigedh nEreand*, 'of the provinces of Ireland' ; read 'the province' LL.

Stanza 2. (*a*) *Isin*, which the metre demands, for *I* of LL. ; (*b*) *flaithius* ; (*c, d*) *i náemad trichaid re thest | du flaithus Cesar Aughest*, 'In the thirty-ninth, according to testimony, of the reign of Caesar Augustus.' This reading is not traceable as such in LL.

Stanza 3. (*a*) *Aenbliadain deg is derbh libh*, 'Eleven years, assuredly' ; *is derb lib* would seem to be the reading of LL. also ; (*c*) *i comré*, as conjectured.

Stanza 4. (*b*) *a athar*, as conjectured ; (*c, d*) *ocht mbliadna do is Crist rocess | a comre robo choimhdes*, 'eight years to him and Christ .   coexisting, it was evenly matched.'

Stanza 5. (*b*) *i comre 7 Concobhar*, 'contemporary with Conchobor' ; (*c*) *cle* for *holc*, ''twas no ill' ; and so LL. ; (*d*) *i comflaithius a comre*, 'co-sovrans, contemporary.'

Lightning Source UK Ltd.
Milton Keynes UK
UKHW011820030621
384869UK00001B/39